INTRODUCING CATHOLIC THEOLOGY
Revelation and its interpretation

INTRODUCING CATHOLIC THEOLOGY

Revelation and its interpretation

Aylward Shorter

GEOFFREY CHAPMAN
LONDON

9954863

8-15-84 JH

A Geoffrey Chapman Book published by
Cassell Ltd
1 Vincent Square, London SW1P 2PN

© Aylward Shorter 1983

Cum permissu superiorum

First published 1983

ISBN 0 225 66356 2

Nihil obstat: Anton Cowan, *Censor*
Imprimatur: Monsignor Ralph Brown, *V. G.*
Westminster, 20 December 1982

The *Nihil obstat* and *Imprimatur* are a declaration that a book or pamphlet is considered to be free
from doctrinal or moral error. It is not implied that those who have granted the *Nihil obstat* and
Imprimatur agree with the contents, opinions or statements expressed.

British Library Cataloguing in Publication Data

Shorter, Aylward
    Revelation and its interpretation.—(Introducing
    Catholic theology; 1)
    1. Revelation   2. Theology, Catholic
    I. Title   II. Series
    231.7′ 4   BT127.2

Phototypesetting by Georgia Origination, Liverpool

Printed and bound in Great Britain at
The Camelot Press Ltd, Southampton

FOR
DEODAT MSAHALA

Contents

Foreword

Introducing Catholic Theology has been conceived and planned in the belief that the Second Vatican Council provided the Church with a fundamental revision of its way of life in the light of a thorough investigation of Scripture and of our history, and with fresh guidelines for studying and reflecting upon the Christian message itself. In common with every other form of human enquiry and practical activity, the Christian faith can be set out and explained in ways appropriate to human intelligence: it calls for scientific textbooks as well as for other forms of writing aimed at expressing and conveying its doctrines.

It is hoped that these volumes will be found useful by teachers and students in that they will supply both the information and the stimulus to reflection that should be taken for granted and counted upon by all concerned in any one course of study.

Conceived as expressions of the Catholic tradition, the books draw upon the contribution to the knowledge of God and the world made by other religions, and the standpoint of other patterns of Christian loyalty. They recognize the need for finding ways of reconciliation where differences of understanding lead to human divisions and even hostility. They also give an account of the insights of various philosophical and methodological approaches.

The series opens with an examination of the Christian understanding of the process of revelation itself, the special communication between God and humanity made available in the history of Israel and culminating in the person of Christ; its second volume is about the Catholic understanding of Christ, the Word of God and the source of the New Testament faith. The volumes immediately following will deal with the human person as understood in the light of that faith and with the work of the Holy Spirit through whom the Word is continually made present and comprehensible to humanity.

Michael Richards

Introduction

A book about revelation and its interpretation belongs to the field of fundamental theology which, as its name implies, should provide an initiation into the whole study of Christian theology. Fundamental theology necessarily trespasses on a number of scientific and theological domains: social and cultural anthropology, the history and scientific study of religion, the exegesis and interpretation of Old and New Testaments, the Christian theology of revelation/salvation and of religions, ecclesiology, evangelization and apologetics. One cannot aspire to expertise in all these areas – at least within the span of a single human lifetime. The most one can do is to rely upon one's own specializations – in the present case, history, cultural anthropology and mission theology – and to read and consult as widely as possible in other fields. It is recognized that one should not write fundamental theology nowadays without an anthropological perspective and a review of the history and interaction of world religions. I hope that my own specializations confer the desired relevance and direction to the other subjects treated in a fundamental theology.

My aim has been to produce a readable textbook which will introduce students in the English-speaking world to modern approaches in the study of Christian revelation. I have tried to eschew altogether the *a prioristic* or definitional textbook style, and to offer an experiential theology with arguments of a more inductive nature. The book begins with a chapter on revealed religion and its relevance in the contemporary world. Two chapters follow, dealing with the nature and content of Old Testament revelation. The fourth chapter is Christological and constitutes, as it were, the 'watershed' of the whole book. Thereafter, successive chapters deal with the role of Scripture and tradition in the Church, the relation of Christian revelation to divine revelation in other religions, the act of faith and its expression in Christian life and liturgy, and finally the question of evangelization in a divided church and a divided world.

I began to collect material for this book while teaching African Christian Theology at Kipalapala Senior Seminary in Tanzania in 1980. However, the writing was done at Downside Abbey in England in 1981, while I was carrying out my functions as Downside Visiting Fellow in the Department of Theology and Religious Studies at the University of Bristol. I am grateful to the Abbot and Community at Downside for allowing me to stay on after term, so that I could continue writing. I am indebted to them and to my colleagues at the University of Bristol for many helpful suggestions about reading and about the shape of the book.

The work of writing was interrupted by a stay of nearly three months in Jerusalem in the summer of 1981, during which I visited sanctuaries and archaeological sites throughout the Holy Land and made contact with Fr P. Benoît and Fr M. E. Boismard of the École Biblique. This period of pilgrimage, prayer and study has profoundly influenced the writing of the last two chapters of the book, as well as the revision of the earlier chapters. I am grateful to Fr Pierre Simson W. F., of St Anne's, Jerusalem, for his careful reading of the Biblical sections and for his guidance in their revision. I wish also to thank Fr Bernard Brown W.F. of the Missionary Institute, London, for reading drafts of the theological sections and for his helpful critique. I am indebted to Fr Gerald O'Collins S.J. of the Gregorian University for the suggestions and references he gave, both in correspondence and in personal conversation. Finally, I wish to acknowledge my indebtedness to Fr Michael Richards of Heythrop College, the General Editor of the series to which this book belongs, for inviting me to write it in the first place, for preparing the typescript for the publisher and for being a continual source of help and encouragement.

Bristol, October 1981   *Aylward Shorter*

1
Receivers of God's Word

REVEALED RELIGION, A SOCIAL REALITY?

Methodological atheism and the study of religion

Preaching at Oxford in 1830, John Henry Newman declared:

> It is not here meant that any religious system has been actually traced out by unaided reason. We know of no such system, because we know of no time or country in which human reason *was* unaided.... No people (to speak in general terms) has been denied a revelation from God... (Newman 1909, p. 17).

The future cardinal was speaking out of his own Christian faith in an authenticated revelation, but for his description of what he termed 'natural religion' he appealed to human experience. There was scarcely a people in the world that did not hold a tradition about a supreme power, exterior and superior to the human conscience and to the visible world. Religion, said Newman, was the system of relations between human beings and this power.

Half a century after that Oxford sermon, the German philosopher Friedrich Wilhelm Nietzsche wrote:

> The greatest modern event – that God is dead, that belief in the Christian God has become unworthy of belief – has now begun to cast its first shadows over Europe (Nietzsche 1901, p. 80).[1]

Nietzsche's dramatic announcement was the last phase of a movement of thought beginning with the philosophers of the eighteenth-century Enlightenment who had denied the possibility of revealed religion and had enthroned reason in the place of faith. Nietzsche was certainly right to say that belief in God can die – perhaps, that in Europe it was already dying – but history proves again and again that the ability to believe does not die and that the sense of God so far survives each crisis of plausibility that a new characterization appears. The question, as Professor Bowker has explained, is not whether gods die, but whether people have correctly or satisfactorily identified the divine reality (Bowker 1978, p. 27).

Newman spoke of 'a supreme power, exterior and superior' of which religious believers are conscious, and he called religion a 'system of relations between human beings and this power'. In terms of a contemporary sociology of religion, this is a perfectly acceptable definition of what most religious people believe, but it begs the question of whether there are, or are not, strictly religious determinants of behaviour. There is no doubt at all, from a phenomenological point of view, that people believe in an external divine reality which engages with them in a powerful, self-authenticating way, and to which even the changes in the beliefs which people have about this same reality (one instance of which interested Nietzsche) are ultimately attributed. The existence of religious beliefs and systems as a social reality of the logical order, which can powerfully affect human thought and behaviour, is not questioned by social scientists. Controversy centres on whether one can accept religious determinants, or divine reality itself, as an independent, non-empirical category or variable in social analysis, leaving to faith the question of its truth or falsity; or whether, on the other hand, a strictly scientific study of religion demands the adoption of a methodological atheism.

There are two logical disadvantages entailed by methodological atheism. One is that the denial of the object of religious faith is gratuitous. On the face of it there is no reason at all why religion should be judged 'guilty' until proved 'innocent'. There are a great many gaps and limitations in our experience of a world perceived by the senses alone, and some of these limitations may be overcome by the application of technology. Many of our limitations, however, are intransigent and these tend to be overlooked or conveniently forgotten by the spirit of evolutionary optimism that pervades contemporary science. Whether we like it or not, we cannot eliminate suffering and death or go back in time to live our lives all over again and presumably do better on the second time round. But religion would not of course be credible if it were merely a 'God-of-the-gaps' religion, exploiting the limits of human endeavour and the human failures in coping with a hostile environment. Methodological atheism also overlooks the fact that religion offers resources for constructing a more human way of life and that it has inspired artistic creativity and cultural traditions of great worth in the history of humankind. The acceptance of a religious explanation which transcends the data of sense perception is certainly more logical than the mentality which assumes that only scientific facts are real truths.

The second logical disadvantage is that methodological atheism leads to reductionism (cf. Mills and Pickering 1980, p. 19; Bourdillon and Fortes 1980, p. 6). In other words, it purports to explain religion in terms of another, non-religious, phenomenon. Most of the early social anthropologists and scholars of religion were reductionists, whether they wore their atheism on their sleeves, or justified it as a methodological necessity.

Thus Sir Edward Tylor and Sir James Frazer reduced religion to a form of primitive science, an attempted rational explanation of sense phenomena based on a logical error, and so resulting in the positing of non-existent realities, such as souls, ghosts or gods. Much of their thinking derived from the earlier writing of positivists such as Auguste Comte and Herbert Spencer, with their somewhat mechanistic understanding of social and psychological processes and their presentation of the science of society as 'social biology'.

For the great sociologist Emile Durkheim, religion was simply the form taken by human social consciousness; and religious rituals, such as the totemic celebrations of the Australian aborigines, had the function of strengthening social solidarity. Durkheim ignored the specificity of religious beliefs and the reasons why religious rituals should generate feelings and emotions which strengthen social bonds, but it is not clear that he reduced religion entirely to the worship of society. If Durkheim did not clearly assert that religion was an epiphenomenon of socio-economic life, Ludwig Feuerbach and Karl Marx, however, certainly did. For both of these philosophers religion was the fruit of a malfunctioning sensibility, but, whereas Feuerbach saw religion as an early form of self-consciousness belonging to the childhood of the human race and exercising a curative influence, inculcating true social values through a holy make-believe, Marx's view was that religion was a social disease, perverting the human consciousness and contradicting secular reality – in the classic phrase, it was 'the opium of the people'.

In Sigmund Freud's psychology, religion was traced back to infantile fantasies about the sexual life of one's parents. Religious beliefs were 'projections' and 'compensations', which offered an explanation of experience and an illusion of human control over phenomena. Gods, spirits and demons were necessary inventions to help human beings come to terms with their experience. Eminent scholars of religion have also frequently offered what is basically a psychological explanation for religious systems. Rudolf Otto saw religious beliefs as generated by a feeling of awe in the presence of unusual natural phenomena. His description of the 'Holy' or the 'Sacred' as a mystery that is both fear-inspiring and fascinating has become a classic. Even Mircéa Eliade makes the experience of the sacred the source of all religion (cf. Vergote 1980, p. 38).

The basic flaw in such reductionist theories is that they do not touch or describe the reality of religion itself. Religious experience is mediated in countless different ways, social, psychological, political, economic. There is also no need to claim that natural laws or scientific truths must be suspended, if the divine reality exists and exerts an influence on humanity. The divine is not an 'intervention' or an 'addition' to reality, and it does not compete with social consciousness or psychoanalysis.

Religion as a symbol-system

The atheistic assumption and the scientific inaccessibility of divine reality – its non-empirical character – have led many contemporary social anthropologists to consider merely the secondary question of the influence of religion on other aspects of social life. Since there was no sociological answer to the question: 'Is this religion true?', it could be replaced with the question: 'Is it useful?'; and pragmatic social scientists could afford to ignore people's religious motivations while concentrating on the (usually) latent social functions of religion (Bourdillon and Fortes 1980, pp. 6-7). Thus A. R. Radcliffe-Brown emphasized the way religion strengthened social values and provided psychological security in moments of danger. Bronislaw Malinowski showed how religion supports structure and order in society and Godfrey Lienhardt explained how religion controls the way in which people experience the world.

Sir Edward Evans-Pritchard took the view that religion was a fit subject for study in its own right. It was, he said, *sui generis*; and he made no apology for giving us a study of Nuer theology and religious practice (Evans-Pritchard 1962). It was Clifford Geertz, however, fifteen or so years ago, who gave clearest expression to the contemporary concern for taking religion seriously. He discerned a return to the hermeneutic interpretation of ritual and the explication of religion as a coherent system of thought:

> Religion is a system of symbols which acts to establish powerful, pervasive, and long-lasting moods and motivations in men by formulating conceptions of a general order of existence and clothing these conceptions with such an aura of factuality that the moods and motivations seem uniquely realistic (Geertz 1966, p. 4).

Religion, therefore, is a 'symbol-system' which functions, as Geertz explains, like a 'model'. A model can be either a 'model of' or a 'model for'. It can be a replica or a mock-up, evoking either what is or what may be. The symbol-system, then, gives meaning by shaping itself to psychological reality, and by shaping that reality to itself. As it does so, it motivates the believer to seek truth and to analyse his experience. It helps him cope with suffering and gives him an insight into the reality of evil.

Geertz offers us a structural study of religion. In the language of contemporary anthropology, religions have a 'structure'. Their different parts relate to one another in view of a final purpose which unites them all. A structure is an integrating theory in the minds of people, helping them to make sense of experience. In the minds of the believers it may be only partially or intermittently conscious. (As we shall see, symbols make a specific appeal to the subconscious.) But the structure is discernible and plausible when it is made explicit. Within this total system religious experience occurs. It is not necessarily (though it can be) a direct intuition or perception or mystical experience. Rather it is a conviction born out of a cumulative appeal to the believer's imagination. The divine reality is experienced within a system that makes it imaginatively credible. John Bowker employs a vocabulary borrowed from communications theory: 'Religions are bounded systems of information' (Bowker 1978, p. 8). They transmit and process information in a sufficiently plausible way for individuals to allow the system to become informative in the construction of their lives, and they are the outcome of a lengthy accumulation of tradition. Religious experience is commonly mediated by such systems, and phenomenological analysis of the evidence suggests that religious determinants may really exist, although natural science is not (yet) able to identify them.

Although, as we have seen, analysis of experience may be one of the functions of a religious system, such systems are not just comprehensive explanatory systems. Robin Horton has coined the formula 'EPC' for those aspects of a religion which respond to the human need for 'explanation', 'prediction' and 'control' (Horton 1971). Undoubtedly, such elements are present in religious belief-systems, particularly in their more popular forms; and undoubtedly also 'EPC' can threaten the very essence of religious belief if it pervades the entire system. However, as Horton argues, the 'EPC' aspect of religion chiefly flourishes in situations where science and technology are undeveloped, and as a substitute for rational thinking and effective human action. In any case, he says, even in the sphere of analysis of experience, science and technology have their limitations, and a much more fundamental aspect of religion takes over. This is 'communion', which is both presumed by, and transcends, 'EPC'. Horton's notion of religion as essentially a 'communion' or a 'sharing of life' with divine reality echoes an older definition by F. Heiler of prayer as the central phenomenon of religion:

> . . . a living communion of the religious man with God (conceived as personal and present in experience), a communion which reflects the forms of the social relations of humanity (Heiler 1932, p. 358).

Heiler speaks of 'God', conceived in a 'personal' way, and these are terms which, for the purposes of our argument here, we are not yet ready to use. What is important for us is that Heiler sees prayer or worship as the heart of religion and the essential disposition of the religious man, and that he conceives it as a 'living communion' with the divine reality, reflecting the forms of ordinary human social relationships. Religion, in other words, is a dimension of life as it is lived by the believer and it is doxological or 'worshipping'.

This takes us back, not only to Tylor's definition of religion as the belief in, and worship of, spiritual beings, but to the very basic understanding of religion as the experience of an action done to the subject by an external reality (cf. Tylor 1903). Before there is religious response or commitment, there is a passive and even a submissive quality in religion as worship. Freud, in the context of sexual love, described how the initial appetite or libido is transcended because of an action upon the subject by the one who is loved. The same thing, argues John Bowker, happens in worship and prayer (Bowker 1978, p. 25); at least, believers experience such feelings of related-ness to what Newman called 'a superior and exterior power' (Newman 1909, p. 18).

The encounter with divine reality

Up to this point we have spoken about 'the sacred' and about 'the divine reality' which is the object of religious belief and worship. It is important not to confuse the two concepts. The sacred is a psychological sphere or zone; and a sense of the sacred is a mental disposition in a believing person. The sacred is also a social category which is applied relatively to things, places, actions, persons – and to divine reality itself. The sacred is the form taken by recognition of a divine quality or dimension in experience, and while religious symbols express and awaken a sense of the sacred, this sense is not necessarily antecedent to experience of divine reality itself.

It is also important not to confuse the notion of sacred and secular, or sacred and profane, with that of clean and unclean. Anthropologists have made this mistake because of an over-emphasis on the factor of prohibition, or setting apart, in their definition of the sacred. In many religious traditions sacred persons, objects, actions, places and times are hedged round with pro-hibitions carrying a mysterious, automatic sanction. Such prohibitions are commonly called 'taboos', and experience shows that unclean things are also frequently tabooed. Hence the odd deduction that the sacred can be unclean. Without in any way wishing to deny the ambivalent character of the sacred, nor the fact that it may be the subject of taboos, one cannot define it by reference to the taboo-mentality alone, and similarly one cannot restrict the application of the concept of taboo exclusively to the sacred. All is called sacred which pertains to the divine reality and to the system of relations with this reality which constitutes religion. The sacred inspires feelings of awe, feelings which are a mixture of fear and fascination, but ultimately it reflects divine reality as a unifying principle of order, as Geertz pointed out, even if this order is dark and obscure to the human mind. In so far as what is unclean represents disorder and dissolution, it is inappropriate to predicate it of the sacred.

This brings us to the object of religious belief and worship, the divine reality which is experienced in, and mediated by, the sacred. The sacred is a kind of intermediate zone between divine reality and the profane, everyday world. As we have said, it is a quality or dimension of experience perceived by the human individual in the depths of his being and in the external world, a dimension associated with the mystery of existence and the deep source of everything that is. In this dimension, zone or sphere, the divine reality is intimately present (Vergote 1980, p. 39). It is the basis of all reality, the ulti-mately real, the ultra-real or *realissimum*. To describe it in terms of ultimacy or finality is not to say that the believer can speak about it with finality or that he can in any way begin to comprehend it. It is, as Rudolf Otto insisted, 'wholly other', and yet, through the sacred, the believer has access to this Other, and 'recognizes' its otherness. Furthermore, in this recog-nition, the human individual is addressed and summoned. A new level of meaning is imparted and he is somehow, in one degree or another, 'enlightened'.

All religious sytems interrogate existence, and all offer to the human individual a balance between hope and despair, a rule by which to live. 'Religion', writes Kenneth Cragg (1977, p. 111), 'is the capacity to say "yes" to mystery, to wonder, to curiosity, to hope and to say "no" to travesty, to futility, to cynicism.' Religious belief is not mere submissive piety; it is a questing and questioning. It is not a reckless and unrealistic opti-mism; on the contrary, it is often a temptation to revolt or a deep sense of shared tragedy. It hovers between affirmation and negation and, as John Coulson points out, this is the peculiarly intensifying and unifying power of imaginative symbolism, and it explains why religious systems are symbol-systems (Coulson 1981, pp. 63-72).

Cardinal Newman thought that the personal conception of the Godhead and what he called 'the method of personation' carried through the whole system of theology was one of the special strengths of Christianity (Newman 1909, p. 28). Yet he was the first to admit that the application of the human being's experience of himself as a person to ultimate reality, while refuting certain objections, was also 'the confession of an insoluble question'. The human being experiences himself as an identity, as a self-conscious being endowed with freedom and responsibility, an inalienable or incommunicable existence. Yet there are obvious limitations when this experience is transferred to ultimate reality and a 'person' is identified as 'God', 'Yahweh', 'Allah', 'Shiva', 'Vishnu' or 'Maha Brahma' – even more so when, as in Christian Trinitarian theology, more than one person is predicated of God. The limitations of the personalization of divine reality in the Judeo-Christian tradition have been partially overcome, as Piet Schoonenberg has shown, by the use of the *passivum divinum*, whereby the 'it-ness' (as opposed to the 'thou-ness') of God is represented (Schoonenberg 1977, p. 86). God is somehow a universal, unlimited and mysterious activity. He is identified with abstract qualities, like Truth, Spirit and Love. Whatever he is, he is not just another person, or even another being. In the Buddhist tradition the limitations of a personal approach to the ultimate have been much more strongly felt. Even though gods and god-relatedness are acknowledged in the Buddhist world-view, these are subordinated to the higher ideal of the human being's seeming annihilation and the cessation of all perception and feeling – a state of release or 'dreamless sleep' which is by definition unqualifiable. Nevertheless, it is probably true to say that the 'personation' of ultimate reality, commonly referred to as theism, is the most frequent form adopted by religious symbol-systems, and this lends itself more readily to a metaphorization rooted in human experience, even though the 'otherness' of God inevitably means knowing him, as it were, in a void.

Religious symbolism and divine self-revelation

At various times in the course of this book we shall return to the importance, the nature and the function of symbols in human experience. Symbols are a species of sign, but they are not the product of an arbitrary, conventional signification, such as the ordinary metaphor, simile or allegory. Symbols are instances of experience and true appearances of reality. Everything that exists is a symbol of itself, an epiphany or manifestation of what is. Such symbols communicate and impose themselves because they are part of a context which we experience. But we can enlarge our experience of reality – make it more real – and discover further depths of meaning in it by our perception of overlapping contexts. Consequently, symbols communicate a further range of meaning because they participate in a further reality. They are multivocal, calling up a variety of experiences. Moreover, symbols have reference to one another, so that together they form a system or pattern.

If there is a basic given-ness in symbolism, whence does it derive its form and content? Symbols appeal to a form of non-discursive logic that is built into human minds. They are a conscious elaboration of what is, to some degree, unconscious, but when they are given an explicit narrative form, they are put into a more or less rational-logical order. Dreams, like symbolic stories or myths, also possess an involuntary character and a non-discursive logic. If, as Claude Lévi-Strauss declared: 'Myths think themselves in men', then C. G. Jung's statement is equally true: 'One does not dream, one is dreamed'. Dreaming is a normal aspect of our thought processes, providing problem-solving messages from one part of ourselves to another and offering us food for conscious thought. There is plenty of evidence, from the way dreams are used socially and religiously in pre-literate or recently literate societies, for a connection between dreams and myths.

We owe a great debt to Jung for helping us to take a positive view of dreams and dream-symbolism and for his hypothesis of the collective unconscious. The way dreams are told and used corresponds to the collective concerns and expectations of a specific culture, and many psychologists and social scientists do not feel that symbolism can be explained by psychology alone, and they suspect that there is a circularity in arguments for the existence of universal symbolic archetypes. Symbols present an objective cultural reality which has psychic implications for the members of a particular culture. Nor can social science do more than identify the forms which symbolism is likely to take, as a result of a collective socio-psychological response to given physical environments or to definable categories of social experience. As Mary Douglas has shown, even the basic unity of form in the human body and the basic identity of human biological functions can be interpreted differently in different symbol-systems, though there may often be a similarity of fundamental interests in this area (Douglas 1970, pp. 65-81). The truth is that a symbolic universe emerges with man himself and with his own self-awareness, a universe of signs that is comparable to language and which transcends both man and human society. Neither psychology nor sociology can satisfactorily explain the difference of content between one symbol-system and another, any more than they can explain the differences in meaning between words of different languages, whatever their similarity of form. Karl Popper has even suggested the existence of a symbolic order as a mental 'Third World', distinct from the physical world and the world of socio-psychology (Vergote 1980, pp. 28-29).

Be that as it may, symbol-systems are certainly a dynamic and historical phenomenon. Human societies interact with their physical environments, and these environments offer a limited number of choices for solving the problem of basic material needs. The way a human society chooses, arranges and modifies (e.g. through migration, trade and diffusion of techniques) the materials offered by its physical environment is what we call its economy – at least, in its most fundamental form. A human society must adapt its social patterns of living and its social institutions to its chosen economy, and it thus establishes a tradition which is nothing other than the story of its choices, of historic innovations and historical contacts with other human societies. All these influences combine to create a human tradition, replete with symbols, and capable of an independent existence long after members of a given society have become separate from the physical environment in which their cultural tradition originated. The classic example is that of the Jewish people who, after their dispersal into the ghettoes of medieval Europe, continued to treasure the names of Palestinian geography: Zion, Horeb, Hermon, the river Jordan and the cedars of Lebanon, etc., and celebrated seasonal festivals totally inappropriate to the climate of northern Europe.

Since the symbols of a cultural tradition appeal to a collective memory of real experience, it is inevitable, as Johann Baptist Metz insists, that they have an essentially narrative structure, and that the narrated memory has a cognitive primacy over rationally classified thought and objectivized or 'scientific history' (Metz 1980, pp. 195-196). There is also a sense of effective memory or *anamnesis*, that experiences can be repeated or re-invoked.

This is an idea common to many, if not most, cultures and religions, even those in which the depth of historical consciousness is relatively shallow.

Up to this point we have been dealing mainly with the ways in which human beings come to terms with earthly or secular realities through symbolism and stories, and through their re-enactment in symbolic action or ritual. Earlier we spoke of the apprehension of ultimate or divine reality within the socio-psychic zone known as the sacred. For certain privileged individuals, the divine or paramount reality is perceived through some form of immediate intuition or mystical experience. For them it is massively and overwhelmingly real. These are the 'religious *virtuosi*', as Peter Berger, echoing Max Weber, calls them (Berger 1980, p. 33). There is no language in which to speak of such experience, and the first impulse is to remain silent. It is the silence, as John Bowker recalls, of Jesus before his judges, of Al-Ghazali overwhelmed by the conviction that Allah *is*, and of Gautama, the Buddha, fearing that his understanding of the enlightenment would cause fear and misunderstanding (Bowker 1978, *passim*). It is also the silence of the African sage from Rwanda who justified his failure to verbalize his traditional faith with the words: 'When I contemplate the work Imana [God] has accomplished in my house, I have no need to tell him about it. Before him I keep silence, and I offer him in silence the house over which he has made me the head' (Kayoya 1968, p. 46; my tr.).

For the vast majority of believers who, of course, are not religious *virtuosi* and who apprehend the divine reality within an inherited, total system of symbols, there is a need to verbalize the experience. The religious *virtuosi* themselves, if they are religious innovators or if, for one reason or another, they are prevailed upon to break their silence, must also try to say what divine reality is for them and for their fellow human beings. This cannot, of course, be described in anything but an indirect or oblique manner and so appeal is made to the universe of secular symbolism. Such an appeal is justified by the knowledge that divine reality underlies all human experience and also by the fact that one would otherwise be forced to adopt a purely negative speech – the option taken, perhaps, by Buddhists and by some mystics of other traditions. As Antoine Vergote shows, it is when the two chains of expression have been placed in 'chiasm' or intersection, and when the attempt is made to speak about religious experience in terms of secular symbolism, that a specifically religious symbolism emerges (Vergote 1980, pp. 33-34). It is then that new significations appear and that the 'revelation' of divine reality receives tangible expression. The process is altogether different from the process of comparison (poetic or otherwise) which John Hick equates with religious language and which he opposes to 'literal' propositions (Hick 1977, p. 32). It is in a very real sense an 'unveiling' or *revelatio* of certain aspects of divine reality. Taken literally, there is nothing in common between, say, a shepherd or a fortress on the one hand, and God on the other. Yet it is a fact that the meaning of the metaphorical words is enhanced when they are spontaneously applied to the experience of God. New meaning is present and new information is received.

All experience is an immediate experience, even when the interpretation of that experience and the language in which the interpretation is expressed are influenced by a collective cultural tradition. There are no second-hand experiences. Moreover, experience is a total phenomenon. It is not the conclusion of a reasoning process, because we do not really 'experience' mental objects in the same way as we experience concrete objects. On the other hand, experience is not just 'sense experience'; it involves our whole existence, our humanity. We apprehend events, and we apprehend the active presence of divine reality in events in an imaginative way which stimulates our conduct and our commitment. Experiences, both positive and painful, impose themselves upon us and condition our interpretation of them. As we experience them, we also 'know' them, imparting a meaning which renders them authentic, that is to say, derived from the reality which we take to be their origin. All valid religious experience is taken to be a self-revelation of divine reality (O'Collins 1981, pp. 32-52).

Gods die and are replaced by others. That is to say, characterizations of divine reality are replaced by more plausible ones. What is at stake, as between one generation and another, and increasingly in the modern world, as between each religious system and its contemporaries, is the continuity and identity of the experience – the sense of God.

SOCIAL PROCESSES IN THE MODERN WORLD

An outline history of religion – traditional religion

Johann Baptist Metz has spoken of the 'silent atrophy of the religious consciousness' in the modern world (Metz 1980, p. 155). This observation applies primarily to what is known as 'the West', the North Atlantic world of Europe and North America, but it also applies in varying degrees to other countries and continents in so far as social processes at work in the West have radically affected them. Is the assurance of religious identity progressively disintegrating on a world-wide basis, as Metz believes? Is the survival of the sense of God now in doubt?

To answer these questions we must first sketch the history of religion and civilization, and then assess the impact of the modern consciousness on the contemporary heirs of the great religious traditions, including the Christian tradition itself. It is customary to begin a survey of the world's religions with a description of the ethnic religions of small-scale, pre-literate and pre-industrial societies. It is also customary to dub them 'primitive' or 'primal'. The usage is unfortunate because it carries overtones of prejudice, implying that such religions are crude and undeveloped, or at least primitive in time. While it is probably safe to describe man's earliest religious systems in terms of small-scale ethnic groups, it must not be forgotten that religion is a non-simultaneous phenomenon and that one cannot subject it to a neat theory of unilinear evolution. Ethnic religions flourish today in many parts of the world: mainly in Africa, but also in Oceania, parts of India and in Asia generally, Australasia, the Caribbean and the Americas. In default of historical evidence one cannot draw any specific conclusions from the nature of these religions today about ethnic religions at the dawn of recorded history. There will be occasion later in this book to discuss the nature of traditional ethnic religions and their relationship to Christianity, but it should be pointed out here that they exhibit an immense variety of theologies and forms of religious practice, although the majority of them can be termed theistic.

Many descriptions of so-called 'primitive' religions exhibit a scarcely disguised prejudice, be it Christian, evolutionist or simply Western ethnocentric. They are frequently called 'nature religions' and it is alleged that their objects of worship are the phenomena of nature. It is also alleged that there is relatively little notion of divine reality revealing itself in human events or in historical traditions of any depth. The worst caricatures, alas, are to be found in the pages of secular theologians and of Biblicists, anxious to emphasize the uniqueness and exclusive character of God's self-revelation in the history of Israel. The truth is that, although such religions flourish among eminently rural people whose closeness to nature encourages them to turn to creation for their religious symbolism and theological vocabulary, there is plenty of evidence in a great many instances of a clear distinction being made between the symbol and its referant, and of tribes whose religious beliefs and practices are a veritable map of historical migrations and socio-political events. There is no denying that a sense of closeness to nature breeds a sense of closeness to eternity and that modern Western man feels himself distanced by technology and urban living from the physical environment in which his religious symbols are grounded. The independent life of his symbolic tradition is undergoing severe strain and it can be relevantly asked whether a sense of closeness to nature is not a necessary ingredient in any religion, not least in Christianity.

When so-called 'primitive' religion is contrasted negatively with so-called 'higher' religion, one has the distinct feeling that the basis of this contrast is really other than religious. The critic does not have in mind the mental complexity of Australian Aboriginal beliefs, for example, or the subtlety of the African Dinka religion, imaging the human experience of unity and diversity. He is thinking in terms of technology and of political sophistication, rather than in those of theological ingenuity, refinement of spiritual experience or beauty of poetic imagery. In the final analysis, literacy and sacred

books, temples, vestments, hierarchies of religious specialists and the manipulation of precious materials in worship are secondary in religious experience
and in the functioning of religious systems. However, it is undeniable that
religious belief-systems have spread as a result of a growth in the scale of
socio-political relationships and of a development in technology, even if
these factors are not the ultimate criteria for making comparisons or value
judgements between one religion and another. Of course, there is a connection between religion and the advance of material civilization, a connection
we shall later explore, but the two are not inexorably linked and it is a
commonplace of religious history that the highest flights of religious experience (by the religious *virtuosi*) have occurred in conditions of ascetical
poverty and a denial of material values.

What characterizes the traditional ethnic religions of the world is that
their symbolic universe is derived directly from the historic interaction of a
human society with a given physical environment. What we witness in
these religious systems is a peculiar density of symbolism, a peculiarly unified
world-view, a refusal to make objective distinctions. Physical well-being is
bound up with social harmony, and human bodily existence is somehow
continuous with the created elements in which it exists. Man, says the
Caribbean poet Aimé Césaire: 'is flesh of the flesh of the world'. Human
society being undifferentiated and homogeneous, there is no incentive towards mental differentiation, and the whole of experience tends to be
'humanized' or personalized, not because of any intellectual incapacity or
inferiority, but because of recognizable socio-cultural realities.

It is reasonable to conjecture that it was against a tribal religious background of this kind that the great civilizations of Ancient Egypt and Meso-
potamia emerged in the fourth millennium B.C., the Indus Valley civilization before the middle of the second millennium B.C. and the Aryan civilizations which followed it and which gave birth in the fifteenth century B.C.
to the Vedic religion of India, and before the twelfth century B.C. to the
religion of the ancient Greeks. Finally, this kind of religious background lies
behind the formation of the Neolithic and Bronze Age dynasties of the Far
East and the rise of Shintoism in Japan towards the end of the first millennium B.C., and the appearance of Confucianism and Taoism in China in the
middle of the first millennium.

An outline history of religion – Judaism, Islam, Hinduism, Buddhism

As we have seen, 'gods die', and we are not primarily concerned here with
ancient religions which have no present-day adherents. In some cases, however, it is necessary to trace historical developments of present-day religions
from those which are no more (cf. Smart 1977). This book is essentially

about the Judeo-Christian revelation and its interpretation, and all the following chapters will deal with aspects and implications of this revelation.

The Hebrew sense of God finds expression in the Book of Exodus, which echoes the experience of Moses at Sinai about 1250 B.C. This experience is also the religious source of Israel's national identity. Although the mono-theistic Egyptian Pharaoh Akhnaton (Amenhotep or Amenophis IV) carried out his reform of Egyptian religious cults not much more than a century before the time of Moses, there is no reason to suppose a direct Egyptian influence on Mosaic Yahwism. However, Egyptian influences made them-selves felt in other ways, particularly later in the Jewish wisdom traditions. The Mosaic covenant was retrojected upon the religious traditions of Abraham and the patriarchs (who lived between 2000 and 1500 B.C. and) who were part of a nomadic movement from Chaldea to Canaan pre-cipitated by barbarian invasions of Mesopotamia. The writings of the Old Testament supply abundant evidence for the action and reaction upon one another of Judaism and the successive forms taken by religion in Meso-potamia and Canaan.

By the sixth century B.C. the religious vision of the poet Homer, who had lived some three centuries previously, was shaping the Olympian religion of the Greeks at Athens, and Hellenic culture made itself felt throughout the Mediterranean world, including post-exilic Israel during most of the three hundred years which preceded the birth of Christ. Ancient Rome was the political heir of ancient Athens, but the confrontation of the two cultures resulted in the identification of the Roman gods with those of Greece and the gradual submergence of Roman religion and culture within Hellenism, Christianity therefore appeared within a partially Hellenized Judaism and gradually established itself as the religion of the later Roman Empire, while Jewish hopes of a national revival were finally extinguished by Hadrian's conquest of Palestine in A.D. 135. Henceforth the Torah replaced the Temple as the unequivocal focus for Jewish religion and identity in their dispersal throughout the Mediterranean and European world.

The Islamic sense of God takes its origin in the experience of Muhammad when he was overwhelmed by the revelation he received on Mount Hira and received his mission as a prophet. The unique poetic power of this revelation recorded in the words of the Qur'an and its self-authenticating character are the basis of Islamic belief. Muhammad had witnessed Christian disunity and the proselytism of both Monophysites and Nestorians in north-western Arabia. Judaism, however, was a stronger influence in the towns of the Hejaz which were the centres for the Arabian caravan routes. Stronger still was the ethnic polytheism which Muhammad inherited from his family and tribe. Muhammad's mission radically transformed these tribal traditions at the turn of the sixth and seventh centuries A.D. There are many similarities between Muhammad's prophetic role and message and those of the prophets of ancient Israel. Indeed, the Qur'an itself situates the Islamic faith within the history of Israel and reinterprets the person and teaching of Jesus.

The simplicity of Muhammad's proclamation of the uniqueness and majesty of Allah and its power over the imagination of nomadic desert peoples was probably the chief factor in the creation and expansion of an Islamic spiritual empire. At its most powerful this empire stretched from the Himalayan mountains to the Pyrenees, and, although by the fourteenth century it had lost Spain, it gained the Balkans, Asia Minor, and Christian Byzantium itself; this continuous land mass in Europe, North Africa and the Near East has remained the historic patrimony of Islam. Peripheral to this patrimony are what might be termed the 'Muslim missions' which are the outcome of trade across the Sahara to West Africa and by sea to the East African coast and the East Indies. Although another attraction of Islam is its offer of a practical social ideal, the seeds of disunity already appeared in the eighth century, and today the three great manifestations of the Muslim religion and way of life are the Arab, the Persian and the Indian.

The only other strand of religious tradition emanating from the Near East which we shall consider here is that of Zoroastrianism. Zoroaster or Zarathustra was a holy man who lived at the turn of the seventh and sixth centuries B.C. and whose religion became that of the ancient Persian Empire and of the Cyrus who restored Israel after the Babylonian captivity. Despite the monotheistic emphasis in Zarathustra's teaching, the central problem of evil remained unresolved. However, like the Judeo-Christian tradition and Islam, it also possessed an eschatological character, with a belief in judgement after death. After the triumph of Islam in Persia (now the modern Iran), Zoroastrians went into exile in India, where they continue to survive in relatively small numbers as Parsees in the region of Bombay.

To understand the religious experience of India we must return to the ancient religion of the Aryans celebrated in the hymns we know as the Vedas. This was a theistic religion with a profusion of cults, myths and deities, celebrated by the collection known as the Rig-Veda, containing more than a thousand hymns. The organization of Indian society into castes also goes back to these very early times. In about 500 B.C. Vedic religion was transformed by writings concerned mainly with ritual, writings known as the Upanishads. In these writings the sacred principle Brahman is identified with a divine being or self that pervades the whole world and is found eternally within the individual. In its supreme form this self is known as Atman. Classical Hinduism is a devotional development of Vedic religion, reorganized by the religious philosophy represented by the Upanishads and by belief in cycles of rebirth operated by a principle of material force known as *karma*. In about the second century B.C. there appeared the *Bhagavad Gita* or 'Song of the Lord'. This religious epic presents a theistic religion in which Brahman becomes the creator, and other Hindu gods appear as alternative ways of thinking (mythologically) about him. It is Krishna who is the in-carnation of the god Vishnu and who is celebrated by the *Bhagavad Gita*. The bonds of *karma* can be overcome by loving devotion towards him and by doing good for his sake. He is a God of terror and majesty, but also of gentle love and compassion. In Hindu tradition Vishnu's great rival and alternative is Shiva, the god of fertility and dance, and yet, paradoxically, also the patron of Yoga, the Hindu tradition of asceticism.

In the history of Hinduism there has been an interaction between the popular devotional religion and the experience of holy men, ascetics, mystics and philosophers. The three personalities who have had the greatest in-fluence on Hinduism in its modern form are Shankara, Ramanuja and Madhva. Shankara, who lived at the turn of the eighth and ninth centuries A.D., emphasized the monistic aspect of the Upanishads and evolved a 'higher' understanding of the popular theism. This philosophy diminished the personal aspect of Brahman and taught the basic identity of the soul, the world and God, leading in practice to an extreme form of quietism. In the twelfth century, Ramanuja returned to the theistic mainstream of Vedic religion and sought to reconcile both the monistic and dualistic aspects of the Upanishads, while a century later Madhva abandoned monism altogether.

Shankara's philosophy was certainly influenced by Buddhism, and it is interesting to note that his tradition of Hindu monism influenced Sufi mysticism in Islam, while the Muslim religion in its turn had repercussions on Hinduism, producing a remarkable synthesis in the religion of the Sikhs.

A Hindu monastic asceticism called Jainism, which sought liberation from *karma*, the endless cycle of rebirth, was the starting-point for Buddhism. Siddartha Gautama, called Buddha or 'Enlightened One', was born in the sixth century B.C. and began by studying the cause of suffering within the total world process of change and again-becoming. He eventually gained enlightenment and taught that the way to end suffering was the removal of desire or craving. The goal of existence is total release or *nirvana* that comes about through final death when there is no further physical or psychological existence. *Nirvana* is thus a mystery which the Buddha could only describe in the negative terms of a deathless realm of the unborn and the uncreated. The Buddha bequeathed techniques of contemplation and medi-tation and these are practised by monks who follow his teaching in all its strictness, the form of Buddhism known as Theravada or Hinayana.

The Buddha's teaching was not esoteric or quietist. The cycles of rebirth are governed by the moral actions of the individual and his Noble Eightfold Path was one of purity, temperance, non-violence and compassion. He him-self was held to have postponed his *nirvana* out of compassion for his fellow human beings who needed his guidance. The monasteries, in their turn, be-came focal points for social order and popular devotion in a way that was more highly institutionalized than that of the Hindu holy men and their schools of meditation. This was especially due to the cult of the Bodhisattvas or 'Buddhas-to-be', the holy men who were consenting to rebirth and to the postponement of *nirvana* for the compassionate service of humanity. As we have already remarked, theism was not absent from even the most orthodox or conservative Buddhist world-view, but god-relatedness and rebirth as a god was made subordinate to the total goal of *nirvana*. Divinization was a halfway house to perfection, even though it might be the experience of a large proportion of mankind. At the Buddha's death in the fifth century B.C. his cremated remains were dispersed and buried in shrines, and statues began to be made of him. It is clear that, even in the conservative form of Buddhism which spread to Sri Lanka and Burma, the Buddha himself is equal in force, vitality and significance to God and that he attracts to himself the awe and gratitude which, in theistic religions, is directed to God (Bowker 1978, p. 250; Gombrich 1971, pp. 140–142).

Popular, or Mahayana, Buddhism made much of the cult of Bodhisattvas and even of celestial Buddhas who could be worshipped and invoked. In India Mahayana Buddhism became submerged in popular Hindu devotion, but it became the dominant religion in South-East Asia, and spread also to China and Japan. In Tibet the so-called Tantric Buddhism assembled a vast pantheon of celestial Buddhas, emanating from a single, theistic figure; while in China and Japan Amidism or 'Pure Land' Buddhism focused on Amitabha, creator of a 'heaven' in which *nirvana* could be more easily attained, and who, as 'Buddha of Boundless Light', could transfer merit to unworthy people. In China Buddhism dovetailed with Confucian ideas of correct behaviour and with the mystical techniques of Taoism, a religious philosophy that originated in the fourth century. In Japan it merged with Shintoism, originally the traditional religion, especially in the form of Buddhist meditation, known as Zen, which was brought from China at the beginning of the thirteenth century A.D. and which teaches a way of harmony in every department of life.

This historical and theological sketch reveals that the Christian is confronted by five basic non-Christian worlds. The first is that of traditional ethnic religion in its varied cultural forms, but distinguished by a symbolic universe derived from close human interaction with a specific physical environment and by certain forms of (small-scale) social experience. The second is Judaism, ancestral to Christianity and Islam, and now a world within a world. The third is Islam, and the last two are comprised by the Oriental traditions of Hinduism and Buddhism. We now return to Christianity and the birth of modern Europe, and thence to the effects of modern social processes on Christianity and on its five non-Christian contemporaries.

Christianity and the birth of modern Europe

The Roman imperial conquest resulted in the imposition of a Hellenistic culture on heterogeneous tribes over a major part of western Europe. This culture had become Christianized by the time the Roman Empire collapsed in the West during the fourth and fifth centuries, and the Church, with its powerful monarchical papacy and episcopate, inherited the mystique and the reality of Roman imperial power, while continuing to attract the migrating 'barbarians' to this same culture. 'Christendom' in the last quarter of the first millennium A.D. was a socio-political reality, as well as a religious one, uniting small, feudal communities which were hostile, or potentially hostile to one another. The high Middle Ages witnessed a contest for the substance of power between Church and State. This contest ended in a Pyrrhic victory for the Church, which was accorded spiritual supremacy but was effectively robbed of political dominance. This development was succeeded by the growth of nationalism in Europe and the emergence of the European nations in their modern form. The twelfth-century renaissance saw the partial recovery of the Greek philosophical and scientific patrimony and the appearance of competing schools of Christian theology. The sixteenth-century Renaissance encouraged a new spirit of rationalism and scientific criticism which helped to justify the Reformation. The zeal of the Reformers, coupled with the rivalry of competing nationalisms, resulted in the dismemberment of the Church in Europe, as well as the disappearance of any hope for an early *rapprochement* with the churches of the East. To theological pluralism was added ecclesial pluralism.

The wars of religion and the persecution of religious minorities led inevitably to the secularization of the state and to the discrediting of Christianity as an indisputable criterion for judging human thought and action. The eighteenth century was the age of 'Reason' and 'Enlightenment', symbolized at the height of the French Revolution by the enthronement of a 'Goddess of Reason' upon the high altar of Notre Dame Cathedral in Paris. This act was eminently symbolic of the dethronement of faith in divinely revealed religion by the philosophers. Meanwhile the effectiveness of human reason was daily demonstrated by the march of the physical sciences and the advances in technology, all of which received an overwhelming impetus from the discovery of evolution. Evolutionism bred a spirit of optimism and enquiry that promised an endless future for human invention. In the early stages of this process, long before the agricultural and industrial revolutions were in full swing, the possession of a developing technology and the need for markets and raw materials drove the nations of Europe into their first colonialist phase. The foundations for a secular state were laid in North America and gradually footholds were obtained in Latin America, in India, the East Indies and China. Meanwhile the human capital of Africa was drained in the murderous slave traffic across the Atlantic.

The excesses of the French Revolution were no tribute to the nobility of human reason, and German Idealist philosophers demonstrated its limitations. They were, however, divided as to what should replace it. For Johann Gottlieb Fichte the Absolute was a a moral world order. For Immanuel Kant, the greatest name among the Idealists, it was the practical moral imperative that governs the individual. For Friedrich von Schelling, it was 'Nature', while for G. W. F. Hegel, it was the 'World', and ultimately in practice, the State. Arthur Schopenhauer took a completely pessimistic view of reality, pitting the reason against a totally irrational will. The Christian theologians who conducted the debate with German Idealism, particularly the Lutherans, tended to invoke a transcendent and irrationally capricious God, or else to reduce him to a subjective religious experience, while Catholic theology became identified with neo-Scholasticism, in the final analysis a regressive movement, isolated from theological and political involvement.

Reactions to philosophical or theological idealism took two main forms, the existentialist and the positivist. Existentialism became a form of optimistic nihilism with Nietzsche, and a pessimistic, but equally radical, atheism with Jean-Paul Sartre. Nietzsche's supreme value, 'the eternal return', denied the finite, and made of truth the 'dance' of appearances and illusions. The liberated 'superman' who affirms his existence, according to Nietzsche, must run the supreme risk of recognizing the illusion as illusion. Nietzsche's ideal turned out to be no less irrationally capricious than the God whose existence he denied (Coplestone 1942, pp. 116-119). It is difficult not to be pessimistic, unless – with the German existentialists – one harks back to the human possibilities offered by history. One thing is sure, this kind of philosophy favours the rise of totalitarian regimes for which truth and falsity are equally illusory.

Auguste Comte and the positivists since his day have simply asserted that theology and metaphysics are meaningless, and that all knowledge is factual knowledge. In their conception, nature provides a coercive mechanism for technological progress. At most, with Ludwig Feuerbach, theology can be equated with anthropology. It is against this background of thought that the teaching of Karl Marx must be seen. Of German-Jewish descent, Marx was in many ways a prophetical figure of Old Testament proportions. He proclaimed, in almost eschatological terms, that a totally new world order was close at hand. He preached a radical – even a violent – break with the socio-political establishment of nineteenth-century Europe with its exploitation of the working class and its inequitable division of material wealth. He called for a total eradication of previous theologies, philosophies and irrelevant historical memories. What mattered was not theory, but practice. The only bearers of historical meaning were the members of the working class and, as Metz has pointed out, history was rewritten by Marx in an evolutionary way (Metz 1980, pp. 125-127). The triumphant proletariat was the final outcome of a kind of historical survival of the fittest, and the vanquished classes were blamed for every failure. With the end of capitalist society, Marx believed, ultimate human freedom and happiness would be assured.

Without underestimating the importance of Marxism for world history or the many truths that underlie the Marxist analysis of modern society from a socio-economic point of view, it has to be recognized that Karl Marx was a false prophet. The Marxist 'Second Coming' has not happened. In Marxist countries the old religious allegiances have not automatically disappeared and material prosperity for all has not been achieved. As an eminent Czechoslovak Marxist, Milan Machoveč, has written, modern Marxists are in a situation comparable to that of the early Christians who discovered that the parousia was taking its time and who became more favourably disposed towards the culture, the disappearance of which they had foretold (Machoveč 1977, pp. 26-27). One might be pardoned for thinking that the comparison ends there. The mistake of Marx was not to see that, after the revolution, human beings would still be egotistical, cowardly, cruel and power-hungry, and that the violent expropriation of one class by another was a recipe for totalitarianism, arbitrary bloodshed and the abuse of power. Marx also failed to foresee the coming of the welfare state in which petty bourgeois as well as proletariat would enjoy many of the social reforms intended as by-products of the revolution, and he could not know of the awakening of a political consciousness among colonial peoples.

Christianity and the contemporary world

Writers and thinkers of the twentieth century have proclaimed again and again that man is liberating himself from his old fears and superstitions and that he 'has come of age'. Yet, behind this façade of the rational, liberated man, this 'new man', there lurks, as Johann Baptist Metz reminds us, the middle-class, bourgeois society of the Western world (Metz 1980, pp. 32-47). This society grew out of a historic struggle with the social and economic structures of an earlier feudal and absolutist world. Its principles are materialist: the principles of production, trade and consumption. Everything that has no value for this 'exchange game', religion, tradition, traditional authority, is relegated to the private sphere. This relativization and privatization of religious traditions and authorities is further accelerated by the revolution in communications technology and by the increased mobility and the enlargement of social scale that this revolution has entailed. Middle-class Western man is not being expropriated by the proletariat; he is swallowing up the proletariat, and he is himself the victim of new forms of authority, bureaucratic, hierarchical, anonymous – a faceless totalitarianism. In his hurry to control the resources of nature in the interest of his markets, he has lost interest in human freedom and sensibility and his understanding of life, of love and of suffering is diminished.

The race to control natural and human labour resources was not far beneath the surface in the great movement of colonial expansion which characterized the ending of the nineteenth century. The colonial empires of Spain and Portugal were already disintegrating into new nationalities and cultural amalgams, when Britain, France, Germany, the United States and – to a lesser extent – Holland, Belgium and Italy parcelled out the remainder of the world. Interest was focused on the exploration and annexation of the African interior. No doubt there were genuinely altruistic motives involved, such as the desire to end the Arab slave trade across the Sahara and the Indian Ocean, and to raise the material standard of life of indigenous peoples unwillingly placed in colonial tutelage. But altruistic motives alone would not have been enough to sustain the colonial movement. Colonialism was a form of aggressive nationalism, and, in spite of the material benefits it conferred on subject peoples, it was an alienating and divisive experience which also generated racialist antagonism. The colonial powers found the indigenous peoples of their colonies socially heterogeneous, and technologically weak. Not only did colonial borders create further divisions, but the colonial policy of 'divide and rule' (sometimes elegantly named 'indirect rule') heightened tribal consciousness.

The relationship of the nineteenth-century missionary expansion of Christianity to the colonialist movement was a complex one, but there was a relationship. Although the one cannot be simplistically explained in terms of the other, there is no doubt that the churches rode out from a Europe, increasingly hostile to their teaching, upon the crest of the colonial wave. Without the support and protection of their compatriots, the Christian missions might not have survived, let alone have achieved success. Yet, in spite of having the colonial power in the background, the impact of Christianity was uneven. This was partly because Christian missionaries themselves offered a divided witness. It was also due to the varying strengths of the non-Christian worlds with which they were confronted. A fundamental ethnocentrism at home foiled the early attempts at cultural adaptation by missionaries in China, India and Ethiopia. The Buddhist cultures of China, Japan and South-East Asia were impervious to Christian evangelism, and conversions were marginal. In India European colonialists and missionaries arrived in the wake of an earlier Islamic expansion which had left Hinduism weakened and vulnerable. However the ultimate effect of Christian evangelism and education was to stimulate Hinduism and Indian nationalism. Muslims, from the beginning, were deeply disturbed by their contact with a technologically superior Europe. They were unable to reconcile their own passionate faith in Islam with their experience of political weakness, so powerful a cohesion was there between religion, politics and society in their minds. Again, there was never a question of Christianity making any impact within the Islamic world. The tensions in contemporary Islam derive from an access of economic and political power, rather than from religious dialogue.

In the world of traditional ethnic religions, typified best by Africa, the cultures were highly absorbent and vulnerable to a Christianity allied with modern education and technology. But even here ethnic diversity was bewildering and there has been a failure to Christianize in depth, so much so that there is an ever-present danger of grass-roots heterodoxy and the spontaneous generation of new Christian movements. Parallels can, no doubt, be provided from the relatively small populations of the Oceanian archipelagoes and the Aborigines of Australasia. It must, however, be said that Christianity was an important factor in the political awakening of many colonies, and often the first generation of nationalist leaders were deeply convinced Christians. In Latin America the Amerindian and Black ex-slave populations remained very much the exploited classes, although they adopted the religion of the colonists from Spain and Portugal. Catholicism remains the dominant religion in these – often politically unstable – countries, although it exhibits a considerable degree of syncretism in its popular forms (cf. Bastide 1978).

Totalitarianism is a superficially attractive option in a modern, open, pluralistic and disorientated society. It offers a political formula that is at once simple and ruthless. The origin and aftermath of the two twentieth-century World Wars were bound up with totalitarianisms of different kinds, the militarism and fascism of the defeated European powers and the rise of the Soviet dictatorship and its satellites. The First World War brought about the end of the German empire; while the Second World War, with its strongly racist issues, sounded the death knell for the other remaining empires, British, French, Portuguese and Dutch. The newly independent countries of India, Africa, Asia, Oceania and the Caribbean either found a nationalist ideology in their own religious culture, or tended to create a totalitarian system with either a socialist (often a Marxist) ideology or a political creed invented to justify a given alignment. Judaism also found political expression again in the independent state of Israel.

The immediate post-war period saw an enormous upsurge in technological development which vastly increased the capacity to produce goods and services. New electronic, metallurgical and pharmaceutical discoveries were made, while the population of the world doubled in thirty years. The establishment of a welfare state in Western countries was accompanied by a massification of industry and urban living and the industrialization of agriculture. Enormous concentrations of economic power appeared in the hands of massive enterprises known as multi-national companies; and these rapidly became a new and more insidious form of imperialism. In fact they represented a network of domination according to which decisions concerning the income, investment and trade of three-quarters of the world were made by about one quarter. Multi-national companies are one thing; another facet of modern world organization is multi-national blocs; mutual defence pacts, economic communities, international cartels operate against the background of the ever-present threat of a nuclear war.

The United Nations Organization and its various agencies have become the principal forum for public protest against a world divided into rich and poor nations, dominators and dependents. The West, it appears, is continuing – by its policies – to keep the 'Third World' countries poor, that is, continuing to underdevelop them. So far, there is no sign of a new social and economic order in which the world community can become a collection of truly interdependent nations. In the West industrialization is dehumanizing mankind; there is a constant threat to the environment, and a new form of violence, outside the bounds of legal warfare, is taking place in the heart of towns and cities.

We asked, at the beginning of this section, whether the survival of the sense of God was in doubt. It looks now as if it is a question of the survival of man himself. It seems that technological man has lost his nerve and that his machine is about to veer out of control. Certainly modern social processes and the modern consciousness have no room for a sense of God, but equally we should not assume that the modern consciousness spreading from the West has captured all the peoples of the world. There are many people who still value human dignity and freedom, many who cry out for liberation from the depths of suffering, poverty and humiliation, and their desire for liberation breeds the still more fundamental desire for redemption. A sense of God is still deeply relevant to the human situation, but what forms can it take in the modern world, and what credibility remains to the Christian sense of God?

THE CREDIBILITY OF CHRISTIAN REVELATION

Christianity and pluralism

Credibility and plausibility are closely related ideas. We shall study the act of faith at a later stage in this book, but it is enough to say now that a person believes what is credible; and what is credible appears plausible on the basis of social experience. A religious belief, expressed in symbolic terms, appeals primarily to that part of our thought process which we call the imagination, and our imagination evokes experience. We learn our symbols and our interpretation of experience in a social way, and we therefore depend upon a 'symbol-system' or upon a 'system of information' which is plausible because it is part of our experience. Today we have to deal with a crisis in religious plausibility. This has come about because of religious pluralism and human mobility. Before the revolution in communications technology, before the improvement in land and sea travel, before the invention of air travel, radio and electronic communications media, not to mention communications satellites, people lived in relatively isolated, homogeneous communities and plausibility was not a problem. Organizational change has now brought different 'plausibility groups' into proximity with one another. This is the phenomenon known as pluralism. The modern consciousness, of which we have spoken above, gives people not only a facility for handling, using or 'consuming' the new technology, but it also relegates non-material values to a secondary or private sphere. An individual is therefore likely to fall under the influence of different plausibility groups at different times of his or her life, and their information content tends to be mutually conflicting. The pace of change and mobility in the modern world tends to make our allegiances transient and superficial. Over and above all this is the primacy of the materialistic modern consciousness in which the churches and religious faiths become (in Peter Berger's phrase) 'cognitive minorities', and people feel free to choose, or not to choose, a religious allegiance (Berger 1980, pp. 32-65). All this is what we mean when we speak of 'religious consumerism' or of the relativization and privatization of religion in the modern world.

Westerners are apt to overestimate the power and depth of the modern consciousness, because the rest of the world has been obliged to become a passive consumer of Western technology. Yet there is not only less facility for handling Western technology in Third World countries (and it is hardly likely to improve as long as the West remains the almost exclusive source of this technology), but a strong sentiment of revolt against cultural alienation is growing in the aftermath of colonialism. Not only are Hindus, Muslims, Buddhists and Jews reaffirming their religious traditions, but Africans, in a continent fraught with ethnic heterogeneity, are also taking their stand on a not easily definable African culture. What is more, mobility from and between all the points of the compass is bringing non-Christian cultures to Europe and North America. Small Muslim communities, often associated with immigrant workers from North Africa, Turkey and Pakistan, are springing up. Hindu techniques of meditation are making their appeal and the more conservative forms of Buddhism are attracting the Western atheist intellectual.

One cannot, it appears, describe the modern experience of pluralism in wholly negative terms. On the contrary, one of the aspects of contemporary society is that of specialization and the interdependence and complementarity which this entails. There is also a degree of overlapping, or congruence, between different systems and experiences and this can be discerned by reflective people. There is also a process of 'incorporation', the term applied to the degree to which different systems and institutions have a mutual influence. In the 1960s Marshall Murphree demonstrated, in what he called a 'synthetic' study of religion among the Shona people of Zimbabwe, just how a process of dialectical interchange took place between Catholics, Methodists, Independent Church members and Traditional Religionists in that area, even though each denomination had a relative degree of self-encapsulation (Murphree 1969). It was a thoroughly realistic approach to the study of religion in the modern pluralistic situation.

Of course, the churches and faiths have been able to meet the challenge of pluralism in a way similar to that of secular states and communities – the formation of blocs; and this has had very positive results for Christians where the ecumenical movement has been concerned. United churches, world federations and alliances of different wings within a particular church tradition, national Christian councils, continental conferences of churches and the World Council of Churches itself are all examples. Catholic participation in such bodies is so far small, but the Catholic Church regularly sends official observers, holds joint working parties and ecumenical discussions, and in some cases has taken membership of joint Christian Councils. It has, in any case, its own lateral blocs: national episcopal conferences, regional and continental associations and its Vatican Secretariats for Christian Unity, for Non-Christian Religions and for Non-Believers. Other faiths, too, have seen the need to form blocs and secretariats. In Britain, for example, there is the British Board of Jews; in Tanzania, the Supreme Council of Muslims of Tanzania. In the case of Islam, in which religion and politics are closely interwoven, one is not surprised to find conferences of Muslim Heads of State.

Christianity and secularism

All this activity in the cause of greater religious unity, however, is only a partial answer to the ever-present problem of pluralism, and this problem is compounded – particularly in the case of Christianity – by an appearance of counter-witness which further weakens the grounds for credibility. We have spoken of modern secularism and materialism. How far, it may be asked, has Christianity itself been bound up with the processes which have brought about the materialist and secular outlook? We have spoken about colonial alienation, about injustice in the world, about rich and poor nations. Where does Christianity stand in all of this? Is the Church perhaps on the wrong side? There are no easy answers to these questions, and they are not such as to contribute unequivocally to a restoration of credibility.

Theological interpretations of secularization have adopted different standpoints (and we shall return to the question in Chapter 7). The traditional point of view in Catholic theology has been that secularism is opposed to a sense of the sacred and to religious faith, that it is a form of human egoism, a replacing of God by man. The more recent view of the 'secular theologians' has been that it is a reaction to sacralism, to an unbalanced domination of human thinking by the sacred, and they point to factors within Christianity itself which favour secularization. Some would like to begin with Genesis and the divine command to Adam 'to fill', 'to conquer' and 'to master' the earth. Others would begin with the Christian mystery, the incarnation and resurrection by which human nature and secular realities have been transformed and God himself brought down to earth. It is not a question of anthropomorphism, of talking about God in a human or secular way, but of anthropogenesis – of man, becoming, through embodying the divine reality, more truly himself. Western philosophers of history, like Christopher Dawson or Arnold Toynbee, trace the technological development of the Western world back to the liberating effect which Christianity has had on the human mind, and predict world unification under the spiritual, as well as the technological, aegis of the West. Some anthropologists and missiologists see Christianity as the only form of religion which can cope with the modern consciousness.[2] Because of its Western origin and form, it alone can articulate religion in a technological society. The great palaeontologist and Christian philosopher of evolution Pierre Teilhard de Chardin saw the technological unification of humanity (by the West) as culminating in Christogenesis, Christ becoming all in all.

Yet somehow this optimism of the secular theologians fails to satisfy. Somehow it fails to do justice to the actual facts as we experience them. The secular reaction has clearly gone too far if no explicit reference need be made to God at all, or if God becomes a dream that nobody remembers, but which does its work nonetheless in the subconscious mind. In any case, if one accepts secularization as a divine work of liberation, creating an increasingly open society, this comfortable view would appear to be belied by the scandal of pluralism.

Some would plausibly argue that the Church itself is inherently pluralistic, but that the Reformation was simply an occasion when it was unable to control or contain open discussion. There is certainly a grain of truth in Max Weber's classic bracketing of Protestantism and capitalism, and in the idea of a link between the liberty asserted at the Reformation and the growth of a secular society.

If the whole meaning of human history and existence is to be discovered from within, as secular theologians propose, without any reference to an 'outside' or transcendent God, human life would not appear to have any meaning at all. Any experience, even the most trivial, can only be fully understood by going beyond it and by placing it in a new and larger context. Those who deny a transcendent principle are making the impossible claim that man and his world are self-explanatory, with the further implication that Jesus is no more than a comparative example of a successful human being (Williams 1966, pp. 75-103). It was logical, therefore, that the secular theology of the 1960s was followed by the 'Death of God' school in which the paradoxical attempt was made to take the death of God as the starting-point for a 'theology'. In our experience things *are* explained in terms of other things; and it is reasonable to believe that everything is only explicable in terms of a transcendent principle which reveals itself in the oblique language of mythology, a mythology formed by, and forming, our experience.

Christianity and counter-witness in the Third World

If Christianity is only meaningful in terms of a revelation, what about the charge that the Church is frequently on the wrong side? We have already seen that Christian missionary activity was related in complex ways to the whole movement of colonialism by which the West turned the world into a 'white minority régime', and that this domination persists in the form of economic and technological power. In the early days missionary evangelization was fraught with Western ethnocentric prejudice. Seventeenth-century missionaries and nineteenth-century missionaries were children of their time, convinced that technological superiority implied moral superiority – the 'Protestant ethic', if you like. Theologically, non-Christian religions had no rights. It took time for an effective confrontation to take place between Christianity and other religions and for the development of a nuanced theology of salvation, a nuanced theology of religions and an ecclesiology that was multi-cultural. The question arises whether Christianity, as a kerygmatic and universalist (Catholic) religion, does not have a built-in aggressivity that has come to bring 'not peace, but a sword'. Certainly, the message of Christ is a challenge to human wickedness, human complacency and human irrationality. It demands a *metanoia*, or change of heart; and it provokes the hostility of those for whom the ideal is too high or too censorious of their own lives. But there has also been misplaced zeal on the part of the missionary, and an unjustified intolerance at variance with the spirit of the Gospel.

It would be invidious to apportion blame too specifically, or to make odious comparisons between one century and another. However, different epochs had different failings. In the sixteenth and seventeenth centuries, the era of the Reformation and the wars of religion, when governments took up the cudgels on behalf of the denomination of their choice, it was almost impossible for a missionary to distinguish between colonization and evangelization. Moreover, the Church cherished the 'Constantinian' or Christendom image of the relationship between religious and secular power, long after it had ceased to be a reality. In a historical church which values tradition, there is, perhaps, also a built-in tendency to be conservative, to support the establishment and justify the *status quo*. That is the origin of the Latin American paradox, the paradox of a church divided between a repressive, rightist ruling class and a poverty-stricken populace clamouring for civil liberties and social justice. It is perhaps also the paradox of Southern Africa or the 'Deep South' of the United States, where Christians are divided by racialist attitudes or racial policies. In the same Church, Christians flirt with Marxism in Nicaragua or El Salvador but fight it in the militant free trade unions of Communist Poland. Christian statements about social principles sometimes reflect the concerns of Western bourgeois society. Equally, at other times they reflect the interests of the worker and peasant classes and their desire for liberation. Christians are bound to support the cause of the poor and the suffering. They should not uphold – or appear to uphold – the claims of oppressors.

Missionaries of the last 150 years, we might like to think, had a better record than those of the Reformation period. Yet there is still a sizeable gap between theological theory and actual praxis. A distinguished Catholic missionary bishop has recently suggested that one of the main areas of tension in the Church is the relationship between the Church as universal and the local churches; and that another area of crisis is the character of missionary agencies, particularly their economic and cultural role in the present neo-colonialist situation (Blomjous 1980). But in the end, it is not a weighing-up of the successes and failures of Christians to live up to their own ideals which creates or dissipates credibility. Conversions are made because a Christian explanation of experienced relationships is plausible, and for the same reason people remain loyal to the Christian tradition they have adopted in spite of the mistakes of their co-religionists.

Interculturality and historicity – human bases of a Christian revival

We still have to ask ourselves: What is the Christian to do in the face of contemporary pluralism, privatization and relativization of religion, and in the face of occasional counter-witness by his fellow-Christians? How can he continue to assert the credibility of his religion? Peter Berger has recently suggested three courses of action (Berger 1980). The first is simply to reaffirm the old certainties and to bypass or to ignore modern realities. This is done by an appeal to authority. The authority, he suggests, might be the authority of God's Word in the Bible appealed to as completely transcending human understanding, and as something wholly and exclusively true. This would be the position, he thinks, of the great German Protestant theologian Karl Barth, and he dubs this line of thinking 'neo-traditionalism', the prefix 'neo-' suggesting an unrealistic revival.

Berger does not offer a specific Catholic example, but the Catholic reading his words will think immediately of 'neo-Scholasticism', the anti-modernist form of theology which dominated the final years of the nineteenth century and the first decades of the twentieth. We shall deal at length with the whole modernist controversy later in this work, but it should be said at once that, though the opinions of individual modernists constituted a challenge to received Catholic teaching, there was no single integral theory called 'modernism' which was held by all modernists. It can also be said that neo-Scholasticism evaded the awkward questions of the modernists by returning to the system of thought which prevailed among Catholic theologians three or four centuries earlier. In particular there was a nostalgia for the magisterial and coherent theological system of St Thomas Aquinas, for Thomism was a symbol of an age of certainty and faith.

Similarly, the neo-traditionalist tries to revive past certainties, to recreate a world in which he can feel at home once more. He simplifies the problem by artificially thinning the ranks of his enemies. Everyone must be classified as either for or against. And he appeals to the very authority which is being questioned, ignoring history and the fact that times have changed. His transcendentalism takes him out of the world of present-day reality. Berger includes in this tendency those who make – what is called – 'the leap of faith'. Like Søren Kierkegaard (or even like Nietzsche), they prefer to leap out of a hopeless situation and into an unknown world. It is an irrational, escapist act and, like the other forms of neo-traditionalism, it provides no lasting answer to the basic problem of modern disorientation.

The second choice is that of the reductionist. We met him earlier in this chapter, both in the shape of the methodological atheist studying religion and of the secular theologian. The reductionist decides to accept modernity and all its presuppositions. He accepts modern man's opinion of himself, as 'a man come of age'. He is the classic demythologizer, determined to strip away layer after layer of mythology and poetry (for these, in his opinion, have nothing to do with factual reality) and to try to reach the core of the message, the originating experience of Christianity. If this is historically elusive, according to modern criteria of scientific history, then it becomes a question of how far one can go. The important thing is to 'translate' anything otherworldly, or transcendent, or supernatural, or mythological into terms which are acceptable to modern, secular man. What is one left with? One is left with a 'God of the gaps', an anonymous factor to which all the gaps in our knowledge are referred. Or, like Rudolf Bultmann, the well-known demythologizing Biblicist, one again makes 'a leap of faith'. In his case, the Biblical events carry no revelatory meaning in themselves. The only saving reality is the faith of the believer who responds to the events. Or, with the secular theologians, Harvey Cox, C. van Peursen, A. van Leeuwen, or Colin Williams and many others, God is replaced by an existentialist anthropology.

However, as we enter the 1980s, all is not well with secularism. Man cannot cope with his own technology. It is destroying the environment and it threatens to destroy man himself. Mankind is in a state of shock about its own future; in Alvin Toffler's memorable phrase, it suffers from 'future shock'. Toffler's message was simply: Learn to live with it. Accept the transience and the superficiality and the disorientation. Grasp the nettle! But why, we ask, should humankind not look for further and wider horizons? Why should we accept that a man who uses a telephone, or watches television or drives a car is more of a man than, say, Socrates, or the Buddha, or the prophet Isaiah, or the author of St John's Gospel? It seems, Berger concludes, that modern man has a great 'hunger for redemption and transcendence'.

Berger's final course of action, the one he recommends, is to accept the fact that theology follows faith, and then, true to St Anselm's dictum of *fides quaerens intellectum*: 'faith seeking understanding', to look for evidence to strengthen and clarify our faith. There is nothing new about such a conclusion, though we seem to have lost sight of it in the contemporary welter of semi-rationalist theology. This proposal, of course, assumes that there is faith left in the world – even the Western world – and it raises the further question that interested Newman, as to how faith arises. Faith needs roots – roots in a community, roots in an authority. Faith is not a mere assent to intellectual propositions, but a living communion with the God in whom one believes and whom one trusts and loves. It is an experience and it is found in fellowship, in the encounter with other people and other communities. Faith appeals firstly to that part of our mental process that we call 'imagination', and it does so – as we have already often pointed out – through symbols, which are instances of experience. The authority to which faith appeals is not an authority of the past or an authority placed outside one's experience. It is the authority of a community that lives imaginatively, sacramentally and in a posture of worship (Coulson 1981, pp. 161-163). Faith needs an authority which inspires trust, a present, self-authenticating authority, and this is found in the experience of community and of the communion among communities.

This last phrase suggests Christianity's final answer to pluralism. Even though much stress is being laid on basic community-building in the Christian Churches today, as a means of combating superficiality in relationships and the anonymous 'crowd Church' of the past, such communities are essentially open, or they are not Christian at all. We saw that there is a possibility – indeed, an often disguised reality – of dialectical interchange between religious traditions and cultures. Contrary to recent suppositions by missionaries and others, such interpenetration is of the essence in Christianity. The Catholicity of the Church is not merely defined in terms of its kerygmatic vocation, to proclaim the Good News to the uttermost ends of the earth, but by its 'conditioning by strangers', by its essential interculturality (Metz 1980, p. 98). This again is a theme to be taken up later in greater detail.

We have spoken of faith in a transcendent God, revealing himself, a faith symbolically credible. Johann Baptist Metz defines faith as a *memoria* or 'memorial', that is, a memory made present, an *anamnesis* (Metz 1980, pp. 184-187, 195-197). This memory differs from the rationally classified or objectivized 'cybernetic use of memory' by scientific history. It is the Church's public and collective memory of Jesus Christ, continually kept alive by his personal presence. It is a narrative memory; and Christianity is a community 'remembering and narrating'. As Edward Schillebeeckx has pointed out, scientific historians, Biblical exegetes and systematic theologians have lost their 'narrative innocence' (Schillebeeckx 1979, p. 79). Of course, we cannot pretend Biblical or philosophical or historical criticism has not happened, but we do need to regain that 'narrative innocence', and we do that primarily in worship. Our memory is a repetitive memory that goes forwards, an 'eschatological memory', a hope with roots in the past. We do not, like the Marxists or any of the positivist or evolutionist philosophers, deny the relevance of the past towards the future.

What do we remember, and what do we celebrate when we remember? We remember and celebrate the suffering and the freedom of Jesus Christ, and, with his suffering and freedom, we celebrate the history of human suffering and human freedom. The contemporary philosophies have no use for those who suffered in the past or for those who are dead. Even contemporary theologians often ignore them. Christians believe in universal justice and that means justice for those who suffered in the past. Christians believe in the historic unity of mankind and of a God who is God of the living and the dead. Suffering has always been associated with guilt. As long as men believed in God, they could exonerate themselves by blaming God for suffering. Once the philosophers had declared that God was dead, they either invented a new transcendent principle, such as 'Nature' or 'the World' or 'Matter', which could take the blame, or else they followed up the abolition of God with the abolition and oblivion of man, thus suspending man's historical responsibility or negating him as an acting person.

Jesus's passion gives us a new vision of man and a new hope. By taking suffering upon himself and by dying, he has taught man to take suffering upon himself, by recognizing that he is a sinner. Only then does man become free. The history of suffering is not merely the history of conquest and domination, but the history of the cause of freedom. Thus liberation is really redemption and in celebrating it and experiencing it with greater awareness of its reality, we express our solidarity with the dead and the conquered, and our resistance to everything that reduces the human being to an unremembered step in an evolutionary process. Every human life has meaning for the whole of history. God's self-revelation in Jesus, therefore, not only tells us who God is and what he is like; it tells us who we are and what we are like, and it transforms us by conferring meaning and hope on our lives. This is the Word God speaks to us in the collective memory of the Christian tradition.

NOTES

1 Nietzsche was naturalized Swiss.
2 Swantz 1970 takes this view, and Horton 1971 comes near to it.

QUESTIONS FOR DISCUSSION

(1) To what extent is it necessary to affirm that religion is a distinct category of experience?

(2) Why is symbolic language (rather than language that is purely subjective or completely literal) apt for the expression of revealed religion?

(3) What are the effects of modern social processes on contemporary Christianity?

(4) For further enquiry: In your experience, is religious consciousness becoming atrophied in the modern world? What kinds of experience can strengthen and clarify the Christian faith today?

SELECT ANNOTATED READING LIST

J. Bowker, 1978: *The Religious Imagination and the Sense of God* (Oxford). This book begins with a discussion about the plausibility of revealed religion and the shortcomings of methodological atheism. It then demonstrates how the sense of God has survived crises of implausibility in Judaism, Christianity, Islam and Buddhism.

J. O. Mills and W. S. F. Pickering (eds), 1980: *Sociology and Theology: Alliance and Conflict* (Brighton). This symposium deals with several aspects of the relationship between these two disciplines. The contributions of Eileen Barker (especially pp. 18–22) and Timothy Radcliffe (especially pp. 151–160) deal with sociological approaches to the study of religion and the problem of pluralism.

C. Geertz, 1966: 'Religion as a Cultural System', in *Anthropological Approaches to the Study of Religion*, ed. M. Banton, A.S.A. vol. 3 (London). This classic study offers an accurate picture of the psycho-social reality constituted by the phenomenon of religion.

C. Rycroft, 1979: *The Innocence of Dreams* (London). Dr Rycroft gives a readable summary of the development of psychological theory concerning dreams and their symbolism from Freud and Jung to our own day. He does not neglect the aspects of religion and literary imagination.

N. Smart, 1977: *The Religious Experience of Mankind* (Glasgow). A comprehensive synopsis of the whole history of religions.

P. Berger, 1980: *The Heretical Imperative* (London). A readable and succinct analysis of the modern consciousness and the problems it poses for Christianity. He presents the options before the Church with equal clarity.

G. O'Collins, 1981: *Fundamental Theology* (London). This book is intended to be a guide to the teaching of the theology of Revelation. It is relevant to every chapter of our book, but it would suffice to begin by reading Fr O'Collins's chapters II and III on 'Human Experience' and 'The Divine Self-Communication'.

J. B. Metz, 1980: *Faith in History and Society* (London). This is a practical, fundamental theology which analyses the complex social and political structures of the modern world, as well as the current Christian crisis of identity. He shows how the Christian message must be disengaged from irrelevant structures, and he explores the relevant categories of salvation.

2
God's Word, Our Guide

THE PRE-HISTORY OF CHRIST

The religious experience of ancient Israel

Karl Rahner represents the whole Biblical age from Abraham to the birth of Jesus Christ, some two thousand years in all, as nothing other than the brief moment that inaugurates the Christ-event (Rahner 1978, pp. 166-167). Of all human history, it is the most immediate and proximate preparation for the life and death of Christ. It is Christ's 'pre-history', and for Christians that is its value. If God speaks his word to us in the collective memory of the Christian tradition, then we must go back to the history of ancient Israel, to Moses and to Abraham in order to understand that tradition, and the process, as well as the product, of that revelation. But first let us briefly summarize the argument that has brought us to this stage in the discussion.

We began with Newman's dictum: 'No people has been denied a revelation from God' and with the modern challenge to revealed religion. We then considered the psycho-social reality of religions as symbol-systems and their capacity to generate new knowledge about ultimate reality. This new knowledge comes about not because of the mere application of some attributes of our experience of the world to religious experience, but because of the interaction of two verbal schemes which in itself produces a distinct category of information. This is described by the believer as an 'unveiling', a 'revelation', an experience of God speaking and calling. It is an experience that takes place, with varying degrees of intensity, within the framework of a symbolic universe that is inherited by a community. We then examined religious identity in the contemporary world and concluded that, although it was in crisis, it was not in a state of total disintegration. The modern consciousness has not eliminated either the faith or the foundations of Christianity, nor has it destroyed those of the other major religious traditions of the world. On the contrary, processes of modernization, coupled with the wider impact of Christian missionary activity, have even provoked a revival of non-Christian religions.

In discussing Christian credibility, therefore, we begin with a faith that is not only still alive but is particularly relevant to the positivist, materialist situation in which we find ourselves. It is a faith that claims to cater for a world that hungers after transcendence and redemption, a faith that expresses solidarity with the suffering (in spite of lapses in practice), a faith that is characterized by its interculturality and its relevance to other religious traditions, and a faith that unites both living and dead through the saving event of Jesus Christ. It is his memory that Christians narrate and celebrate with practical effect on their lives. It is a faith that confers meaning and hope.

In order to understand Jesus Christ and to test the claims of Christian faith, we turn to the Old Testament and to the religious experience of ancient Israel, for it is this tradition and this experience which constitute the symbolic universe inherited by Christians and which help us to discover what they mean by revelation. It has been said that while the ancient Greeks bequeathed many books to us, the fruit of profound human thinking and equally profound debate between individual thinkers, the ancient Israelites had, on the other hand, one single book, the Jewish Bible of the Old Testament. This Bible (and the word itself means: 'The Book') was, in fact, a whole literature. Some of it is clearly poetry or hymnody. Some parts are oracular. Some purport to deal with historical events in chronological order. Some sections are simply fiction, while others are collections of proverbs and wise sayings. But all of it possesses an impressive unity, a growing comprehension. The writings which comprise the sacred books of the Old Testament and which came to be known collectively as 'the Word of God', are the result of a lengthy and complex process of editing and revision. They are compilations and re-compilations which represent different layers of theological thought, and a constant re-reading of older texts in the light of later events. These books which constitute the Bible of the Jews are the cumulative reflection of a whole people and that is why, for example, the compilations of post-exilic scribes were ascribed to the great leaders of Israel's history, to Moses, Joshua, Samuel, David and Solomon, who were not necessarily writers at all, let alone the authors of the books ascribed to them.

The idea of the Old Testament as an authoritative collection of sacred *writings* can, perhaps, obscure the very real sense in which they are God's Word. Not only are they, in the main, a series of 'congealed' or 'frozen' oral traditions, but they are traditions about historical events, and their unity derives from the perception that these events form an intelligible unity in the light of religious faith. The events of Israel's history are the 'words' of Yahweh, Israel's God. For the Israelites the spoken word had a dynamic entity, as it has among many pre-literate peoples. We who live in a literate culture believe that *scripta manent*: 'that which is written remains'. In the oral culture, it is the spoken word which has permanence. Thus the Pygmy of Zaïre compares God with the spoken word:

> He has no body.
> He is as a word which comes out of your mouth.
> That word! It is no more.
> It is past and still it lives! (Young 1940, p. 23).

The word is a release of psychic energy from a person, and when it is uttered with power it effects the reality which it signifies. The word is a 'thing' or a 'deed' according to this mentality. The Israelites believed that all the realities of nature had come into existence because of Yahweh's creative word:

> For he spoke, and it came to be;
> He commanded, and it stood forth (Psalm 33:9).

Furthermore, the whole of history was also thought by the Israelites to be the word of Yahweh. Human history is first of all God's history and there is no distinction between sacred and profane history. It is Yahweh's word which renders history intelligible, for words are also names and it is the naming of a thing which renders it meaningful. Yahweh's word also offers guidance, the disclosure of his plan, the moral teaching according to which humanity must live. The Law then is also the Word of Yahweh, and the commands of the Decalogue are his 'Ten Words'. For the Israelites the word of Yahweh was intensely compelling. It was a fire, a sword, a hammer. It always accomplished what it was sent to do. It was explosive. It was eternal. The word of Yahweh was the beginning, the end and the whole process of history – of man's activity in the world.

Every problem, every event in human history was referred back by the ancient Israelites to the basic meaning of existence and that meaning was provided by God himself. God had spoken his word, and the religious faith of Israel rested on his acts in history. Of course, it took centuries before Israel really began to piece things together and to appreciate what it had discovered. Every act of God said something to the people of Israel, but as Wolfhart Pannenberg has pointed out, no one act was a full revelation (Pannenberg 1969, p. 9). Concentrating upon a single event in the history of Israel could produce a distorted view. It could even be idolatrous, because in the end the word of God was infinitely elusive. It was God who took the initiative and God who was in ultimate control. Many religions of the world have believed in some degree of manipulation of divine power by human beings, some degree of control over events, some application even of magical techniques to the deity; but in Israel this was entirely and fundamentally excluded, and the history of Yahwistic religion is in part a long-standing battle against such an idea. The Old Testament concept of revelation was overwhelming and absolute. It is hard, if not impossible, to find in any other religious tradition such a comprehensive and such an overpowering sense of the presence and authority of God.

It is clear, then, that in the Old Testament we are dealing with an interpretation of history, an interpretation of human events and of man's experience of nature. Indeed, human history unfolds against the backdrop of created nature and is continuous with it, and this, as we noted in the previous chapter, is an understanding that is common to the ethnic religions of pre-literate societies. The difference with ancient Israel lay in the quality and intensity of its theism, the depth of its historical memory, and the clarity of its developing pattern of interpretation. Yahweh was the single, the exclusive, the all-pervasive principle of interpretation. It was almost as if, in the symbolic universe of ancient Israel, there were no purely secular experiences; and yet it would be wrong to level a secularist accusation against the Israelites and convict them of sacralism. Their understanding of reality was nothing if not concrete and objectified, and it was always possible for the Israelite to take the secular option, to close his eyes and ears to the action and voice of Yahweh and to say, like the fool in his heart: 'There is no God'.

History and mythology in the Jewish Bible

It could be said, therefore, that the Old Testament interpretation of history was theological, but it was not theological in the received meaning of that word. We shall have occasion in a later chapter to offer a critique of the popular understanding of the discipline known as theology, but even in the light of that critique, the religious interpretation of the Old Testament was not a theology. That is to say, it was not an attempt to explicate or clarify, to make abstractions, to analyse or to impose any human mental order or pattern on the objects of faith and experience. The religious interpretation offered by the Old Testament was basically a mythology – a system of interlocking and overlapping symbols. It was not a rational elucidation of the analogical elements in a symbol already apprehended. It was the symbolic apprehension itself of reality and its inner meaning which is logically and chronologically prior to all theological explanation.

Mythology is not mere poetical comparison, nor a mere figment of the creative imagination. It is already – in a sense – given. As John L. McKenzie has explained, it is an expression of 'the total psychic experience of the object' (McKenzie 1974, p. 175). The Greeks made the error of thinking that mythology was attempting to explain phenomena as experienced by the senses or as a philosophical abstraction of universals, and their mistake ultimately destroyed the influence of mythology in the Western world. There are still people who want to treat the Bible as a scientific encyclopaedia, as a literal record of history (like the Cecil B. de Mille films of Biblical epics!) or as a source-book for theological proof-texts. In fact, they would treat it as anything other than what it is – a mythology. Mythology attempts to conceive of the divine in terms of the human. Myth dares to speak the divine word in human words – and it succeeds. It is a whole experience, a unity, even an actual participation in the inner meaning of reality. It states the incomprehensible. How can we express the unworldly in terms of the worldly, the transcendent in terms of the immanent? It is impossible to answer that question 'How?' All we know is that the question is both posed and answered in mythology. To demythologize, it has been said, is to condemn every religion to silence. To theologize is to embark upon a process of comprehending clarification which has no ending in this world and no role in the next.

The myth or symbol-system attempts to grapple with the inner nature of experience; the religious symbol, with that of religious experience. In many religions of the world, myths are archaic events, the historicity of which may or may not be ascertainable. However, their historicity is unimportant and these events are retold as symbolic stories and ritually re-enacted according to the collective memory of a people, and, what is more, that people's social and political institutions are patterned after these archetypes. In their traditions myths are turned into historical events which thereby acquire both factual existence and ulterior meaning. It is not to be denied that there were myths of this kind in the experience of ancient Israel, but the peculiar insight of the Israelites was not to historicize myth but, as McKenzie has pointed out, 'to mythicize history' (McKenzie 1974, p. 182). That is to say, they conferred a mythological quality, and therefore a deep ulterior meaning, upon historical events as they actually experienced them, and as they reflected upon their outcome. Israelites had an intuition of the ultimate meaning and purpose of events as they experienced them, and this form of mythology assumed the position and function of theology. Questions which a modern believer handles theologically, the ancient Israelite handled mythologically.

Hence it came about that the mythical dimension received emphasis in the Bible, that historical events were embroidered mythologically and that even historical narrative itself was retold in mythological form. This is very far indeed from saying that history was unimportant to the Jews. On the contrary, it was of such supreme importance that it was the subject of repeated and renewed reflection and re-interpretation. However it does mean that the Old Testament understanding of Yahweh and his word – his revelation – in history cannot be measured by scientific knowledge. In many, if not most cases, the historical facts, as they happened, are not accessible to us because of the very nature of the Biblical texts themselves. Bible scholars and theologians today hold different views about how far one can apply modern methods of historical criticism to the texts of the Bible and about how far one can find out what *really* happened. But what do we mean when we ask what *really* happened? If this is the question of a positivist historian, seeking the bare phenomena or the naked facts of history, then it exhibits a superficial understanding of reality. As the great philosopher of history R. G. Collingwood suggested, history is always *for* something, and the very least one can say is that it is for an understanding of what man is and of what man can do (Collingwood 1963, p. 10). The naked fact is always clothed with an interpretation by the historian, as well as by the writer who has a religious interest. However, there *is* a difference between the writing of history and the writing of religion. The historian attempts to answer questions about past human actions through the interpretation of different types of historical evidence. Religious writing is about God's self-revealing and about human beings, believing or not believing, accepting or not accepting that God who reveals himself. Religious writing is ultimately about the actions of someone who eludes the grasp of historical criticism.

Myth is not opposed to history in the Bible. The Old Testament has a historical basis; and for Christians this historical basis is just as important as it was for the ancient Jews. The Old Testament is about the experience of God by man, but it has both the quality of history and the quality of religious interpretation or myth. It is a unified duality. A purely historical approach to the Bible is an inadequate approach, and, unless it takes into account the mythical thought processes of Biblical writers, it can achieve nothing even in terms of scientific history. The Bible, then – we repeat – is about human actions and historical events, but it presents them as 'words' or deeds of Yahweh, Israel's God.

To believe in a God who transcends is, as Cardinal Newman pointed out, to believe in a Being that is at once exterior and superior to the human conscience and the visible world (Newman 1909, p. 17). This is how the Bible presents the experience of Yahweh from the beginning. The factual self-revelation of God was not the subjective experience alone of a few mystics or religious *virtuosi*, not yet was it merely the inherited thought-pattern of successive generations, trying to make sense of, and to cope with, their experience of the visible world. It was the direct and actual experience of a 'living God', of a personal reality that was paramount and unique, and that, without being irrational or capricious, acted in events with total freedom and with a directly intended goal or purpose. This goal towards which Yahweh was moving the history of mankind was not always understood even partially by the Israelites, let alone comprehended by them. Furthermore, they frequently did not co-operate with the known will of Yahweh, but ancient Israel believed that Yahweh was in control, that he took the initiatives and made the fundamental choices even when men did not co-operate, and that he could even use constructively the failures and wicked actions of mankind.

In the history of ancient Israel it was always God who called, God who commanded, God who guided and led his people. Old Testament history begins 'out of the blue', as it were. God's word always comes 'from outside', unexpectedly. In Hebrew imagery, 'it leaps down to earth'. Thus we begin tangibly with Moses and the group of Israelites who had emigrated to Egypt, a people enslaved in a foreign land. Moses was their first missionary, the emissary sent to them by Yahweh, to deliver them and win them over to his service. The vocation and religious experience of Moses was collectivized at Sinai, during the journey back to their homeland.

The non-Mosaic traditions of other groups and earlier periods were reinterpreted in the light of the Mosaic covenant and the Exodus from Egypt. The patriarchs begin from 'nowhere'. Abraham has no genealogy, apart from the Table of the Nations in Genesis 10, which sought to tabulate the peoples who were Israel's neighbours. In fact the whole genealogy of the patriarchs is an artificial reconstruction, linking personalities in the popular memory who were the ancestors of the different groups from which Israel was descended. It is typical that the patriarchs were 'sojourners' or 'resident aliens', people from another place. Abraham is a nomad on the move from Ur to Haran and from Haran to Canaan, and the period of the patriarchs appears to coincide with the Aramaean and Amorite migrations of 2000 to 1500 B.C. Jacob is called a 'wandering Aramaean' and Laban, too, is an Aramaean.

> Now the Lord said to Abram, 'Go from your country and your kindred and your father's house to the land that I will show you' (Genesis 12:1).

That is how the Bible begins the story of the peopling of Canaan by the ancestors of the Israelites; and that is the constant way events happen in the pages of the Bible. We shall see it in greater detail in Israel's history. We shall see it in the phenomenon of prophecy. And we shall see it in Israel's understanding of nature and cosmic events. Always, the initiative lies with Yahweh. God's word comes from outside.

THE BIBLICAL VIEW OF GOD'S SELF-REVELATION

Revelation: a personal communion with God

The Bible shows us God 'speaking', and it is the characteristic of spoken language not merely to communicate a message, but also to reveal the personality of the speaker. Furthermore, the process of speaking is a two-way process, because it involves a listening and it invites a response. Speaking reveals the speaker. As we have seen, it is a release of psychic energy. When God spoke to Israel, he revealed himself as a 'living God', whose vitality was apparent in his actions. Thus revelation for the Hebrews was the self-manifestation of God – a real meeting with him. It was the historical self-communication of this God to a people who were made particularly aware of his presence and his activity, a people deeply marked by extraordinary religious experiences. Since this self-revelation was historical, it was bound by the limitations of a language, a culture, a particular time and place. Reading the Bible, we become contemporaries of the ancient Israelites and we, too, meet God through their culture and their history.

Revelation, therefore, as presented in the Bible, involves a number of related ideas. Revelation is fundamentally God himself in his own self-manifestation; but it is also the process of that self-manifestation. This process involves man's experience of God's self-manifestation and it also involves the disclosure of a message, purpose or plan for mankind. Revelation takes place through and within human experience, an experience which invites reflection, understanding, concern and, ultimately, decision. The notion, and very etymology, of 'revelation' denotes an 'unveiling' of something hidden, a mystery that requires a special perception in order to fathom it. It has an ambiguous quality and it is an invitation to probe further. The call of God revealing himself is aptly depicted in the fascination of Moses on Mount Horeb or Sinai.

> And the angel of the Lord appeared to him in a flame of fire out of the midst of a bush; and he looked, and lo, the bush was burning, yet it was not consumed. And Moses said, 'I will turn aside and see this great sight, why the bush is not burnt.' When the Lord saw that he had turned aside to see, God called to him out of the bush, 'Moses, Moses!' And he said, 'Here am I' (Exodus 3:2-4).

Revelation is given especially to a few, chosen, perceptive or charismatic individuals who develop a special relationship with the Divine and a consistent response to it. This response they feel compelled to communicate to others, so that others become aware of the actuality of God's presence, of his will and his promise, and they, in their turn 'see' and 'hear' something of what has first been revealed with such intensity. They also receive the message and the interpretation of the historical events they are experiencing.

However, more than mere communication of meaning, of truths or propositions, more than the communication of a divine vitality, Biblical revelation is interpersonal. It is a personal communion between God and man. It is the discovery of who Yahweh is and what he is like. It is a non-verbal self-disclosure. God is known, as we know other persons – through a relationship of affection, of loyalty, of acceptance. Even more than this, it is *belonging* to the Other, being completely possessed by someone or something beyond ourselves. It creates trust, security and joy, even in suffering, incomprehension and trials. God is blessedness for us, 'a physical totality', as Walter Eichrodt calls it, which awakens not merely our curiosity, but enlarges our understanding of a mystery, *the* mystery which underlies all else in our whole experience – God's self-giving to us (Eichrodt 1961, p. 40). This personal communion between God and his chosen one(s) implies two important further ideas, those of election and covenant. The second of these belongs, perhaps, more properly to a detailed consideration of Israel's history in a later section of this chapter, but the first can be conveniently treated here. God's revelation or gift of himself is a completely, an infinitely, free act. Although God is presented in the Old Testament as the Holy One and the source of holiness itself, this is not really a question, as Eichrodt shows, of an elevated moral standard (Eichrodt 1961, p. 276). God is holy because he is 'other' and 'separated'. His holiness is an overwhelming power, an unapproachable majesty which is simply one of his qualities as God. In the priestly tradition of·the Bible which places the emphasis on worship, God's holiness appears as 'perfection', as cultic purity and integrity. In this tradition the various taboos or prohibitions which surrounded the Temple worship and gave physical expression to God's holiness and otherness, were given a conscious meaning and an eventual moral explanation. It was only by slow degrees that the idea of Yahweh as being 'moral' and 'good' permeated the religious thinking of Israel and acted as a corrective in its ideas about how he behaved.

In the experience by Israel of God as a person, the concept of election was dominant. Whenever God acted it was the voluntary engagement of his sovereign freedom. God had unlimited power and yet he freely limited that power and bound himself by promises when he chose a person or a nation and committed himself in fidelity to them. Moreover, Yahweh did not choose anyone because of his or her merits. No one deserved to be chosen. On the contrary, Yahweh's fidelity was only matched by the recurrent – one might say, the constant – infidelity of those he chose. Even Moses, the first 'missionary', as we have called him, to Israel, the one who spoke 'face to face' with Yahweh, was unfaithful and was not allowed by Yahweh to enter the promised land. It was eventually the prophet Hosea who reflected most deeply on the motive behind God's paradoxical choices and who saw that motive as one of love – a love that was unrequited, the wooing of a 'wanton'. This idea was carried over (as we shall see in the next chapter) into the Deuteronomic revision of the Law, which stresses God's love and his pure favour of grace in choosing Israel. God's free choice was exercised in love. His choice was disconcerting and unexpected. He chose a rootless and enslaved people, a people wandering and lost in a desert wilderness. He chose prophets in spite of their reluctance, or even against their will: Moses, Isaiah, Jeremiah. He chose leaders from their childhood, even from their mother's womb, Samson and Samuel for example. He chose Saul as king from the smallest tribe, that of Benjamin; and he chose David, the shepherd-boy, whom everyone had forgotten, to be Saul's royal successor. God's favour made weak people strong and gave them victory against all odds.

All these stories celebrate one basic idea – the sovereign freedom of God.

Revelation as God's judgement

The Bible shows us God's freedom exercised in love; but it also shows us that same freedom exercised in wrath. God's choice or 'election' of people confronted them, in their turn, with a chance to choose freely and to remain faithful to their choice. God's self-revelation to mankind in the history of Israel was a confrontation, even a head-on collision with human ideas, with human selfishness and human materialism. What else could one expect from the inconceivable 'otherness' of God but a radical clash with all that human beings expected and held dear? God revealed himself, therefore, not only in election, but also in judgement, and that judgement fell most heavily on his chosen ones. When Yahweh acted, his actions were 'judgements', and the theme of judgement runs right through the whole of the Old Testament.

The Biblical idea of judgement is basically one of vindication, according to which the victor is proved right by his victory. God is on the winning side, as it were. This could work both ways in the historical experience of Israel. When Israel won its battles, Yahweh was on its side, fighting with them and for them; but when Israel was defeated it was because God had changed sides, and God changed sides because Israel had been unfaithful. A judgement was a defence of the righteous, the faithful, the weak, a proof of God's fidelity and consistency and a sign of his providence and lordship over human history. The fact that all events were judgements showed God's ultimate control over everything that happened and gave everything a meaning through reference to him. A judgement was both a punishment and a deliverance. 'Vindicate me, O God,' prayed the psalmist, 'and defend my cause against an ungodly people; from deceitful and unjust men deliver me!' (Psalm 43:1).

One of the clearest – and seemingly most simplistic – examples of the Old Testament view of judgement comes from the Book of Judges, so called because it is about the 'deliverers' who were raised up by God to save Israel. The book has a single recurring pattern. The Israelites betrayed Yahweh, so he handed them over to their enemies. They pleaded with him and he sent a saviour – the judge. The deliverance was effected and there was an interval of peace before the Israelites relapsed once more and the cycle started all over again.

> And the people of Israel did what was evil in the sight of the Lord and served the Baals; and they forsook the Lord, the God of their fathers, who had brought them out of the land of Egypt; they went after other gods, from among the gods of the peoples who were round about them, and bowed down to them; and they provoked the Lord to anger. They forsook the Lord and served the Baals and the Ashtaroth. So

the anger of the Lord was kindled against Israel, and he gave them over to plunderers, who plundered them; and he sold them into the power of their enemies round about, so that they could no longer withstand their enemies. Whenever they marched out, the hand of the Lord was against them for evil, as the Lord had warned, and as the Lord had sworn to them; and they were in sore straits.

Then the Lord raised up judges, who saved them out of the power of those who plundered them. And yet they did not listen to their judges; for they played the harlot after other gods and bowed down to them; they soon turned aside from the way in which their fathers had walked, who had obeyed the commandments of the Lord, and they did not do so. Whenever the Lord raised up judges for them, the Lord was with the judge, and he saved them from the hand of their enemies all the days of the judge; for the Lord was moved to pity by their groaning because of those who afflicted and oppressed them. But whenever the judge died, they turned back and behaved worse than their fathers, going after other gods, serving them and bowing down to them; they did not drop any of their practices or their stubborn ways. So the anger of the Lord was kindled against Israel; and he said, 'Because this people have transgressed my covenant which I commanded their fathers, and have not obeyed my voice, I will not henceforth drive out before them any of the nations that Joshua left when he died, that by them I may test Israel, whether they will take care to walk in the way of the Lord as their fathers did, or not'. So the Lord left those nations, not driving them out at once, and he did not give them into the power of Joshua (Judges 2:11-23).

Thus the changing fortunes of war between Israel and its neighbours were interpreted in the light of Israel's cultic fidelity or infidelity to Yahweh; and their tendency to lose faith in him explained why they had failed to oust the foreign nations from their land.

This example, linking every reversal in battle with a specific bout of infidelity on the part of the ancient Israelites, is the concept of judgement at its most literal and naïve. Ancient Israel never worked out a systematic development of this idea of the wrath of God, punishing them for violating the covenant. It was simply a spontaneous reaction to the adverse event, an event which revealed their infidelity, the fact of which there is no reason to doubt. The wrath of God could also be exercised, as they later learned to distinguish, in the experience of the innocent sufferer, as well as in that of the sufferer who was guilty. In that case, it was an expression of the unsearchable greatness of God, and the human response was not that of contrition and repentance but one of continuing hope and trust in a new and incomprehensible experience of God. In any case wrath was not a permanent attribute of God and it was false to believe that it was purely capricious. Even Job, the innocent sufferer, went on invoking God as his 'judge' and 'deliverer', refusing to accept his 'comforters'' view of a cruel God. At the end of it all, God was still supremely credible. Israel surely achieved a more subtle understanding of God's self-revelation as judgement through the greatest judgement of all – the greatest test in its history. That was when Yahweh fought on the side of Babylon and the Assyrians. The defeat of Israel at the hands of the Assyrians in the sixth century B.C. and its total annihilation as a nation was a completely new revelation of the mighty providence of Yahweh. But that incredible event, too, had to be interpreted with reference to God – had to be understood. The destruction of Jerusalem, of the Temple and of Israel as a nation inaugurated a radically new understanding of God's dealings with mankind, an understanding that was at once more interior and more other-worldly and a hope that looked towards a final day of judgement when a future world would be redeemed from God's wrath.

It is already clear from what we have been saying that the concept of God's self-revelation as judgement is very closely related to that of redemption or salvation, and therefore to God's plan. If the events of history were seen as words and deeds of God, as a communion with him, as his supremely free choices and as his judgements, they were also seen as his saving acts. As we shall shortly see, the fundamental event in Israel's history, the starting-point for their whole theological reflection, was the Exodus. Yahweh delivered the Israelites from their bondage in Egypt, welded them into a nation and led them into the land of promise. This was the great saving manifestation of Yahweh to his people, the sign of his power and his will to save them. This event became the type of all other experiences of deliverance in Israel's history and finally of the second great saving wonder, the restoration of Israel after the exile to Babylon. The Exodus was closely linked with the covenant and with Israel's election by Yahweh. It was therefore the revelation of Yahweh as a God who saves, a God who intervened on their behalf, and this was the foundation of their faith in an ultimate salvation from a final annihilating judgement.

The concept of salvation underwent greater refinement as time passed and Israel reflected more deeply on its accumulated experience. It became clearer to the Israelites just what dangers God was delivering them from. The plan of salvation began to unfold for them and they placed themselves in God's hands, to be led and guided by him. Various themes came to their minds as they tried to think of the future, themes borrowed and reinterpreted from the past history of their nation. Towards the end of the Old Testament period there were several competing ideas about the end times, but Israel knew that God was himself the future, that he was salvation in person. So in the end, their future was in his hands, from their point of view, an open future – but a future with a sublime climax.

The consequence of seeing Yahweh's hand in every historical event and of regarding Yahweh himself as the only, and the total, explanation and significance of history, had a profoundly creative and liberating effect on Israel. God was essentially a 'deliverer' or a 'liberator', and the ancient Israelites achieved liberation by sharing in God's own freedom, and God's own work of liberation. God revealed himself in the actual fact of liberation and in the progressive history of liberation. The situation and Israel's own reflective involvement in it mediated this self-revelation of God.

The Old Testament view of revelation, therefore, can be summed up in the statement: 'God spoke to Israel'. Israel knew God through his word, and that word was Israel's guide. Every historical event was a 'word' which disclosed the living and personal God – a meeting with Yahweh. God's word was also a call and a guide to action on the part of man. It demanded a conversion and it offered a vocation. It was a free self-gift – a gratuitous choice – by God. It was a promise and a plan. It was the unveiling of a mystery of both love and wrath. It was a judgement and a deliverance – a saving mystery. Israel lived in communion with its God, accepting either his guidance or the consequences of rejecting it. In Chapter 3, we shall be concerned with the content of Old Testament revelation, revelation as a category of information or a communication of meaning. In particular, we shall be concerned with the notion of salvation and with answering the question: 'From what, in the last resort, did Israel expect Yahweh to save them?'

For the remainder of this present chapter, we shall discuss Israel's history in greater detail, particularly in the light of the foundational event – the covenant. This became an interpretative theme throughout Old Testament history, and it was also the starting-point for Christian reflection on the life and teaching of Jesus, as 'a new and everlasting covenant'. This is not at all to say that the New Testament can be deduced from the Old, as conclusions are drawn from premises. There are discontinuities as well as continuities between these two parts of Scripture, and the New Testament is yet another re-interpretation in the light of yet another foundational event. For Christians, however, this event and this new interpretation have a definitive quality which was lacking in the message of Old Testament history.

It will also be necessary in this present chapter to consider the notion of prophets and prophecy, the idea that the perception of God and his activity in human history has been mediated in a special way by a few perceptive or charismatic individuals who were the messengers or missionaries of Yahweh to Israel. Finally, there is the consideration of created nature as yet another 'book' revealing the presence and purpose of God and of the God-given wisdom required for the reading and expounding of this further book of God's mighty deeds.

REVELATION IN COVENANT AND CULT

God's self-revelation in the covenant

It is difficult, if not impossible, to exaggerate the importance of the Covenant of Sinai in the history of Israel. In the event of the covenant all the elements of God's self-revelation of which we have been speaking came together. What happened at Sinai was the real entry of God into human history, as far as the ancient Israelites were concerned; and it confirmed for them the factual, rather than the purely speculative, character of revelation. These things really happened to Moses and to the group of people that he led out of Egypt to the sacred mountain of Horeb or Sinai, the focal point of worship for the tribes that had come down from Canaan to Egypt. The covenant was a gratuitous act on the part of Yahweh in electing Israel to be his people. Henceforth, Israel's destiny was to be bound up with the will of God. It is true that in the beginning the Israelites had no thought for the other nations of the world and that, even though Yahweh was the only real or 'living' God, they considered their relationship with him to be an exclusive one. However, they were gradually led to understand that what had happened to them in the Exodus and at Sinai, and in all their subsequent history, had made of their nation a microcosm of God's dealings with the whole of mankind. The Old Testament does not, of course, give us a factual history, but Israel's interpretation of the facts.

The Exodus and the Covenant constituted a decisive moment of revelation, a dramatic intervention by Yahweh on behalf of Israel. A series of dramatic events, miraculous – at the very least, when considered in their opportuneness and in their conclusive effect – had delivered them from Egypt and broken their connection with their slave-masters. The crossing of the Red Sea or 'Sea of Reeds' and the destruction of the pursuing Egyptian army as their horses and chariots became clogged in the sea bed and the returning waters covered them and washed their corpses upon the shore, was such an amazing feat, such an extraordinary experience of liberation, that it became the foundation of Israel's faith.

> Thus the Lord saved Israel that day from the hand of the Egyptians; and Israel saw the Egyptians dead upon the seashore. And Israel saw the great work which the Lord did against the Egyptians, and the people feared the Lord; and they believed in the Lord and in his servant Moses (Exodus 14: 30-31).

One can only recapture the mood of the Israelites as they contemplated the sudden and totally unexpected destruction of their cruel pursuers, by thinking of modern parallels. One reads in newspapers, or sees on television, interviews with people who have survived a terrible disaster – an air crash, an earthquake, a hotel fire. One sees their bewilderment, their overwhelming sense of relief, their release of emotion, at having been snatched from the jaws of certain death. That is what the Israelites felt. It was so extraordinary that they knew God had plucked them from the danger. Israel had become in real truth God's 'first-born son'.

> And the Lord said to Moses, 'When you go back to Egypt . . . you shall say to Pharaoh, Thus says the Lord, Israel is my first-born son, and I say to you, Let my son go that he may serve me; if you refuse to let him go, behold I will slay your first-born son' (Exodus 4: 21-23).

Thus Israel had been rescued by Yahweh and led into the wilderness to offer worship at the mountain where he had first revealed himself to Moses in the burning bush. What happened at Sinai was a profound religious experience – with Moses as mediator – of divine revelation as radical interpersonality. Moses appears to us today as a towering figure, a strong leader of his people, yet the Book of Exodus shows him as a diffident man, protesting to God: 'Oh, my Lord, I am not eloquent, either heretofore or since thou hast spoken to thy servant; but I am slow of speech and of tongue'. And God agrees to make Aaron, his brother, to be the 'mouth' of Moses:

> And you shall speak to him and put the words in his mouth; and I will be with your mouth and with his mouth, and will teach you what you shall do. He shall speak for you to the people; and he shall be a mouth for you, and you shall be to him as God (Exodus 4: 15-16).

We are also told in the Book of Numbers that Moses was 'very meek, more than all men that were on the face of the earth', and yet God's 'spirit' rested on him and 'the skin of his face shone because he had been talking with God'. No one among the Israelites had such a profound experience of God as Moses:

> Hear my words: If there is a prophet among you, I the Lord make myself known to him in a vision, I speak with him in a dream. Not so with my servant Moses; he is entrusted with all my house. With him I speak mouth to mouth, clearly, and not in dark speech; and he beholds the form of the Lord (Numbers 12: 6-8).

God spoke to Moses 'face to face, as a man speaks to his friend'. Yet even in God's self-revelation to Moses there was still mystery. Nevertheless, by proclaiming his divine name, he communicated something of his very personality.

> Moses said, 'I pray thee, show me thy glory.' And he said, 'I will make all my goodness pass before you, and will proclaim before you my name THE LORD; and I will be gracious to whom I will be gracious, and will show mercy on whom I will show mercy. But', he said, 'you cannot see my face; for man shall not see me and live.' And the Lord said, 'Behold, there is a place by me where you shall stand upon the rock; and while my glory passes by I will put you in a cleft of rock, and I will cover you with my hand until I have passed by; then I will take away my hand, and you shall see my back; but my face shall not be seen' (Exodus 33: 18-23).

Moses communed with God upon the mountain and then descended to disclose the covenant and to ratify it with the whole people.

The idea of covenant in the history of ancient Israel derives from the speaking of a 'word' with ritual solemnity, a word which was effective or instrumental in bringing about a blessing or a curse. In legal terms, the covenant was a most solemn and binding ritual agreement between two parties – not necessarily two equal parties – who bound themselves to one another under terrible imprecations if the promise was broken. In the ancient East such covenants governed the relationships of vassals and over-lords. In this case, the covenant was between Yahweh and Israel. Yahweh bound himself to be Israel's God, to lead, guide and exercise dominion over them. Yahweh's part of the agreement was the promise to guard Israel, to lead them to the land he had prepared for them, to be an enemy to their enemies, to bless them with prosperity, to take away sickness, to give them a numerous progeny. In a word, Yahweh promised Israel 'life'.

> You shall walk in all the way which the Lord your God has commanded you, that you may live, and that it may go well with you, and that you may live long in the land which you shall possess (Deuteronomy 5: 32-33).

Israel, in accepting God's dominion, promised to carry out his ordinances, the 'covenant-law', to have no god but Yahweh himself, and in particular to be faithful to the 'Ten Words' of Yahweh, the Decalogue. This covenant was ratified sacrificially at the foot of the mountain of revelation, the place where God's name had been proclaimed and his reality experienced. The account of this solemn undertaking as we have it in the Book of Exodus is a mixture of different traditions, but they converge to communicate a single meaning. Israel ate and drank in the presence of Yahweh. The interpersonal communion was expressed by a shared meal, a fellowship in eating and drinking – in nourishing the very processes of life. In the tradition which stresses the sacrificial element and turns the covenant meal into a ritual banquet, Moses builds an altar and then sprinkles the blood of a single sacrificial victim upon both altar and people. The altar, at the foot of the mountain, was the symbol of God; the blood, the symbol of life and the principle of life.

> And Moses wrote all the words of the Lord. And he rose early in the morning, and built an altar at the foot of the mountain, and twelve pillars, according to the twelve tribes of Israel. And he sent young men of the people of Israel, who offered burnt offerings and sacrificed peace offerings of oxen to the Lord. And Moses took half of the blood and put it in basins, and half of the blood he threw against the altar. Then he took the book of the covenant, and read it in the hearing of the people; and they said 'All that the Lord has spoken we will do, and we will be obedient.' And Moses took the blood and threw it upon the people, and said, 'Behold the blood of the covenant which the Lord has made with you in accordance with all these words' (Exodus 24: 4-8).

The covenant is therefore not only a ceremonial agreement, but 'a relation-ship of communion' (von Rad 1965, I, pp. 129–135). It is also a legal relationship and a balancing of claims of each party against the other. It is a question of decision or choice, a contract freely entered into by either party. For Israel it was truly a question of either 'a blessing or a curse', and this is shown in the account of Joshua's renewal of the covenant at Shechem.

> But Joshua said to the people, 'You cannot serve the Lord; for he is a holy God; he is a jealous God; he will not forgive your transgressions or your sins. If you forsake the

Lord and serve foreign gods, then he will turn and do you harm, and consume you,
after having done you good.' And the people said to Joshua, 'Nay, but we will serve
the Lord.' Then Joshua said to the people, 'You are witnesses against yourselves that
you have chosen the Lord to serve him.' And they said, 'We are witnesses'. He said,
'Then put away the foreign gods which are among you, and incline your heart to the
Lord, the God of Israel.' And the people said to Joshua, 'The Lord our God we will
serve, and his voice we will obey.' So Joshua made a covenant with the people that
day, and made statutes and ordinances for them at Shechem (Joshua 24: 19-25).

The covenant law was elaborated in all its detail of positive, as well as negative, prescriptions in the so-called 'Book of the Covenant' which constitutes
chapters 21 to 23 of the Book of Exodus. In these chapters the Decalogue
was amplified and applied by later hands to a settled, non-nomadic community, and consequences were drawn for civil and criminal law. When
Israel entered the land of promise and Shechem became the first place of
ritual gathering, the covenant was solemnly renewed there every seven
years. But there was a sense in which the covenant could never be repeated, a
sense in which it was irreversible. It was a factual saving event of the first
rank, and very far indeed from being a theological reflection on created
nature or a celebration of a cosmobiological relationship with God. For the
Jews, the primary sacrament of their relationship with God was not nature
but this historical event.

So important an experience for Israel was the covenant at Sinai that it was
used as a theological model for interpreting earlier religious traditions. The
Biblical story of Noah and the flood is probably derived from the same
source as the Babylonian flood stories. Thus Noah is a parallel figure to the
Mesopotamian Ut-Napishtim, and all these traditions may go back to the
memory of a disastrous flood in the valley of the Tigris and Euphrates. In the
Biblical account, the idea of covenant is retrojected upon Noah and his sons
and involves the whole of creation.

Then God said to Noah and to his sons with him, 'Behold, I establish my covenant
with you and your descendants after you, and with every living creature that is with
you, the birds, the cattle and every beast of the earth with you as many as came out
of the ark. I establish my covenant with you, that never again shall all flesh be cut off
by the waters of a flood, and never again shall there be a flood to destroy the earth'
(Genesis 9: 8-11).

The story then goes on to relate how God set the rainbow in the skies as a
perpetual sign of this covenant with the whole of creation.

The covenant with Abraham, retold in a Yahwistic narrative, is a
covenant with a family, the family of Israel's most memorable ancestor. It is
basically a promise and a bestowal of land and of physical progeny, after
Abraham had been tested. Abraham's humility and trust in God were such
that he believed in the promises, even though they were impossible of realization in purely human terms. In ancient covenant ceremonial, animals were

slaughtered and the parties to the contract passed between the pieces of the victim, calling down upon themselves the same fate, should the covenant be violated. Yahweh did this in the shape of fire.

> When the sun had gone down and it was dark, behold, a smoking fire pot and a flaming torch passed between these pieces. On that day the Lord made a covenant with Abram, saying. 'To your descendants I give this land . . .' (Genesis 15: 17-18).

Yet another covenant account – this time in the priestly tradition – is associated with Abraham. In this narrative God is called 'El Shaddai', which possibly means 'mountain God', but the same promises of a land and multitude of descendants are again made. Abram receives his new name of Abraham, interpreted as 'father of a multitude' and undertakes the obligation of circumcision as a 'sign of the covenant'. Originally, male circumcision was simply, as it still is among many peoples of the world, part of an initiation rite before marriage, but for the Israelites – particularly after the exile – it assumed a religious significance, as a sign of belonging to the people of the covenant.

God's self-revelation in ancient Jewish worship

In the first chapter we spoke of *memoria*, of effective memory, or memory made present. This is an idea which occurs with varying degrees of intensity in different religions. In the ethnic religions of pre-literate societies, for example, it is frequently assumed that God's favour will be enjoyed by worshippers who re-enact the prayers and rituals of their ancestors who are now the 'friends' of God. The Israelites possessed a very strong idea indeed of memorial, and they applied it in the first place to their experience of the Exodus and the Sinai covenant. By remembering these events ritually at stated intervals of time, they believed that they were entering into the experience of salvation, into the saving acts themselves, in a real and actual way. The mountain of revelation on which Moses had met God face to face and spoken with him as to a friend, received a kind of permanent extension in the 'tent of meeting' where Moses spoke 'mouth to mouth' with the Lord, and on which the cloud-emblem of the divine presence descended, as it had done upon Sinai.

The Israelites, moreover, carried a permanent reminder of the covenant with them in the shape of the 'Ark of the Covenant' which contained the tables of their law, and other relics of their marvellous journey from Egypt. One of the 'Ten Words' revealed on Sinai had been the commandment to keep holy the Sabbath or seventh day. This was a direct reminder of the Exodus:

> You shall remember that you were a servant in the land of Egypt and the Lord your God brought you out thence with a mighty hand and an outstretched arm; therefore the Lord your God commanded you to keep the sabbath day (Deuteronomy 5: 15).

The Sabbath was also a sign of sanctification, a 'tithe of man's days' or a sacrificial offering to God of his time. It was a sign between God and his faithful people, and was therefore another echo of the covenant.

> And the Lord said to Moses, 'Say to the people of Israel, You shall keep my sabbaths, for this is a sign between me and you and throughout your generations, that you may know that I, the Lord, sanctify you . . . Therefore the people of Israel shall keep the sabbath, observing the sabbath throughout their generations, as a perpetual covenant' (Exodus 31: 12-13, 16).

The Sabbath made God's people holy, like himself – set apart and belonging to him.

Religions are symbol-systems; and rituals, which are a typical form of religious practice, are symbols in action. They are celebrations of life and dramatizations of experience. They help people to cope with events, to remember and to rehearse their concerns, their hopes, their beliefs. Rituals are an important bridge between faith and everyday life. They are at once the high point of activity and the most explicit and concrete statement of belief. As prayer or worship, religious ritual is instrumental, for it purports to align itself with the effective will of God and his saving activity. As we saw in the first chapter, for most individuals religious experience is dependent on social experience and collective traditions in which they relive the metaphorical process which first gave rise to the religious symbols of their tradition. The whole of life and experience of the world, therefore, can become a theatre for ritual action.

The ancient Israelites inherited from the peoples of Canaan rituals and festivals which were celebrations of human and natural cycles. However, as the covenant tradition of the nomadic group from Egypt mingled with the religious traditions of the agricultural peoples already settled in their land, the ancient rituals received a new, historical significance. There were three basic agricultural festivals whose Canaanite fertility aspects had been set aside by the Israelites. The Feast of the Unleavened Bread originally celebrated the holiness of the grain as it came straight from the hand of Yahweh. This was later subordinated to the memorial of the Exodus, the last meal in Egypt and the miraculous feeding of the Israelites on their journey with bread from heaven, in the historic festival of the Passover. Another nature festival was that of the First Fruits, a harvest ritual. This became the Feast of Weeks, celebrated seven weeks after the beginning of the harvest and effectively commemorating the enjoyment of the land of promise and the first harvest there. Finally, there was the Feast of Ingathering, when the harvest was completed, and this became the Feast of Booths or Tabernacles, a commemoration of how Israel had dwelt in tents and shelters on the journey from Egypt. It is significant that these feasts were basically family feasts.

Sacrifices were performed by the priestly caste and reflected the concept of ritual handling of the blood which symbolized life. Sacrifices were also family events, even though they came to be celebrated exclusively in the Temple. They tended to express thanksgiving, joy and peace, rather than penance; and the family celebrated its own micro-historical events as guests in God's house. The great festival and solemn assembly on the Day of the Atonement was a post-exilic ritual, a collective acknowledgement of guilt which may have had archaic precedents. At any rate, it is clear from this varied cultic experience of Israel throughout its history that God revealed himself to ordinary individuals in and through the experience of ritual and worship, and through the sacramental renewal of the covenant.

Generally speaking, the covenant tradition received a setback from the institution of monarchy in Israel, and particularly after the division into two kingdoms. Yahweh, after all, was Israel's king, and he had no need of house or temple, let alone of an image, which had always been strictly prohibited lest he be assimilated to other gods. The building of the Temple was closely associated with the monarchy and was a deliberate imitation of non-Israelite symbols. It was not a building for sacred assemblies of worshippers, but 'the palace' of Yahweh, an earthly counterpart of his heavenly abode. It was the dwelling-place of his name and therefore, in some measure, of his personal presence. It stood upon Zion, later identified with the legendary mountain of Abraham's sacrifice; and the Ark of the Covenant, set up in the Holy of Holies, became Yahweh's footstool. Above the Ark were the figures of the cherubim, the winged mythological creatures that symbolized the wind and cloud, the heavenly chariot of Yahweh or his 'mercy seat'.

> When Solomon had finished building the house of the Lord and the king's house and all that Solomon desired to build, the Lord appeared to Solomon a second time as he had appeared to him at Gibeon. And the Lord said to him, 'I have heard your prayer and your supplication, which you have made before me. I have consecrated this house which you have built, and put my name there for ever; my eyes and my heart will be there for all time' (1 Kings 9: 1-4).

McKenzie has called the building of the Temple 'the climactic act of sovereignty', and he reminds us that it was incorporated into the buildings and courts of the palace (McKenzie 1974, p. 52). Zion was not only the residence of Yahweh, but also the residence of the kings of Judah.

The Temple, therefore, took on a further significance. It was not so much a house built for Yahweh by the king – for who could build a house for God? – but rather, a symbol of the house that Yahweh would build for the Davidic dynasty, a dynasty which, according to the oracle of the prophet Nathan, would last forever.

> But that same night the word of the Lord came to Nathan, 'Go and tell my servant David, "Thus says the Lord: Would you build me a house to dwell in? I have not dwelt in a house since the day I brought up the people of Israel from Egypt to this day . . . the Lord declares to you that the Lord will make you a house . . . And your

house and your kingdom shall be made sure forever before me; your throne shall be established forever'' ' (2 Samuel 7: 4-6, 11, 16).

And once again, this revelation is described in terms of the covenant model. Among the last words ascribed by the Second Book of Samuel to David are these:

> The Spirit of the Lord speaks by me, his word is upon my tongue . . .
> Yea, does not my house stand so with God?
> For he has made with me an everlasting covenant . . . (2 Samuel 23: 2, 5).

Before the extinction of the monarchy and the destruction of the Temple of Solomon, the Temple had clearly become a place of God's self-revelation and of covenant-renewal. Nothing could be more dramatic than the discovery of the Book of the Law in the Temple itself, the renewal of the covenant that followed and the reform which it inspired in the days of King Josiah:

> And the king went up to the house of the Lord, and with him all the men of Judah and all the inhabitants of Jerusalem, and the priests and the prophets, all the people, both small and great; and he read in their hearing all the words of the book of the covenant which had been found in the house of the Lord. And the king stood by the pillar and made a covenant before the Lord, to walk after the Lord and to keep his commandments and his testimonies and his statutes, with all his heart and all his soul, to perform the words of this covenant that were written in this book; and all the people joined in the covenant (2 Kings 23: 2-3).

The reform of Josiah and the Deuteronomic re-editing of the historical books of the Old Testament tried to give binding force to the broken pattern of national life by a strong affirmation of the power of love. 'With all his heart and all his soul', the words used by King Josiah, are like a recurring refrain in the pages of Deuteronomy. This period stands at mid-point in the classic age of prophecy in Israel, and it is to prophecy as the high point of Old Testament revelation that we must now turn.

REVELATION THROUGH PROPHECY

Divination and early forms of prophecy

Like the ethnic religions of many pre-literate peoples in the world, prophecy in Israel took the form of divination in early times. Divination is a technique – often magical or with magical overtones – for discovering hidden knowledge. Sometimes it consists of a ritual or symbolic action, sometimes it relies on the clairvoyance of a human oracle or seer. In many cases divination appeals to God or to spiritual beings for the revelation of hidden knowledge, either through divinatory techniques employed in prayer and worship, or through the possession of the seer by the spirit concerned. Much of worship in ethnic and popular religion is of a divinatory kind, and there is no question but that this characteristic of 'seeking a sign' through an immediately tangible answer is prejudicial to the nature of true prayer, although in many instances it may be difficult to draw a clear line between superstition and simple faith. Divination caters for the everyday needs and decisions of ordinary people, as well as – in more primitive forms of government – for those of chiefs and rulers. Hence the relative, and sometimes crucial, importance of oracles and seers in the political affairs of the ancient world.

Since divinatory or oracular activity was often associated with spirit possession, forms of mental dissociation or ecstasy were often held to be evidence of the spirit's presence. Such ecstasy was, and is still in many preliterate societies, a collective phenomenon. Group ecstasy has a kind of contagious character and can often be induced by drugs and by ritual and mesmeric techniques. Such was the type of 'prophecy' practised in the kingdoms and religious systems of Canaan – a group ecstasy associated with religious cult and induced by narcotics and self-inflicted torture. Such, for example, was the behaviour of the prophets of Baal on Mount Carmel when Elijah had his famous contest with them.

> And they cried aloud, and cut themselves after their custom with swords and lances, until the blood gushed out upon them. And as midday passed, they raved on until the time of the offering of the oblation, but there was no voice; no one answered, no one heeded (1 Kings 18: 28-29).

Israel inherited some of these divinatory ideas but rapidly transformed them in accordance with its own religious belief. In early times there was a divinatory technique – a form of casting lots – known as the Urim and Thummim, which, like so many magical oracles or spiritist techniques, yielded a 'yes' or 'no' answer to the questions put to it. Eventually it sank into disuse and became simply a part of the ornaments of the high priest. There were also frenetic prophets who employed music and dance to induce group ecstasy, but this phenomenon was attributed by the Israelites to possession by the spirit of Yahweh. An example is provided by Saul, who, after his anointing as king by Samuel, fell into ecstasy in the midst of a troop of prophets.

> When they came to Gibeah, behold, a band of prophets met him; and the spirit of God came mightily upon him, and he prophesied among them. And when all who knew him before saw how he prophesied with the prophets, the people said to one another, 'What has come over the son of Kish? Is Saul also among the prophets?' (1 Samuel 10: 10-11).

It is clear from the context that such bands of prophets aroused a measure of disdain among ordinary Israelites because of their seemingly irrational behaviour. We have a further reference to a band of prophets – 'the sons of the prophet' – who met Elisha at Bethel and foretold to him the death of his master Elijah. 'And he answered, "Yes, I know it; hold your peace"' (2 Kings 2: 3).

The 'sons of the prophet' who met Elisha were associated with the ancient sanctuary of Bethel, which had become a rival to the Temple of Jerusalem after the political schism and the establishment of the northern kingdom. It was clear that such bands of ecstatic prophets were associated with the cult of Yahweh. The prophets whom Saul had joined were also associated with a sanctuary, that of Gibeah or Gibeath-Elohim, 'the Hill of God'. Such temple prophets would have had a role in worship and hymnody, and as intercessors. They were both men and women, and they had a long history before them, stretching even into New Testament times. In the infancy narrative of Luke's gospel, we are introduced to a prophetess named Anna, the daughter of Phanuel, who 'did not depart from the temple, worshipping with fasting and prayer night and day' (Luke 2: 37).

Besides the ecstatic groups and the temple prophets, there were also individual, wandering prophets. These did not go in for ecstasy, but for direct oracular utterance, and they were at people's service as 'seers'. Samuel is introduced to us as a seer who is expected to find lost animals, just like any Mesopotamian diviner, while the prophet Gad was David's own personal seer. All the prophets could exercise a political role, but the wandering prophets were typically charismatic figures, rather than hereditary 'sons of prophets'. They could be associated with dynastic revolutions and *coups d'état*. Early prophets were miracle-workers and men of action, not writers of books. Samuel was a 'judge' over Israel; Eichrodt calls him 'the uncrowned king of Israel', but, for all that, he failed to depose Saul and enthrone David in his place (Eichrodt 1961, p. 299). Elijah and Elisha were more successful in overthrowing the northern house of Omri. John McKenzie notes a developing antagonism between the prophets and the monarchy in Israel (McKenzie 1976: 'Prophet, Prophecy'). Just as Nathan rebuked David for his murder of Uriah because of his lust for Bathsheba, Ahijah rebuked Jeroboam and Micaiah predicted the defeat and death of Ahab. Jehu, who usurped the royal power, was also himself a prophet.

The seers were endowed with divine power. They had the charisma of the word of Yahweh, delivering his judgements and his censures, struggling against the corrupting influence of the religion of Canaan and against the equally pernicious influence of the royal court which corrupted the court prophets and turned them into sycophantic supporters of infidelity. The prophet possessed, or was possessed by, the spirit of Yahweh, but there was an ambivalence about this spirit. It could be a 'lying' spirit or a 'spirit of evil' like that which entered into Saul and made him try to kill his rival David. The spirit of Yahweh could lead people astray and turn them into false prophets. It could harden men's hearts; and it did this because people did not exhibit an unconditional dependence upon Yahweh. This was the touchstone of prophetic authenticity – a total dependence upon the will of God. This was what the prophets proclaimed, not a foretelling of the course of Israel's fate, but a willingness to be guided by the revealed word of Yahweh. Once again, prophecy in Israel was a historical phenomenon. The prophets were concerned to interpret the immediate events that were happening in their own historical surroundings. As Gerhard von Rad reminds us, there was nothing speculative, or even strictly mystical about the prophetic charism (von Rad 1965, II, p. 62).

Nevertheless, the prophets did have a divine call or commission, and, to the extent that they enjoyed an immediate and ineffable experience of God, their charism was parallel, as John McKenzie claims, to mystical experience (McKenzie 1976: 'Prophet, Prophecy'). The fact, however, was that it went beyond mysticism and led to entirely new vistas of religious belief. They held conversations with Yahweh as Abraham and Moses had done, and both Abraham and Moses as well as other early figures in Israel's history were accorded the title of 'prophet' in the light of this later experience of prophecy. But whatever insights they themselves gained, whatever profound religious ideas they had, what counted in the final analysis was that they did not speak their own words, but the word of God. They lived by that word and became, in the phrase of Walther Eichrodt, 'speaking-tubes of God' (Eichrodt 1961, p. 340). The false prophet was the one who gave ready acquiescence to human wishful thinking, who was insincere or fanatical, or who gave vent to his own feelings and his own private delusions. He was himself a man of evil deeds, who followed the dictates of a hardened heart. In short, he was one who put man – and especially the king – in the place of God. The Old Testament does not despise visions and dreams. On the contrary, great importance is attributed to the subconscious aspects of human thought processes. Many revelations occurred in dreams, and many conflicts and problems were solved at the subconscious level through the interpretation of a dream. But the false prophet accepted any dream, and was unable to make the discernment necessary to distinguish one dream from another, or to see when a dream was the vehicle of the revealed will of God. Jeremiah was, perhaps, the most devastating critic of the false prophet.

> Thus says the Lord of hosts: 'Do not listen to the words of the prophets who prophesy to you, filling you with vain hopes; they speak visions of their own minds, not from the mouth of the Lord. They say continually to those who despise the word of the Lord, "It shall be well with you", and to everyone who stubbornly follows his own heart, they say, "No evil shall come upon you."
>
> 'I have heard what the prophets have said who prophesy lies in my name, saying, "I have dreamed, I have dreamed." How long shall there be lies in the heart of the prophets who prophesy lies and who prophesy the deceit of their own heart, who think to make my people forget my name by their dreams which they tell one another, even as their fathers forgot my name for Baal? Let the prophet who has a

dream tell the dream, but let him who has my word speak my word faithfully. What has straw in common with wheat?' says the Lord (Jeremiah 23:16–17; 25–28).

Classical prophecy in ancient Israel

The era of classical prophecy in Israel began about the middle of the eighth century B.C. with Amos and Hosea in the northern Kingdom, and then continued with Isaiah in Judah. Amos was the first of the 'writing prophets', because, before his time, we do not have an entire book of prophecy – merely the written record by others of the words and deeds of the prophets. But even in the case of Amos and the great prophetical writers, their words and actions are logically and chronologically prior to their writings. We shall examine the content of the prophecies in the next chapter. Here we are primarily concerned with the phenomenon of prophecy itself, as a form of revelation. However, it is useful to list the prophets and refer briefly to their main interests.

Amos is concerned with oppression of the poor by the wealthy, while Hosea compares Yahweh's experience of Israel's infidelity with that of a man whose wife is faithless. By the end of the eighth century B.C. the Assyrians had extinguished the northern kingdom, deported its inhabitants and installed foreign colonists in Samaria. Meanwhile, in the surviving kingdom of Judah, Micah rebukes the Israelites for their polytheism and their oppression of the poor while threatening the destruction of Jerusalem as well as Samaria. Isaiah rebukes the nation for its immorality and issues a call to repentance. Zephaniah returns to the charge of polytheism and oppression shortly before King Josiah's religious reforms, and Habakkuk, on the eve of the siege of Jerusalem, identifies the imminent Chaldean scourge as the judgement of Yahweh for Israel's wickedness. It was left to Jeremiah to interpret the most shattering event in the whole of Israel's history, the destruction of the nation and the end of the monarchy, the Davidic dynasty, the Temple, the priesthood, the Ark of the Covenant and the Law itself. Jeremiah's prophecies were a complete reversal of Israel's experience as the chosen one of Yahweh, whose enemies were their enemies and whose adversaries were their adversaries. Yahweh was now fighting for the Babylonians and to resist them was to resist Yahweh himself. The kingdom of Judah, said Jeremiah, had forfeited all claims of allegiance upon its subjects. Ezekiel joined his voice to that of Jeremiah before, during and after the destruction of Jerusalem and the deportation to Babylon. For Ezekiel, the whole history of Israel had been an apostasy from first to last, but he predicts the restoration of Temple, monarchy, priesthood and covenant in ideal forms.

The Second Isaiah wrote his Book of the Consolation of Israel with its remarkable Servant Songs during the Babylonian captivity itself. This work concentrates on the future of Israel and offers the profoundest and most inspiring understanding of the salvation wrought by Yahweh in the whole of the Old Testament. The prophecies of Baruch and Obadiah are related in different ways to the message of Jeremiah, while all the remaining prophets (with the exception of Nahum) are post-exilic: Haggai, Zechariah, Malachi, the collection known as Third Isaiah, Jonah and Joel. These books are mainly concerned with the present restoration and future destiny of Israel. They exhibit a variety of interests: the rebuilding of the temple, cultic observances, religious integrity; but they are characterized also by a strong sense of universalism and of the outpouring of the spirit. At length in post-exilic Israel the written word of the Law replaced the spoken word of the prophet, and the assembling of a canon of Scripture encouraged the idea that God had, as it were, finished speaking, and that the age of prophets was over.

The classical prophets show a very marked individuality, not only in their reaction to their times, the morality of their contemporaries or the degeneration of worship, but also in their own imagination and creativity. Their prophetic utterances took on a distinctive style, delivered in their own names and bound up with their own personalities. They did not preach, but used popular literary forms, poetry, oracles, promises and threats. The personal character is nowhere more evident than when they employed symbolic actions to make their points. Jeremiah is always resorting to prophetic actions in which a concrete symbol is manipulated to draw attention to a key word in the subsequent message. The almond-tree branch, the boiling pot, the loincloth, the shattered wine jars, the yoke are all such symbols. In the case of Hosea, it was the prophet's own matrimonial experience which provided the prophetic action. Israel, like his own wife, was a prostitute. It is clear then that in this Biblical notion of prophecy, God shared in the prophet's own way of thinking, acting and living, illuminating his own mind and his own understanding of events.

Yet, Yahweh was not said to have addressed himself *to* the prophets, but to have spoken *through* them, even though the conception and formulation of their utterances were their own. They felt that they were drawn into the emotions of God himself. They identified themselves with his designs in history, and, as Gerhard von Rad describes their prophetic inspiration, they shared in the feelings of God's own heart, his wrath, his love, his sorrow, his revulsion and even his doubts (von Rad 1965, II, p.63). God's own sensibility flowed into the prophet's psyche. However, this inspiration was not a psychological condition of the prophets themselves. It was a message and a revelation. To be a prophet was to hold an office, to be a messenger or a communicator of God's word to other people. The prophets were free agents of Yahweh, living sometimes, like Jeremiah, on the borderline between obedience and disobedience, but there was an otherness in their utterances which did not come from themselves. They felt under compulsion from an external force they could not overcome. In the inaugural visions which describe their call to be prophets, their lips are purified, or the word of Yahweh is put into their mouths as if it were a concrete object. In the case of Ezekiel, he is even made to eat a written scroll.

> And he said to me, 'Son of man, eat what is offered to you; eat this scroll, and go, speak to the house of Israel.' So I opened my mouth, and he gave me the scroll to eat. And he said to me, 'Son of man, eat this scroll that I give you and fill your stomach with it.' Then I ate it; and it was in my mouth as sweet as honey (Ezekiel 3:1–3).

The prophet in Israel was, then, a man of God, whose life was bound up with Yahweh's dealings with his people, a man who had been vouchsafed a special insight into the divine reality, who shared in the awareness of God himself. He was a man who had received God's own word – his self-revelation – in order to speak that word for him, as Aaron spoke for Moses. Prophecy in Israel was just one further instance of the interpersonal character of God's self-revelation. In the next section we shall see how God's own gift of wisdom was thought by the Israelites to be available to every individual for the discernment of his self-revelation in nature and how every man, in his own turn, was called to be a prophet to himself.

GOD'S SELF-REVELATION IN NATURE

Nature, history and transcendence

Interpersonality or personal communion is the great characteristic of Israel's concept of divine revelation. In prophecy, God used the persons of certain charismatic individuals, speaking his own word with their voice and penetrating their own mental life. Through these individuals, their messages and their political and/or moral leadership, Israelites discovered the religious meaning of the historical events that occurred. For ancient Israel, the conception of God's self-revelation in created nature was different from his self-revelation in history. Nature, in their thinking, was an impersonal bearer of revelation, a challenge offered to ordinary individuals. A principle of rationality existed in the world which complemented, or at least supported, the principle of religious faith, and ordinary men and women had to be, as it were, 'instant prophets', making the connections and the applications themselves. Created nature was 'another book' beside the sacred texts which recounted and interpreted the religious history of Israel, a book to be read by everyone. Yet even here, there were certain privileged individuals who reflected more deeply on the message proclaimed by nature, certain 'wise men' who committed their experiences and their thoughts to actual writing and who created the Biblical books which we know as Israel's wisdom literature.

The difference in approach, by ancient Israel, to history on the one hand, and to created nature on the other, is ultimately traceable to a more fundamental factor in its whole religious confrontation with life. This factor is best expressed by the personal character of Yahweh: his supreme autonomy, freedom and unpredictability – in a word, his otherness. It was therefore through personalities and human events that he most clearly revealed himself. Events in nature were interpreted through personalizations and with reference to persons – at least in the beginning of Israel's history. This does not sound very out of the ordinary. After all, the traditional ethnic religions of the world also go in for personalizations and develop a pan-sacralist world-view. But Israel's pan-sacralism was unusual in several ways.

For Israel it was a historical God, a Lord of History, whose history was their own history, who was also Lord of the World. This God was definitely not a remote 'clock-maker' God, who had set the world machinery in motion, and left it to follow the laws he had laid down. Yahweh was a God who created and renewed his creation. The creative process was continuous. Total disasters happened because humanity was wicked, but certain individuals were innocent and they were spared to make a new beginning. Thus the great flood showed the wickedness of the world except Noah and his family, while the destruction of Sodom and Gomorrah, the cities of the plain, also revealed that their inhabitants, with the exception of Lot and his family, were sinners. New 'creations' and new peoplings of the earth took place after these catastrophes. Even the historical destruction of Israel's monarchy and of the Temple and city of Jerusalem was seen as a return to primeval chaos, and the restoration was a creation more wonderful than the first.

Natural phenomena were subordinated to historical events. Thus, at the Exodus of Israel from Egypt and in the making of its covenant with Yahweh, nature was turned upside down and extraordinary phenomena occurred. Seas fled before the approach of God, as he led his people; rivers flowed backwards, mountains skipped like flocks of sheep; hard rock turned into water.

> The sea looked and fled,
> Jordan turned back.
> The mountains skipped like rams,
> the hills like lambs . . .
> Tremble, O earth, at the presence of the Lord,
> at the presence of the God of Jacob,
> who turns the rock into a pool of water,
> and flint into a spring of water (Psalm 114:3–4; 7–8).

The geography of the Holy Land was a mystical geography, a map of the nation's collective religious experience. Yahweh dwelt on the mountain of revelation, Sinai or Horeb, and he was pictured as coming from that mountain, or at least from that direction – from Teman or Paran, southern places which evoked the experience of the Exodus. Later, Mount Zion definitively replaced Mount Sinai as the dwelling-place of Yahweh.

> . . . the Lord came from Sinai into the holy place.
> Thou didst ascend the high mount,
> leading captives in thy train,
> and receiving gifts among men,
> even among the rebellious, that the Lord God may dwell there (Psalm 68:17–18).

> God came from Teman, and the Holy One from Mount Paran.
> His glory covered the heavens,
> and the earth was full of his praise.
> His brightness was like the light,
> rays flashed from his hand;
> and there he veiled his power (Habakkuk 3:3–4).

In the viewpoint of Israel, therefore, everything that had happened and continued to happen in nature was directly due to the actual decision of Yahweh, and that decision was bound up with his plan for mankind. The order of the world rested on his fidelity and on his love. As John McKenzie has written, describing the Jewish understanding of nature: 'Nature was not morally neutral' (McKenzie 1974, p. 198). As Psalm 145 put it: 'The Lord is faithful in all his words and gracious in all his deeds' (Psalm 145:13).

Israel's pan-sacralism was also unusual because of the extent to which it revealed a God who transcended the experience of nature, and who, therefore, acted as a principle of unification. Bible scholars are sometimes tempted to play down the religious experience of non-Israelites in their desire to emphasize this point about the religion of Israel. It is perhaps a moot point whether such a thing as 'nature religion' exists, or has existed, that is to say, whether any people of the world has ever worshipped the sun as sun, or the storm as storm. The evidence seems to show that natural phenomena were, at the very most, viewed as external manifestations of the deity, or at the very least, as powerful symbols (among many) of the deity. The fact that religious systems turn to nature for their theological vocabulary, or that human existence is seen to be somehow continuous with the world of nature, or that a symbol-system of extreme density has been built up, are not signs of a crude, nature religion. To take a recent example from the study of African ethnic religion, Raimo Harjula demonstrated (Harjula 1969) that the Meru people of Tanzania were not sun-worshippers, and that when they addressed their God as 'sun', they had in mind a very clear distinction between the object in the sky and the divine reality which that object revealed.

The point at issue is really: 'How far is a religion monist? How far does its distinction between God and nature go?' The malice of idolatry is unlikely to reside in the foolish mistake of taking a piece of wood for God, or even a mountain, or a storm or a celestial body for God. It is more likely to reside in the error of associating God too closely with material things, things which man can manipulate or upon which man can impose laws and regularities arrived at by his own observation. Israel satirized the idolaters, and, while its satires should be accepted for what they are: satires, the truth of the basic critique should not be overlooked. Idols were not merely unauthorized 'sacraments', they were perverted 'sacraments', and the temptation of idolatry was one to which the followers of any religion could succumb. Israel's concept of God was not pantheistic, that is to say, it did not identify God with the world itself, let alone any aspect of the world. Nor was its concept of God pan-entheistic, that is to say, it did not divinize the world to the extent of making it reside within God. On the contrary. God and the world were separate entities which, nevertheless, possessed a real and actual relationship. The world was the theatre of God's activity, and his salvation was effected in the world. Mythology provides, in every religion, the means by which a diversity of contradictory human experiences can be unified. It is not to be condemned on this account. By Israel's standards, it is to be judged, however, according to the extent to which it sacrifices God's unity by emphasizing experiential diversity, the extent to which it sacrifices God's spirituality by 'tying him down' to material forms of his self-expression, and the extent to which it sacrifices God's freedom and autonomy by denying him an on-going plan and the possibility of further revelatory surprises. Idolatry was a strong temptation for the followers of Israel's religion, as it is for those of all religions.

Nature's testimony to those with faith

It is against this background that the theophany or manifestation of Yahweh to Israel in the experience of cataclysmic natural events, such as thunderstorms and earthquakes, must be seen. At Sinai, Israel's originating experience of Yahweh took place through such a theophany, and there is a multitude of passages in the Old Testament in which Yahweh's presence is described in terms of storm, thunder, thunderbolts, lightning, rain, smoke, darkness, cloud, fire, wind, natural convulsions, earthquakes, volcanic eruptions, the shattering of rocks and trees. One example must suffice here.

> In my distress I called upon the Lord;
> to my God I cried for help.
> From his temple he heard my voice,
> and my cry to him reached his ears.
>
> Then the earth reeled and rocked;
> the foundations also of the mountains trembled
> and quaked because he was angry.

Smoke went up from his nostrils,
and devouring fire from his mouth;
glowing coals flamed forth from him.

He bowed the heavens and came down;
thick darkness was under his feet.

He rode on a cherub and flew;
he came swiftly upon the wings of the wind.

He made darkness his covering around him,
his canopy thick clouds dark with water.

Out of the brightness before him
there broke through his clouds
hailstones and coals of fire.

The Lord also thundered in the heavens,
and the Most High uttered his voice,
hailstones and coals of fire (Psalm 18:6–12).

The cherub (plural: cherubim) was a mythical hybrid creature like a sphinx which, in Mesopotamian religions, was a symbol of the wind and sometimes also of the storm-cloud. These cherubim became a motif of God's presence. In Ezekiel's theophany these winged creatures form a living chariot for Yahweh, and there were, of course, representations of the cherubim above the Ark of the Covenant in the Temple, denoting the presence of Yahweh in the Holy of Holies.

There was no question but that Yahweh's presence in nature was a universal presence. He was not simply another storm-god, like the storm-gods in the pantheons of neighbouring peoples. The storm and the earthquake, however, revealed his divinity, his inscrutability and, above all, his power. In the theophany God was seen as truly Lord and Master over nature. However, his power and mastery were not blind and purposeless. This is shown in the very interesting symbolic reversal of the theophany by Elijah. The prophet Elijah, escaping for his life from the wrath of Jezebel, came to Mount Horeb in the Sinai desert, and climbed up to the cave or cleft of rock in which Moses had been vouchsafed his sublime vision of God.

And behold, the Lord passed by, and a great and strong wind rent the mountains, and broke in pieces the rocks before the Lord, but the Lord was not in the wind; and after the wind, an earthquake, but the Lord was not in the earthquake; and after the earthquake a fire, but the Lord was not in the fire; and after the fire a still small voice (1 Kings 19:11–13).

That still small voice of calm, that whisper of a gentle breeze, succeeding the fury of wind and earthquake and fire, was symbolic of God's spirituality and intimacy – of his immanence, as well as of his transcendent power.

At the time of Solomon, Israel's primitive pan-sacralism was challenged by a spirit of secularization and realism. Not only was it a materialistic age, an age dominated by worldly concerns, but it was one which saw a relative determinism in events. Israel came under the influence of neighbouring 'wisdom' traditions which taught the science of a successful life. These traditions included a discipline and a conceptual framework for defining and classifying the real. They spoke the practical language of proverbs, aphorisms, numerical sayings, dialogues, fables and allegories – a didactic language. The wisdom literature of the Bible was, as Gerhard von Rad demonstrates, the result of bringing the Yahwistic faith into contact with this altered understanding of reality (von Rad 1972, p.60). Faith in Yahweh meant faith in an order controlled by him, for Yahweh was the final and ultimate wise one. This faith could liberate human wisdom and intellectual knowledge, could enable it to discover the divine order in the world of nature and encounter God there in the individual act of experience. Thus the search for wisdom begins with the fear of God, and practical atheism is folly. 'The fear of the Lord is the beginning of wisdom and the knowledge of the Holy One is insight' (Proverbs 9:10). Wisdom, real wisdom, is therefore God's self-revelation, the gift for which Solomon prayed. 'Behold', said Yahweh, 'I give you a wise and discerning mind, so that none like you has been before you and none like you shall arise after you' (1 Kings 3:12).

The Israelites believed that the mysteries of nature derived ultimately from the mystery of God and that he was present in all causes and effects. One can see this very clearly, for example, in a passage like that of Sirach 38:1–15 which deals with the work of the physician. There we are told that his skill comes from Yahweh, as well as the medicines which he employs, but so also does the sickness which he strives to cure. Both doctor and patient must therefore call upon Yahweh for health, healing and successful diagnosis. The 'wise man' who knows nothing of God, or who refuses to acknowledge him in life, is really the epitome of the fool, because to deny reality to what one does not understand is to deny intelligibility to the world and to undermine wisdom itself.

Biblical wisdom taught that the world is not dumb, but that it has a message; moreover, this message is self-evident and self-manifesting.

> The heavens are telling the glory of God;
> and the firmament proclaims his handiwork.
> Day to day pours forth speech,
> and night to night declares knowledge.
> There is no speech, nor are there words;
> their voice is not heard;
> yet their voice goes through all the earth,
> and their words to the end of the world (Psalm 19:1–4).

The true wisdom is thus God's self-revelation in created nature. In the Book of Proverbs and in Ben Sirach this wisdom is personified as a kind of female companion of God himself. Lady Wisdom who is the adversary of Dame

Folly. Reading such passages one might almost think that wisdom was being presented as a personified entity immanent in creation or a divine attribute that had been given an independent personal existence. However, it is clear that wisdom is a creature; 'The Lord created me at the beginning of his work' (Proverbs 8:22). Wisdom was created with the world itself and was assigned to her proper function. It is clear, therefore, that this wisdom is more than a mere principle of rationality in the cosmos, and that it is the fact that God has made creation bear witness of himself to those who have faith.

There is an element of what McKenzie calls 'anti-wisdom' in the Book of Job and in Koheleth (Ecclesiastes, or the 'Preacher') (McKenzie 1974, p.225). Job's incomprehensible experience as an innocent sufferer is an invitation to go beyond wisdom. His so-called 'comforters' cannot make that journey with him. They are insensitive to suffering because they are smug and prosperous and they cannot envisage Job's idea of a God who enters into the experience of suffering. Their view of God is of a cruel and capricious God, a view that Job refuses to endorse. God's ironical reply to Job: 'Where were you when I laid the foundation of the earth?' prompts Job's act of faith: 'I had heard of thee by the hearing of the ear, but now my eye sees thee' (Job 42:5). Job had felt the finger of God in terror and had accepted the mystery.

Koheleth does not question or attack God but seems to accept Job's God from the start. For him the world is an unfriendly place. As von Rad points out, Koheleth tries to answer the question about the meaning of life with a reason unsupported by confidence in life (von Rad 1972, p. 235). One aspect of the traditional wisdom was the teaching that every activity and experience has its proper time, but that the ultimate meaning and content of time was of divine determination – the *kairos*. Yet, for Koheleth, it was impossible to discover this 'time of God'. God had put eternity into man's mind, but had made it impossible to comprehend. If Koheleth was not an atheist, he certainly did not expect God's help. 'Vanity of vanities. All is vanity.' Koheleth's discourse is evidence that a dialogue with the world is necessary if we are to know God. It was Israel's faith that God had addressed humanity through the medium of this world, and that man can only discover the *kairos* by coming face to face with him.

QUESTIONS FOR DISCUSSION

(1)   What do we mean when we say that, in the history of ancient Israel, there were no purely secular experiences?

(2)   'Not historicized mythology, but mythicized history' – what do you understand by this phrase as applied to the Bible?

(3)   Why and how is the concept of covenant central to ancient Israel's experience of revelation?

(4) For further enquiry: What is the relationship between prophecy and revelation in the Old Testament? Has it any significance for us in the modern world?

SELECT ANNOTATED READING LIST

Pope Pius XII, 1943: *Divino Afflante Spiritu* in *Selected Letters and Addresses of Pius XII* (C.T.S. London, 1949), pp. 111–146. The encyclical which was the charter for modern Catholic Biblical studies, and which recognized the need to study the texts according to their different literary forms.

K. Rahner, 1978: *Foundations of Christian Faith – An Introduction to the Idea of Christianity* (London). Karl Rahner situates the Biblical history of salvation/revelation in the whole of world history and in the context of the multiplicity of religious histories.

J. L. McKenzie, 1974: *A Theology of the Old Testament* (London). The first ninety-five pages enumerate the different vehicles of Old Testament revelation and especially the experience of prophecy; pp. 131–161 on Israel's history, 174–201 on Nature and 205–230 on Wisdom are relevant to our chapter.

1976: *Dictionary of the Bible* (London). The following entries should be consulted: 'Revelation', 'Covenant', 'Election', 'Word', 'Theophany', 'Prophet, Prophecy'.

W. Eichrodt, 1961: *A Theology of the Old Testament* (London). Sections on the covenant and on prophecy – pp. 36–68 and 244–370 are especially relevant. Eichrodt places his theological emphasis on the theme of covenant.

G. von Rad, 1965: *Old Testament Theology* (London), 2 vols, especially vol. II. This gives a very detailed exposition of the nature and historical development of prophecy in Old Testament Israel.

1972: *Wisdom in Israel* (London). Though this book deals more with the subject-matter of our next chapter, it introduces the reader to the wisdom literature of the Bible with considerable thoroughness and explains the Old Testament attitude to created Nature as a vehicle of revelation.

3

God's Word in the World

REVELATION, THE LANGUAGE OF EVENTS

The mystery of God in the appropriateness of events

The Greek word *kairos,* as used in the Bible, is not an easy word to render into English. It has nothing essentially to do with theories of time, whether endlessly linear or endlessly cyclical. Taken in itself, it does not refer exclusively to the end of time, an idea which happens to be rather rare in the history of religious thought. It alludes to a Jewish idea that time has a content or a meaning intended by God. It is the 'hour', the 'moment of truth'. It refers to the timeliness of events, to the 'fullness of time'. It is the 'proper' or 'appropriate' time. Basically, it conveys the idea that the world has a meaning and that history has a purpose. It is the very opposite of the popular evolutionist and/or determinist idea that every step in the history of the earth and of sentient and animal life was due to pure chance, or else that human choice and activity are fundamentally determined by blind economic necessity. By definition, chance is not a principle of causality. It does not make anything happen, nor does it explain anything. It is merely a word that designates a coincidence or an accident without saying anything more about it. And yet the human yearning for meaning and interpretation is such that popular writers about the origins of animal and human life bestow a misplaced concreteness upon the process of evolution. If they do not actually give it a capital 'E', they make evolution get up and do things. Imperceptibly, evolution – which, after all, is only a pattern of events discerned by ourselves who are wise after they have happened – is made to become a bearer of meaning. 'Evolution' or 'Nature', although subject to pure chance, is made into a coercive mechanism, and it is a poor substitute for faith in a God who imparts meaning to events and who proves his deity in the language of facts.

To the eyes of faith the events of nature and of history have a transforming power. For ancient Israel the content of history, the appropriateness of events, stood in a real and actual relationship to the God in whom they believed; and they came to understand, as Wolfhart Pannenberg has put it, that the end or goal of history 'is at one with the essence of God' (Pannenberg 1969, p. 131). A little over thirty years ago, a Christian historian, Herbert Butterfield, tried to express the Judeo-Christian understanding of history. In a celebrated passage (Butterfield 1949, pp. 94–95) he compared the human story to an orchestra in which each of us is playing his part (for example, that of the second clarinet) and of which God is the conductor and composer. It is a continuous piece of music that we are playing together and, as we are sight-reading, we do not know what is coming next, nor how it will all end. We can only see our own part and know what note we have to play next, following the music on the page and the baton of the divine conductor. However, were we to page forward in our music score, we would find only blank pages, because God is actually only composing this music note by note as the orchestra is playing it. We do not know what is in the composer's mind, but we *do* see how, when one of the musicians plays the wrong note, God adjusts the music he is composing and somehow gives a different turn to the bars that come immediately afterwards. Brilliantly, he straightens things out, incorporating our false notes, by – for example – passing from the major to the minor key. When the music has actually been played over and has become a thing of the past, we can begin to see the pattern of the whole symphony.

This modern analogy of the universal symphony and the divine conductor-composer may help us to appreciate the Jewish understanding of history and the way, in their thinking, that God directs his creatures in freedom and reveals his purpose to them. Like the *rapport* between conductor and orchestra, revelation is essentially dialogue. It is a revelation 'to' or 'for' others, and these others, through their own imaginative response, became a part of the revelation process.

In the preceding chapter we saw how the Israelites believed that God personally addressed them in his word. His words were the phenomena of created nature, particularly cataclysmic events. They were also the events of human history. All these events were given meaning through a mythological interpretation which referred them to the ultimate reality of God. Myth, as we saw, is not only *not* opposed to factual knowledge; it is the instancing and illumination of facts. It is a language of fact. Not all these facts were historical in the Israelite case. In many instances, the Israelites remodelled unhistorical, symbolic stories in order to convey the meaning of the human experience of nature (including human nature) and human dealings with God in general. But typically, the Israelites sought to interpret historical facts and to retell their history in symbolic form in order to understand how God revealed himself in particular historic instances and what God's pattern or plan was.

In particular events, especially in the Exodus and the covenant, God revealed himself as a person and as a vindicator or saviour. 'God spoke to

Israel.' In the cultic celebration of Exodus and Covenant, the symbols provided by monarchy and Temple, and more particularly in the pheno-menon of prophecy, according to which certain charismatic individuals spoke and lived by God's word, Israel encountered God, discovered who he was and what he was like. The age of classical prophecy coincided more or less with the most shattering event in Israel's history, its destruction as a nation and its eventual return from the Babylonian captivity. Most of this present chapter will be concerned with how God manifested himself to Israel in this traumatic experience and in its aftermath. But it was the prophets who were most aware of the divine determination of time, and who could read 'the signs of the time'. These perceptive minds were the privileged vehicles of revelation, for they had been given a special insight into God's awareness. They experienced truly great moments in rising to the challenge of events, somewhat like the experiences in time which the poet Wordsworth celebrates:

> There are in our existence spots of time,
> That with distinct pre-eminence retain
> A renovating virtue . . . (*The Prelude*, XII, 208–210).

or like T. S. Eliot's 'moment in and out of time' (*Four Quartets: The Dry Salvages*, V, 24). It is perhaps no accident that many poets envisage their vocation as prophetical and that the classic prophets of Israel were themselves poets.

The mystery of God and man's self-revelation

In the preceding chapter we noted how, according to Israel's way of thinking, God revealed himself in his transcendence through the cataclysmic events of nature. These awe-inspiring phenomena participated in the speci-ficity or 'one-off' character of historical events, and were, indeed, on occasion associated with them. Such was the case with the theophany and covenant at Sinai, and probably with the crossing of the Sea of Reeds. We also noted, however, that the theophany could be reversed and that God's immanence in the world could be detected by the man of faith, reflecting upon the order and harmony of the cosmos. God's wisdom was the fact that creation itself bears witness to an order controlled by Yahweh and to his active involvement in the world he has created. The dialogue which consti-tutes God's self-revelation to man necessarily implies a dialogue with created nature, and it was Koheleth's tragedy that he could only see a dark world in which true wisdom consisted in the acceptance of transience and pain as inevitable.

Other wisdom writers lay emphasis on the sense of joy and liberation which comes from the recognition of Yahweh's governance of the world.

Wisdom is active, calling men and promising them life, happiness and the security of divine favour. Wisdom trains her human children for the encounter with the imponderable mystery of God. She wants men to feel at home in the world and to surrender to the glory of full human existence.

> Blessed is the man who meditates on wisdom
>   and who reasons intelligently.
> He who reflects in his mind on her ways
>   will also ponder her secrets.
> Pursue wisdom like a hunter,
>   and lie in wait on her paths.
> He who peers through her windows
>   will also listen at her doors;
> he who encamps near her house
>   will also fasten his tent peg to her walls;
> he will pitch his tent near her,
>   and will lodge in an excellent lodging place;
> he will place his children under her shelter;
>   and will camp under her boughs;
> he will be sheltered by her from the heat,
>   and will dwell in the midst of her glory (Sirach 14:20–27).

Many scholars have come to think that the personification of wisdom in certain passages of Ben Sirach and the Book of Proverbs is influenced by the cult of the Egyptian goddess Isis. Isis was proclaimed by her devotees as the divine agent who created and who sustains the universe and as teacher of morality and the arts of living to mankind. Undoubtedly, the Biblical wisdom literature draws very freely upon the sources of non-Jewish religious thought and philosophy and borrows images and forms from other cultures and traditions. However, there is no real doubt that the Old Testament authors were attempting to make the worship of Yahweh as attractive an alternative as possible to the other cults and philosophies then prevalent. There is no question of making wisdom into a goddess or turning an attribute of God into an independent being. On the contrary, the fact that Ben Sirach associates wisdom very closely with the Law or Torah shows that these images were given a different connotation within the monotheistic religion of Israel. Having described wisdom in profoundly personal terms, as having come forth 'from the mouth of the Most High' and as having been created from eternity for an eternal existence, Ben Sirach proceeds:

> All this is the book of the covenant of the Most High God,
>   the law which Moses commanded us
>   as an inheritance for the congregations of Jacob.
> It fills men with wisdom, like the Pishon,
>   and like the Tigris at the time of the first fruits,

It makes them full of understanding, like the Euphrates,
    and like the Jordan at harvest time.
It makes instruction shine forth like light,
    like the Gihon at the time of vintage (Sirach 24:23–27).

In the same passage, although wisdom is equated with the Mosaic Law itself, it is also presented as the key to the Law. It is wisdom who explains the Law and who has been assigned a special place in the providential history of Israel: 'Make your dwelling in Jacob, and in Israel receive your inheritance' (Sirach 24:13). Thus wisdom interacts with the special and heaven-sent guidance provided by the Law of Moses.

It is also suggested very often that the figure of Wisdom in the Old Testament can be identified with the Logos of Stoic pantheism and Platonic idealism. In Greek thought the Logos was certainly less personal than 'Lady Wisdom' of the Bible. It was a kind of principle of rationality or order in the cosmos. There is little doubt that later pre-Christian Judaism was strongly influenced by Hellenistic ideas, but, since *logos* means 'word', there is also no doubt that Greek and Jewish concepts of 'Word' differed sharply. According to Thorlief Boman, *logos* derives etymologically from a root meaning 'to gather' or 'to arrange' (Boman 1960, p. 67). Thus, 'speaking' in the Greek way of thinking referred to the meaning of the word spoken. When the ancient Greeks spoke of Logos, they had in mind the ordered and reasonable content of the Word.

For the ancient Hebrews, as we have seen, it was totally different. When they thought of 'speaking', they had in mind, not the content of speech, its rationality or intelligibility, but its function. The Word was for them the function of speaking, a dynamic force which issued in deeds, rather than reasons. As we have seen, the whole of creation was understood by the Israelites as being the outcome of the effective and dynamic word of Yahweh. 'And God said, "... let the dry land appear". And it was so. God called the dry land Earth ... ' (Genesis 1:11–12). Wisdom comes forth from the mouth of the Most High, and, as Yahweh's Word, represents his will to create and to govern events. Much later, the Jewish theologian and philosopher Philo of Alexandria, who was a contemporary of Jesus and of Paul, used the Greek concept of Logos, identifying it very clearly with the Mosaic Law, but using the word 'wisdom' as an occasional varient for Logos. Once again, we see a very different approach to the Logos idea from that of Greek philosophy. Although he seems to have accepted the Stoic Logos, Philo felt it was most clearly and fully embodied in the Torah of Israel (Dunn 1980, pp. 221–228).

Wisdom was therefore a way of speaking about God's active involvement with the world and with humanity, without, however, compromising his transcendence. It was also a charism or gift from God for understanding this involvement. As such it was a created, rather than a creative, word, like the self-evidence of Yahweh 'written into' or 'spoken into' creation itself. Nevertheless, it shares in the dynamism of the creative word, for it brings about a transformation, a whole cosmological process of becoming. God's wisdom fills the whole earth and reflects back his glory. Israelites came to look forward to a new creation, a radical renewal, in which the knowledge of the Lord would change the whole face of earth and restore the peace and harmony of the garden of Eden.

> The wolf shall dwell with the lamb,
>   and the leopard shall lie down with the kid . . .
> The sucking child shall play over the hole of the asp,
>   and the weaned child shall put his hand on the adder's den.
> They shall not hurt or destroy in all my holy mountain;
> for the earth shall be full of the knowledge of the Lord
>   as the waters cover the sea (Isaiah 11:6–9).

Through the knowledge God gives him, man becomes himself a bearer of revelation.

In the Biblical wisdom literature we find a paradigm for the theology of revelation, as it was later developed within Christianity. We quoted Cardinal Newman's view that faith is essentially belief in a Being 'exterior and superior', a transcendent and absolute reality. Further, Newman believed that conscience was the 'essential principle and sanction of religion in the mind' (Newman 1909, p. 18). Conscience testifies to a *relationship* with this exterior and superior Being. This was Newman's approach to the problem of immanence. The Bible teaches us very clearly that the basis of revelation is experience itself and that God's person and God's dynamic activity are experienced and communicated by human beings. The transcendent lies *within*, that is to say, is *immanent* to, human experience and is expressed in words of faith. Faith, thought Newman, implies obedience to conscience (even to an unformed and incomplete conscience) and also a 'triumphing' over reason and a 'quieting' of its murmurs.

Pope John Paul II, in the first encyclical letter of his pontificate, took up an idea of the Second Vatican Council, that the revelation of the mystery of God is inextricably bound up with the revelation of man to himself. God penetrates the mystery of man and enters his heart with his own mystery of love:

> Man cannot live without love. He remains a being that is incomprehensible for himself, his life is senseless, if love is not revealed to him, if he does not encounter love, if he does not experience it and make it his own, if he does not participate intimately in it (*Redemptor Hominis*, 10).

In so far as all religions are successful up to a point in confronting this mystery and making it their own, then revelation is a part of their own self-understanding, and all religion is revealed religion. In true revelation, God communicates himself to man. As Edward Schillebeeckx makes clear, God offers both a self-revelation and a human interpretative experience of this revelation, at one and the same moment (Schillebeeckx 1980, p. 50). Revelation is not the quantitative addition to truths known by unaided reason of 'supernatural' truths. The unaided reason does not, in fact, exist, as Cardinal Newman pointed out in the university sermon just quoted. Religion and the language of faith are expressions of a unique encounter with the world and with history, a unique interpretative experience. As the Old Testament teaches us, God is actively involved with the world and with human activity. This involvement was both self-evident in the structure of cosmic and historical events, and intelligible to man through a participative understanding of it. Moreover, as humanity reflected, even more clearly, on this divine self-communication, it was transformed.

The next stages of our investigation will help us to understand how the people of the Old Testament saw this transformation which resulted from their historical encounter with the living God, how they saw God's self-revelation at work in the histories of other nations, and how their expectations of God developed. The ancient Israelites certainly understood the whole of creation in the light of God's self-communication to them, but this self-communication came to them in the uniquely tangible manner of their history as a nation.

REVELATION, LANGUAGE OF SALVATION

Salvation as God's fidelity and love

Israel's experience of a living God was the experience of a God who saves. His activity and involvement in their history was a saving activity. The Torah or Pentateuch, the five books which make up the so-called 'Book of the Law', are all centred upon the life and teaching of Moses and the primordial experience of salvation, the Exodus from Egypt. Of course, the Torah is an amalgam of traditions of great antiquity, and it is more important for us to know the experiences to which these traditions refer than to try and work out how the documents attained the form in which we now have them. It is clear, however, that Moses and the Exodus are central to the Torah.

As we have already seen, the essential character of Yahwistic religion was summed up in the covenant, the agreement according to which Yahweh promised his people a land, long life, prosperity, a numerous progeny and victory over their enemies, in return for fidelity to him, to his worship and to his moral laws. If the Exodus was the primordial experience of Yahweh's saving power, there was another primordial experience in the desert, even at the very foot of Mount Sinai itself. This was Israel's immediate infidelity to

Yahweh, its lapse into idolatry with the making and the adoration of the golden calf. This event became the perennial archetype of all infidelity in Israel. As Psalm 106 describes it:

> They made a calf in Horeb
>   and worshipped a molten image.
> They exchanged the glory of God
>   for the image of an ox that eats grass.
> They forgot God, their Saviour,
>   who had done great things in Egypt.
> wondrous works in the land of Ham,
>   and terrible things by the Red Sea (Psalm 106:19–22).

For Jeremiah, what happened at Sinai or Horeb foreshadowed Israel's later infidelities and was, in fact, a double evil. Israel had forsaken Yahweh on the one hand; while on the other, it had put itself in his place. Idolatry was self-worship and attempted auto-salvation.

> Has a nation changed its gods,
>   even though they are no gods?
> But my people have changed their glory
>   for that which does not profit.
> Be appalled, O heavens, at this,
>   be shocked, be utterly desolate, says the Lord,
> for my people have committed two evils:
>   they have forsaken me,
> the fountain of living waters,
>   and hewed out cisterns for themselves,
> broken cisterns,
>   that can hold no water (Jeremiah 2:11–13).

The Book of Deuteronomy, the so-called 'Second Law', re-words the first commandment of the Decalogue, basing it upon the actual theophany or manifestation at Sinai.

> Since you saw no form on the day that the Lord spoke to you at Horeb out of the midst of the fire, beware lest you act corruptly by making a graven image for yourselves, in the form of any figure ... (Deuteronomy 4:15–16).

It was the continual transgression of the first commandment and the assimilation of all infidelities and infractions of the Law to that first and basic one at Sinai that triggered an increased understanding of Yahweh himself and of the salvation he offered. Yahweh punished his people for their infidelities, but he always relented and forgave them in the end. He was the faithful partner to the covenant, whereas Israel was the unfaithful one. In the consciousness of their own sin, the Israelites were more than ever conscious of the righteousness and justice of their God.

This was the message of Amos, the shepherd-prophet sent to the northern kingdom. Amos preached against Israel's idolatry, its formalism and self-deception even in the worship of the true God, and against its corruption and oppression. God is presented by this prophet as the all-powerful defender of justice who will call Israel to account. Israel looked forward to a day of Yahweh, which would be a day of vindication for itself, a day of liberation from the yoke of its enemies. Amos tells them that this day will be one of vengeance against Israel itself, but that a remnant – those who have remained faithful – will be saved. 'The Lord God has sworn by his holiness . . . prepare to meet your God, O Israel! . . . For thus says the Lord to the house of Israel: "Seek me and live . . ."' (Amos 4:2, 12; 5:4).

The prophet Hosea, another of the northern prophets, belongs to the same period as Amos, and yet his insight into the righteousness of Yahweh is more profound. God's righteousness is a personal quality, transcending all laws and standards, supreme, exclusive, jealous, universal. This is the quintessence of traditional Yahwism. Hosea, guided by his own emotional life and his own experience of marriage, brings out the paradoxical quality of God's fidelity and goodness. It is the forgiving love of a marriage partner. It is the tender love of bridegroom for bride, speaking to her heart.

> I will betroth you to me forever; I will betroth you to me in righteousness and in justice, in steadfast love, and in mercy. I will betroth you to me in faithfulness; and you shall know the Lord (Hosea 2:21–22).

It is also like the love of a father for his infant son:

> When Israel was a child, I loved him,
>   and out of Egypt I called my son.
> The more I called them,
>   the more they went from me;
> they kept sacrificing to the Baals,
>   and burning incense to idols.
> Yet it was I who taught Ephraim to walk,
>   I took them up in my arms;
>   but they did not know that I healed them.
> I led them with cords of compassion,
>   with the bands of love . . .(Hosea 11:1–4).

Yahweh is pictured by Hosea as a fond father, lifting his infant up to his cheek and stooping down again to give him food. 'How can I give you up?', Yahweh asks. 'My heart recoils within me, my compassion grows warm and tender . . .' (Hosea 11:8).

Salvation in Hosea proves to be reconciliation with Yahweh, sincere conversion and a healing of the heart which brings true happiness.

> Return, O Israel, to the Lord your God,
>   for you have stumbled because of your iniquity . . . .

I will heal their faithlessness;
  I will love them freely,
  for my anger has turned from them.
I will be as the dew to Israel;
  he shall blossom as the lily . . .(Hosea 14:2, 5–6).

In the following century, after the fall of the northern kingdom, the religious reform associated with the name of King Josiah of Judah took place. This led to the Deuteronomic formulation of the Mosaic inheritance, which again saw the bequest of the Law as the gift of Yahweh's love. Set within the framework of a Mosaic discourse, Deuteronomic teaching returns again and again to the same theme. Israel has been chosen by God in a spontaneous act of divine love and it is its duty to return that love by remaining faithful to the law and the worship which God prescribes.

> And now, Israel, what does the Lord your God require of you, but to fear the Lord your God, to walk in all his ways, to love him, to serve the Lord your God with all your heart and with all your soul, and to keep the commandments and statutes of the Lord, which I command you this day for your good? Behold, to the Lord your God belong heaven and the heaven of heavens, the earth and all that is in it; yet the Lord set his heart in love upon your fathers and chose their descendants after them, you above all peoples, as at this day. Circumcise therefore the foreskin of your heart, and be no longer stubborn (Deuteronomy 10:12–16).

Deuteronomy does not have so refined an understanding of salvation as Hosea. Salvation is definitely to be found in a spiritual understanding of the Law and a loving motivation for fidelity to the covenant. Deuteronomy appeals again and again to the gratitude and praise that should be on the lips of the Israelite, but the reward for fidelity remains the ideal of a successful – even a materially successful – earthly life, while the punishment for infidelity is death and destruction. 'See I have set before you this day life and good, death and evil' (Deuteronomy 30:15). The characteristic message of Deuteronomy is that the good life is tied inexorably to the love of God.

With the traumatic experience of the Babylonian captivity, the Second Isaiah was inspired to return to Hosea's theme: 'Speak tenderly to Jerusalem'. According to Walther Eichrodt, Second Isaiah elevates the concept of Yahweh's righteousness to the status of a key concept for understanding the whole divine work of salvation (Eichrodt 1961, p. 246). God's righteousness and loving kindness are shown in his redemptive acts. In a later section we shall consider the universalist implications of Second Isaiah's teaching; it is enough to notice here that he proclaims a new and 'everlasting covenant' which echoes the highly personal and heartfelt religion of Jeremiah and that he continually promises strength and courage. Thus Israel's fidelity and hope rest on the very strength that God himself gives.

Fear not, for I am with you,
  be not dismayed for I am your God;
I will strengthen you, I will help you,
  I will uphold you with my victorious right hand (Isaiah 41:10).

Strengthen the weak hands,
  and make firm the feeble knees.
Say to those who are of a fearful heart,
  'Be strong, fear not!
Behold, your God
  will come with vengeance,
with the recompense of God.
  He will come and save you' (Isaiah 35:3–4).

Jeremiah re-thought the traditional teaching of Israel, not only in the light of contemporary events – the destruction of Temple, monarchy and nation – but also in the light of his own personal sufferings. This led him to an understanding of religion, and of salvation in particular, which was peculiarly spiritual and inward. He realizes, more clearly than the prophets who have gone before him, how Israel's infidelities stem from a perverted heart and will.

The heart is deceitful above all things,
  and desperately corrupt;
  who can understand it?
'I the Lord search the mind
  and try the heart,
to give every man according to his ways,
  according to the fruit of his doings' (Jeremiah 17:9–10).

This prompts him to proclaim the new covenant which is the very highest peak of Jeremiah's spirituality.

Behold the days are coming, says the Lord, when I will make a new covenant with the house of Israel and the house of Judah, not like the covenant which I made with their fathers when I took them by the hand to bring them out of the land of Egypt, my covenant which they broke, though I was their husband, says the Lord. But this is the covenant which I will make with the house of Israel after those days, says the Lord: I will put my law within them, and I will write it upon their hearts; and I will be their God, and they shall be my people. And no longer shall each man teach his neighbour and each his brother, saying, 'Know the Lord', for they shall know me, from the least of them to the greatest, says the Lord; for I will forgive their iniquity, and I will remember their sin no more (Jeremiah 31:31–34).

True salvation, then, consists in a total conversion of the heart, not in submission to an externally imposed law. This is the new covenant or testament.

Humanity as divine icon and as idol

Reflection on Israel's infidelity to Yahweh, as a repetition of the primordial apostasy in the desert, led the Hebrews to consider human nature itself and the experience that this nature is deeply flawed. This conclusion, as we have just seen, received full expression in the prophecy of Jeremiah. In the books which make up the Torah there is another primordial apostasy, the very first sin ever committed by a human being. Of course, sin is as old as man himself, and there must have been a 'first' sin. The authors of Genesis described this sin in symbolic terms, through a process of etiological history. In their poetic conjecture, the collective noun *adam,* 'the man', became the proper name of the first ancestor of the whole human race, and his sin not only exemplified all sins committed after his time, but inaugurated a reign of sin throughout the world, in which man made war on his fellow man, after his revolt against God.

In the Book of Genesis man is not created out of God's substance, nor is his creation a work of evil, or of some lesser god or demiurge. Instead, a remarkable balance is held between monism and dualism. Humanity, male and female, is created in the 'image and likeness' of God himself.

> Then God said, 'Let us make man in our image, after our likeness; and let them have dominion over the fish of the sea, and over the cattle, and over all the earth, and over every creeping thing that creeps upon the earth.' So God created man in his own image, in the image of God he created him; male and female he created them (Genesis 1:26–27).

'Image and likeness' means that man is an *icon* of God, that he really makes God present in some way, that he participates in the nature and creative freedom of God. The *icon* is akin to the symbol or sacrament. We have already seen (in the preceding chapter) how an idol is a 'perverted sacrament'. It is perverted because it is not really the image of something else. It stops short at itself and does not show forth the nature of God or make him present. It is an idol, because it is not a true *icon* or image. Idols were therefore relentlessly forbidden by the Mosaic law.

Man, on the other hand, had started out as a true image or *icon* of God. Genesis postulates a homogeneity between man and God, a homogeneity which, as Raimundo Panikkar points out, is the very condition of religion itself. It is this homogeneity

> that 'binds together' God and Man so that they are not totally separate and hetero-geneous realities. If God were *totally* other, there would be no place for love or for knowledge, or for prayer and worship, no place, indeed, for Himself-as-Other (Panikkar 1973, p. 15).

Thus, without being part of the divine substance (as Brahmanism suggests), man was divinized from the beginning, called to an actual relationship or union with God, as God. Creation itself is thus an act of grace. There is no such thing as a purely natural condition of man. Man is not God, but neither is he an animal or any lesser kind of creature, He is created out of the pure love and favour of God for a supernatural destiny, orientated towards God. Anthropogenesis, or the fulfilment of man in himself, can only come about through communion with God. Since we know man only as actually called to meet God, there is now, as Gustavo Gutiérrez remarks, a reluctance to use the word 'supernatural' (Gutiérrez 1973, p. 71). Theologians today favour the word used by the Second Vatican Council's Pastoral Constitution on the Church in the Modern World (*Gaudium et Spes*): the word 'integral'. Man is called to be more integrally, more fully, human. That is why theologians from St Thomas Aquinas in the thirteenth century to Karl Rahner in the twentieth have seen the human orientation towards God as an innate or constitutive element of the human spirit.

Unlike the Upanishads, for example, or the Orphic myth, or the idealism of Plato and those influenced by his thought, Genesis presents the creation as an irreversible process. It is not an 'everlasting return', a cyclical development, or an illusion or dream of the absolute. It is real and tangible and concrete. True, man's integral destiny is described in poetic language. That is because, as we have had occasion to point out more than once, directly descriptive language is inadequate to express the experience of the divine, or indeed to express any significant interpretation of a profound human experience. The Old Testament turns to the language of symbol and metaphor. The communion between God and man is expressed through the image of a garden, an oasis in the eastern desert, in which animals did not prey on one another but were satisfied with plants for their food. It was a garden in which Yahweh walked in the cool of the day, under the shade of symbolic trees. Among these were the tree of life and the tree of the knowledge of good and evil. The tree of life; the promise of immortality, was – as it were – an extra gift bestowed upon man who was by nature mortal. The tree of the knowledge of good and evil, on the other hand, was reserved to God alone, for it represented the fact that God was, in his very nature, the ultimate measure of what was good or bad. It represented God's sovereignty and his unlimited goodness. Psalm 8, another poem, celebrates the divine plan for humanity and the privilege bestowed on him at his creation. Man is 'little less than God', or 'than a god'. In saying this, the psalmist had in mind the angelic creatures who were pictured as being closest to God and who were part of his heavenly court.

> What is man that thou art mindful of him
>   and the son of man that thou dost care for him?
> Yet thou hast made him little less than God,
>   and dost crown him with glory and honour.
> Thou hast given him dominion over the works of thy hands;
>   thou hast put all things under his feet (Psalm 8:4–6).

The tragedy recounted by Genesis is that Adam was not content to be little less than God. He and his wife Eve ('the mother of all living') took and ate the fruit of the forbidden tree. By this act the first man and the first woman tried to claim moral independence from God. They accepted the lie of the serpent: 'You will be like God', and distorted God's image in themselves. They put themselves in the place of God, committing the supreme act of idolatry. That is why, in Israelite thought, the idolatry of the golden calf at Sinai and the sin of the first human parents were so closely associated. Both were acts of rebellion, pride and ingratitude. Both were a refusal of obedience and true worship and both jeopardized the communion of life existing between themselves and God.

As a result of his disobedience, Adam and his wife were expelled from the Garden of Eden; and they and their descendants were not given the chance of by-passing natural death. Death, suffering and the struggle for survival were the direct results of this human rebellion and perverted human will. Throughout their history, the ancient Israelites always associated death and suffering with actual sins of disobedience to Yahweh and his covenant. As we have seen in the preceding chapter, the case of the innocent sufferer posed a problem for them, and they began to grope their way towards the notion of a suffering that was salvific. Suffering and death were the universal lot of man, and the fall of Jerusalem and subsequent deportation and exile caused them to reflect more deeply on their own relationship to other nations, and on the universality of the salvation which was embodied in the self-revelation of Yahweh.

REVELATION, LANGUAGE FOR THE UNIVERSE

The nations as instruments of God's judgement and mercy

Already implicit in the Genesis story of the fall of man is the idea that the Jewish historical experience is 'of the world', that it is a microcosmic history. In the history of Judaism there has always been a tension between the election of Israel as God's people and the universality of God's salvation. The idea that Yahweh's gift of salvation was offered to the Gentiles was more easily accepted at the time of exile and restoration than it was in later Judaism, let alone in the earlier pre-exilic period of Israel's history.

God had spoken to Israel and not to other nations. The consciousness of this privilege was bound up with the historical character of their encounter with the living God in the unique event of the Exodus. It was when their historical horizons were forcibly widened that they discovered this election to be a mission and even a service. This happened when either they had no further need to struggle to preserve a precarious national identity among the other nations, or their nation had simply ceased to exist. Thus it comes about that other nations are ignored by the Torah in the whole story of the development towards the Sinai covenant. For Israel, idolatry, as we have seen, was the basic sin, and idolatry was the normal religious condition of other nations. Other nations were the enemies of Yahweh. This assumption prompted a self-righteousness and narrowness, a religious and ethnic prejudice.

The first glimmerings of a different attitude come about when Amos condemns Israel and tells them they cannot presume on their election by Yahweh. Amos compares the Israelites to the people of Cush, the Ethiopians who inhabited the furthest limits of the known world in Africa. He compares the Exodus to what God has done for Israel's traditional enemies the Philistines and for the migrant Aramaeans.

> 'Are you not like the Ethiopians to me,
>   O people of Israel?' says the Lord,
> 'Did I not bring up Israel from the land of Egypt,
>   and the Philistines from Caphtor and the Syrians from Kir?
> Behold, the eyes of the Lord God are upon the sinful kingdom.
>   and I will destroy it from the surface of the ground;
>   except that I will not utterly destroy the house of Jacob,' says the Lord
> (Amos 9:7–8).

Yahweh, says Amos, brought all these Gentile nations to their present lands, and the prophet implies that a single moral standard is valid for both Israel and the Gentiles. This idea is taken up in First Isaiah and other prophets with oracles delivered against Israel as well as against the nations, although ultimate pardon and victory are foretold for God's chosen people.

We are already familiar with the idea of Yahweh deserting his own people in battle, as a punishment for their infidelity. This concept, of course, says little of Yahweh's relationship to the victorious enemies. With the rise of Assyria, however, and the approaching destruction of the Jewish kingdom, God is seen, not merely as withdrawing support from Israel, but as actively using the enemy as an instrument in his plan. First Isaiah calls Assyria the 'rod of anger' of Yahweh.

> Ah, Assyria, the rod of my anger,
>   the staff of my fury!
> Against a godless nation I sent him,
>   and against the people of my wrath I command him,
> to take spoil and seize plunder,
>   and to tread them down like the mire of the streets (Isaiah 10:5–6).

But Assyria will be punished after Jerusalem, for not recognizing that it is but Yahweh's instrument. In Jeremiah, Yahweh's alliance with Assyria is even more explicit. To resist Assyria is to resist Yahweh himself; Israel must simply submit to the punishment it deserves. For Nebuchadrezzar is Yahweh's 'servant' and God will send for him and for all the tribes of the north to do his work of vengeance. Babylon's supremacy, says Jeremiah, will last for seventy years.

If foreign nations execute Yahweh's punishments, they are also the instruments of his mercy. This is supremely true of Cyrus, the conqueror of Babylon and the restorer of Israel. Second Isaiah pictures Yahweh granting victories to this Persian king, so that he can restore Israel. In a reference to Cyrus's lightning victorious advance, Yahweh asks: 'Who is the author of this deed?'

> Who stirred up one from the east
>   whom victory meets at every step?
> He gives up nations before him,
>   so that he tramples kings under foot;
> he makes them like dust with his sword,
>   like driven stubble with his bow.
> He pursues them and passes on safely,
>   by paths his feet have not trod.
> Who has performed and done this,
>   calling the generations from the beginning?
> I, the Lord, the first,
>   and with the last; I am He (Isaiah 41:2–4).

In an even more famous passage, Second Isaiah calls this pagan king God's 'shepherd' and 'anointed' whose right hand he has grasped. Cyrus is therefore hailed by the very same title as the kings of Israel, and one which came to be reserved for the Messiah to come.

> 'I am the Lord, who made all things . . . .
> who says of Cyrus, "He is my shepherd,
>   and he shall fulfil all my purpose"';
> saying of Jerusalem, "She shall be built",
>   and of the temple, "Your foundation shall be laid".'
> Thus says the Lord of his anointed, to Cyrus,
>   whose right hand I have grasped,,
> to subdue nations before him
>   and ungird the loins of kings,
> to open the doors before him
>   that gates may not be closed:
> 'I will go before you
>   and level the mountains . . .'   (Isaiah 44:24, 28 – 45:2).

Universal salvation through the destruction of Israel

We have seen how the new covenant foretold by Jeremiah consisted in a moral regeneration for Israel. Ezekiel, the prophet of the exile, and Zechariah, the prophet of the restoration, both took the same theme. For Ezekiel it was a cleansing and a renewal:

I will sprinkle clean water upon you, and you shall be clean from all your unclean-
ness, and from your idols I shall cleanse you. A new heart I will give you, and a new
spirit I will put within you; and I will take out of your flesh the heart of stone and
give you a heart of flesh. And I will put my spirit within you, and cause you to walk
in my statutes and be careful to observe my ordinances (Ezekiel 36:25–27).

Zechariah itemizes the good deeds that will be done by Israel:

These are the things that you shall do; Speak the truth to one another, render in your
gates judgements that are true and make for peace, do not devise evil in your hearts
against one another, and love no false oath, for all these things I hate, says the Lord
(Zechariah 8:16–17).

Throughout the three parts of the Book of Isaiah there is a clear theme of
universalism. At times it is expressed through a crude ethnocentric outlook.
At the restoration, Israel will become the centre of the universe and all the
nations of the world will be its slaves, flocking to Jerusalem with riches and
tribute. It is a new golden age, more glorious than the height of material
splendour enjoyed by King Solomon. We shall discuss the themes of
monarchy and messiahship more fully in the next section of this chapter, but
it should be pointed out here that often, in the pages of Isaiah, it is Yahweh
who is proclaimed the true king of Israel, rather than a human descendant of
the house of David. It is, perhaps, this everlasting, universal reign of
Yahweh which prompts a more religious interpretation, for we find an
increasing emphasis on the moral conversion of the Gentiles, rather than on
their subjugation. Or rather, perhaps one should say: Subjection to Yahweh
means moral conversion, and that new spirit spoken of by Jeremiah, Ezekiel
and Zechariah.

In Isaiah, God's gift of salvation is for the whole world, and his covenant
is no longer with Israel alone, but with all the nations. It is not simply that
the nations which formerly enslaved Israel will now be humiliated and
enslaved in their turn, or that Israel will be vindicated for having remained
faithful to God in her captivity and exile. Israel will not merely be 'leader
and master' of the nations, but will be a 'witness' to them. Israel has a
mission and a vocation towards the foreign peoples.

Behold, I made him a witness to the peoples,
  a leader and commander for the peoples.
Behold, you shall call nations that you know not,
  and nations that you knew not shall run to you (Isaiah 55:4–5).

The heathens will come to Zion in order to worship the true God, to learn
the ways of Yahweh and be converted. From Zion, the Law will go out to
the whole world.

It shall come to pass in the latter days
  that the mountain of the house of the Lord

shall be established as the highest of the mountains,
    and shall be raised above the hills;
and all the nations shall flow to it,
    and many peoples shall come, and say:
'Come, let us go up to the mountain of the Lord,
    to the house of the God of Jacob;
that he may teach us his ways
    and that we may walk in his paths.'
For out of Zion shall go forth the law,
    and the word of the Lord from Jerusalem (Isaiah 2:2–3).

The degree to which this proselytism is stretched is quite remarkable, even if ethnic and nationalistic considerations are still strong in the picture that is presented. Israel is to become a kingly nation, a nation of kings, but their kingship is a moral one, drawing others, by their example, to be converted to the religion of Yahwism. It is a spiritual imperialism, not always easily discernable from the political variety, but definitely assuming dominance. This in itself was a noteworthy development in a world where political and religious domination were usually identified. Of course, in the Servant Songs of Second Isaiah, Israel's vocation reaches a final height of sublimity, but, before turning to them, it is worthwhile considering the universalism explicit in two other post-exilic books, those of Ruth and Jonah.

Although there is argument about the date of the Book of Ruth and its action is placed in the period of the Judges, there is no doubt whatever about its message. This little book tells the story of the loyalty and piety of a foreigner from Moab who trusted in God and who was rewarded by him. When her husband, who hailed from Bethlehem, died, Ruth refused to leave her husband's family, invoking the law of the levirate so that seed could be raised up for the dead man. Boaz, a relation of her husband's, had the claim on her, and he rewarded her loyalty and persistence by taking her to wife. Ruth's song, addressed to Naomi, her mother-in-law, is touching and full of faith:

Where you go I will go,
and where you lodge I will lodge;
your people shall be my people,
and your God my God;
where you die I will die.
and there will I be buried . . . (Ruth 1:16–17).

The purpose of the story is transparent. Trust in Yahweh is rewarded, and his love crosses over frontiers to members of other nations. The book ends by recalling that Ruth, the woman of Moab, was privileged to become the great-grandmother of King David.

The story of Ruth is still centred on Israel, the nation favoured and chosen by God. With the Book of Jonah it is otherwise. This fictitious didactic story is wholly centred on the country of Israel's greatest enemy, Assyria. All the characters in the story are pagans, with the exception of Jonah himself, and he is an Israelite prophet sent to preach repentance to the citizens of the great Assyrian city of Nineveh. All the pagan characters in the story are sympathetic, men of goodwill. Only Jonah, the prophet, is the odd man out, rebelling against his mission. The sailors are anxious to do the right thing and are horrified at Jonah's disobedience to Yahweh in fleeing his mission. They are loath to make Jonah the scapegoat, and they pray, and make sacrifice and vows to Yahweh. God is merciful to Jonah, saving him by means of the great fish, and sending him out again on his mission to convert Nineveh.

The people of Nineveh are no less admirable than the sailors. They repent at once and a fast is proclaimed which includes even the animals. God's mercy is shown once more and the threat of destruction, proclaimed in Jonah's prophecy, is withdrawn. Only Jonah remains dissatisfied.

> Is not this what I said when I was yet in my country? . . . I knew that thou art a gracious God and merciful, slow to anger, and abounding in steadfast love and repentest of evil . . . (Jonah 4:2–3).

Jonah complains that his mission has been useless, and goes out of the city, still hoping to see fire and brimstone descend upon the town and its inhabitants. In the final incident Yahweh makes Jonah angry over the trivial withering of a castor-oil plant and then draws the moral:

> You pity the plant, for which you did not labour, nor did you make it grow, which came into being in a night, and perished in a night. And should not I pity Nineveh, that great city, in which there are more than a hundred and twenty thousand persons who do not know their right hand from their left, and also much cattle? (Jonah 4:10–11).

Jonah is the epitome of Israel's narrowness and exclusiveness, but Yahweh's compassion extends even to the Assyrians and the cattle of the Assyrians! In Israelite eyes, surely compassion could go no further than that? The moral of the Jonah story – 'the sign of Jonah' – is the unexpected deliverance wrought by Yahweh's universal and compassionate love, and also the effectiveness of his word in his prophet's preaching, bringing about the conversion of Israel's greatest enemies. McKenzie sums up this prophecy when he calls it 'a great step forward in the spiritual advancement of Biblical religion' (McKenzie 1976: 'Jonah').

In the Servant Songs, Second Isaiah gives evidence of an understanding that Yahweh's final purpose is not merely the existence or the survival of Israel as a nation. Nor is it necessarily a spiritual purpose centred on Israel as a historical and political phenomenon. It is in the destruction of Israel that he accomplishes his purpose and that the nations recognize him as God. Israel's service to the world is one of vicarious, atoning suffering. At the basic level, the title 'Servant' applies to Israel and yet there is also a suggestion of what Wheeler-Robinson called 'corporate personality'. Though not distinct from Israel, the Servant is larger than Israel. In him Israel is somehow transcended.

In the first song, the Servant appears with the diffidence and humility of Moses. His task is to establish justice on the earth and to proclaim the law to the islands or coastlands – an image of the universality of his mission. In the course of the song, God proclaims his own name Yahweh, the name he revealed to Moses, and he constitutes the Servant in himself 'a covenant' to the nations.

> I am the Lord, I have called you in righteousness,
>   I have taken you by the hand and kept you;
> I have given you as a covenant to the people,
>   a light to the nations,
>   to open the eyes that are blind,
> to bring out the prisoners from the dungeon,
>   from the prison those who sit in darkness (Isaiah 42:6–7).

In the second song, the Servant of Yahweh himself speaks, recounting his vocation and calling upon the remotest peoples to listen to his message. Yahweh is quoted at the end of the song:

> It is too light a thing that you should be my servant
>   to raise up the tribes of Jacob
>   and to restore the preserved of Israel;
> I will give you as a light to the nations,
>   that my salvation may reach to the end of the earth (Isaiah 49:6).

Once again, the world-mission of the Servant is affirmed. In the third song, the Servant appears as a disciple of Yahweh and a preacher inspired by him. Yahweh has given him both hearing and speech so that he may strengthen those who are weary. This time the Servant's meekness extends to his submission to blows, insults and shame. All this he can bear, because the Lord God helps him.

In the fourth and longest song, parts of which may have been inspired by the experiences of the prophet Jeremiah, the atonement is at its clearest. There is no beauty in him. He is despised and rejected by men, 'a man of sorrows and acquainted with grief'. He was 'smitten by God'. He was oppressed and afflicted and yet like a lamb that is led to slaughter 'he opened not his mouth'. He was cut off out of the land of the living, and 'they made his grave with the wicked'. Why all this? 'He has borne our griefs and carried our sorrows . . . wounded for our transgressions . . . bruised for our iniquities.' 'Upon him was the chastisement that made us whole and with his stripes we are healed.' 'The Lord laid on him the iniquity of us all.' More than that: 'He makes himself an offering for sin . . . he poured out his soul to death'. And what, finally, is it all for? 'He shall see the fruit of the travail of his soul . . . my servant (shall) make many righteous . . . he bore the sin of many and made intercession for the transgressors' (Isaiah 52:13 – 53:12).

The fourth Servant song lays great emphasis on the stupendous nature of this atonement. It is a cause of astonishment and speechlessness, disbelief and misunderstanding – in short, a scandal. Yet in all of this Yahweh is glorified and the recompense of his Servant will be very great, although that recompense is hardly specified. Walther Eichrodt is surely right in seeing the Second Isaiah as the summit of the Old Testament understanding of the divine work of salvation (Eichrodt 1961, p. 246). Israel's encounter with God, revealing himself, led them to go beyond their own nationalism and their pride in being Yahweh's 'first-born son'. It led to a belief in their mission towards the moral regeneration of humanity, through suffering and annihilation as a nation. In the fourth song of Yahweh's Servant, the questionings of the Book of Job are answered, and the acceptance of suffering and death finds a place in the divine plan of salvation – all this, without any clear promise of immortality or heavenly reward.

We have said that the New Testament cannot be deduced from the Old Testament. That is true; and not all the writers of the Old Testament, particularly in the later period, could rise to the level of the Second Isaiah. But the New Testament is the fulfilment of the Old, and the early Christians turned almost naturally to Second Isaiah, as they did to other Old Testament texts we have been considering, in their effort to express the significance of the event of Jesus Christ. Meanwhile, we shall now examine other versions of Israel's future, other expectations indicative of God's plan for humanity which were popular in post-exilic Israel.

REVELATION, LANGUAGE OF THE FUTURE

Messianism

It is clear from Second Isaiah that some Israelites did not believe in the eternity of Israel. In his Book of the Consolation of Israel, there is a new Exodus and a new covenant and frequent mention of Zion, but we do not have any hope that the monarchy or the Temple will be restored or that the future of Israel is bound up with these historic institutions which perished at the hands of the Assyrians. In the Third part of Isaiah (as we have seen) the whole nation seems to share in the charism of kingship. Yet there were still some people, during and after the exile, who centred their hopes on the restoration of the monarchy and who saw Yahweh's identification with Israel as taking the shape of a promised King-Saviour, a Messiah or anointed one.

Messianic tradition goes back to the oracle of Nathan which promised

David that his kingdom and his throne would last forever. Yet nothing could be more obvious or more brutal than the extinction of that same kingdom and that same throne in 587 B.C. It was clear to most people that the monarchy in Israel had been a failure. However, King Jehoiachin was pardoned and released by his captors, and the Davidic line survived, even if the monarchy was not restored after the exile. Henceforth, the political power was to be largely in the hands of the priests.

When the southern kingdom was already in danger and even during the exile itself, prophecies were made which described a fulfilment of Nathan's oracle in political terms. First Isaiah foretells the birth of Immanuel, 'God-with-us'. Probably, there is a historic reference here to a specific royal birth which Isaiah saw as ensuring the continuity of the monarchy – perhaps the birth of Hezekiah, son of Ahaz. At any rate, Isaiah paints a picture of the ideal king who is the special recipient of God's blessing on behalf of his people, God's representative on earth. He is given resounding royal titles: 'Wonderful Counsellor, Mighty God, Everlasting Father, Prince of Peace'. The rule of this king, thinks Isaiah, will inaugurate a reign of universal peace that will last forever, an age of the 'anointed one', a messianic age. This prophecy was certainly not fulfilled in any literal way through the Kings of Judah themselves, and the political kingdom collapsed. Isaiah had looked beyond the actual kingdom to what it stood for, and the hope it engendered.

During the exile, Ezekiel centred the national hope – at least to some extent – upon the restoration of Israel as a nation and upon the reunification of the two kingdoms in one. There can be no more dramatic symbol of Yahweh's ability to perform the seemingly impossible than Ezekiel's vision of the 'valley full of bones'. There is a rattling as the bones come together and the whole house of Israel stands up to live and breathe again.

> Behold, I will open your graves, and raise you from your graves, O my people. And
> I will bring you home into the land of Israel (Ezekiel 37:12).

Then there is the prophetic action of Ezekiel in joining the two sticks, symbols of the two halves of the divided nation, joined now in one stick. Finally, Ezekiel envisages a descendant of David sitting again upon the throne of Israel:

> And I, the Lord, will be their God, and my servant David shall be prince among
> them; I, the Lord, have spoken (Ezekiel 37:23–24).

The Book of Psalms contains a number of royal psalms or songs connected with the monarchy. Some of these are prayers for the king or songs of thanksgiving for him; others are prayers put into the mouth of the king himself. There is also a royal song and a song for a royal wedding; but, perhaps most striking of all, there are two great oracles addressed to the king by Yahweh himself.

'You are my son,
  today I have begotten you.
Ask of me and I will make the nations your heritage,
  and the ends of the earth your possession' (Psalm 2:7–8).

The Lord says to my lord:
  'Sit at my right hand,
till I make your enemies your footstool.' ...
The Lord has sworn,
  and will not change his mind,
'You are a priest for ever
  after the order of Melchizedek' (Psalm 110:2, 4).

The reference to Melchizedek king of Salem, the place which Biblical tradition identifies as Jerusalem, is to a mysterious figure described in Genesis as 'priest of God Most High'; and the inference is that the prerogatives of the Davidic king are divinely bestowed. Long after the destruction of the monarchy, Israelites continued to sing these royal psalms. Undoubtedly, for many the divine oracles had to be fulfilled literally, in the coming of a future king who would restore the kingdom to Israel. But there was a more sublime level of fulfilment for others, with either the whole nation reigning as kings, or, as in Second Isaiah and the psalms of God's universal sovereignty, with Yahweh as Israel's true 'king and redeemer'. 'Say among the nations, "The Lord reigns" ' (Psalm 96:10); 'The Lord reigns, let the earth rejoice' (97:1); 'The Lord reigns, let the peoples tremble!' (99:1). Thus messianism was no mere nostalgia for a vanished glory, but a faith seeking understanding, a belief in God's fidelity to his promises and speculating on the ways in which they might be fulfilled. One thing Israel had learnt in its encounter with the living God was 'to expect the unexpected'. Revelation was always a surprise.

Spiritual worship

Some of Israel's exilic and post-exilic spokesmen envisaged a religious, rather than a political future. This was centred on the Temple. The short prophecy of Haggai, which exhorts the returned exiles to redouble their efforts in the building of the second Temple, foretells a building the glory of which will surpass the old; and the Books of Chronicles, which retell the story of the ancient kingdoms, subordinate the monarchy to the Temple, to the extent that temple-building becomes the main purpose of kingship. The Temple of Zerubbabel, however, turned out to be a poverty-stricken affair, and the Book of Ezra tells how old people who remembered the Temple of Solomon wept aloud at its inauguration. It was left to Herod the Great to demolish the second Temple and rebuild it on a scale which was at once vaster and more sumptuous than even the Temple of Solomon. Work began in 20 B.C. and continued up to six years before its final destruction by Titus in A.D. 70.

From what can be seen of the masonry today, the great platform on which it was erected, it must have been one of the architectural wonders of its time. All during the lifetime of Christ, this colossal building project dominated Jewish public life, until the preoccupation with a material sanctuary threatened to become a new form of idolatry.

Yet the Temple represented the presence of God among his people, and there were those who had taken a more spiritual view of its importance to Israel. The prophet-priest Ezekiel describes his vision of a Temple that is perfect in its proportions, a purely imaginative construction, the dimensions of which are measured by an angelic interpreter. Out of this utopian Temple, and from its very threshold, flows a stream which regenerates the whole country, turning the stagnant waters of the Dead Sea into a lake that is fresh and sweet, so that fish and animals, trees and fruit will live and flourish. Ezekiel's teaching, however, centres on a moral regeneration of which all this pictorial writing is a symbol. What counts for him is the inner conversion, the 'new heart' and the 'new spirit'. What was important was true worship that was a real spring of life, not the hollow mockery of triumphalist ceremonial. Nothing could, in fact, be further from Ezekiel's vision than the ostentation of Herod's Temple. When Israel sinned, God's glory departed from the Temple, leaving it an empty shell.

This spiritual view of the future as a quiet, worshipping community was also taken by other post-exilic writers. Chief among these was Malachi. This prophet was part of a long tradition among the Jewish prophets, representing a critique of externalism and formalism in temple worship. For Malachi, the Temple was still the place of revelation *par excellence*. It was even the place of future, decisive judgement, when God's messenger would 'suddenly come to his temple' to purify the Levitical priesthood with a fire like that of a refiner of gold or silver. This imagery and its message belong to the next section of the present chapter, when we shall consider the eschatological character of Old Testament revelation. At the moment we are concerned with Malachi's ideal for the immediate future and his critique of contemporary worship.

The burden of Malachi's message is that, as H. H. Rowley puts it, 'an imperfect faith that is the true spring of life is better than a hollow profession of a richer faith which proves itself to be no faith, because it does not become the spring of life' (Rowley 1944, p. 75). The outer profession of ritual is meaningless; it is the quality of worship that counts, a worship in spirit. Yahweh rejects the 'orthodox' worship of Israel, but he accepts the 'unorthodox' worship of the pagans. This is a 'pure offering'. Thus in Malachi spirituality and universalism come together.

I have no pleasure in you, says the Lord of hosts, and I will not accept an offering from your hand. For from the rising of the sun to its setting my name is great among

> the nations, and in every place incense is offered in my name, and a pure offering; for my name is great among the nations, says the Lord of hosts. But you profane it when you say that the Lord's table is polluted, and the food for it may be despised. 'What a weariness this is', you say, and you sniff at me, says the Lord of hosts (Malachi 1:10–12).

True religion is not merely a question of getting God's name right! Perhaps this is the very extreme of broadmindedness that we encounter in the pages of the Old Testament.

Malachi's spirituality echoes that much earlier message of the prophet Micah, who was a contemporary of First Isaiah before the exile in Babylon. Micah inveighs against the corruption and oppression practised by Israel's rulers and he evokes a combination of universalism and messianism that is similar to that of Isaiah. However, the true religion of Yahweh is described in highly spiritual terms. In the dialogue with God, Yahweh asks: 'My people, what have I done to you?', and the repentant Israelite answers: 'What shall I do?'

> Shall I come before him with burnt offerings,
>   with calves a year old?
> Will the Lord be pleased with thousands of rams,
>   with ten thousands of rivers of oil?
> Shall I give my first-born for my transgression,
>   the fruit of my body for the sin of my soul?
> He has showed you, O man, what is good;
>   and what does the Lord require of you
> but to do justice, and to love kindness,
>   and to walk humbly with your God? (Micah 6:6–8).

Justice had been the theme of Amos; tender loving-kindness the theme of Hosea. Was the humble walking with God perhaps already a forerunner of the salvific and vicarious suffering proclaimed by Second Isaiah? Micah is not explicit; in fact, he goes on to paint the proverbial picture of Israel's enemies being eventually defeated and licking the dust at its feet, after Yahweh has pardoned his people. But for a moment, the veil of revelation had been raised upon a religious ideal that was both spiritual and highly personal, and one that came to express a less triumphalistic religion after the experience of exile.

Personal religion and the Law

Yet another expectation of the future, and one which proved to be more lasting, centred on the Law. Ezekiel's vision of a future utopian Temple took its place within a larger framework, the 'Torah of Ezekiel' which represented the restoration, reform and adaptation of the ancient Mosaic legislation. This became the starting-point for a pietistic movement within the restored Israel. This pietism was greatly assisted by the development of the synagogue. Synagogues, or places of assembly for the study of the Torah and for prayer, may have had a pre-exilic existence. They certainly came into their own and existed side by side with the second Temple. After the Temple's destruction in A.D. 70, they came to replace the Temple completely, and are indeed referred to today by some Jews as 'temples'. In these democratic places of instruction and worship were kept the scrolls of the law and the other sacred books. Jesus himself, we are told in the Gospel of Luke, was invited to read and expound the prophecy of Isaiah in the synagogue at Nazareth, and picked out a passage from Third Isaiah about the prophet's mission, which he proceeded to apply to his own. In modern synagogues there is still an 'ark', containing the scrolls of the Torah.

Devotion to the Law reached heroic extremes with the Hasideans, who allied themselves with the Maccabees in their struggle against the persecutors in the Greco-Roman period. They were ready to suffer excruciating tortures and even death itself rather than countenance a material or apparent infringement of the law. Typical of this attitude is that of Eleazar who died in defence of the 'holy God-given law' and the martyrdom of the seven holy Maccabees, sons of an equally courageous mother, who exhorted them to die one after another and finally went to her own death. The Hasideans were the spiritual ancestors of the Pharisees who appeared in the second century B.C. and who figure largely in the pages of the New Testament. The Pharisees believed not only in the meticulous observance of the letter of the Law, but in the observance of the whole law – all the oral traditions and interpretations of the Torah. They were the pious people *par excellence,* the conscientious respecters of the Law. They advocated a strongly personal religion of salvation and a belief in the immortality of the soul, or, more correctly, in the bodily (personal) resurrection of the individual. The Synoptic critique of Pharisaism is in some points a caricature which does not do them full justice. Paul (Saul) of Tarsus was a devout Pharisee, before his conversion to Christianity, and there is no doubt that the party of the Pharisees saved Judaism after the destruction of the Temple in A.D. 70, and that their piety has been an influence in modern Judaism and even in Christianity itself.

Ranged against the Pharisees was the party of the Sadducees, the priestly, conservative and autocratic guardians of the Temple and its official structures and ceremonies. They were also the ones who encompassed the death of Jesus of Nazareth, according to the Gospel accounts. For the Sadducees, only the written Torah could be recognized. This was a minimalist – perhaps even a reductionist – approach to Jewish tradition which did not admit of any speculation or devotional practice which was not explicitly contained in the written word. The Sadducees were ready to compromise with the

Roman occupiers of their land, in order to ensure the survival of the Law and the Temple worship at all costs.

As John Bowker has put it (Bowker 1978, p. 37), whereas the Sadducees built a 'wall' around the Temple, the Pharisees built a 'wall' around the Torah. For the latter, closeness to God was a personal matter, which did not depend on the structures of priesthood and Temple ritual, but on the meticulous observance of the law. For the Jews, the question of God's immanence was bound up with his people, Israel. God's immanence became problematical when his effects were either not seen or appeared to be irregular. In other words, in her history Israel experienced various crises in the plausibility of God. One of these, the problem of the innocent sufferer, was expressed in the Book of Job; another was the experience of desertion by God in defeat and captivity and especially in the destruction of the Solomonic Temple and Davidic monarchy. To the implausibility of Yahweh, there were, argues John Bowker, two solutions. One was to demand more dramatic effects of God in the visible cultic and political sphere; the other was to demand a more dutiful and thoughtful approach to the Torah (Bowker 1978, pp. 118–119). When the soldiers of Titus fired Herod's Temple and those of Hadrian ploughed up the Temple site, the future of Judaism lay with the second alternative. But, as H. H. Rowley remarks, the religion of Israel was too bound up with the history and future of a particular nation for it ever to become a kerygmatic or missionary religion, in spite of the profound insights of a Jeremiah, a Second Isaiah or a Malachi. Nevertheless, if Judaism 'is not essentially and notably a missionary religion . . . [the] Old Testament is a missionary book' (Rowley 1944, p. 75).

In the next section of this chapter, we shall deal with Old Testament apocalyptic and eschatology. Of course, this is a subject which overlaps with the present topic, the future expectation of later pre-Christian Judaism. It is, in any case, difficult to avoid overlap in any division one makes when treating the character and content of revelation in the Old Testament. However, as we said at the beginning of the chapter (quoting Pannenberg), the Jewish understanding of God's self-revelation was not simply a question of a process of becoming. It was a process which had a climax in God.

REVELATION, LANGUAGE OF FINALITY

God revealed as the end of history

Not even modern science is convinced of the eternity of the earth or even of the universe. There has to be a limit, whether it be in a final fragmentation or explosion, or in the annihilating engulfment of a black hole. *A fortiori* there has to be an end to human history, a moment when the earth, at least, is no longer habitable, and there is no longer a foothold for man. But even if the fantasies of science fiction were to be verified and humanity could migrate endlessly to other planets and galaxies, this would change very little in our contemporary human outlook. If we are to be realistic from a chronological point of view, our objectives are short-term. The finality or endlessness of time are scarcely relevant to human activity and human ambition. Time, in fact, is not a mode of viewing reality, and certainly not of understanding it. Western man has inherited Greek concepts of cyclical time, of an astronomical time that can be spatially or quantitatively measured, and, as Claude Tresmontant has stated, fixed cycles of time militate against the notion of human freedom (Tresmontant 1962, p. 64). Theoretically, the possibilities of human invention may be endless, but as long as we are time-bound, the ultimate fruits of our invention elude us. They are like Macbeth's dagger of the mind: 'Come let me clutch thee! I have thee not, and yet I see thee still!' Moreover, as Metz demonstrated, the past has no further relevance of its own, since in an evolutionary scheme. it merely prepares the path for the present (Metz 1980, pp. 106–109). Without in any way questioning the scientific basis for evolutionary hypotheses, it is nevertheless true that evolutionism in its popular form can quickly become triumphalist. The 'fittest' who survive are the ones who write the history of science in linear fashion, forgetting the crises, the revolutions, the discarded views of the world and the abandoned avenues of enquiry which might live again in a future renaissance (Metz 1980, pp. 124–127). One cannot break through fixed spatio-temporal cycles, any more than one can finally escape (in Buddhist fashion, for example) the process of becoming.

At least, that was the ancient Israelite view. Ancient Israel certainly had a dynamic view of history as a process of becoming, but it was a qualitative becoming. Humanity was certainly pressing forward, and the language of revelation had to do with the future. But the obscurity of the future had nothing to do with the endlessness of time or with a spatio-temporal horizon. The end or goal of history, according to Hebrew thinking, was a matter of decisiveness, of God's light being progressively revealed in a darkness not fathomable by man. The end of history 'is at one with the essence of God' and God reveals himself in the actuality of present experience. In the light of this revelation, past meanings are being continually revised and the goal of history is being anticipated. Revelation is both a past record and a future reference. It is also a cosmic drama, an 'end-myth' of God's complete, universal sovereignty. Revelation provides an overall perspective on past and future; a new, a final world order, which is outside time. This is what is meant by eschatology: God leading the world, through the influence and transforming power of his active personality, towards its goal. Revelation is not the mere perception of God's being, but the experience of his power and grace, his loving-kindness and fidelity, and the sense of ultimacy, of finality and absoluteness that this experience conveys.

We have already seen Israelite conceptions of the future which had eschatological implications. Messianism, in particular, with its certainty that God would restore the kingdom in one form or another, was one of these. The new world order of messianic times was often pictured, especially in Isaiah, as a return to the peace and harmony of Eden – the communion of life between man and God. These pictures may well have been influenced, as is now thought, by the corpus of psalms devised for Temple worship under the monarchy, the royal psalms especially, and the psalms, to which we have already alluded, of the universal sovereignty of Yahweh. There was also the image of the 'Day of Yahweh' which first appeared in Amos, and which was taken up again and again by different prophets, by Obadiah, Joel, Malachi. This dread day of judgement for the nations and for Israel itself is described in terms of cataclysmic cosmic events, the shaking of the heavens and the earth, the sun and moon growing dark, the coming of plagues and the spread of consuming fire.

> For behold, the day comes, burning like an oven, when all arrogant and all evildoers will be stubble; the day that comes shall burn them up, says the Lord of hosts, so that it will leave them neither root nor branch (Malachi 3:19).

Other images, too, appear: the laying waste of the land, the treading down in the wine-press of God's anger, human slaughter and destruction by invading armies, famine and drought. However, the victory of Yahweh is assured and, in so far as it is identified with him, of Israel, or at least of the 'true Israel', the faithful remnant.

The cosmic drama of good and evil

The word 'apocalypse' comes from a Greek word meaning 'revelation' and referring especially to the revelation of hidden things and events of the future. It is typically the revelation of the Day of Yahweh, the day of judgement, and of vindication or liberation of his elect. There are several apocalypses or apocalyptic passages in the Old Testament and they claim to derive from visions, rather than from a 'word of the Lord'. The visions are described in complex and cryptic imagery. This is because they were coded messages for a persecuted people. Apocalyptic literature flourished in times of persecution, giving hope for a reversal of fortunes and promising the putting right of present wrongs. Persecution often carries with it predictable theological repercussions. There is an enlargement of theological scale and a deepening of spiritual insight. As we have seen, the Jewish experience of exile brought a new spiritual certainty and a new sense of the reality of God. After the restoration of Israel, the religious horizons tended once more to shrink, as people equated the divine plan with the political and institutional survival of God's people. However, Israel again experienced persecution at the hands of the Seleucid rulers in the third and second centuries B.C. and once more the experience stimulated apocalyptic writing in the shape of the Book of Daniel and (in part) the apocryphal Book of Enoch.

Apocalyptic writers describe the cosmic drama, the conflict between good and evil which will issue in a totally new world order. Their view is of a God who is utterly transcendent, whose dealings with humanity are mediated by angels and obstructed by demons. Their stance is above, or outside, time, contemplating past, present and future through the eyes of this transcendent God in the light of a divine secret which contains the true significance of history. They proclaim the finality of history, the everlasting and universal reign of the saints presided over by mysterious eschatological figures.

The Book of Daniel envisages a resurrection of the dead and everlasting life for all whose names are written in the Book of Life.

> At that time shall arise Michael, the great prince who has charge of your people. And there shall be a time of trouble, such as never has been since there was a nation till that time; but at that time your people shall be delivered, everyone whose name shall be found written in the book. And many of those who sleep in the dust of the earth shall awake, some to everlasting life, and some to shame and everlasting contempt. And those who are wise shall shine like the brightness of the firmament; and those who turn many to righteousness, like the stars for ever and ever (Daniel 12:1–3).

The most celebrated passage in Daniel, however, is the description of Daniel's dream about the four beasts and the 'ancient of days'. The series of beasts evidently signify the successive empires of the Middle East, while the fourth beast in particular stands for the Seleucid dynasty, the final representative of which – Antiochus IV Epiphanes – is symbolized by the 'little horn' with eyes and 'a mouth speaking great things'. The narrative of the dream then goes on to describe a judgement scene which became one of the most evocative passages in later Israel and in the inter-testamental period.

> As I looked
> thrones were placed
>   and one that was ancient of days took his seat;
> His raiment was white as snow,
>   and the hair of his head like pure wool;
> his throne was fiery flames,
>   its wheels were burning fire.
> A stream of fire issued
>   and came forth from before him;
> a thousand thousands served him,
>   and ten thousand times ten thousand stood before him;
> the court sat in judgement,
>   and the books were opened.
>
> I looked then because of the sound of the great words which the horn was speaking. And as I looked, the beast was slain, and its body destroyed and given over to be

burned with fire. As for the rest of the beasts, their dominion was taken away, but their lives were prolonged for a season and a time. I saw in the night visions,

and behold, with the clouds of heaven
    there came one like a son of man,
and he came to the Ancient of Days
    and was presented before him.
And to him was given dominion
    and glory and kingdom,
that all peoples, nations and languages
    should serve him;
his dominion is an everlasting dominion,
    which shall not pass away,
and his kingdom one
    that shall not be destroyed (Daniel 7:9–14).

That the 'Ancient of Days' is Yahweh himself, there can be no doubt, since he is described in the language and imagery of eternity and is seated upon a fiery chariot, redolent of Ezekiel's inaugural vision. The mysterious eschatological figure, *bar nasha* or *ben adam,* 'the son of man', is not only presented to God, but seems to share in divine privileges. He comes 'with the clouds of heaven', always a divine prerogative in the Old Testament; and there is at least the implication that he shares in the divine judgement, since there is mention of more than one throne..A passage in the Book of Enoch, which is probably not earlier than A.D. 70, clearly associates the mysterious 'son of man' with the process of judgement. Furthermore, in the Danielic passage, he is given an everlasting and universal dominion. In other words, he is made to share in the complete and final sovereignty of God.

Eschatological figures

Like the 'Servant of Yahweh' in Second Isaiah, the 'son of man' has a connotation that seems to go beyond Israel as a collectivity. The Servant of Yahweh seemed not only to evoke each and every Israelite as an individual, but to possess a corporate personality which transcended the collective Israel. The Son of man certainly represents Israel, because the text itself goes on to make the identification: ' . . . the saints of the Most High shall receive the kingdom, and possess the kingdom forever, for ever and ever'. And:

As I looked, this horn made war with the saints, and prevailed over them, until the Ancient of Days came, and judgement was given for the saints of the Most High, and the time came when the saints received the kingdom (Daniel 7:21–22).

It was perhaps inevitable that the Son of man should be eventually identified with a particular individual. The same passage from the Book of Enoch cited above equates the Son of man with 'the Chosen One', that is to say, with the future anointed king or messiah. However, the writer of Daniel did not himself draw that conclusion. In the inter-testamentary period, no doubt stimulated by very early Christian speculation, Jews began to evince a special interest in certain heavenly individuals, deemed to be dwelling with God and, perhaps, to have a future role to play in the divine plan for humanity as eschatological figures. One of these was the prophet foretold by Moses in the Book of Deuteronomy:

> And the Lord said to me, ' . . . I will raise up for them a prophet like you from among their brethren; and I will put my words in his mouth, and he shall speak to them all that I command him. And whoever will not give heed to my words which he shall speak in my name, I myself will require it of him' (Deuteronomy 18:18).

In its context this passage refers to the institution of the prophetical office by Moses, but Jewish expectation came to read more into the passage and to look for the coming of a second Moses. Elijah was another eschatological figure. Like Moses, he had been vouchsafed a vision of God upon Horeb, and he disappeared in mysterious fashion. The Second Book of Kings tells us that a chariot of fire and horses separated Elijah and his servant Elisha, and that 'Elijah went up by a whirlwind into heaven' (2 Kings 2:11). The conclusion was later drawn that Elijah did not die, although this is not said explicitly in the text, which merely records his disappearance. The expectation that Elijah would return became an important feature of Jewish eschatology and was expressed by Malachi:

> Behold, I will send you Elijah, the prophet, before the great and terrible day of the Lord comes. And he will turn the hearts of fathers to their children and the hearts of children to their fathers, lest I come and smite the land with a curse (Malachi 3:23–24).

Sirach also addressed Elijah, and, in a passage the sense of which is uncertain, seems to suggest that those who see him on his return will live forever like him.

> You who were taken up by a whirlwind of fire,
>   in a chariot with horses of fire;
> you who are ready at the appointed time, it is written,
>   to calm the wrath of God before it breaks out in fury,
> to turn the heart of the father to the son,
>   and to restore the tribes of Jacob.
> Blessed are those who saw you,
>   and those who have been adorned in love;
> for we also shall surely live (Sirach 48:9–11).

Even more mysterious among the eschatological figures of later Judaism was that of Enoch. Like Elijah, he was assumed to have been taken bodily up to heaven by Yahweh. The passage in Genesis is cryptic in the extreme:

> Enoch walked with God; and he was not, for God took him (Genesis 5:24).

In one Genesis account, Enoch is the seventh generation from the creation and he is distinguished from the other patriarchs by his piety and by the fact that his span of years equals the number of days in the solar year. In another genealogy fron Genesis, Enoch is the son of Cain and builder of a town. Commentators have seen a parallel with a Sumerian king who was the seventh to reign before the Mesopotamian flood, and whose town was the centre of a sun-worshipping cult. He was also alleged to have a special wisdom and to have been the first to practise divination. The Old Testament has taken this ancient tradition and made it a symbol of piety and the reward for piety. Sirach also has praise for Enoch:

> Enoch pleased the Lord, and was taken up;
>   he was an example of repentance to all generations (Sirach 44:16).

Apocalyptic writing is more truly a theological and literary *genre* than any other writing in the Old Testament. It is an interpretation of history, as well as of those who have already interpreted it – the prophets. As Edward Schillebeeckx has pointed out, at bottom, the apocalyptic experience is an essentially 'modern' experience (Schillebeeckx 1979, p. 124). It is a wrestling with the problem of cruelty, pain, inequality and injustice. It proclaims a radically new order in which roles will be reversed, in which those who suffer now will soon laugh for joy. It is a yearning for a Utopia, as human beings have always yearned for a Utopia when life became unbearable. It is a commonplace of religious sociology that millenarian or messianic cults flourish in conditions of extreme dislocation. It is also a commonplace of social history that such cults fail to satisfy in the end, and that the promise remains 'utopian', which is to say: a question of wishful thinking.

It is of immense significance to people of the twentieth century that the earthly life of Jesus of Nazareth began in an era of apocalyptic expectation, that his preaching was addressed to people who posed apocalyptic questions, the questions which interest us moderns, questions about suffering and questions about the meaning of the individual human life for the whole of history, questions about justice and inequality, about liberation and peace. The utopias of the twentieth century are pragmatic, and the goals which they try to realize are presupposed – that is to say, they are either left to the individual conscience (a conscience frequently stifled by materialism), or to the conscience of an élite who interpret a dogmatic blueprint for the future. There is not only a difficulty in choosing from among the countless possibilities and innumerable goals which the future offers us, but there is the further difficulty of planning for a future that we cannot ultimately foresee or control in all its details. It is only in looking back that events fall into place, and in facing the challenging realities of the present, which defy human explanation and control, that we can work towards a worthwhile and realistic future.

We are back at Herbert Butterfield's analogy of the orchestra with which we began this chapter, for the music, when we finally hear it being played, is always a surprise. Yet to play the music, and to be an active member of the orchestra, our eyes must follow the conductor's baton. We must discover the *kairos,* the timeliness of events, the content of time, as we try to read the signs. We must discover the salvific or transforming power of events. If it is liberation that we desire, what are we to be liberated from, and what are we to be liberated for?

In this chapter and the previous one, we have been preparing to hear Christ's answer to these questions. In these chapters we have been sketching the 'pre-history' of Christ, examining the character of God's self-revelation in the Old Testament and its all-important content. It has not ended in a unified conclusion. Rather it has issued in a welter of speculations and expectations, out of which both Christianity and modern Judaism have sprung. The important fact for our purpose is that God's self-revelation in Jesus Christ – the climax, as we believe, of that self-revelation – was understood and expressed in the language and in the light of Old Testament traditions.

QUESTIONS FOR DISCUSSION

(1) How does Biblical wisdom literature offer a paradigm for the complementarity of 'transcendence' and 'immanence' in modern theology?

(2) What is the nature of the salvation offered to man in the writings of the Old Testament?

(3) Do you agree with H. H. Rowley that the religion of ancient Israel was 'not essentially or notably a missionary religion but the Old Testament is a missionary book'?

(4) For further enquiry: Explore the relevance of apocalyptic thought and writing to the situation of the modern world.

SELECT ANNOTATED READING LIST

G. von Rad, 1972; *Wisdom in Israel* (London). Attention should be paid especially to the whole section (the latter portion of the book, from p. 144) which deals with God's self-revelation in creation and the actual concept of wisdom.

W. Eichrodt, 1961; *A Theology of the Old Testament* (London). All that Eichrodt has to say about the salvific message of the classic prophets is worth reading (pp. 244–285), as are the final pages, which deal with Israel's 'end-myth' and its new sense of the reality of God after the end of the monarchy.

J. L. McKenzie, 1974; *A Theology of the Old Testament* (London).
From p. 267 onwards Fr McKenzie deals with Old Testament speculation on the future of Israel. Our chapter draws extensively on his ideas.

H. H. Rowley, 1944; *The Missionary Message of the Old Testament* (London).
This is a short but important (and very readable) account of missionary and universalist themes in the history of Israel from Abraham to Malachi.

J. Bowker, 1978; *The Religious Imagination and the Sense of God* (Oxford).
In connection with this chapter, Professor Bowker's sections on Judaism (pp. 31 ff.) and Christianity (pp. 123 ff.) are especially useful.

4

The Word Made Flesh

THE 'EXEGETE' OF THE OLD TESTAMENT

Jesus of Nazareth and the Old Testament

Reversing Rahner's dictum that the Old Testament is the 'pre-history of Christ', René Latourelle has called Jesus of Nazareth the 'exegete' of the Old Testament. In other words, while the New Testament cannot be understood except with reference to the Old Testament, it is the New Testament which is normative.

The Old Testament begs for fulfilment and it is abundantly clear that the texts of the New Testament regard Jesus of Nazareth as being – in a very special way – the 'fulfilment' of the Old Testament. Why that should be so is no less explicitly stated. Even the earliest texts of the New Testament, the Pauline Epistles, approach Jesus theistically. As C. F. D. Moule remarks, Paul thinks of the risen Christ as a theist thinks of God, as personal and yet supra-individual (Moule 1977, p. 107). The results of his death are available universally and those who believe live 'in' him. This is because, to use John Bowker's somewhat diffuse phrase, Jesus claimed 'direct input from theistic externality' (Bowker 1978, p. 182).

We shall examine the nature and extent of Jesus' claim later in this chapter. For the moment, we are noting the attitude of New Testament writers towards him from the point of view of God's self-revelation. In the Letter to Titus there is a probable reference to Jesus Christ as God: ' . . . the appearing of the glory of our great God and Saviour Jesus Christ . . . ' (Titus 2:13). However, the reading is not entirely certain and the interpretation depends on a possible late dating for this letter. It was only in Christianity's second generation that Jewish monotheistic inhibitions were overcome and John could put the words: 'My Lord and my God!' into the mouth of Thomas the apostle, confronted by the apparition of the risen Christ (John 20:28).

The truth is that the immediacy of the relationship between Jesus of Nazareth and the God invoked by the Jews of the Old Testament was a profound mystery which Old Testament models alone were incapable of expressing. Jesus, unlike the Old Testament prophets, was not a mere 'speaking-tube' for God. He was himself the epiphany or manifestation of God. In him, in his very own person, in his humanity and in the events of his human life and death, his contemporaries had a direct experience of God. James Dunn says that Jesus was thought of as 'the climactic embodiment of God's power and purpose... God's clearest self-expression, God's last word' (Dunn 1980, pp. 211, 262). Jesus did not merely reveal what God was like, he revealed God. Edward Schillebeeckx describes Jesus as communicating in his person the communion of God with humankind, the unexpected grace of God's free and benevolent love (Schillebeeckx 1980, p. 468). It is this loving favour of God, revealed in Jesus Christ, that the author of the prologue to John's Gospel opposes to the Mosaic law. For the New Testament writers, this particular event – the historic life of Jesus of Nazareth – was an event of decisive importance for the salvation of the world. 'Jesus Christ', writes Walter Kasper, 'is the final self-definition of God, of the world and of man.' The Christ-event was 'the moment of final truth', the *kairos,* the fullness of time (Kasper 1977, p. 185).

There is, therefore, a specifically Christian exegesis of the Old Testament – not the only possible exegesis, but the only possible one in the light of Jesus Christ's life and death. Many of the specific New Testament claims that Jesus fulfilled this or that 'prophecy' or 'promise' appear superficial to us. Many ignore the original context, or smack of manipulation, to make the events fit the prophecy. It would be naïve for us, nevertheless, to dismiss the argumentation as irrelevant or untrue. The specific instances of fulfilment cited by the New Testament writers are indications of a deep-rooted faith that Jesus is the fulfiller of the Scriptures in a profoundly relational and organic sense. The fundamental claim is being made that God's active involvement with human history and the created world, instanced over and over again in the Old Testament, is now centred upon the human life and death of Jesus. He interprets the Scriptures for us, but he also 'interprets' us! He confronts and challenges us through the New Testament texts, forcing us to a decision. Jesus, therefore, is our 'exegete' also, telling us who and what we are, and what our destiny is, what choices lie before us. It is this central position of Jesus in our history that gives the Old Testament an importance for Christians, and which allows us to see God's final self-revelation as having its beginning in the history and culture of Israel.

The mediator *is* the message

Jesus' life was a once-for-all event, therefore, which constituted a final interpretation of human existence, according to the New Testament authors. The proclamation of this interpretation was called 'Gospel' or 'Good

News', long before the word 'Gospel' was applied to the literary form which bears the name, that is to say, the canonical Gospels attributed to Matthew, Mark, Luke and John. Paul speaks continually of the Christian proclamation as the 'Gospel' he is sent to preach, and Mark regards the 'Gospel' as an event, beginning with the preaching of John the Baptist (Mark 1:1).

The word 'Gospel' or 'Good News' is a technical term which goes back to the tradition of Isaiah and the Psalms. It refers to the messianic good news, the glad tidings that God's universal reign has begun. In Second Isaiah we find the words:

> How beautiful upon the mountains
>   are the feet of him who brings good tidings,
> who publishes peace, who brings good tidings of good,
>   who publishes salvation,
>   who says to Zion, 'Your God reigns' (Isaiah 52:7).

Psalm 96 celebrates the proclamation of Yahweh's final reign with the same enthusiasm. This good tidings is news of God's favour, of comfort and gladness to those who mourn, encouragement to the afflicted and the brokenhearted, liberty to captives and those in prison. Third Isaiah describes the good news brought to the afflicted in those terms (Isaiah 61:1–3). Jesus not only preached God's kingdom in these same terms, but spent his public life among the sick, the mentally handicapped, the cripples and the outcasts of society. All the written Gospels testify to Jesus' preoccupation with such people and the cures he effected among them.

The teachings of Jesus which the early Christian communities are most likely to have preserved intact, portions of the sermon on the Mount, the parables and the sayings concerning the Kingdom, all reflect a consciousness in Jesus that he was bringing the 'Good News' in word and work. The Beatitudes, in the forms given by Matthew and Luke, describe the spirit in which the children of God's kingdom are to live. In Matthew, they are followed by the antithesis to the Mosaic law. 'You have heard that it was said to the men of old . . . But I say to you . . .' (Matthew 5:21–22). In these sayings, Jesus sets himself up as a new source of revelation, a greater-than-Moses, and he demands faith in himself as the bringer of the messianic Good News.

The New Testament presents Jesus as the conscious vehicle of a new revelation from God. It is a revelation which owes nothing to human wisdom or perspicacity.

> At that time Jesus said, 'I thank you Father, Lord of Heaven and earth, because you have hidden these things from the wise and prudent, and have revealed them to mere children' (Matthew 11:25).

When Peter professed his faith in the messiahship of Jesus at Caesarea Philippi, Jesus made the same point again:

> Blessed are you, Simon Bar-Jona; for flesh and blood have not revealed it to you, but my Father who is in heaven (Matthew 16:17).

Antedating even the Synoptics, Paul stresses the Gospel's revelatory character as a 'mystery', a hidden and incomprehensible plan which has now suddenly been revealed by God in Jesus Christ.

> Now to him who has power to establish you according to my Gospel and the preaching of Jesus Christ, according to the revelation of the mystery, which was kept secret since the world began, but now is made manifest, according to the commandment of the everlasting God, made known to all nations for the obedience of faith: to God only wise be glory through Jesus Christ forever. Amen (Romans 16:25–26).

Passages in both Matthew and Luke make the deliberate connection between the words and works of Jesus and the messianic Good News described by Isaiah.

> Now when John heard in prison about the deeds of the Christ, he sent word by his disciples and said to him, 'Are you he who is to come, or shall we look for another?' And Jesus answered them, 'Go and tell John what you hear and see: the blind receive their sight and the lame walk, lepers are cleansed and the deaf hear, and the dead are raised up, and the poor have good news preached to them. And blessed is he who takes no offence at me' (Matthew 11:2–6).

Nothing could be more dramatic than the scene in the Nazareth synagogue where Jesus deliberately takes the words of Isaiah 61:1–3 and applies them himself, to the astonishment of his hearers.

> And he came to Nazareth where he had been brought up; and he went to the synagogue, as his custom was, on the sabbath day. And he stood up to read; and there was given to him the book of the prophet Isaiah. He opened the book and found the place where it was written,
> 'The Spirit of the Lord is upon me,
> because he has anointed me to preach good news to the poor.
> He has sent me to proclaim release to the captives
> and recovering of sight to the blind,
> to set at liberty those who are oppressed,
> to proclaim the acceptable year of the Lord.'
> And he closed the book, and gave it back to the attendant, and sat down; and the eyes of all in the synagogue were fixed upon him. And he began to say to them. 'Today this scripture has been fulfilled in your hearing' (Luke 4:16–21).

'The Gospel of Jesus Christ' proclaimed by Paul and described by Mark, as beginning with the activity of John the baptizer, is not simply a message in words. Jesus *is* himself the Good News. He *is* the Gospel that he and his followers preach. Jesus is what is offered to the world in Christianity. As

Edward Schillebeeckx has rightly said: 'Christianity is not the religion of a book, but of a person' (Schillebeeckx 1980*, p. 33). To speak, therefore, of the Gospel of Jesus Christ is to speak of a message and a messenger, but also of a messenger who is himself the subject of his message. The message is that God has made him 'Lord and Christ', the unique mediator of divine salvation.

An important corollary of this understanding of 'Gospel' is that in the writings of the New Testament we are not simply dealing with words, names and sayings. God's final self-revelation in Jesus of Nazareth is not merely discovered in words attributed to him, whether they are authentic or not. The revelation takes place in an acting person, in deeds as well as words, in a life and a life-style. Jesus reveals who and what he is through his actions, and these actions are entirely consistent with the words attributed to him.

Another corollary is that, in accepting Jesus, we must be prepared to follow where he leads and to be surprised by him. Jesus does not simply correspond to people's expectations, he transcends them. We should not need him at all, if he were merely a receptacle for our own projections and wishful thinking. As a convinced Marxist, Milan Machoveč, has pointed out (Machoveč 1977, pp. 89–90), Jesus incarnates the messianic event. He lives in his own life the very future which he preaches to humanity. His story is an illuminating and transforming energy in our own lives. Machoveč, however, declares that the miraculous is irrelevant to an understanding of the phenomenon of Jesus. He is one of those who hesitates on the brink of the transcendental (Machoveč 1977, p. 204). Of course, 'miracles' present more of a problem to us moderns than they did to Jesus' contemporaries and they must be seen in the right perspective. But that is a very different thing from approaching the story of Jesus with the small-mindedness of the positivist, who has decided *a priori* that anything which transcends his sense-experience has no existence or meaning. Some Biblical scholars today are reductionists, seeking at all costs to escape the transcendental and to inhabit what Moule calls 'the safer territory of the rational and the intelligible' (Moule 1977, p. 5). The Gospel miracles, closely linked though they are to the life and message of Jesus, pale into insignificance beside the miracle that is Jesus himself. In Jesus 'the grace of God has appeared for the salvation of all men' (Titus 2:11).

History, theology or both?

According to John Hick, to call Jesus 'God, Son of God, God incarnate etc.' is a poetic form of language which expresses 'loving devotion and commitment', but which is not a language of 'literal propositions' (Hick 1968, p. 32). The imagery of the incarnation, he writes, 'lacks non-metaphorical meaning'. It is a language of personal commitment which need not – should not – be dogmatized. Quite apart from the fact that the doctrine of the incarnation is logically and chronologically secondary to the experience of Jesus of Nazareth as God in the evolution of Christology, Hick's view bristles with unacceptable assumptions. The most basic one concerns the relationship between poetic or metaphorical meaning and 'literal' or non-metaphorical meaning. Of course, there can be bad literature, but poetry and literature which are successful succeed precisely because they make real experience more real for us. They intensify an experience through their use of symbols and bring its meaning out more clearly.

Are we to assume, with Hick and several other modern commentators, that there are such things as 'bare facts', devoid of any interpretation? Not at all. Experience tells us again and again that interpretation is a part of that experience. Nothing happens which does not carry with it some meaning or other for us. Doubtless, there can be several possible interpretations, according to context. Doubtless, too, further opinions may serve to change or to deepen our religious interpretation of the experience, but all this does not alter the fact that interpretation is dovetailed with experience. Poetic meaning may not be palpable to our material senses, nor need it be scientifically demonstrable, but to limit it to a mere interest, a 'devotion' or a 'commitment', is to deny to artists, writers and musicians any capacity to convey true meaning through the exercise of the creative imagination.

Symbolism, as we have pointed out several times, is of the essence of human experience. Everything that exists conveys meaning because it is a symbol, or manifestation of further or deeper reality. It follows that symbolism is *par excellence* the language of divine revelation.

In speaking of the character of the Old Testament books, we have already pointed out that some mythologies or symbol-systems are profoundly true, but general, statements about human life and human destiny. In other cases, however, they are attempts to grapple with the meaning of particular historical events. In both cases, the symbolism is not only true but also to some degree 'given' to us by the real order of things. To say that Jesus was not 'literally' God may mean that his contemporaries never historically experienced him as God, or that the interpretation which declares his Godhead had no foundation in the actual life and personality of Jesus himself. At most, it may mean that faith in the divinity of Jesus relates to a generalized subjective experience, or else to a personal and untypical one.

In the later sections of this chapter we shall demonstrate the falsity of these propositions. Allowing for a development of interpretation, there is no discontinuity between 'the Jesus of history' and the Jesus of 'post-resurrection faith'. Jesus' death was a recapitulation of the life he had lived. Without denying the objectivity of a new – and indeed supreme – revelation in the event of his resurrection, the Easter faith was so congruent with the life of Jesus that some writers appear to lay greater stress on the 'confirmation' aspect of this faith – a faith confirming what the life and death of Jesus had meant for his followers. There is no 'Jesus of history', as opposed to a 'Jesus of faith'. The Jesus of history is already an object of faith. As Edward Schillebeeckx has put it rather startlingly, dogmatic theology began before the New Testament was written! (Schillebeeckx 1980*, p. 30).

On the other hand, it is extremely important to affirm that the Jesus of faith was historical, even if it is difficult to reconstruct that history scientifically, and even if our faith does not rest on a mere 'scientific' historical reconstruction which tries to make abstraction of all interpretation. The Christian faith rests on a revelation that took place in and through the historical life of Jesus of Nazareth.

But, it may be objected, does not history disappear altogether in the so-called 'kerygmatized' or 'theologically interpreted' narratives of the New Testament? In the post-Bultmann era the pendulum has tended to swing away from such a minimalist interpretation of the historical basis of the New Testament writings. Granted that they were written in the light of an Easter faith. Granted, also, that the writings of Christianity's second generation tend to be more 'theological' and interpretative. But there can be no doubt at all that a real Jesus determines all this development, and a real originating experience underlies it all.

Whether we can ever reach the authentic *ipsissima verba* of Jesus himself is, of course, highly questionable, but there are indications that the texts recapture the authentic content of that teaching and that the *kerygma* is in continuity with it. The aim of the New Testament writers was pastoral, or it was kerygmatic or catechetical. An idea which was very strong in the early Christian communities that produced these writings and the oral traditions on which they were based was the idea of *paradosis,* or handing down of tradition. According to this idea there must be a correspondence between receiving and transmitting the tradition. This is especially noticeable in the writings of Paul:

> For I delivered to you as of first importance what I also received, that Christ died for our sins in accordance with the Scriptures, that he was buried, that he was raised on the third day in accordance with the scriptures . . . (1 Corinthians 15:3–4).

> So then, brethren, stand firm and hold to the traditions which you were taught by us, either by word of mouth or by letter (2 Thessalonians 2:15).

Once again, this is no mere handing-on of verbal instructions. It is an entry into the experience of Jesus through his effective, narrative memory. It is a memorial – a typically Jewish idea:

> As therefore you received Christ Jesus the Lord, so live in him, rooted and built up in him and established in the faith, just as you were taught, abounding in thanksgiving (Colossians 2:6–7).

Paul frequently warns his hearers not to accept a false tradition, a Gospel other than the one he has himself handed on, and he exhorts others, such as Timothy, to guard what he has entrusted to him and to 'follow the pattern of the sound words which you have heard from me' (Timothy 1:13; 2:2). Timothy is intructed to entrust the same 'deposit' to faithful men who will be able to teach others. Here Paul is borrowing the word *parathēkē* from the juridical vocabulary of the Greeks. The Gospel, in his view, is a 'trust' or a 'deposit' to be kept faithfully and preserved unchanged. All of this suggests an extreme and scrupulous fidelity to the Good News of Jesus.

The work of H. Reisenfeld (1957) and Birger Gerhardsson (1979) has given us an idea of the principles at work in the early Christian communities which preserved the tradition about Jesus. There existed in contemporary Judaism schools for the study of the oral materials which interpreted and complemented the written Torah. In these schools extreme respect was shown for the actual words of an author and these were carefully memorized, repeated and recited. Various mnemonic and didactic techniques were employed to make the work of memorization easier. The oral material was not preserved in a continuous, literary style but in a structure which relied upon the association of ideas, or which was numerical, alphabetical or dependent upon parallels. Above all, there were proverbs, aphorisms, parables, pithy and picturesque sayings. Anyone who (like the present author) has studied the oral traditions of a pre-literate society (e.g. rural Africa) will testify to the lengths to which people will go in order to preserve the exact wording of an oral tradition and to resist any interpretation by the oral historian which appears to modify it.

It seems that the early Christian communities functioned in similar fashion to the contemporary rabbinical schools and that the sayings of Jesus had been formulated in such a way as to be suitable for transmission. Jesus himself was regarded as a teacher, and his sayings were evidently repeated and explained with great fidelity. The written Gospels, which are very far from being a continuous presentation of Jesus' teaching, bear evidence of the form in which that teaching was originally given, to the use of key words, images and parables. They are different groupings of the events and sayings of the Jesus tradition, and there is a strong presumption in favour of a desire and motivation for historical fidelity to Jesus and to the content of his teaching. Even Paul, whose essential proclamation was that of the resurrection and who has often been held to have ignored the pre-resurrection Jesus tradition, was entirely familiar with the rabbinical schools, having himself sat at the feet of Gamaliel. His letters contain references not only to the tradition about Jesus before the resurrection but also to the manner in which he himself received the teaching about that tradition – from the apostles, older than himself. Gerhardsson goes so far as to speak of evidence for a 'conscious, deliberate and programmatic transmission' in Paul's time of the Jesus tradition (Gerhardsson 1979, p. 28). The apostle was 'sent' to witness to this tradition and the community shared in this function.

René Latourelle lists a number of criteria, current among exegetes today, which indicate the historicity and authenticity of actions and word-content attributed to Jesus (Latourelle 1978, pp. 220–237). The writers of the Gospels acted as compilers or editors. Their individual styles are recognizable and it is possible to discern a tension between their own editorial activity and the materials they handled. This in itself testifies to a tradition or traditions, the historicity of which is presumed in default of evidence to the contrary. This presumption, of course, becomes stronger when a tradition is reiterated by other, independent sources. Another criterion of historicity is when a passage or usage attributed to Christ is irreducible to the practice of contemporary Judaism or even that of early Church communities. Examples would be: 'Amen, Amen, I say unto you' or 'Abba' ('Father'): Jesus' acceptance of John's baptism, when there was considerable rivalry at a later stage between the disciples of John and his own; Jesus' command during his public ministry not to preach the Gospel to non-Jews; Jesus' unusual practice of calling his disciples, when other rabbis were sought out by theirs; passages which show up the apostles in an unfavourable light; the sayings about the Kingdom; the parables, with their conformity to the homely details of the rural and lower-class life of Jesus' Palestinian background; the Beatitudes; the original proclamation of the Good News ('The time is fulfilled, and the kingdom of God is at hand; repent, and believe in the gospel': Mark 1:15), significantly different from the post-Easter proclamation; the consistent refusal of Jesus to show signs and to work miracles in proof of his claims; his emphasis on a spiritual and interior kingdom, rather than on a political messianism; the use of the phrase 'the son of man'; the confrontation between the Kingdom of God and the kingdom of Satan in the words and cures of Jesus.

Another criterion discerned by Latourelle in contemporary exegesis is that of necessary explanation. Many events in the New Testament are not immediately intelligible in themselves, but demand an explanation or a basis in a historical personality. Here the link between the miracles and the proclamation of the messianic Good News is one of the most obvious examples. Also the fact that the earliest formulas of faith were: Jesus is 'the Christ', 'Lord', 'Son of God', in the Acts of the Apostles and in the hymns and preaching of Paul's Letters. Again there is the distinctive 'style' of Christ, which must be a very early formulation of his own personal and vital impact on others: his dislike of falsity and hypocrisy and his equal love of all people. The convergent use of all these criteria by modern exegetes is our basis for affirming historical authenticity in the Gospels and other New Testament writings. Though the history is a 'kerygmatized' history, the picture given to us is not an exclusively kerygmatic picture.

The primacy of ecclesial communities in the Jesus tradition

In Chapter 1 we pointed out that the narrative memory which constitutes a religious tradition is the property of a community. Nothing could be more true than in the case of Christianity. The Christian tradition about Jesus does not begin with the writing of the New Testament. On the contrary, the New Testament is evidence for a previously existing oral tradition which was the property of early Christian communities. The Church community, its faith and life, was therefore at the heart of the process of transmitting the Good News of Jesus. These communities remembered the past experience of Jesus with 'an eye to acting in the present for a liberated future' (Schillebeeckx 1980*, p. 54). Jesus delivered his teaching openly and deliberately in a community context. His Word gave the hearers an identity and a structure; the listening crowd of the Gospel text later become the assembly, *ecclesia* or 'church'. Christianity was a 'way' or a 'way of life' that took its origins in the life and life-style of Jesus. Such a way of life implied putting oneself under the guidance of Jesus Christ who revealed the benevolent and merciful love of God for humanity. This was faith – a loyalty to the community formed by Jesus, a new way of life, even a new mode of existence in communion with God. Faith seeks, and indeed implies, understanding, so it was inevitable that there should be speculation, that early followers of Jesus should respond imaginatively to their experience of him.

For early Christians, Jesus had a focal connection with their experience of God and of the salvation that comes from God. 'For in him', says Paul, 'the whole fullness of deity dwells bodily, and you have come to fullness of life in him . . . ' (Colossians 2:9–10). In view of the self-authenticating impression that 'external, theistic reality was the informing construction of his [Jesus'] life and actions', it was inevitable, argues John Bowker, that Christological and Trinitarian reflection should take place (Bowker 1978, pp. 126, 179, 185). A 'theology' of Jesus – or a 'Christology' – was unavoidable. It was unavoidable that questions should be asked about the relationship of the man Jesus to God, and about the continuing Christian experience of him. And it was inevitable that these questions should lead directly to the formulation of the classical Christian doctrines.

There are two consequences of accepting the primacy of the early communities in the formulation of Christian faith. One is that this formulation was a progressive or developing phenomenon. the other is that it was – at any rate, in its beginnings – a pluralistic phenomenon. A theological synthesis is always temporary. Questions elicit answers, and answers evoke new questions which must be answered in their turn. The texts of the New Testament bear witness to the Church's struggle to express its developing understanding of Jesus of Nazareth. Christians of the first generation centred their interest on the resurrection and exaltation of the man Jesus, on a man being taken up into the Godhead to become the life-giving Son of God, the first-born of God's eschatological family, and also the embodiment of God's own cosmic action through his Spirit. As James Dunn has suggested, the alternatives of a mere man being given this heavenly, cosmic role, or of a heavenly being becoming man, after pre-existing in the Godhead, probably did not occur to Paul (Dunn 1980, pp. 211–212).

What is clear, however, is that the 'Son of God' formulation was pushed back to the beginning of Christ's public ministry, and then to his birth and conception, by evangelists writing for early second-generation Christians. For them, not only was the death and resurrection of Jesus a manifestation of God's grace, but his whole life and ministry. With the prologue to John's Gospel, we find the explicit affirmation of Jesus' pre-existence in the Godhead from all eternity, and this Johannine presentation eventually predominated. As James Dunn explains, the early Christian communities had a variety of kerygmas and Christologies, none of them invalidating the others.

> Clearly, here in this kaleidoscope of imagery we see earliest Christianity searching around for the most suitable way of understanding and describing Christ, ransacking the available categories and concepts to find language which would do justice to the reality of Christ (Dunn 1980, p. 265).

These differing formulations arose in primitive communities which were in different regions and which had different preoccupations. As time went on, they developed a deeper sense of the meaning of the past. Their formulations cannot be artificially harmonized, nor can a common denominator do justice to their particular insights.

The early Christians, as the New Testament itself bears witness, regarded the books of the Jewish Old Testament as inspired (2 Timothy 3:16). That is to say, they held that God had revealed himself in word, action and purpose in these ancient writings: that he was, in the final analysis, their author. They knew that God had willed all things to be summed up in Jesus Christ, and that the Old Testament could only be finally interpreted in the light of his mystery. They also knew that the Gospel was a living word, that Jesus Christ was accompanying them and guiding them into all truth through the Spirit. The reflection on the reality of Christ which engaged all the attention of the early Christian communities was led by the apostles themselves and their associates, and was mirrored in the apostolic preaching and in the liturgical formulas they used. Certain written texts came to be respected as being, in a broad or strict sense, of apostolic origin, and were preserved with great care for liturgical reading, becoming the basis for a living experience of faith. Already, before the last documents of the New Testament had been written, earlier ones had come to be placed on a par with the books of the Old Testament, as an authoritative self-revelation of God and a divinely willed norm of faith (cf. 2 Peter 3:16). Although the death of the last apostle and the end of the apostolic preaching was deemed to have closed the final and fullest moment of God's self-revelation in Jesus Christ, the manner of the formation of the New Testament texts in the first ecclesial communities had, as we shall see in later chapters of this book, important repercussions for Christian faith and teaching in the later centuries.

THE LIFE, DEATH AND RESURRECTION OF JESUS CHRIST

The Galilean background

Jesus of Nazareth appeared in first-century Galilee as an itinerant teacher and charismatic healer. Geza Vermes, a Jewish writer who is unsympathetic to arguments for Jesus' divinity, gives us nevertheless a graphic picture of Galilee in Jesus' time (Vermes 1973, pp. 46–57). It was a relatively remote rural area, separated from Jerusalem and Judea by the land of the heterodox Samaritans. Galileans were peasants who 'dropped their aitches' and who adopted their own dialectal forms for ordinary Jewish names, such as 'Lazarus' instead of 'Eleazar'. The Aramaic words which are preserved in the Gospels show that Jesus spoke the Galilean dialect of Aramaic. Although Galilee was a hotbed of Jewish resistance to the Romans, this earned it little respect from the élite of the metropolis. Sporadic missionary journeys by the devout Pharisees had made little impression on the Galileans and they were regarded by law-abiding Jews as guilty of cultic uncleanliness – a cursed, unclean, lawless rabble. The Talmud says of them that they are 'unclean animals and their wives are like reptiles' (Vermes 1973, p. 74). It even applies to them the Deuteronomic injunction: 'Cursed be he who lies with any kind of beast' (Deuteronomy 27:21). To marry a Galilean was to commit bestiality. The Gospel of John reflects this prejudice a little less crudely:

'Is the Christ to come from Galilee?' ... 'Have any of the authorities or of the Pharisees believed in him? But this crowd, who do not know the law, are accursed.' ... 'Search and you will see that no prophet is to rise from Galilee' (John 7:41–52).

Jesus was a healer and a teacher with a liberating style of life. He broke cultic regulations deliberately. He consorted with the ritually unclean, with public sinners, as well as with people who suffered from loathsome diseases such as leprosy. He had no fixed address, but walked with his followers from village to village. He was disowned by the inhabitants of his home town; his own family thought him mad. But one thing stands out clearly from the life and teaching of Jesus: he was Good News for the poor, the sick and the suffering, Good News for the despised, the aliens, the rejected, the sinful. Jesus experienced a deep personal relationship with God, a relationship which we shall explore in a later section of this chapter. It was Jesus' Good News that God – through him – was diametrically opposed to suffering and evil. He sought at all costs to relieve suffering. He denounced the imposition of suffering on others. He revealed God as 'pure positiveness' – to use the phrase of Edward Schillebeeckx (Schillebeeckx 1980, p. 675). He refused to make God in the image of man who can choose between good and evil, but that is not to say that he offered an explanation of suffering and evil. There was no question of blaming God, or of transferring the ground and source of evil in the world to God himself.

But equally, although Jesus linked suffering with sin, he refused to blame man for every instance of suffering. He condemned the suffering caused by human wickedness, but he refused to look for a culprit in every case. On the contrary, he saw suffering as an invitation to repentance in general and to a healing, liberating love.

> There were some present at that very time who told him of the Galileans whose blood Pilate had mingled with their sacrifices. And he answered them, 'Do you think that these Galileans were worse sinners than all the other Galileans because they suffered thus? I tell you, No; but unless you repent you will all likewise perish. Or those eighteen upon whom the tower in Siloam fell and killed them, do you think that they were worse offenders than all the others who dwelt in Jerusalem? I tell you, No; But unless you repent you will all likewise perish' (Luke 13:1–5).

People were expected to accept suffering in order to end suffering, not only by refusing to judge others, but by showing them compassion, by going out of their way to draw near to a neighbour in distress and taking their neighbour's sufferings upon themselves. More than this, one was expected to 'love' one's enemies rather than to return evil for evil. This was far from being an invitation to passivity or compromise in the face of hatred or evil, but a call to faith in one's fellow human beings and in their capacity to change and be converted. Finally, one was called to forsake one's own possessions, and even one's life itself for the sake of others. One was called to a poverty of spirit which implied on the one hand uncompromising demands upon oneself and a radical change in outlook, and on the other hand, a liberation of oneself for others. That Jesus actually lived this liberated life himself, there can be no reasonable doubt.

Jesus, therefore, offered no explanation of the so-called 'problem of evil'. It may be, as Brian Hebblethwaite and many others before him have speculated, that suffering and evil are a necessary concomitant for a world in which organic sentient life – and ultimately persons who are not moral puppets – has come into existence (Hebblethwaite 1976, pp. 40ff.). But Jesus did not speculate. He accepted the fact that good and evil are mixed in what Schillebeeckx has called the 'ecology' of salvation (Schillebeeckx 1980, p. 697). What he offered was not to explain evil and suffering, but to break their power. The Marxist writer Milan Machoveč is right to draw our attention to Jesus' very un-Jewish attitude to children (Machoveč 1977, p. 99). Not only did he love to fondle them and lay his hands upon them in blessing, he made them a theme in his teaching. Childhood became for him the model of the changed human being. The truly liberated person must have the simplicity, the innocence, the trustfulness, even the 'strength-in-weakness' of the child. In contemporary Jewish society children were loved and cared for, but they had no social significance. Like children in every age and place, they were dependants, without an effective title to property, without the intellectual riches of knowledge and experience. Yet for Jesus the child was a favourite example of spiritual poverty.

The heart of Jesus' teaching was that not all the suffering and evil in the world were equal to the loving mercy and forgiveness of God. God, in Jesus, overcomes our suffering and accepts us in our sinfulness. It is here that the miracle stories have their relevance. Jesus was a healer and he effected cures. The Gospel texts do not allow us to judge how far his cures defied the explanations of modern medical science. There are healers today who effect scientifically inexplicable cures. Were the dead people whom he raised to life really dead, or were they in a coma? Jesus himself said of Jairus's daughter that she was asleep, and described his raising of the dead Lazarus as a 'waking' from a rest. One thing is certain, that Jesus' followers and the crowds that accompanied him regarded him as a wonder-worker. It is equally certain that wonder-workers were not uncommon in Jesus' day. There were many healers who were reputed to effect cures and to cast out demons. Aesculapius, who was apparently a historical physician before he was deified by classical antiquity, was credited with as many miracles as Jesus, if not more.

Once again, to repudiate the miraculous, the supernatural, the transcendental a priori is a mark of intellectual myopia. It may well be, as exegetes point out, that some of the miracle stories are doublets, that others are modelled on legendary miracles performed by Elijah or Elisha in the Old Testament, that others are due to the well-known tendency in popular miracle traditions for tall stories to grow taller. Some of these factors may account for the nature miracles, for the multiplication of loaves and fishes and for the raising of the widow's son and other dead people to life. But whatever grounds of historical fact lie behind the miracle stories, these stories are there because Jesus was experienced as a wonder-worker and people strove to describe him as such.

Jesus, however, always transcended people's expectations of him. The cures which he effected were not done merely to demonstrate a mighty power for its own sake, or even simply to help particular people in their infirmities. They were performed to elicit faith in God's power to overcome our limitations and our finitude, faith in God's power to forgive sins, in God's power communicated through Jesus himself. The wonderful cures performed by Jesus were part of the great apocalyptic battle waged between God and the forces of evil in the world. Geza Vermes rightly points out that repentance for sin was a disposition frequently demanded in the person seeking a cure from disease by the Jewish healer (Vermes 1973, pp. 67–68). This was because a strict causal link was assumed between suffering and sin. As we have seen, Jesus repudiated this strict causal link, and did so explicitly on several occasions. The point which Vermes has failed to grasp is that Jesus reversed the order of things in the healing process. Repentance was not required as a condition for healing, but physical healing was an outward sign of the more profound inner healing wrought by repentance.

Again, Jesus of Nazareth was an exorcist, and used the techniques of contemporary charismatic exorcists. He dealt with people – perhaps schizophrenics – who felt themselves externally oppressed or internally submerged by moral evil in a personal form. He also dealt, no doubt, with people whose afflictions were popularly personalized or demonized, epileptics and the like. Jesus used these exorcisms to dramatize the conflict between good and evil. But, unlike his contemporaries, Jesus evinced no interest in demonology. His exorcism involved no elaborate naming of demons. Nor did he name a human or angelic mentor, like other exorcists, in whose name the demon was cast out. For Jesus, Satan was already conquered and insignificant. 'I saw Satan fall like lightning from heaven' (Luke 10:18). He simply prayed, laid his hands upon the sufferer and rebuked the demon, while his apostles used the name of Jesus himself when they practised exorcism. In Jesus of Nazareth the eschatological battle over all such powers had been won. Charismatic healer and exorcist Jesus certainly was, but this activity was for him a means of proclaiming the messianic Good News.

The Kingdom of heaven

Jesus was proclaiming the messianic Good News. Was he called, and did he call himself, Messiah? Did he accept the title of the 'Anointed One' *par excellence,* the 'one who is to come', the 'Son of David' who would finally restore the monarchy in a golden age of peace and plenty? The Gospels present him as actually being called Messiah in his lifetime, not simply being made 'Lord and Christ' at the moment of his resurrection. It seems probable that Jesus accepted the title, while at the same time being reluctant to use it and giving it an entirely new interpretation – or at any rate, an interpretation that differed from the political expectations of his contemporaries. As Walter Kasper indicates, the earliest passion kerygma (1 Corinthians 15:3–5) asserts that the Christ suffered, that messiahship involved suffering as well as exaltation (Kasper 1976, p. 106). All the four evangelists describe Jesus as accepting the title of Messiah during his trial before the Sanhedrin. In Mark, the earliest account, Jesus says quite simply 'I am', when asked if he is the Messiah, but immediately reinterprets the title in terms of the Danielic 'son of man' figure, which he also slightly adapts (Mark 14:62). In a later section of this chapter, we shall explore this apocalyptic title.

Jesus' final entry into Jerusalem is also presented as having been something of a messianic demonstration, with the crowd shouting:

> Hosanna! Blessed is he who comes in the name of the Lord! Blessed is the kingdom of our father David that is coming! Hosanna in the highest! (Mark 11:9–10).

Yet it is clear that Jesus claims no political messiahship. He comes, riding upon a colt, and goes straight up to the Temple to drive out the buyers and the sellers and to quote (in Mark's version) the words of Isaiah:

> My house shall be called a house of prayer for all the nations (Mark 11:17; Isaiah 56:7),

in this way announcing the messianic era of a single, universal worship.

Again, in Mark's version of the dialogue between Jesus and Peter at Caesarea Philippi. Peter's response to the question: 'Who do you say I am?' is uncompromisingly stark: 'You are the Christ' (Mark 8:29). But Jesus not only follows up this reply with a warning that the title must not be used; he immediately (in all the Synoptic parallels) goes on to speak of his rejection, suffering and death at the hands of the Jewish authorities.

Jesus probably accepted the title, although he did not like to use it, because he repudiated the idea of a political Messiah who would lead a rebellion against the Roman colonialists. Jesus had not come to fight the Romans, but, as C. F. D. Moule puts it, to fight 'abuse at the heart of Judaism' and to risk the vengeance of the Jewish establishment. Instead of a victorious, political king, Jesus knew that the messianic kingdom would be ushered in by a suffering leader, by one who had to face, and undergo, death. That Jesus died in the end is a fact. We cannot doubt the factual nature of the Last Supper either, with the institution of the distinctive Christian ritual, the Eucharist.

Whether or not the Last Supper was a Passover meal, it had a distinctly messianic character. The texts which describe the institution of the Eucharist allude to Exodus, to the meal which followed the communion sacrifice at the foot of Mount Sinai; but they also allude to Jeremiah's 'new covenant' and, possibly, to Second Isaiah's Servant who would be 'a covenant to the people'. Bread and wine were traditionally associated with the messianic banquet at the end of time (Isaiah 55), and were used by Jesus' contemporaries, the members of the Qumran sect, in order to anticipate the liturgy of the messianic age at every meal. At every ordinary Jewish meal a ritual took place in which a blessing preceded the eating of every dish and the filling of each cup (Guzie 1974, pp. 43, 48). At the last Supper Jesus did what every Jewish householder did at mealtimes, he blessed bread and wine, but he also added a formula of his own:

> This is my body which is for you. Do this in remembrance of me . . . This cup is the
> new covenant in my blood. Do this, as often as you drink it, in remembrance of me
> (1 Corinthians 11:24–25).

All the Synoptic Gospels add a messianic reference to the institution account.
Mark's version runs as follows:

> Truly, I say to you, I shall not drink again of the fruit of the vine until that day when
> I drink it new in the kingdom of God (Mark 14:25).

Jesus was denounced to the Romans because he had challenged the Jewish
establishment, and a case was made out to Pilate that he was a malefactor, a
political agitator and would-be king. The title 'King' was even placed
derisively over the cross on which he died. Numerous are the references in
the New Testament to a suffering Christ. Luke 24:26 and Acts 8:32–35 are
two well-known examples, the latter being an explicit interpretation of
Second Isaiah's fourth Servant song. Even before the narrative of the passion
itself, there are several references to the suffering Servant in Matthew. There
are also numerous references in the New Testament to messianic passages in
the other sections of the Book of Isaiah, some of which we have already considered. As Edward Schillebeeckx reminds us (Schillebeeckx 1980*, p. 64),
we should not underestimate the redactional element in the whole book of
Isaiah, even if exegesis distinguishes three sections or phases in the material
of which it is made up. The way in which the three Isaiahs have been
brought together and in which different sections influenced each other may
have already suggested to Jesus and his followers the link between suffering
and messianism.

If Jesus was reluctant to call himself Christ/Messiah or King in his
lifetime, he certainly identified with the coming Kingdom that he preached.
'The time is fulfilled, and the Kingdom of God is at hand. Repent and
believe in the Gospel' (Mark 1:15). The Kingdom was the rule of God trans-
figuring the present, orientating it towards an absolute future. The
Kingdom was here and now, within and among people, but it was also yet
to be fulfilled finally and forever. Jesus did not refuse the world by merely
promising a consoling future to those who suffered now. The future was
not a substitute for the present. People had to work *now* for the future, and
the future was everyone's business. The Kingdom was where God's name
was hallowed and God's will done, where sins were forgiven and evil
overcome. The Lord's Prayer was the manifesto of the Kingdom. Jesus
described the Kingdom in terms of stories and everyday experiences,
through image and symbol, not in terms of philosophy, or law, or ritual.
Jesus was not drawn to politics. He was neither political nor unpolitical; he
simply believed in the imminence of the Kingdom and in the total para-
mountcy of the Kingdom. By its standards all social institutions and social
behaviour were to be judged.

To enter the Kingdom one had to open up to God and to other human beings – love, forgive, serve without limit and . . . follow Jesus himself. One day, in a dispute over which was the greatest commandment of the Law, Mark records that Jesus answered by quoting the *shema* text of Deuteronomy (6:4). Whereupon the scribe who had posed the original question replied:

'You are right, Teacher; you have truly said that he is one, and there is no other but he; and to love him with all the heart, and with all the understanding, and with all the strength, and to love one's neighbour as oneself, is much more than all whole burnt offerings and sacrifices.' And when Jesus saw that he answered wisely, he said to him, 'You are not far from the Kingdom of God' (Mark 12:32–34).

To enter the Kingdom one had to become a disciple of Jesus and this entailed total fidelity and total renunciation:

So therefore, whoever of you does not renounce all that he has cannot be my disciple (Luke 14:33).

Jesus, in fact, seems to have regarded riches as a danger, and the story of the rich young man illustrates this poignantly. The young man had asked: 'What must I do to inherit eternal life?', and Jesus replied by enumerating the commandments.

And he said to him, 'Teacher, all these I have observed from my youth.' And Jesus looking upon him loved him, and said to him, 'You lack one thing; sell what you have, and give to the poor, and you will have treasure in heaven; and come, follow me.' At that saying his countenance fell, and he went away sorrowful; for he had great possessions. And Jesus looked around and said to his disciples, 'How hard it will be for those who have riches to enter the Kingdom of God' (Mark 10:20–23).

Entry into the Kingdom was not a search on the part of man, but a call from God through Jesus, to follow him and to share his life-style and his attitude towards people and things.

Passion, death and resurrection

As we saw at the end of the previous chapter, Jewish expectation about the future included not only the messianic restoration of David's dynasty, but also the coming of the Deuteronomic 'prophet' who would be another Moses and would perform again the wonders of the Exodus. It also included the return of Elijah, as the precursor of the Day of Yahweh, and perhaps the return of the prophets and Old Testament figures. It was natural that people should identify both Jesus and John the Baptist as Elijah, or one of the prophets, or even *the* (Mosaic) prophet. With characteristic humility, John the Baptist refused all these labels. He was but 'the voice of one crying in the wilderness' (John 1:23; Matthew 3:3). Yet Matthew makes Jesus identify

John very clearly as Elijah, citing the relevant passage from Malachi (Matthew 11:9–14), and much of the New Testament is constructed in such a way as to present Jesus as the second Moses. In the accounts of the transfiguration vision, Jesus appears between the two forerunners, Moses and Elijah.

Jesus seems to have called himself 'prophet' (Luke 4:24), and the crowds gave him this title again and again. Even a modern Jewish critic like Geza Vermes is happy to confer this title on him (Vermes 1973, p. 225). Jesus' picture of the prophets with whom he identified was that of the messenger from God, rejected and even martyred by the Israelites to whom he was sent.

> O Jerusalem, Jerusalem, killing the prophets and stoning those who are sent to you! (Matthew 23:37).

> Woe to you, scribes and Pharisees, hypocrites! for you build the tombs of the prophets . . . . Thus you witness against yourselves, that you are sons of those who murdered the prophets. Fill up, then, the measure of your fathers (Matthew 29–32).

Luke presents Jesus as telling the crowds that he is greater than Solomon and Jonah. As Jonah was a sign to the Ninevites, so Jesus is a sign to his contemporaries, with the difference that Jonah was accepted, whereas Jesus was rejected (Luke 11:29–32).

However, the greatest contrast that Jesus drew was between his own teaching and that of the Mosaic law, and it was inevitable that there should be a clash between him and the authorities who sat in 'the chair of Moses'. In Jesus' day there were a number of élitist religious communities with ascetical or ritualistic traditions, such as the Essenes and the community of Qumran, yet Jesus did not belong to any of these, and, in any case, his liberated way of life contradicted the exclusivist spirit of these movements. The groups with whom he had to do were more closely identified with the establishment. These were the Herodians who supported the ruling dynasty, the politically-minded priestly party of the Sadducees, the scribes or *literati* who were learned in the Law, and above all the scrupulous observers of the Law known as the Pharisees.

Jesus did not identify with the anti-Roman Zealots or 'freedom fighters' of the day, though one of his disciples bore the epithet 'Zealot'. In some ways he was closer in outlook to the Pharisees, who believed in a resurrection and in the existence of spirits. However, it is significant that he was especially critical of them. They were the epitome of the devout, and it was precisely because of their claim to righteousness, which led them to discriminate against their fellows, that Jesus was scathing in his denunciation of them. The Pharisees stood for the Law, the Sadducees for the Temple; and Jesus relativized both these things. What was important was the lordship or rule of God – the Kingdom. Paul would later on oppose life 'in Christ Jesus' to the Mosaic law (Romans 8:1) and speak of the Christian community as the temple the cornerstone of which is Christ (cf. e.g. Ephesians 2:20–22). In the Johannine writings Christ's body was the new Temple. At any rate, it was clear that the old Jewish Temple was superseded.

In the end, the debate centred on the question of authority: 'By what authority are you doing these things, or who gave you this authority to do them?' (Mark 11:28).

> And they were astonished at his teaching, for he taught them as one who had authority, and not as the scribes (Mark 1:22).

In other words, he made no appeal to traditions or to ancient schools or teachers. He simply proclaimed his message as God's. The possibility of death was not only the outcome of a clash with the Jewish establishment of the day; it was a logical consequence of Jesus' whole attitude and teaching. As prophet, he could not but be an eschatological martyr-prophet, *the* prophet.

If Jesus presented himself as the 'One who is to come', the messianic Suffering Servant, the second Moses who would lead his people in a final eschatological Exodus, then it is inconceivable that his death could be thought of as the end of the story. If his message was that of a final Exodus, a final salvation in which God overcomes all evil and all suffering, then death – and especially the death of Jesus – makes nonsense of his Good News. Death had to be overcome. Jesus had to be vindicated and to be given a victorious throne. His 'coming' – his *Parousia* – had to triumph over the suffering and death which he accepted in order to end all suffering and all death. The resurrection has been presented by Rudolph Bultmann as being nothing more than the eschatological faith of Jesus' followers, a new subjective state of consciousness on the part of the disciples; but resurrection and faith in the resurrection are obviously distinct, even if that faith proves to be unfounded (Bartsch 1972, pp. 42, 69; Schillebeeckx 1980*, p. 79). In fact the New Testament makes it clear that the faith of the disciples was engendered by an event, and that this event was a supreme moment of revelation, the climax of God's self-revelation in Jesus.

The vindication of Jesus, his being 'raised up' by God was not seen visibly by his followers. It was an event beyond history and beyond time – or at most it was a kind of interaction between men in time and the timeless itself. It was not the mere resuscitation of a corpse; it was the transformation of Jesus' humanity into a vehicle of salvation for the world. Jesus became Lord, with all the accompanying effects associated with Yahweh himself in the Old Testament, and his promised universal reign over the hearts of all individuals and peoples. This event caused a realization among the followers of Jesus that in him God had been man's fellow-sufferer, that in his humanity God had tasted death. The Old Testament prophets had glimpsed a tender, forgiving love as the motivation behind all Yahweh's deeds. Now, 'God so loved the world that he gave his only Son, that whoever believes in him should not perish but have eternal life' (John 3:16). The love which Jesus showed in his passion and to the point of death itself was now an all-embracing means of salvation.

> God has made him both Lord and Christ, this Jesus whom you crucified (Acts 2:36).

> Christ died for our sins in accordance with the scriptures, . . . he was buried, . . . he was raised on the third day in accordance with the scriptures (1 Corinthians 15:3–4).

The resurrection revealed the final, eternal and universal lordship of Jesus, conferring upon him the title of Christ/Messiah which he had been reluctant to use in life. It now became his new, his second, personal name. Even his first name, Jesus, a common Jewish name meaning 'salvation', took on its new and fundamental meaning. For, in virtue of his resurrection, Jesus was clearly seen not only as the final source of revelation, the final object of revelation, but the final goal of revelation. The risen Christ realized the Jewish expectation of a radical renewal of the world, and the salvation he brought was a return to the supernatural destiny of man inherent in the process of creation. Christ was seen to have had a role in the whole of God's plan for creation and salvation.

The resurrection was not an event visible on earth, and none of the canonical Gospels has attempted to describe it visually. It happened 'beyond' the death of Jesus and even formed one mystery with that death. Although Luke, in his writings, separates out Death, Resurrection, Ascension and Out-pouring of the Spirit (Pentecost), and the Church has adopted Luke's scheme for the purposes of liturgical celebration, the Johannine community saw all these as aspects of a single mystery, not as separate events. John speaks of the 'lifting up' of Jesus (e.g. John 8:28), and implies both the raising of the cross on Golgotha and the exaltation and enthronement of Jesus in divine glory. Again, according to the author of the Johannine Gospel, it is the risen Christ who breathes forth the Holy Spirit upon the disciples (John 20:22). The shape of the appearances is one thing, the fact of the resurrection is another.

To describe the resurrection – as Hans Küng does (Küng 1978, p. 359) – as a 'dying into God' could, perhaps, lead to a misunderstanding. The resurrection was more than a 'dying into God', it was a 'rising into God'. The 'into God' part of Küng's phrase must be seen to imply a new life and existence that is continuous with the old. Neither the empty tomb nor the apparitions of the risen Christ are to be equated with the resurrection mystery itself, but it seems to me that they are indispensable to the genesis of the apostles' Easter faith and/or the Easter proclamation. It is difficult to accept Küng's view that the empty tomb story is a 'legendary elaboration' (Küng 1978, p. 364). The tomb story is incidental to the narrative of the apparitions and may, indeed, reflect a particular cult tradition that was in existence before the Gospels were written. However, it is impossible to conceive of the apostles, with their Jewish understanding of personal, bodily existence and with their conviction that the same Jesus they had known was alive and in touch with them through a radically new relationship, proclaiming the resurrection of Christ when it was well known that Christ's corpse lay in a clearly specified tomb.

Of course, the role of the dead body (which had been buried in the sepulchre) in a resurrection which was bodily in a spiritual or non-spatio-temporal sense, is perhaps a secondary problem, but the empty tomb story is there, and a sceptical writer like Vermes regards it as the most likely historical event connected with the resurrection accounts (Vermes 1973, pp. 39–40). More important is the status of the appearances. Edward Schillebeeckx attempts to relativize these (Schillebeeckx 1980*, pp. 80–83). He does not deny the personal, objective, corporeal resurrection of Jesus, nor the probable historicity of psychological or emotional and visual elements in the apostles' experience of the resurrection, but he appears to regard the appearances as phenomena which are concomitant to the grace which seized the apostles' hearts at Easter, and the accounts of them as 'models' of their conversion. Schillebeeckx calls this a 'hypothesis in systematic theology', but it must be admitted that it is a hypothesis which is not grounded in an exegesis of the Gospels themselves. As Raymond Brown demonstrates, the appearances are crucial to the genesis of faith in the resurrection, as the Gospels present the process (Brown 1973, p. 127). One cannot hope to harmonize the different experiences, but it is clear that they describe the dawn of faith in the resurrection among people who were previously doubting and despondent. It is clear that they convinced people of the corporeal continuity of the risen Jesus with the Jesus who had suffered and died. And it is clear that they were not merely internal psychological experiences, otherwise how could they have occurred to several people – even more than five hundred – at once? The appearances not only convinced the apostles of the fact of the resurrection, they also inaugurated their mission to the world, and brought into existence a 'people', 'a community' or 'church'. The resurrection was an eschatological event, the appearances were an eschatological encounter with the risen Christ, an encounter which cannot be reduced to a pre-existing faith in the *parousia,* nor to a psychological epiphenomenon of such a pre-existing faith. There is absolutely no reason to disregard the structure of the appearance stories or to detach them from the real experiences in which the resurrection was revealed to the apostles. To do so is gratuitous. The models used to describe the encounter with the risen Christ by the writers of the Gospels must be considered appropriate until exegesis can demonstrate otherwise.

The disciples of Jesus saw the resurrection as an eschatological happening – a new and final Exodus. They also saw themselves as an eschatological community or Exodus community, a new 'people of God' analogous to the old Israel. Jesus was himself a 'paraclete' or legal advocate on man's behalf, at 'the right hand' of God, but his resurrection released God's Spirit as 'another paraclete' (John 14:16; 1 John 2:1). It is the Spirit who incorporates the believer into Christ and secures his entry into the Kingdom of God. This entry is achieved actually and eschatologically, that is to say, what is not yet fully complete has already begun. The redemption by Christ is therefore not just potential, it is already an available fact. As C. F. D. Moule says: it is both 'an anchor' and 'a goal' (Moule 1977, p. 122). The doctrine of the Trinity is essential to an understanding of the resurrection belief. Of course, it is not a consequence of it, in the sense that God became three persons at the birth of Christ or at his death and resurrection! It is a mystery of relationship and of authentic understanding, a mystery of the relationship of Jesus and of God to ourselves, and it is a question of how this relationship is to be explained in a logical way, while remaining completely faithful to the experiences and formulations of the New Testament.

THE CHRISTOLOGIES OF THE NEW TESTAMENT

Son of God, Son of man, Son

In the high Christology of the early Church awe-inspiring titles were applied to Jesus. In the context of the Johannine writings for example, there can be little doubt that the title 'Son of God' refers to Jesus as a pre-existing, divine being – in fact, God himself. But the raw material for this title is found in the tradition of Jesus' earthly life, as is the case with the other titles. The phrase 'son of God' was, as we have seen in an earlier chapter, applied by the Old Testament to Israel as a collectivity. It was also the designation of the ordinary righteous Israelite. In a special sense it was applied to the king and to the expected Messiah of the Davidic dynasty.

> I will tell of the decree of the Lord:
> He said to me, 'You are my Son,
>   today I have begotten you.
> Ask of me, and I will make the nations your heritage,
>   and the ends of the earth your possession' (Psalm 2:7–8).

Jesus did not refer to himself as 'Son of God', but when the title was applied to him in the Gospels, he is usually shown as reinterpreting it by using the phrase 'Son of man'. This is what happened, for example, in the Marcan version of his trial before the Sanhedrin.

The text of Psalm 2 is however used in the early forms of the Easter proclamation. Paul, for example, in his speech in the synagogue at Pisidian

Antioch, quotes the very words of the psalm in order to describe the resurrection, implying that Jesus had become Son of God and Messiah at that moment. The other uses of the word 'Son' in the Pauline writings (even that of Galatians 4:4) do not allow us any other interpretation. In the Gospel of Mark, Psalm 2 is apparently quoted to show that Jesus' sonship/messiahship began with his baptism in the Jordan and his public ministry. 'A voice came from heaven, ''Thou art my beloved Son . . .'' ' (Mark 1:11). Matthew's infancy narrative pushes the sonship/messiahship of Jesus back to the moment of his conception. Without, however, using the title 'Son of God' at all, he describes Jesus as having a divine origin, being conceived by the power of the Holy Spirit, and he interprets Isaiah's Immanuel prophecy in the light of this event. Luke's infancy narrative also describes a divine conception for Jesus, but seems to place the title 'Son of God' in the future:

> therefore the child to be born will be called holy,
> the Son of God (Luke 1:35).

It is the begetting of one who will be called – and will in fact be – the Son of God.

As Raymond Brown has said, scientifically controllable evidence does not allow us to see what actual facts lie behind the accounts of the virgin birth (Brown 1973, pp. 66–67). Geza Vermes has offered the view that a 'virgin' according to the Talmud was a girl who had not menstruated, even though married before puberty (Vermes 1973, p. 219). However, the virginity of Mary was intended to serve the divine origin of Jesus and it is clear what the evangelists are teaching us, namely that no mere man brought about Jesus' historical presence on earth, and that, in view of his messianic function, his human origin was unique, The story also emphasizes the central role of a woman, the mother of Jesus, in co-operating with God's plan.

It would seem that Jesus preferred to refer to himself as 'the son of man'. 'Son of man' can, of course, simply mean 'man', as it does repeatedly in the prophecy of Ezekiel, and it has been argued that Jesus was merely emphasizing his humanity, or at most his being the representative of humanity. It is not a title which was used in the early Church. However, in Jesus' own day it would have carried dramatic significance if a referance to the Danielic eschatological figure was intended. C. F. D. Moule thinks this is likely, in view of the use of the definite article, *the* Son of man (Moule 1977, pp.12–17). Even if Jesus himself used the phrase as a title and was referring to Daniel 7:9–14, it is far from certain that he would have given the referance a messianic interpretation. As we saw in the previous chapter, that interpretation occurred simultaneously in Christian and non-Christian circles in the inter-testamentary period. In IV Ezra, the Son of man is indeed identified messianically as 'my Son'. Jesus himself would have used it to refer to himself as the vindicated representative of mankind.

Much more significant is Jesus' use of the familiar word *Abba* to refer to God. There can be little doubt that this was an authentic usage of Jesus himself. It is a child's onomatopoeic term for 'father'. ('Daddy' might be a translation.) It was regularly used by children of their fathers, and sometimes by older people of other persons as a title of respectful familiarity. Jesus used it to address God in prayer and, as Luke 11:2 shows, he taught his disciples the same mode of address: 'Father [*Abba*], hallowed be thy name'.

Was the usage unique? It is hard to answer this question. Vermes has claimed that it was a regular prayer usage of contemporary Hasidic piety; yet the only example he is able to cite shows us Hanan being called *Abba* by his disciples and referring to God obliquely as *Abba* for this reason in a prayer which addresses the Almighty as 'Lord of the Universe' (Vermes 1973, pp. 210–211). We do not know enough about contemporary private Jewish piety to be able to judge just how unusual Jesus' usage was. Other texts in the Synoptic Gospels are not really helpful. There are passages in all of them in which Jesus' own sonship is explicitly distinguished from the sonship of his disciples, and there are the parables in which 'the Son' is opposed to the 'servants'. Yet exegetes feel that they are instances of Jesus' sayings which may have been reinterpreted more Christologically in the light of the resurrection.

However, James Dunn is able to write:

> The evidence points consistently and clearly to the conclusion that Jesus' regular use of *Abba* in addressing God distinguished Jesus in a significant degree from his contemporaries (Dunn 1980, p. 27).

And Edward Schillebeeckx is able to speak of the '*Abba*-experience' of Jesus (Schillebeeckx 1979, p. 256). Paul regarded the *Abba* prayer as something which distinguished those who had received a share in Jesus' sonship through the power of the Spirit:

> When we cry 'Abba! Father!' it is the Spirit himself bearing witness with our spirit, that we are children of God . . . (Romans 8:15–16).

> And because you are sons, God has sent the spirit of his Son into your hearts, crying, 'Abba! Father!' (Galatians 4:6).

The *Abba* prayer was therefore presumably characteristic of Jesus, and the earliest Christians retained an awareness of this fact in their own use of *Abba*. We may conclude also that the phrase expressed for Jesus a sense of intimate sonship towards God, and that his disciples' sonship was somehow dependent on his own. Schillebeeckx is right to add that Jesus' own *Abba* experience was not limited to prayer-form alone, but is linked to his whole way of life (Schillebeeckx 1979, p. 256, and 1980*, p. 8). His liberated life-style and message, his healing and reconciling activity, his authoritative teaching – all these things betokened an intimacy with God which no other prophet or rabbi claimed. They were also an invitation to his followers to share in this intimacy as a characteristic of the eschatological times which he was announcing and living.

It might also be remarked here that both Gerhardsson (1979, p. 54) and Moule (1977, pp. 35–43) see an ambivalence in the title 'Lord' which was applied to Jesus in his lifetime. From the very beginning of his public ministry, Jesus was called 'Lord' or 'Master'. In Aramaic this was *maran,* in Greek *kyrios.* It would have been impossible for his disciples to have called Jesus 'Lord' in the sense that Yahweh was called 'Lord' in the days of Jesus' earthly ministry, yet the verbal bridge existed between 'Lord' meaning 'Master' and 'Lord' meaning 'God' in the text of Psalm 110:

> The Lord says to my lord:
> 'Sit at my right hand . . .' (Psalm 110:1).

The title 'Lord'/'Master' was appropriate to Jesus as teacher and leader in his life, and its meaning must have developed as his authoritative teaching and marvellous signs raised him ever higher in the eyes of his followers. The resurrection obviously quickened the pace of this development until Jesus was pictured as exalted and enthroned on the right hand of power as 'King of Kings and Lord of Lords' (Revelation 19:16), and the word 'Lord' was used of him as it had been of Yahweh in the Old Testament. The significant fact is that in this case, as in the case of the other titles, there is no significant break at Easter – no sudden influence from Hellenistic or other non-Christian religious speculation – which altered their meaning. On the contrary, there was an unbroken development of meaning from the earthly life of Jesus into the time of the apostolic teaching of the early Church, and Peter is able to quote Psalm 110 as part of the Easter proclamation (Acts 2:34).

The 'Last Adam' Christology

We have already seen, in the previous chapter, that Israel's oldest dream was of salvation coming from God, and that Adam, the first man, had jeopardized human communion with God by attempting to assert moral independence. Adam plays an important role in Paul's Christology, particularly in the first eight chapters of the Letter to the Romans. Paul uses the Genesis story of Adam's fall to explain the experience which all human beings have of sin and suffering; and he opposes the risen Christ to Adam. Adam disfigured the image of God in mankind; Christ, on the other hand, has re-made man in the image and likeness of God, by restoring him to communion with God. In Christ, we are being reshaped and remodelled, as Adam was shaped by God from the clay of the earth. After Adam's fall, creation was subjected to futility, for the whole of creation was caught up in the fall of him who had been the priest of creation, the one destined to subdue the earth and make it fruitful. Now, in Christ, creation regains its purpose and is renewed. Christ is opposed, as 'Last Adam', to the 'First Adam', and the salvation he brought is the reversal of Adam's fall.

As James Dunn points out, Psalm 8 provided a ready vehicle for Adam Christology (Dunn 1980, p. 109).

> [Thou] dost crown him with glory and honour.
> Thou hast given him dominion over the works of thy hands;
>   thou hast put all things under his feet (Psalm 8:5-6).

This was a description of God's purpose for man, as well as of Christ's lordship. The author of the Letter to the Hebrews argues that God's purpose was not fulfilled until Christ was exalted (Hebrews 2:8-15). Philippians also returns to this idea:

> But our commonwealth is in heaven, and from it we await a Saviour, the Lord Jesus Christ, who will change our lowly body to be like his glorious body, by the power which enables him even to subject all things to himself (Philippians 3:20-21).

Earlier in the psalm, man was described as being 'little less than God' or 'little less than the angels'. This was the first Adam's condition which Jesus, according to the thought of Paul and the author of Hebrews, shared even to the point of death. However, in contrast to Adam's disobedience which led to death, Jesus' obedience to death led to life for himself and for all who are recreated in him.

Following James Dunn (1980, pp. 114-121) and J. Murphy-O'Connor (1976, pp. 25-50), one can see that this is the meaning of another passage in Philippians:

> Have this mind among yourselves, which was in Christ Jesus, who though he was in the form of God, did not count equality with God a thing to be grasped, but emptied himself, taking the form of a servant, being born in the likeness of men. And being found in human form he humbled himself and became obedient unto death, even death on a cross. Therefore God has highly exalted him and bestowed on him a name which is above every name, that at the name of Jesus every knee should bow, in heaven and on earth and under the earth, and every tongue confess that Jesus Christ is Lord, to the glory of God the Father (Philippians 2:5-11).

Jesus was like Adam, the man made in the 'form' or image of God. Unlike Adam, however, he did not seek 'equality' with God by claiming moral independence from him. On the contrary, being found in this fallen, human form, he humbled himself still more by accepting the most ignominious death possible. For that reason, God has exalted him and made him Lord over creation in a way that is more final and more complete than the first Adam's lordship over creation. Paul is not here dealing with Jesus' pre-existence in the Godhead, but with his salvific role as new man and Last Adam.

Schillebeeckx draws our attention to the parallels of Adam, David and Christ. David was a 'royal Adam', a new and liberated man who, because he was king, could break the ritual taboos of the Mosaic law (Schillebeeckx 1980*, pp. 107–108). The comparison which occurs in the Gospels between Jesus and David is not only in function of the messianic vocation, but in function also of the Adam parallel. David was raised 'from the dust' (like Adam) and made to 'sit with princes' (Psalm 113:7–8). Like Adam, he transgressed and was punished, but, like Adam again, he was never abandoned by God. God never withdrew his trust, and, in Jesus, God again puts his trust in man. This time, man does not fail him.

From what, according to the New Testament, does Jesus save humankind? There are many answers on every page of the Gospels and of the other New Testament documents. Jesus liberates man from sin and guilt, from anxieties of different kinds (including demonopathic conditions), from the fear of death, from sorrow and despair, from hopelessness, from lack of freedom, from egotism and insincerity, from loneliness, from cruelty, from material cares and needs, from jealousy for one's reputation, from merciless condemnation, from fear of war and rumours of war, from sickness of every kind. The list is almost endless. What does he free us for? Well, basically, he frees us to share in his own freedom. We are to adopt his own liberated way of life, his own sense of peace and joy, his own ability to love and be generous. We are freed for equality, for community and reconciliation, for healing and wholeness, for happiness, for hope, for holiness, for eternal glory and for sharing Jesus' own mission to liberate others. All such things are the fruit of the salvation – the redemption or 'buying back' or ransoming – of humanity, brought about by the death of Jesus. With Jesus, we are again raised from the dust and made to sit with princes.

The wisdom and the Word of God

We have already seen in the previous chapter how ancient Israel spoke of God's active involvement with the world and of his plan for his creation in terms of wisdom. This wisdom was often personalized as a picturesque way of speaking, without ever suggesting that it (or rather 'she') was a hypostasis of God, let alone another divine being distinct from himself. In the writings of Paul this outreach of God to the world is regarded as being embodied in Christ. Jesus Christ is therefore the 'wisdom of God'. Jesus Christ fulfils the eternal plan of God for his creation. In a celebrated passage Paul contrasts this true wisdom with the wisdom of the Greeks:

> For Jews demand signs and Greeks seek wisdom, but we preach Christ crucified, a stumbling block to Jews and folly to Gentiles, but to those who are called, both Jews

and Greeks, Christ the power of God and the wisdom of God. For the foolishness of
God is wiser than men, and the weakness of God is stronger than men . . . . He is the
source of your life in Christ Jesus, whom God made our wisdom, our righteousness
and sanctification and redemption . . . (1 Corinthians 1:22–25, 30).

Paul also makes use of a passage in Deuteronomy (Deuteronomy 30:11–14)
which was originally about Yahweh's commandment being possible of
fulfilment because 'the word is very near to you; it is in your mouth and in
your heart, so that you can do it'. In the Book of Baruch, the very same
words are used of wisdom (Baruch 3:29–32), and Paul in the Letter to the
Romans applies the Deuteronomic passage to Christ as wisdom:

But the righteousness based on faith says, Do not say in your heart, 'Who will
ascend into heaven?' (that is, to bring Christ down) or 'Who will descend into the
abyss?' (that is, to bring Christ up from the dead). But what does it say? The word
is near you, on your lips and in your heart (that is, the word of faith which we
preach); because, if you confess with your lips that Jesus is Lord and believe in your
heart that God raised him from the dead, you will be saved (Romans 10:6–9).

Paul is here contrasting a righteousness based on the Law with a righteousness based on faith in Christ, and it is already significant that the Gospel of
Christ is identified with that Deuteronomic 'word'.

It is in Paul's use of the concept of 'mystery' or 'secret plan' of God that
the language of incarnation begins to appear in the New Testament, at least
in an incoherent form. The point is that if the plan which God had from the
beginning of creation is now revealed in Christ in an exhaustive way, Christ
himself was also 'in the beginning'. That this was already dimly seen is
evidenced by the hymns of the later Pauline Epistles:

He is the image of the invisible God, the first-born of all creation;
for in him all things were created, in heaven and on earth,
visible and invisible, whether thrones or dominions,
or principalities or authorities –
all things were created through him and for him.
He is before all things,
and in him all things hold together.
He is the head of the body, the church;
he is the beginning, the first-born from the dead,
that in everything he might be pre-eminent.
For in him all the fullness of God was pleased to dwell,
and through him to reconcile to himself all things,
whether on earth or in heaven,
making peace by the blood of his cross (Colossians 1:15–20).

The thought in this hymn seems to be that Christ is God's intention for his
creation fulfilled. God is already recognizable in Christ, and it is through
Christ that creation now becomes intelligible. Christ was pre-existent in the
creation – at least intentionally – because this creation is now renewed by his

work of redemption. The exaltation of Christ has now fulfilled God's plan for the world, and Christ himself is one with the divine wisdom which gives order and meaning to the whole cosmos.

It was in the Johannine circle of second-generation Christianity that the divine personality of Jesus of Nazareth, together with his pre-existence in the Godhead, was unequivocally affirmed. This community must have enjoyed greater opportunities for reflection on the reality of Jesus Christ, and it was influenced by the Hellenistic thinking of Jewish circles in Alexandria. In the previous chapter we already spoke of Philo's application of the Greek Logos concept to Hebrew wisdom and Torah. Now the Johannine community applied the Logos concept to Jesus Christ. They were encouraged to do this by usages already current in early Christian communities and other New Testament writings. The 'word' was commonly used to refer to the Gospel, as we have already seen in Paul. This was equally true of Matthew, Mark, Luke and Acts. The 'word' is objectified, even seemingly personified. It 'grows'. It 'goes' and 'comes'. It is 'received' and 'served'. It 'runs'. It is free and 'is not bound'. It is a 'sword', even 'a two-edged sword'. This Gospel, then, which is revealed by the apostolic preaching is a distinct dynamic reality and, as John McKenzie points out, 'a revealed judgement' which elicits a decision from those it confronts (McKenzie 1976: 'Word').

In the Gospel of John, the word is generally the teaching of Jesus himself. Jesus' word is not his own, but belongs to his Father. He who listens to this word has life; and the word dwells in him. What is more, the one who hears the word dwells in the word. The word is hypostasized as a permanent reality. The rider on the white horse in Revelation (19:11–16) has the name: 'King of Kings and Lord of Lords', and from his mouth issues a sharp sword of judgement. He, too, is 'the Word of God'.

All of this becomes understandable when we consider the prologue to John's Gospel, for there we see the profound and personal unity of Christ's word and work with that of God himself. The prologue is based on a poem, probably from the Johannine circle itself, which was reworked and placed as a preface to the Gospel by the Gospel's author. In the first part of the poem we are told that the Word was in the beginning, that it was with God and that it was God.

> In the beginning was the Word,
> and the Word was with God,
> and the Word was God.
> He was in the beginning with God;
> all things were made through him,
> and without him was not anything made
> that was made.
> In him was life,

and the life was the light of men.
The light shines in the darkness,
and the darkness has not overcome it (John 1:1–5).

Up to this moment in the poem, and indeed up to verse 14, there is nothing perhaps, in this otherwise highly personal description of God's Word, with which a non-Christian exponent of Logos-Wisdom might not agree, but then the poet lets fall the words which alter all perspectives:

And the Word became flesh
and dwelt among us,
full of grace and truth;
we have beheld his glory,
glory as of the only Son from the Father . . . .

And from his fullness
have we all received,
grace upon grace (John 1:14, 16).

Verse 14, as Dunn points out, reveals not only a transition from pre-existence to incarnation, but from a personification to an actual person, a person who is eternal, identical with God, yet distinct from the Father (Dunn 1980, p. 243). With that dramatic disclosure all the other titles in the Gospel fall into place and the stage is set for a narrative which affirms the divinity of Jesus Christ in one passage after another.

THE MODERN CREDIBILITY OF GOD'S SELF-REVELATION IN CHRIST

A new possibility from God

Various modern writers, Schillebeeckx in particular, have described the modern world in terms of suffering (Schillebeeckx 1980, p. 725). We are confronted at the end of the twentieth century with an excess of suffering and with the possibility – some would say, the certainty – of suffering on a massive scale, brought about by terrifying weapons that have been created by modern technology. Johann Baptist Metz points to the fact that wars to end war and suffering only succeed in generating more war and suffering, and yet we are constantly urged on by the stimulus for liberation and for the conquest of suffering (Metz 1980, pp. 124–133). Karl Marx's insight was that socio-economic systems and structures are a cause of suffering, and his prejudice against religion, as a false solution to the problem, was turned by V. I. Lenin into an atheistic metaphysic. This has led many self-styled 'Marxists' and 'neo-Marxists' to probe more deeply into the meaning of human life. What is human life for, if the door of religious interpretation is to be kept locked? For the impersonal dialectic of history? For the workers' struggle? For work itself? It is significant that Marxist thinkers like Roger

Garaudy or Milan Machoveč have not been content with such goals, but have tended to share Christianity's 'passion for the future', a future with a further and more attractive level of meaning.

The utilitarian individualism of non-Marxist societies is also discovering that science and technology are no substitute for religion. Neither form of pragmatism (Marxist or non-Marxist) can resolve private guilt, explain the fate of individuals, ensure justice and mutual love among human beings, feed the creative imagination and the spirit of openness to the future, let alone justify the untold suffering and innumerable deaths of past history. Modern technological man possesses no integrating theory which links his present life to past and future, and gives him a purpose for living.

The final word spoken by God, the unrepeatable revelation, the 'Word made flesh', offers a new possibility to humankind. It also offers a new understanding of reality in general, for, as Walter Kasper writes: 'Christology is not concerned with the nature of Christ only' (Kasper 1976, p. 38). The life, death, and resurrection of Jesus Christ is liberating because it motivates us and strengthens us to save and to heal – to work relentlessly against suffering. It motivates and strengthens us to show solidarity with threatened humanity and to exhibit what Schillebeeckx calls an 'ethical non-conformity' towards structures of injustice in the world (Schillebeeckx 1980, p. 591). But it also introduces us, more fully than ever before, to the paradox that is God, namely a radical love which is unconcerned about the consequences to oneself or for one's own life, a radical love that shoulders the burden of suffering to end suffering. That *is* a paradox, perhaps, but it is the very opposite of the 'war of liberation', the irrational ideology of inflicting suffering to end suffering, of the war to end war, or the class-struggle to end class-competition.

Jesus' life, death and resurrection proclaims the most basic revolution of all, the *metanoia* or change of heart that is the 'new covenant' or 'New Testament'. It is not only a war against heartless cruelty and senseless injustice; it is a war against impenitence, against hypocrisy and against ethical self-glorification. It is a revolution against the self-sufficiency which feels no need for forgiveness and therefore knows nothing of God's forgiving love. To become a disciple of Jesus Christ, to respond to the call of his teaching, his example and his personality, is to enter upon an adventure which transcends the experiences of this present life. 'God has made him Lord and Christ, this Jesus whom you crucified' (Acts 2:36). In this lordship, which is a lordship over history and a lordship of the living and dead, past and future are united, for he reveals the goal of every human life – the sharing of the life of God.

Christ yesterday and today,
the beginning and the end,

Alpha and Omega;
all time belongs to him
and all the ages . . . (From the liturgy of the Roman Easter Vigil).

Tradition and response

The story of Jesus of Nazareth, and the story of how his followers grasped the reality that he was, contain a number of messages. One, as we have tried to show, is that the tradition of Christianity goes back to an earthly life that was really lived. Another is, as was eventually explicitly discovered by the Johannine circle, that the tradition goes still further back, taking its origin in the Godhead itself and in the eternal generation of the Son from the Father. Jesus is God's Word in a dynamic and distinctly personal sense. But all that Jesus accomplished was accomplished in the Spirit of God, God's utterly free, living, all-pervading power. With that Spirit he was 'anointed' Lord, and it was that Spirit which his resurrection released to his followers, as thereafter empowering them to cry '*Abba,* Father' and to call Jesus 'Lord'. The mystery of awareness, of distinction and of interrelatedness which they called 'Spirit of God' or 'Holy Spirit' came to be understood also as a mystery of personality, and as another distinct divine Person.

These understandings and these successive and overlapping affirmations were made in the 'Exodus communities' of the New Testament. The apostolic preaching took place in a *koinonia* or communion of communities which had received the Word and which, by the power of the Spirit, lived in that Word. The Word was for them the 'Word of Life'. Jesus was alive and personally present among them, bringing about the revolution or *metanoia* of which we have been speaking. How did they experience this life-giving presence of the risen Christ? Through celebrating his narrative-memory, through prayer and worship as expressions of commitment. Typically, through celebrating the Eucharist. Faith was a response to the Word, and it was nourished by the Word. The Word was the criterion of understanding and affirmation. But this Word was a 'Parable', a 'Story', a 'Narrative', even a 'Picturesque Saying' because it appealed to human experience and to human imaginative power, and not merely to human reason and logic. God's wisdom was 'folly' to the philosophers, because truth is stranger than speculation. It is well for us to remember that the Word is the 'Parable of God' when we come to consider the roles and norms that belong to theological formulation and to liturgical celebration.

Another important message from the New Testament is that the developing doctrinal affirmations of the early Christians were made in a climate of interculturation. The Palestine of Jesus' time had been extensively Hellenized and it was in the Greek language that the texts of the New Testament were written. It has been suggested that Jesus himself may have spoken Greek. Certainly, Greek ideas were current among the followers of

Jesus and became more influential as the apostolic preaching spread to the towns and city-states of the Roman Mediterranean world. This world-wide evangelization was inherent in the Christian Gospel itself, which finally and irrevocably broke the link between revelation and the particular history of the people of Israel. The new Israel was not wedded to Temple, Mosaic law or circumcision or to the social institutions of Judaism. It belonged to the whole of the known world at that time. Henceforth, the Good News was to be preached to every creature and every nation in a universal messianic perspective. This was not, of course, to deny the historical character of the Christ-event, its origins from within the Judaic tradition and its factual unrepeatability, extending also to the witness and the preaching of the apostles. But the New Testament does offer a model for the church-building and the activity of evangelization in later ages. It also offers us a model for the so-called 'dependent' or 'participant' revelation of all subsequent history, as operating within human experience and through the inter-penetration of experiences. The early Church was 'Catholic' or universal from the beginning because of its outreach to the world and because of its essential interculturality. These facts lead us on to the questions which must be developed in the subsequent chapters of this book: the nature and scope of dependent revelation, the relevance of Christianity for other religions, the character of faith and sacramental worship, and the shape of Christian evangelization and community-building in the contemporary world. The remainder of this book is in the nature of 'response' to the Jesus tradition, but we have noted that tradition and response are not subsequent to, but are already present at the heart of the proclamation – the *kerygma* of the New Testament.

QUESTIONS FOR DISCUSSION

(1)   What is the evidence in the New Testament that Jesus of Nazareth was conscious of being a new and definitive source of divine revelation?

(2)   What are the arguments for the historicity of the 'Jesus of faith'?

(3)   When and how was the divinity of Jesus clearly affirmed by the early Christian communities?

(4)   For further enquiry: In what ways do the life, death and teaching of Jesus Christ offer our world new possibilities?

SELECT ANNOTATED READING LIST

J. P. Mackey, 1979: *Jesus the Man and the Myth* (London). This is a readable and thorough discussion of all issues relating to the exegesis, and the historical and theological significance of the New Testament.

J. D. G. Dunn, 1980: *Christology in the Making* (London). The author sets out to trace the genesis of the doctrine of the Incarnation, as the Christian communities of the New Testament strove to give full expression to the significance of the Christ-event. The book is a major contribution to Christological studies, and it benefits from its clarity and frequent summaries.

C. F. D. Moule, 1977: *The Origin of Christology* (Cambridge). Here is a convincing attempt to demonstrate the continuities between the historical Jesus and post-Easter faith of the apostles.

B. Gerhardsson, 1979: *The Origins of the Gospel Traditions* (London). It may be that the author overstates the case for identifiable techniques of oral transmission of the Jesus tradition, but this small book is a powerful argument for the historicity of that tradition.

W. Kasper, 1977: *Jesus the Christ* (London). A comprehensive survey of the whole field of contemporary Christology, with a good deal of small print. This book is an outstandingly competent synthesis.

E. Schillebeeckx, 1980*: *Interim Report on the Books: Jesus and Christ* (London). For the reader who has not the courage or inclination to grapple with Schillebeeckx's two large and controversial volumes, this small 150-page book has the merit, not only of setting out the main issues of the other two, but of clarifying many of the questions of his critics.

5

The Church as Word

GOD STILL SPEAKS

History and experience as participation

'The Redeemer of Man, Jesus Christ, is the centre of the universe and of history' (*Redemptor Hominis,* 1). These opening words of Pope John Paul II's first encyclical in 1979 proclaim the definitive character of God's self-revelation in Jesus Christ, its historical unrepeatability. The life, death and resurrection of Jesus Christ were the climactic embodiment of God's self-revelation, as it had unfolded in the history of Israel. But these events were also henceforward normative and foundational. In spite of their factual unrepeatability, they became 'available' to succeeding generations through, and within, the Christian tradition. The Dogmatic Constitution of the Second Vatican Council on Divine Revelation (*Dei Verbum*) declared:

> It pleased God, in his goodness and wisdom, to reveal himself and to make known the mystery of his will. His will was that men should have access to the Father, through Christ, the Word made flesh, in the Holy Spirit, and thus become sharers in the divine nature (*Dei Verbum,* 2).

Sharing in the divine nature, being created in the image and likeness of God himself, 'walking with God' in his garden, is the purpose of human existence according to the Biblical tradition, and it is noteworthy that the language in which that existence is described stresses participation. Human beings are called to live in Christ and to have Christ live in them. They are also called to a fellowship with one another and to a life which is essentially a sharing with others in Christ. John's Gospel puts the very expressive symbol of the vine into the mouth of Jesus at the Last Supper:

> I am the true vine, and my Father is the vine-dresser. Every branch of mine that bears no fruit he takes away, and every branch that does bear fruit he prunes that it may bear more fruit.... Abide in me, and I in you. As the branch cannot bear fruit by itself, unless it abides in the vine, neither can you, unless you abide in me. I am the vine, you are the branches. He who abides in me, and I in him, he it is that bears much fruit, for apart from me you can do nothing (John 15:1–5).

The first hearers of those words belonged to a Mediterranean way of life in which viticulture was well understood. They had seen the annual miracle of the green tendrils issuing from the gnarled vine-stock; and they had been taught to prune it, leaving only those shoots which were closest to the stock, so that the full benefit of the rising sap should be theirs. The vine with its branches was a graphic image of the Christian's closeness to Christ and to his fellows in Christ. This Christian affirmation has shed a unique light on the nature of experience and of history.

To understand this, it is best to recall what was said about history and experience in the first chapter of this book. Human beings experience reality and impart meaning to what they experience from within an inherited tradition of accumulated experiences and meanings. This is particularly true of religious experience or 'revelation', whether it be the expression of a deep or 'mystical' loving awareness of God, or the apprehension of a religious interpretation of ordinary events which stimulates our conduct or our commitment. The tradition from within which we perceive reality as meaningful is historical, in the sense that it is a 'narrative memory' or even 'an eschatological memory' – a hope for the future which has roots in the past. Every religion has a memory of this kind, however shallow in historical depth it may be. In this memory are certain foundational events, certain profoundly revelatory moments, which influence the shape of our contemporary religious perceptions consciously or unconsciously.

It was the recognition of a surviving and living Christian tradition that launched us into an enquiry about the character and content of Judeo-Christian revelation and which has brought us to this point in our discussion.We must now recognize that the Christian tradition has, in fact, contributed to a general philosophical understanding of reality. Because of its emphasis on an unrepeatable self-disclosure of God in history and at the same time on an immediate experience of this unrepeatable event by people at other times and in other places, it helps us to understand the dynamic structure of being. Although Plato put the notion of participation, or the unity-in-difference, of being at the centre of his thought, the actual relationships this implied were never adequately analysed by philosophy. In neo-Platonism it degenerated into a doctrine of unilinear emanation of images from archetypes, while in Aristotelianism the dualistic system of causality could not accommodate the idea at all. St Thomas Aquinas tried unsuccessfully to combine the notions of participation and causality (participation by composition) but fell back upon a more or less Platonic hierarchy of degrees of likeness among beings. Analogical statements, in fact, merely affirm the likeness and the difference, without expressing the relationship. In such a view, the only totalities are abstractions (Rahner 1975, pp. 1160–1163).

In modern structuralism, particular facts are meaningful in so far as they participate in an integrating theory or have a final purpose which unites them all. That is not to say that structures are static. On the contrary, the essential pluralism of reality and the creative interplay between particular facts provoke meaning. Structuralism has revealed more clearly the participatory nature of reality through its analyses of myth and symbolism. Yet the notion of structure belongs to the logical order, and, as such, remains anonymous and impersonal, imparting phenomenal form to the world of appearances. It describes how meaning is created, without offering a meta-phenomenal explanation of why. 'Structure', in so far as it replaces God as the ultimate reality, is not a final explanation.

The reality of participation can only be fully understood in terms of Christian revelation. It is an event, a history, in which the totality who is God reveals himself as radically different. This event actualizes the infinite difference between God and creation, yet does so only through the proportionate self-revelation and self-realization of created reality. The totality (God-in-Jesus Christ) comes to its own fulfilment in the establishment and liberation of its created parts. The Christ-event disclosed once and for all the meaning of the unity-in-difference of God and created reality, the self-imparting of God and the partaking of man. 'And from his fullness have we all received, grace upon grace' (John 1:16).

Participation operates in a vertical-time dimension and in a horizontal space-dimension. Christian revelation accounts for the fact that we are more fully ourselves in the measure in which we genuinely participate in experiences that are spatio-temporally remote. We do not affirm our identities more strongly by pulling up our historical roots, or by practising a cultural ethnocentrism. On the contrary, we are more fully ourselves when we have the self-confidence to seek inspiration from the past or to borrow from other cultures. Our experience is at its richest when it is dialogical, above all, when it is a dialogical partnership with God that is open to the future. The self-revelation of God in Jesus Christ is of a God who reconciles and who calls to unity by liberating.

Participant revelation

The Second Vatican Council's Dogmatic Constitution on Divine Revelation, speaking of revelation and faith, has this to say:

> 'The obedience of faith' must be given to God as he reveals himself. By faith man freely commits his entire self to God, making 'the full submission of his intellect and will to God who reveals', and willingly assenting to the Revelation given by him (*Dei Verbum*, 5).

We shall examine the act of faith in a later chapter; what interests us here is that the Council speaks of revelation happening now, in the present tense. In speaking thus, the Council Fathers actually quote from the First Vatican

Council's Dogmatic Constitution on the Catholic Faith (*Dei Filius*) and borrow the phrase 'God who reveals'. This use of the present tense when speaking of revelation is not accidental. It is echoed in Vatican II's Declaration on Religious Liberty, which speaks of an adopted son of God giving adherence 'to God when he reveals himself' (*Dignitatis Humanae,* 10). The Council's Decree on the Church's Missionary Activity also uses the present tense: 'What Revelation makes known to us is confirmed by our own experience' (*Ad Gentes,* 13). Of even more weight is the Dogmatic Constitution on the Church, which speaks of Christ who 'communicates truth and grace to all men' through the Church (*Lumen Gentium,* 8), and the Pastoral Constitution on the Church in the Modern World, which states that Christ 'can show man the way and strengthen him through the Spirit in order to be worthy of his destiny' (*Gaudium et Spes,* 10).

Even more explicit is the Apostolic Exhortation on Catechesis in Our Time, of Pope John Paul II, who speaks of our own share in the 'revealing' process. 'How are we to reveal Jesus Christ . . . ?' (*Catechesi Tradendae,* 35) asks the Pope. Catechesis, he says, 'will have to reveal . . . all the principal mysteries of faith' (*ibid.* 37). Finally, in catechesis, the mysteries of Jesus Christ are said to 'speak eloquently' to the 'conscience and heart' and to cast light upon suffering and the experience of the created world (*ibid.* 38). How are we to reconcile this revelation by Jesus Christ in the present with the declaration that, since the death of the last apostle, 'no new public revelation is to be expected before the glorious manifestation of Our Lord Jesus Christ' (*Dei Verbum,* 4)?

It is true that the Christ-event, in which the apostles participated as privileged and original witnesses, was a definitive and unrepeatable historical event. But the self-revelation of God in Christ was the revelation of saving Truth, of the God who saves, and the purpose of the apostolic preaching was, as the author of John's Gospel puts it, 'that you may believe that Jesus is the Christ, the Son of God, and that believing you may have life in his name' (John 20:30). This statement is preceded by the words of the risen Christ himself: 'Have you believed because you have seen me? Blessed are those who have not seen and yet believe' (*ibid.* 29). The same divine life is available to all, whether – like Thomas – they have 'seen' Christ, or whether – like ourselves – they have not 'seen' him in the flesh. The self-revelation of God to those who 'saw' Christ in the flesh is still a living and active power among those who have not 'seen' him. This power is contained in a tradition which proclaims the Good News of Christ, which celebrates the historical memory of Christ, and which witnesses to his presence in the life of the individual and the community. Within this tradition, the Christian is able to respond, and within this tradition God reveals himself to him in Christ.

In the first chapter we spoke of the immediacy of experience and of experience itself as the source of all knowledge. We do not, therefore, experience revelation, if we do not experience it immediately. For this reason, Gerald O'Collins rightly rejects the term 'mediate revelation' to describe our own present-day experience of God's self-revelation in Jesus Christ (O'Collins 1981, p. 101). Revelation can never be second-hand, or else it is not really revelation at all. The revelation which we experience today can be called 'derived' or 'dependent' revelation, but, following what we have said about the participatory character of all reality, it is perhaps best to call it 'participant revelation'. This is because God really and actually reveals himself to us in Jesus Christ through the tradition we have received; and our experience of Jesus Christ in the events and relationships of our own life really participates in the foundational revelation bestowed on the apostles and living on effectively in the tradition. Let us examine this fact more closely.

We do not come to our experiences with our minds a blank. On the contrary, we confront reality – the world, other people, our own selves – with a great deal of mental luggage. This mental luggage is the fruit of an accumulation of experiences or of a tradition which our society teaches us, along with a culture or whole way of life. No doubt, there is a logic in this tradition much of which we could reason out for ourselves, but the fact remains that our knowledge comes to us in great part from the testimonies of other people. With this prior knowledge we half-create the reality that we perceive; we make our experiences intelligible. We 'half-create' – that is to say, we both create and discover meaning in our experiences. We participate in God's creative freedom, as beings made in his image and likeness, but our creativity is directed towards the appearances of an already created reality.

To take an example: unless one believes in God, one will not discover his presence and his purpose in the works of created nature. This is well illustrated by two nineteenth-century nature-poets. The American poet Walt Whitman made nature the criterion of all virtue and he sensed a purpose and a presence in nature which he was unable to identify. He wrote:

> The skies of day and night, colors, densities, forms, may-be these are (as doubtless they are) only apparitions, and the real something has yet to be known (*Of the Terrible Doubt of Appearances*).

The English Jesuit Gerard Manley Hopkins, on the other hand, identified that 'real something' in nature as God, and more particularly, as the cosmic Christ.

> All things therefore are charged with God, and if we know how to touch them, give off sparks and take fire, yield drops and flow, ring and tell of him .... God's utterance of himself in himself is God the Word. Outside himself is this world. This world then is word, expression, news of God. Therefore, its end, its purpose, its purport, its meaning is God and its life or work to name and praise him (*Prose Commentary on the Exercises of St Ignatius:* Pick 1966, p. 404, 16).

The difference between the two views is that Whitman considered tradition irrelevant to an understanding of nature, while Hopkins maintained that nature could yield no meaning unless the one who experienced it knew how to 'touch' it, that is, unless he had faith in the divine self-revelation in Christ.

We create meaning by bringing – for example – our religious faith to experience, but we also discover a meaning that is already there. The things we experience are not only apparitions but, as we pointed out in the first chapter, manifestations of reality, and we experience them as 'true' symbols. The word 'symbol' derives from a Greek verb meaning 'to put together'. A symbol is therefore 'a putting together' of two things – a fitting together of pieces in the jigsaw of experience.

We confront reality with our tradition, but we also confront our tradition with the reality we experience. We both discover meaning and create meaning when we profess our tradition, and this, as Gerald O'Collins points out, happens in the case of our Christian affirmations (O'Collins 1981, p. 176). We come to our tradition with new questions and out of new contexts, and so the affirmations of our tradition assume surplus meanings. We shall deal with this question more fully later in this chapter. Let us merely notice that a process of this kind is involved when we make our act of faith in the Christian tradition. It was St Cyprian of Carthage in the third century A.D. who first coined the word 'symbol' for a statement of faith or a creed. He spoke of 'baptizing with the same symbol', meaning that Christians everywhere made the same affirmation of faith as a condition of their baptism (Cyprian, *Epistle to Magnus on Baptizing the Novatians and those who obtain Grace on a Sick-Bed,* 7: Roberts and Donaldson 1868, VIII, pp. 307–308,). Baptism was a sign of faith – a putting together of the Christian and Christ, a participation in him and in his mystery, We, in turn, as Pope John Paul II stated, 'reveal Christ' in new, indeed unique circumstances.

It is important to remind ourselves, before ending this section, that the tradition in which the foundational revelation of Jesus Christ continues to live and which has been so carefully preserved and handed on since the time of the apostles, is not only a verbal tradition (whether it be oral or written). It is also a tradition of community structures and celebrations, and of collective and personal witness. The narrative memory of Jesus Christ is communicated effectively in both verbal and non-verbal forms.

> Do you not know that all of us who have been baptized into Christ Jesus were baptized into his death? We were buried therefore with him by baptism into death, so that as Christ was raised from the dead by the glory of the Father, we too might walk in newness of life (Romans 6:3–4).

> The cup of blessing which we bless, is it not a participation in the blood of Christ? The bread which we break, is it not a participation in the body of Christ? (1 Corinthians 10:16).

According to St Paul, the Christian is so closely united to Christ through baptism and the Eucharist that his personal life and suffering can be attributed to Christ himself.

> Now I rejoice in my sufferings for your sake, and in my flesh I complete what is lacking in Christ's afflictions for the sake of his body, that is, the church . . . (Colossians 1:24).

Not only did the liturgical practice of the early Christian communities influence the shape of the apostolic preaching itself, but the suffering and vindication of Christian martyrs was, as the Book of Revelation shows, visualized and described liturgically, and a close link developed between the celebration of the Eucharist and the tomb cults of the martyrs. *Lex orandi, lex credendi,* 'the rule of prayer is the rule of belief'. That is an ancient saying which is profoundly true of Christianity.

The signs of the times

Jesus chided his hearers because they failed to recognize the messianic climax of God's self-revelation in his own life and person. They could not interpret the signs of the times.

> You know how to interpret the appearance of the sky, but you cannot interpret the signs of the times (Matthew 16:3).

We, in our day, also have to recognize the signs of the times, the signs of the participant revelation. The Second Vatican Council's Pastoral Constitution on the Church in the Modern World recognizes this responsibility:

> At all times the Church carries the responsibility of reading the signs of the times and of interpreting them in the light of the Gospel, if it is to carry out its task. In language intelligible to every generation, she should be able to answer the ever-recurring questions which men ask about the meaning of this present life and of the life to come, and how one is related to the other. We must be aware of and understand the aspirations, the yearnings, and the often dramatic features of the world in which we live (*Gaudium et Spes,* 4).

The Council Fathers then proceed to give an outline of the signs of the times as they see them in the mid-twentieth century: a real but problematical social and cultural transformation; the creation of wealth for some, but the perpetuation of extreme poverty for others; the progress of technology and the human sciences, but, with it, a deep-seated spiritual and moral unease; rapid and far-reaching changes in social structure brought about by communications and by mobility and demography, but a basic dichotomy of power versus weakness, progress versus decline, freedom versus slavery. This dichotomy, argues the Council, stems from a deeper conflict within man himself.

One can, now at the end of the century, add to the Council's list: the growth of violence and systematic torture, the exhaustion of material resources and pollution of the environment, the maldevelopment of poor countries, the growth of sexual permissiveness, the collapse of moral and professional standards and the increase of industrial militancy. If it is objected that these are all negative signs, or signs of crisis, one can name other features which are positive: political independence and decolonization, improved conditions in industry, advances in medicine, the ideals and aspirations of modern youth, the movement for women's liberation, the conscientization of oppressed or disadvantaged peoples, the recognition of cultural values in the Third World, and – in the history of Christianity itself – the spread of charismatic renewal, the growth of ecumenism, and the liturgical renewal and the progress of active participation in worship.

The reader can probably add many more items to this list of features of life in the modern world. The question, however, is: How far are they signs of God revealing himself? Both positive and negative events, as the New Testament shows us, can reveal the lordship of God and the universal salvation brought by Christ. The situations and ideologies of the contemporary world oblige us to see Christ's concern for the poor and suffering, his insistence on moral conversion and his self-forgetting love in a new light. The experience of suffering is obviously a privileged sign, for Christ accepted suffering in order to end all suffering. Where we see suffering being relieved, injustices removed and the reign of peace, freedom and responsibility being established, we see God's lordship in Christ. Where we see a relativization of material wealth, of knowledge, of power, in favour of interior harmony, peace of heart and the prayerful acknowledgement of transcendent values, we witness the reign of God that Christ has brought.

Most of us can say that we have been privileged to meet at least one really holy person in our lives, and it is in people that God reveals himself, in lives that touch our own, but especially in the lives of people who become a sign to many. There are some outstanding examples in the contemporary world. One thinks of Mother Teresa of Calcutta and her Missionaries of Charity, helping the poorest of the poor to die like human beings, giving abandoned children a chance to live, and doing to others all that their love would prompt them to do for Christ. One thinks of Archbishop Oscar Romero of El Salvador, risking his life and even dying at the hands of an assassin, for the cause of social justice and human rights in Latin America. One thinks of the martyred priest Michael Kayoya, the victim of tribal hatred in Burundi, who wrote so movingly about the 'nobility' of death in the pattern of the death of Jesus Christ, and who sealed the truth of his poetry with his own blood.

These people and many others of deep spiritual sensibility, the religious *virtuosi* (as we called them in the first chapter), allow us to see how God's salvific power can shape a human life and make it a vehicle of his self-revelation.

THE BIBLE, BOOK OF THE CHURCH
Scripture and tradition

We have called the Old Testament (following Karl Rahner) the 'pre-history' of Christ. Gerald O'Collins has likened it to a mirror in which the apostles and early Christians saw reflected their own experience of God's self-revelation in Jesus Christ (O'Collins 1981, p. 219). The writings of the Old Testament were held in special veneration by them only because the events they recorded were regarded as inaugurating the event of Christ. In the second and third chapters of this book we attempted to give an account of God's self-revelation as seen through the writers of the Old Testament. The books of the New Testament are a definitive record of the apostolic preaching or proclamation of the Good News about Jesus Christ. In Chapter 4 we tried to give an account of the essential message of the New Testament.

The New Testament is a privileged record of what we have called 'foundational revelation', the self-revelation of God in Jesus Christ to those who 'saw' him. It is the apostolic preaching put into writing by the apostolic church, and it witnesses to the life of the communities which made up the church. As we have seen, it is already an interpretation, a response to the handing down of the Good News. The New Testament is therefore not to be equated with the foundational revelation itself. It is a privileged record and interpretation of that revelation, and as such it is revered as 'sacred' and as 'the Word of God'. The New Testament, together with the books of the Old Testament, was certainly 'the Book of the Apostolic Church'. In what sense is it the Book of the Post-Apostolic Church?

It is probably best to answer this question by beginning with the position of the sixteenth-century Protestant Reformers who saw the Church as the 'Church of the Book'. This conception of the Church came about because of the discovery and diffusion of early texts of the Bible in the original languages, because of the explosion of humanistic learning at the time and because of the invention of printing, which put more emphasis on the written word than ever before and was a powerful stimulus to literacy. Thus the Bible was made available in translation and became the principal reading material for the literate. According to the Reformers, the Biblical texts, which accurately express the saving truth of revelation, bring the presence of Jesus Christ to the believing Christian who reads and interprets them. No other authority is important, only Scripture (*sola Scriptura*).

The principle of 'only Scripture' did not in fact do justice to the ideals of the Reformers themselves and led to positions which many Protestants today have abandoned. The Bible itself does not claim the authority which the Reformers demanded on its behalf. Nor does it anywhere claim to contain the whole of divine revelation. On the contrary, John's Gospel says in a memorable passage:

> But there are also many other things which Jesus did; were every one of them to be written, I suppose that the world itself could not contain the books that would be written (John 21:25).

As we have seen in the last chapter, there are many doctrinal affirmations (including Christological and Trinitarian) which are not contained explicitly in the New Testament. There are also practices, such as infant baptism, which are not explicitly recorded. Yet the Protestant Reformers did not necessarily abandon these extra-Biblical affirmations and practices. However, the problem they set up went deeper than that. Earlier, we said that, when we confront our tradition, we both discover and create meaning. This applies as much to a written text as to an oral tradition, and it means that the Bible alone can never possess an all-inclusive meaning. It is bound to be interpreted differently by different individuals in different times and places. The authority must either be the guidance of the individual reader by the Holy Spirit, or else the deployment of human reason, not the Bible alone.

No one can deny that Protestant preoccupation with the Bible has led us to a much fuller understanding of the texts themselves and of their literary forms, but, as the study of the Bible intensified, insistence on the authority of the Bible alone led to a concentration on its literal meaning and to an erosion of faith in the living presence of Christ.

The Council of Trent condemned the doctrine of *sola Scriptura,* 'only Scripture', and spoke of unwritten, as well as written, traditions which contain the living truth of the Gospel (i.e. foundational revelation). This condemnation was unwarrantably made into the basis for a 'two source' theory of tradition which became widespread in the centuries after Trent, but which did not find its way into the Second Vatican Council's Dogmatic Constitution on Divine Revelation (*Dei Verbum*). At its crudest, the theory looked upon revelation as a collection of doctrinal propositions deriving from the apostles, some of which were to be found in Scripture and some of which were to be found in the unwritten tradition of the Church. On the face of things, it is unlikely that doctrines and practices should have come down to us from the apostles without being recorded in the New Testament or being the result of reflection upon, and interpretation of, the New Testament texts. It is to be expected, rather, that they should have come into existence through the interpretation and application of the Scriptures, especially in liturgical contexts.

After pointing out, with Trent, that our faith has one source, the Gospel, the Second Vatican Council did not define the material content of either Scripture or tradition, but stressed their close relationship.

> Sacred Tradition and Sacred Scripture make up a single sacred deposit of the Word of God, which is entrusted to the Church (*Dei Verbum,* 10).

The New Testament provides evidence for other aspects of the active process of handing on the Word of God, besides that of reading the Scriptures. There are, for example, the administration of the sacraments, preaching, missionary journeys and the witness of the lives of Christians. The Christian communities have the task of handing on the Word of God, and within these communities the apostles possess a special role as bearers of tradition. The post-apostolic Church desires to remain faithful to the privileged record of foundational revelation, but it also has the duty to do what Scripture cannot do by itself, namely, to interpret and apply it in new circumstances so that Jesus Christ reveals himself to subsequent generations. Thus Scripture is a part of the heritage which is handed on, and, in the words of the Second Vatican Council:

> By this [written] Word [sacred theology] is most firmly strengthened and constant-
> ly rejuvenated, as it searches out, under the light of faith, the full truth stored up in
> the mystery of Christ (Dei Verbum, 24).

In the final analysis, the object of the handing-on process is God's self-giving in Jesus Christ, not a quantitative collection of propositions about him (though doctrinal affirmations are, of course, necessary). This is not only the teaching of the Council but it is also the conclusion of the 1963 Faith and Order Conference in Montreal, which illustrates the progress of thought in the Reformed Churches. It means, as Dei Verbum does not fail to point out, that Christ's Spirit guarantees the Church's essential fidelity to the originating experience of God's self-revelation in Christ.

> And the Holy Spirit, through whom the living voice of the Gospel rings out in the
> Church – and through her in the world – leads believers to the full truth, and makes
> the Word of Christ dwell in them in all its richness (Dei Verbum, 8).

How this guarantee operates through the bearers of tradition will be discussed later in this chapter.

The inspiration and truth of Scripture

The term 'inspiration' has been traditionally applied by Christians to the privileged character of the Bible as a record of God's self-revelation which reached its climax in Jesus Christ. The term does not refer directly to that self-revelation, but rather to the Bible as its record. As such, the Scriptures are intimately linked with the mystery of the Word made flesh and with the salvation which he brings to humankind. The books of the Bible were written under the inspiration of the Holy Spirit and they can be truly said (as the Second Vatican Council, echoing earlier papal and conciliar statements, in fact says) to have God as 'their author' (Dei Verbum, 11).

According to Karl Rahner, inspiration belongs to the special divine activity which led to the foundation of the Church with all the various elements, including the Bible, which constitute its total reality (Rahner 1978, pp. 369ff.). The divine authorship of the Bible was part of the providential activity which fashioned the Church as an instrument of communion with God in Christ and of unity in him among all men. It is not merely because the Church recognizes itself in these writings that they are termed 'inspired' but because they had a role in God's providential plan for the Church and because in his providence he employed human authors for this purpose. The human authors wrote in human fashion, using to the full their human faculties, but they wrote for their community and as members of their community. It is of course true that non-Biblical authors may have a providential role to play in God's plan and that their activity of writing may be said to be directed by the Holy Spirit. However, we reserve the term 'inspiration' for the charism exercised by the Biblical authors alone, precisely because their writing was a part of the process of bringing the Church into being and this process did not extend beyond the apostolic age. It was the unique, originating experience of the early Christian communities.

This understanding of the function of inspiration is borne out when we consider the way in which the canon of Scripture was formed, that is to say, the way in which the books of the Bible were selected and judged to be inspired, sacred and 'the Word of God'. In apostolic and sub-apostolic times there was a varied literature in circulation. Some of it played up to public curiosity and tended to deform the message, giving rise to various deviations in faith and practice. Other texts, however, were read during liturgical celebrations. This liturgical reading was one element in the process of fashioning the Christian identity, and the community recognized itself in the content and selection of the writings they deemed to be truly apostolic. Widespread and lengthy liturgical use was the criterion for canonicity. Originally, as Edward Schillebeeckx points out, New Testament books were venerated because they were deemed authoritative in themselves. Ultimately, however, a selection had to be made from the growing literature, and the authority of the institutional Church had to step in to guarantee the inspired character of the books that were selected. Could another inspired New Testament book still be discovered and acknowledged as part of the canon of Scripture? Gerald O'Collins admits the possibility of finding, say, a lost letter of St Paul in an archaeological excavation (O'Collins 1981, p. 246). However, it could only be admitted by the Church to the canon if it were in harmony with the total message of the New Testament and if it were vindicated in liturgical usage.

Factual errors and inconsistencies and even moral and religious errors abound in the Bible. How, then, can we uphold its truth? The Second Vatican Council, following Pope Pius XII (in *Divino Afflante Spiritu*, 1943), exhorts us to pay attention to the variety of literary forms found in the Bible and to the intentions, contemporary presuppositions and modes of expression of the authors of the sacred books. These authors obviously had their own limitations. They wrote poetry, mythicized history, fictional folk-tales, prayers, apocalyptic and so forth. When these forms and limitations are taken into account, many of the difficulties disappear. It is particularly the Western mind, with its scientific prejudice, which does violence to the Bible in expecting it to yield a set of infallibly true propositions. Conservative Evangelicals, or Fundamentalists, also do violence to the texts by their anxiety to iron out all internal contradictions and inconsistencies. They do not, as is often said, hold to a naïve, literal truth of the Bible, but are ready to import all kinds of accommodated meanings in order to make the Scriptures appear consistent.

The authors of the Biblical books recorded, in their human fashion, the experience of divine revelation and divine salvation, as it occurred in the events of their time, in the lives and actions of their contemporaries – good or bad – and in their experience of prayer, reflection and expectation of the future. The human experience in which this revelation occurred was multiple and diverse, positive and negative. All of it, however, served God's saving truth, and that truth was ultimately revealed by and in Jesus Christ (cf. *Dei Verbum,* 11). Biblical truth is found in the person of the Word made flesh. He is the truth and everyone who 'is of the Truth' hears his voice (John 18–37). In many passages of the Old Testament the full truth is obscured or only partially glimpsed. In the end 'the truth is in Jesus' (Ephesians 4–21), and we must not close our eyes to the moral errors and imperfections which the Old Testament contains. Jesus is their judge. A well-known Catholic exegete has remarked that God tolerated much human error in the Old Testament in order to get a little bit of divine truth through.[1]

Interpreting Scripture

From time to time one reads or hears about eminent Scripture scholars and exegetes who have lost their Christian faith and who propound rationalist or reductionist explanations of the texts they study. This is indeed an occupational hazard of those who are concerned with the literal meaning of the Bible. We have already noted that the study of the actual meaning intended by the human author is indispensable. But this literal meaning does not, by any means, exhaust the whole meaning of the Bible. If one believes in inspiration, then one believes that God providentially saw to the writing of these books in view of the founding of the Church, and that the human authors wrote for, and on behalf of, the Christian community. The scientific exegete may be under conscious or unconscious pressure from fellow academics whose outlook, within their own disciplines, is positivist, and he may be tempted to 'demythologize', either in the sense of trying to discount the mythological content of Scripture, or of expressing it in rational, propositional form. Both these approaches are destructive of Biblical meaning and truth.

As we have already seen, the literary forms of the Bible must be respected. The symbolic form of writing expresses the participatory character of reality, and brings us into contact with the more profound levels of experience which cannot be expressed in a rational or propositional paraphrase. The critical exegesis of the texts, involving the analysis of language, style and historical context, is nevertheless necessary if we are to rediscover the symbolic dimension of the Bible, and therefore its originally intended meaning. A large part of humanity has been educated to believe that the only facts are scientific facts, empirically verifiable by the senses. Without scientific techniques of exegesis, they would be faced with the alternative of accepting the Biblical accounts as literally and scientifically true in every detail, or of rejecting them altogether. As Edmund Hill pointed out some years ago, critical exegesis helps us to 'remythologize' ourselves and to get on to the mythological 'wavelength' of the Bible (Hill 1964, pp. 65–75). It should not lead to a minimalism which amounts to a distortion of the original meaning. We must pass through a critical 'phase' in order, as Edward Schillebeeckx puts it, to recover our 'narrative innocence' (Schillebeeckx 1979, p. 79).

Besides the original meaning intended by the human authors, there is also the meaning discovered and created by the reader of the Bible in every age and place. Nietzsche once wrote that, because of what he felt was its lack of humanism, he was compelled to wear gloves when handling the New Testament (Nietzsche 1901, pp. 18–19). He did not, of course, approach the New Testament in a spirit of faith, but the New Testament *should* be handled carefully, indeed, it should be handled in a spirit of great reverence, seeing that it, and the books of the Old Testament also, have provided the divine stimulus for so much prayer and reflection throughout the ages. Scripture enters into a dialogue with the reader, answers his questions and helps him to understand himself – makes an exegesis of *him,* as it were. Scripture puts him before a choice or a decision. Just as Jesus was accepted or rejected in his own lifetime, so also his word in Scripture is accepted or rejected. But it should not be accepted or rejected without taking account of the objective meaning intended by the author. Otherwise, like Nietzsche perhaps, we impose a purely subjective view upon it. Our own lives and problems are illuminated by Scripture, but they are not the key to its understanding. Scripture has an autonomy of its own, intended by God.

Finally, there is the potential meaning of the text itself and this, as Gerald O'Collins rightly insists, is not peculiar to the Bible only (O'Collins 1981, pp. 254–257). Every text acquires further ranges of meaning not foreseen by the human author, but which are consonant with the original meaning. All literature possesses this openness to potential meaning. This outreach of the

Bible towards the future corresponds to God's providential plan for humankind. Scripture offers us its own authentic meaning if we read the whole text in its original context, if we allow it to become a living word that is relevant to our own lives, if we bear in mind that it is part of the total tradition of the Church (and not separate from, let alone opposed to, it), and if we read it Christologically, that is, remembering that all pages of the Bible, Old Testament and New, lead us to the person of Jesus Christ.

PROCLAIMING THE WORD OF GOD

The function and meaning of faith-statements

> Hearing the Word of God with reverence, and proclaiming it with faith, the sacred Synod assents to the words of St John, who says: 'We proclaim to you the eternal life which was with the Father and was made manifest to us – that which we have seen and heard we proclaim also to you, so that you may have fellowship with us; and our fellowship is with the Father and with his Son Jesus Christ' (*Dei Verbum*, 1, quoting 1 John 1:2–3).

With these words the Fathers of the Second Vatican Council opened their Dogmatic Constitution on Divine Revelation. They stress the point that the Christian fellowship has the duty of hearing God's Word and then of proclaiming it with faith. The Church is first of all a 'Listening Church' before it becomes a 'Proclaiming' or a 'Teaching Church'. It has the twofold duty of listening to the Word of God, as it has been safeguarded and faithfully transmitted from the time of the apostles, and also of recognizing the signs of the times, a duty which is demanded by the task of making a relevant proclamation to the contemporary world.

The listening and proclaiming process was already at work before the era of the apostolic preaching was closed. Already the Christian communities were struggling to grasp and to express in word and ritual and way of life what they had seen and heard of Jesus. As the books of the New Testament show, the early Christians made affirmations of faith, statements about what they believed. They said what they believed about the presence of the risen Christ among them, and about their relationship to him and to one another in him. The apostolic preaching continued in the form of the readings of New Testament books in the Christian liturgical assemblies, and – as was necessary – the Christian community continued to interpret and apply what it read to new situations and to new questions. New and successive affirmations of faith were made. As we pointed out in the first chapter, a religious interpretation of reality requires the authority of a community, a community which is the guardian of the collective memory or tradition. How that authority operates will be the subject of the next section.

We have seen that the Trinitarian and Christological implications of the

Christ-event were not fully worked out in the lifetime of the apostles. It was left to Church Councils, such as those of Nicaea in the fourth century or Chalcedon in the fifth, to make further affirmations of Christian faith. Throughout its history, the Church has made many such faith-statements on different aspects of the Word of God which it has received and which it believes it faithfully transmits. Why does it do this? In the first place such statements are a 'confession', that is to say, they affirm before God a partic-ular truth which can be communicated as information. They affirm that Christ is 'consubstantial' to the Father (Nicaea) or that he is 'complete in Godhead and complete in manhood' (Chalcedon).

In the second place, these confessions imply a subjective commitment. They are not merely a definition of truth in itself, but of truth for us in particular, leading to a specific practice or way of life. Thus the creeds which enshrine such faith-statements were inserted into the liturgy and became symbols of allegiance, helping to insert the believer into the community and into Christ. They were not mere intellectual explanations, but participatory symbols of faith. Thus there was an interaction between affirmations of faith and liturgical practice. Of course it was not only creeds which enshrined and enforced these faith-statements, but also the formulas of worship and the liturgical preaching which expounded the Scriptures to the faithful. In many cases, the commitment aspect of a faith-statement is stronger than the confession aspect. Gerald O'Collins cites the Council of Trent's teaching about the sacraments of baptism, confirmation and Orders conferring an 'indelible sign' on the soul, as being directed towards the affirmation of the unrepeatability of these sacraments, rather than towards an exhaustive explanation of the sacramental character (O'Collins 1981, p. 163).

Faith-statements attempt to make sense of reality and they also seek to make others react in the right way to the saving truth which they proclaim. Although we should not ignore the cognitive aspects of such statements, we should also note that they have a function of encouraging, warning, agreeing, denying, reminding, reprimanding, replying and so forth, which shape attitudes and actions in the community.

The meaning of faith-statements cannot, of course, be reduced to the motives or causes which produced them and still less to their actual con-sequences. But we do need to understand them in the light of their historical contexts and of the general linguistic usage of the time. The framers of these statements would not have intended some esoteric meaning, unrelated to general conventions, unless they had given some clear indication of this intention. In fact, even the infallible statements of Popes and Councils do not contain an infallibly guaranteed account of their meaning. If they did, they would, as Gerald O'Collins remarks, require an endless series of infall-ible guarantees (O'Collins 1981, p. 170). A statement can only be under-stood in the light of historical, conventional meanings.

Many faith-statements are a compromise formula worked out by a committee, a formula which possesses a plurality of original meanings, with some members giving a statement the strongest possible meaning, and others a much weaker emphasis. Even so, we cannot reduce a shared statement of this kind to one or another extreme of original interpretation. We must always look for the degree of shared meaning which exists in them, and this shared meaning was at least partly determined at the time the statement was made.

What do the historic faith-statements mean to us now? Inevitably, because of the 'slippery' character of language and the shifts that take place in the meaning of words over space and time, the meaning of a historic faith-statement may be eroded and need to be reformulated. Inevitably also, our own need to create meaning by asking new questions in new circumstances leads to these faith-statements acquiring surplus meanings not foreseen by their human authors. However, we see these affirmations, even in their provisional character, as linking us with the climactic event of God's self-communication in Jesus Christ, and also as pointing forward to a more complete fulfilment at the end of time. Thus, they are truly symbols – a reconciling, a putting together. This means that the faith-statements have a value for us. They can never be interpreted in such a way as to be meaningless for us. Nor can we give them a meaning which conflicts with the degree of shared original meaning intended by the authors. Moreover, we discover their truth by our own confession (orthodoxy) and our own commitment (orthopraxis).

The living teaching authority in the Church

Immediately after the resurrection of Jesus we find in the New Testament that a body of men known as 'the Twelve', or 'apostles', in the strict sense, held authority in the Christian community, as 'witness[es] to the resurrection' (Acts 1:22). Some people have claimed that the college of the 'Twelve' has been retrojected into the life of Jesus by the evangelists. Birger Gerhardsson finds this claim singularly unconvincing, given the somewhat unfavourable picture of the apostles before the death of Jesus and the great authority they exercised after the resurrection (Gerhardsson 1979, pp. 61–65). The facts are better explained by the continuity which the New Testament asserts, As we have seen, the New Testament is venerated as enshrining the apostolic preaching in written form, and the Christian Church can only claim to be in touch with the foundational self-revelation of God in Jesus Christ if it is also apostolic. Apostolic continuity is therefore essential for Christian identity.

The whole Christian community has the responsibility of handing on the tradition, the Good News of Jesus Christ, the Word of God. However, in the apostolic Church a special responsibility was carried by the apostles themselves as witnesses to the Resurrection and bearers of the tradition. The Church today recognizes the bishops as the successors to the apostles. They are not, as Gerald O'Collins rightly says, successors *of* the apostles, but successors *to* them (O'Collins 1981, p. 89). In other words, they do not inherit all the functions of the apostles. They are not, for example, eye-witnesses of the resurrection, nor are they the founders of the Church, but they are true successors to the apostles as bearers and guarantors of the tradition. They are servants of the Word and of the community. The bishops, then, are constituted as an authority in the Church by their office, and, because emphasis has been placed on the character of their authority as a teaching authority, the academic term *magisterium* has been applied to them. Although this authority does not derive from personal qualities, it should not on the other hand be thought of as purely technical and verbal. 'Actions speak louder than words' and bishops teach through their actions and life-witness as much as, if not more than, through their teaching. This is especially true of the Pope who continues the ministry of Peter, the chief apostle, and whose public actions and pastoral journeys to various countries in the world are symbols, carrying extensive meaning.

The bishops are thus 'participant apostles' and in their statements of faith (as opposed to their teaching on practical issues, which does not derive directly from God's self-communication in Christ) they are subordinate to God's Word and to the truth revealed by that Word.

> Yet this Magisterium is not superior to the Word of God, but is its servant. It teaches only what has been handed on to it. At the divine command, and with the help of the Holy Spirit, it listens to this devotedly, guards it with dedication and expounds it faithfully. All that it proposes for belief as being divinely revealed is drawn from this single deposit of faith (*Dei Verbum,* 10).

We have seen that authority to proclaim and interpret the Word of God is given by the Holy Spirit to the community of believers, and the Spirit guarantees their essential fidelity to the original self-communication of God in Christ. John Henry Newman held that there could be no revelation without authority (Coulson 1981, pp. 75–78), and in the end the truth of Christian revelation rests on the authority of Jesus Christ himself, 'who taught them as one who had authority, and not as the scribes' (Mark 1:22). History shows again and again that no authority can coerce human beings to believe things of which they are not convinced. Authority is respected in matters of faith because it has the ring of truth, and the truth imposes itself. It convinces, but does not coerce people. Authority is credible because it inspires trust, and authorities are (as Newman saw them) God's messengers whom we trust (quoted in Coulson 1981, p. 76).

We trust the *magisterium* because it participates in the authority of the apostles, commissioned by Jesus to whom all authority was given in heaven and on earth. The *magisterium* is conscious of possessing a charism of infallibility to ensure that the Church cannot be misled in matters of revealed truth. As defined by the First Vatican Council, it is a rudimentary safeguard, the exercise of which is severely limited. 'Infallibility' is a word which has an uncomfortable ring about it in the English language. It suggests a certain smugness, the attitude of a 'Mr Know-All', rather than humility and deference to the truth. Some prefer the term 'indefectibility'. But whatever term one uses, the reality is that those who possess the charism cannot in their explicit teaching ultimately mislead the Church. They are in the service of the Truth, and the Truth in turn protects them when they express in an authoritative way the faith which all Christians profess.

It follows that absolute assent of mind, heart and will is required when the charism is being exercised. There are three occasions of its exercise. Two belong to what is called the 'extraordinary *magisterium*': solemn definitions by the Pope, speaking *ex cathedra* (from his 'chair' of authority), and solemn definitions by General Councils of the Church (all the bishops with the Pope in Council). The third occasion is when the Pope and all the bishops, dispersed throughout the world, agree in the exercise of their ordinary *magisterium* (or teaching authority) that a certain teaching is to be held definitively as revealed truth. Such a teaching is a 'non-defined dogma', but it belongs materially to the Catholic faith. An example cited by Gerald O'Collins is the teaching that Jesus Christ is the universal Redeemer (O'Collins 1981, p. 188). This has never been defined solemnly by the extraordinary *magisterium*, but it is taken for granted that one could not be a true follower of Christ, if one did not believe it absolutely. It follows, therefore, that the solemn definitions of Popes and Councils (usually on disputed points) are not a guide to the whole deposit of revealed truth. It also follows, now that the Church has explicitly adverted to the charism, that when Popes and Councils speak without invoking their charism of infallibility (and if they do, they must do it 'manifestly', as the First Vatican Council and the Code of Canon Law require), then the charism is not exercised. This was the case, for example, with the Second Vatican Council, which deliberately ruled out from the start any new definitions of revealed truth. Moreover, it follows that the teaching of General Councils which do not invoke the charism, the teaching of Pope and bishops dispersed throughout the world which does not express agreement on whether a certain truth is to be definitively held as revealed, and the ordinary teaching of Popes, episcopal synods and conferences, and of individual bishops in their dioceses, demand religious assent, a minimum of loyalty, obedience and external conformity, rather than the absolute assent of faith.

If authority is to be trusted, it must inspire trust, otherwise it undermines its own credibility. Bishops participate in the authority bequeathed by

Christ to his apostles, and it is obviously a very serious fault in them if they undermine that authority by words and actions which diminish credibility. Part of the problem may stem from the projection of an image of the bishop as a divine oracle, when – in fact – he is but human. 'Even bishops can be fools' remarked the saintly Father Vincent McNabb when shown a photograph of Catholic Bishops giving the Nazi salute. Bishops have to be 'watchdogs' over the deposit of faith, and, as such, they must 'growl' and 'bark', but as Cardinal Newman once wrote, 'the watchdog sometimes flies at the wrong person' (Newman 1961, p. 61). That this can happen must be generally admitted. Bishops are not divinely inspired oracles, they are mere human beings, who, by the grace of God, participate in the apostolic authority. The Second Vatican Council had this advice for the laity:

> . . . let them realize that their pastors will not always be so expert as to have a ready
> answer to every problem (even every grave problem) that arises (*Gaudium et Spes*,
> 43).

When, therefore, the *magisterium* in its ordinary and extraordinary capacities sets forth its teaching, it should do so in such a way that it can be intelligently understood by ordinary people and not wrapped up in difficult and esoteric language. It must express and be seen to express the common faith of the Church and it must be drawn from, and be related to, the lived experience of the Christians to which it is addressed. Appeal should be made to both words and actions in the example offered by the authorities themselves, and it must be freely admitted if they have not, in all respects, lived up to their own teaching. Appeals can and should be made to loyalty, while recognizing that loyalty alone is not the criterion of Gospel truth. It is never enough merely to appeal to authority *as* authority. Only the Word made Flesh could do that.

The role of the laity in matters of faith

The Second Vatican Council spoke of the 'intimate sense of spiritual realities which [believers] experience' (*Dei Verbum*, 8), and it did so in the context of the active guidance of the Church by the Holy Spirit. The consensus of believers is a channel of tradition and, in the words of Gregory of Valence, 'a judgement or sentiment of the infallible Church' (quoted in Newman 1961, p. 67). The consensus of believers (therefore, of pastors and laity) is distinct, though not separate, from the Church's teaching authority. The question which John Henry Newman asked is whether the belief of the laity has any importance in the formulation and handing-on of the Church's teaching, whether the teaching authority is alone sufficient, or whether there is something more in the *conspiratio* or unanimous consensus of pastors *and* laity (Newman 1961, pp. 25, 104).

Of course, the teaching authority would lose its reason for existence if there were nobody to learn! And the reception of the teaching by the laity closes the cycle, as it were, or 'sets the seal' upon the process. On the other hand, the way in which the teaching is received by the Church at large inevitably influences the progress of the tradition itself. The people are a 'mirror' or a 'reflection' of the pastors' teaching, and, as Newman cannily observed, a man may consult his mirror and learn new things about himself from the reflection he sees there (Newman 1961, p. 72). The Second Vatican Council spoke of 'an intimate sense of spiritual realities' (*Dei Verbum*, 8). Newman called it a 'sort of instinct' and referred also to the laity's instinctive feeling of scandal when they encounter error. Newman pointed to the way in which, during the fourth century A.D., Arianism reigned supreme, and it was mainly the orthodoxy of the laity that kept the Nicene faith alive. The laity, therefore, have their own specific testimony to give in matters of faith. Newman would go further. Using his concept of the 'illative sense' or the power to activate or make real the notions contained in the teaching, he is prepared to call the consensus of believers 'the communal conscience of the whole Church'. What is believed and practised by the faithful helps us to discern the truth of what is taught (Newman 1961, pp. 23, 73, 77).

We live today in a Church in which greater emphasis is placed on the witness given by small groups or basic communities than in the past. We also see Roman Catholics expressing their one faith in very diverse cultural forms. What becomes of the consensus of believers under these circumstances? It may well be that one group or one cultural form of Christianity is guilty of error or distortion. But it may also be, as Gerald O'Collins notes, 'a prophetical minority' with a valid message for the Church (O'Collins 1981, p. 216). There are two basic tests to see if it is the work of the Holy Spirit or no. One is to judge it by its fruits. Does it contribute to the unity of heart and mind which should reign in the Church universal, or does it create division and enmity? Another test is to see also how far it depends upon relationships, how far it is intercultural or intersubjective, how far it echoes the sentiments of Christians in past ages and places and how far it exhibits an opening on the future. Above all, how far it is part of the tradition that goes back to the apostles, the continuity which is expressed in Scripture, the Creeds, the *magisterium*, and ultimately the risen Christ himself. In the end, the only criterion of our being in touch with God's completed and perfect self-revelation is Christological, our fidelity to the person and the mind of Christ.

THEOLOGY AND DOGMATIC DEVELOPMENT

The nature and function of theology

From the moment that the followers of Jesus of Nazareth tried to grasp and to express the reality that he was for them, theology was born. Gustavo Gutiérrez, the Peruvian theologian, has written: 'Theology is reflection, a critical attitude, theology *follows*' (Gutiérrez 1973, p. 11). Theology follows faith, experience, praxis. It speculates. It asks questions. It clarifies and it draws conclusions. Above all, it paves the way for more explicit affirmations of faith, for doctrinal or faith-statements. Such affirmations do not drop from heaven. Without theological activity, the *magisterium* could not make its pronouncements and definitions, nor could these statements receive further interpretation and application. Theology is essentially transitory and superficial, serving the final self-revelation of God in Jesus Christ. As a system, there can be no literally 'perennial' theology, because it is successive by nature. As a process of questioning and comprehending, theology never has an end in this life. Theology is for people. It exists to throw light on the object of their faith and to strengthen their union with God, but clarity is not a substitute for certainty, and theology is not a substitute for faith. Freedom of theological enquiry and of theological expression safeguards the faith, for it means that no one fixed set of ideas has the monopoly of explanation. There is a kind of Catholic 'fundamentalism' which would like to reduce all theology to a question of authority and obedience, and which mistakes uniformity of theology for unity of faith. To lock up theology in this way would be a threat to a living and committed Christian faith and widen still more the gulf that separates the Gospel and human cultures – a gulf deplored by the Second Vatican Council (*Gaudium et Spes*, pp. 66–67) and by Pope Paul VI (*Evangelii Nuntiandi*, 20).

Doing theology involves the activity of speculation, and there are different kinds of speculation available to theology. Speculation consists basically in putting experience into a wider or further context, and so obtaining a further depth of clarity and meaning. Employing the distiction regularly made by Newman, following Coleridge, we may speak of first- and second-order language. First-order language is imaginative, not in the sense of being the product of feelings and emotions only, but in the sense of a real apprehension of experience, the images of which strike the mind, engage human affectivity and stimulate action and commitment. First-order language uses images, symbols, parables. It is sensitive to history and to narrative, and it can even 'speak' non-verbally through art forms and ritual action, broadening the human understanding of experience thereby. As we saw in the second chapter of this book, symbolic or mythological expression is in direct contact with reality through a total psychic experience.

Second-order language also tries to express a human understanding of reality, but it does so through discovering and/or imposing a mental pattern on reality which does not spring from immediate experience. It also makes use of images, but it employs them as analogies, not as symbols. Philosophy and science, which use a second-order language, deal in concepts or notions which are inferences or abstractions from reality. They speak of 'matter' and 'form', or of magnetic 'fields', sound 'waves' or atomic 'particles', but these are figures of speech which refer to mental objects. They are analytical statements which strive to define correctly an aspect of reality and they enable human beings to experiment and to construct according to an accepted model, paradigm or disciplinary matrix. In the end, however, it is difficult to draw a hard-and-fast line between the two orders of language, because philosophy and science are nourished by the imagination at their most critical and creative moments. This happens, as Thomas Kuhn describes, when scientific theories or paradigms break down under the weight of growing anomalies, and men of science cast around for inspiration to consult new models. It is then that imaginative insights are gained and real 'discoveries' made (Kuhn 1970). Thus, in the end, second-order language reposes on first-order.

Metaphysical philosophy strains language as far as it will go in order to present an organized body of knowledge about what is ultimate in reality. The clarity of explanation which its method promises is attractive, and, at least since the time of Origen in the second century, theologians in European and Mediterranean countries have turned to successive philosophical systems, not only in order to cultivate their powers of coherent and systematic reasoning, but also to adopt the conceptual language they use and to answer the questions they pose. No doubt this collaboration over the centuries has been fruitful in eliciting what Bishop Butler has called 'a hard currency theology', with a reasoned explanation of revealed truth which is rationally more or less impregnable, but there are also inherent dangers which have not always been overcome, and a philosophical theology poses peculiar problems today for the expansion of the Church into the Third World.

Quite apart from the danger of an assimilation of theology to philosophy, so that theologians are performing tasks set by philosophers, there is the graver danger that theology may fail in its fundamental purpose of bringing about a union of people with God. If theology uses second-order language exclusively, it tends to become static. It does not know what to do with history or the Christian narrative memory, and it cannot address the symbolic 'first-order world' of the ordinary people and their lived experience of faith. This point is made by Johann Baptist Metz. Speaking of the need for a new kind of theology, he writes:

> The critical interest of this theology, however, must be governed by the conviction that the symbols, stories and collective memories of the people in the Church are absolutely necessary to any theology that wishes to avoid losing all foundation. Its critical attitude, in other words, should not lead to direct criticism of the symbolic world of the people. It ought, on the contrary, to lead to making people more and more the subject of their own symbolic world . . . . In order to achieve this, theology must assess the language of narrative differently . . . . This concern is in no way an expression of a theological movement back to a pre-critical attitude (Metz 1980, p. 150).

More basic than the explanatory propositions of philosophical theology are the images and symbols from which they are derived, and which participate in the experience of God's self-revelation in the history of Jesus Christ. This point is made forcefully by the African theologian Bishop Tarcisse Tshibangu:

> The danger for theology is not illusory, if we consider it as a deductive type of discipline, of forgetting that its object is real and personal, and of confining ourselves to the doctrinal and conceptual aspect . . . .
> This revealed object, which is real and personal, is given to us in a human language which uses words and formulas in the form of images and metaphors. The Bible is full of imagery. In the Old Testament doctrine is revealed through imaginative accounts; the prophets teach and transmit the divine message through parabolic language and by presenting symbolic acts and gestures. The revelation of the New Testament is also given to us in large measure through the form of images and symbols. Christ gave his teaching in parables. One has only to think of such expressions as 'Kingdom of God', 'Lamb of God', 'vine', 'body', building'. In their turn, the Fathers of the Church used images and symbols abundantly, in catechesis and liturgy, in order to represent the mysteries of salvation. Given the necessarily partial and more or less abstract character of a conceptual expression of reality, we must see in this mode of teaching a veritable pedagogical intention on the part of God. The imaginative form has the advantage of preserving all the inexhaustible richness of revelation; moreover, it brings home to believers and to theologians the fact that, whatever intellectual instrument they employ, they will never succeed in apprehending revelation adequately or in comprehending it exhaustively (Tshibangu 1980, pp. 163–164; my tr.).

Bishop Tshibangu here echoes an argument put forward already some years ago by Claude Tresmontant, that Christianity possesses its own speculative language and structure, one that is proper to it and which is in the line of Biblical, Hebraic thinking (Tresmontant 1956 and 1962). At the centre of this thinking is the theory of participation, whereby the particular manifests universal truth through its creation by God. Sensory realities are both 'being' and 'sign' at the same time, 'existing words'. All reality possesses 'an immanent signification'. Tresmontant called this 'the metaphysics of sensory reality' (Tresmontant 1956, pp. 64ff.) and the phrase recalls Lévi-Strauss's description of the mode of thought current in pre-literate societies as 'the science of the concrete' (Lévi-Strauss 1966, pp. 1–33). Other writers, such as Thorlief Boman, have underlined the dynamic and functional character of Hebrew thought, as opposed to the static, pictorial thinking of the Hellenic world (Boman 1960). Even when Biblical writers go in for descriptions, they are not really interested in appearances. Thus the 'pictures' of the Ark of Noah or of Solomon's Temple are really blueprints for their construction; while the 'picture' of the beloved bride in the Song of Songs is symbolic and not representational, with its images of unconquered innocence and bodily fruitfulness.

Apart from the possibility of cutting itself loose from its symbolic, Biblical foundations, a philosophical theology also cuts itself off from the world of the poet, the novelist, the dramatist, the artist and the musician. John Coulson has recently drawn attention to the great 'divide' that separates theology in our time from contemporary art and literature. Although Christianity claims to set people free, many artists and writers share the suspicion of Wole Soyinka, the African playwright, that the creative imagination is shackled or 'congealed' by the rigid, metaphysical orthodoxy of the Church. Soyinka's complaint is not unlike that of the Jesuit poet Gerard Manley Hopkins, that theological 'equations' and 'the dull algebra of the schoolmen' cannot create an 'ecstasy of interest' in the human mind. In the same line of thought, another Jesuit, Charles-André Bernard, has demonstrated how philosophical theology has cut itself off from liturgical experience and from the branch of theology which is closely related to it, that of spiritual, mystical or ascetical theology which employs symbolic language by preference (Bernard 1980).

At various times, in an effort to avoid some of the dangers just referred to, the misguided expedient has been proposed of recognizing two 'strata' of theology: a 'kerygmatic' theology of the schools and seminaries, geared to pedagogy and preaching and, therefore, to the first-order requirements of ordinary Christians, and a 'research' theology of the universities which is more inductive and more scientific. Michael Schmauss was right to reject this idea of a double theology which threatens to cut the discipline from its roots still more drastically (Latourelle 1966, p. 222; Schmauss 1968, pp. 263–285). Theology must always be faithful to its object, which is the saving Word experienced in the life of Christians. Obviously, there must be research at university level, and there is a difference between the fruit of research and research itself. The theologian, however, even though he may belong to the class of those who have leisure enough for reflection, must not inhabit an ivory tower, but must have the faith of Christians in view as his starting and finishing points. One respects the attempts of theologians such as Karl Rahner and Edward Schillebeeckx to popularize their theology and to speak down to ordinary Christians.

The Indian theologian Raimundo Panikkar has drawn attention to another defect in traditional theology. Theological language of a high level of abstraction in the Western philosophical tradition has a discriminatory and an oppressive character in a world where Western domination, both technological and cultural, is increasingly resented:

> The moment that words say only exactly what you mean and do not leave room for what I may also mean, the moment that they become only signs and cease to be symbols, the moment that they only signal something else and are no longer the expression, the manifestation and, with it, the veil itself of that 'else', in that moment they degenerate even as words. They become mere tools for transmission of coded messages, open only to those who previously possess the clue. Words may then very easily become means of oppression, tools of power in the mouths or hands of those who dictate their meaning or know the key to decipher the signs. You can neither interpret nor understand those signs; they are only orders or warnings for your orientation, but neither part of you, nor revelations of reality. You can neither play nor pray, let alone be, with those signs. You cannot truly speak those words, but only respect them, aping those who impose such a power on you . . . .
>
> Real words are not mere instruments in your hands or mine, they are part of the human, cosmic and also divine interplay, and they mean what we agree that they mean in the very act of the dialogical interchange, otherwise, they are no longer living words; they are dead (Panikkar 1973, pp. ix–x).

Bishop Tshibangu makes a similar point for African, as well as Asian, theologians:

> One fact is however certain. Priests and Christians of Africa and Asia, even when they succeed in assimilating scholastic philosophy and theology, experience their limits and express their dissatisfaction. On the other hand, the depth of their conviction that they have to 'create' and 'invent' in this domain also raises hopes which cannot be prejudged today (Tshibangu 1980, p. 194).

John Mbiti is an Anglican theologian from Africa who discovered that Christian eschatological symbolism was taken literally by an ethnic group in Kenya, because there was no perception of its meaning at the conceptual level. To achieve this one would not only have to overcome Western theological inhibitions, but also take the African symbol-system itself very seriously. It is interesting that Mbiti envisages a breakthrough only at the liturgical level (Mbiti 1971, p. 183). This point was also made recently by Robert White, a communications specialist:

> All 'communication' has become a form of manipulation. In this context, perhaps the only way to restore trust and real human sharing is through the religious rituals of community in the family, the ecclesial gathering and the nation. The language of these rituals is the *symbol* which functions at the affective level and disarms rationality and manipulation (White 1980, p. 5).

In the final chapter of this book we shall consider the question of intercultural adaptation in the Church and of the pluralism of theological formulations. The fundamental reason for this pluralism was stated in Chapter 1. It is that the universalism of Christianity demands a basic interculturality and interpenetration, a unity in diversity. We must expect to find new, contextual theologies springing up in different corners of the globe, interacting with and challenging the traditional theology of the North Atlantic area. Having no philosophical tradition, indeed, having no predilection for philosophy of a Western kind, but being preoccupied rather with questions of social practice and concrete human circumstances, it is inevitable that Third World theologians should be impatient of merely theoretical reformulations, and should desire to revolutionize the often unjust conditions in which they live their Christian faith. Such theologians seek to know how this faith can be upheld in a world where racism and oppression flourish. This is the interest of Black theology and Latin American liberation theology, for example. Once again, it is ultimately prayer which stimulates hope and commitment, but this language of prayer must not be couched in racist terminology, nor, indeed, in any vocabulary of hatred and resentment which requires an enemy in order to have a reason for existing. The theologian must have the self-confidence to learn from other traditions and from other practical circumstances which shed light on his own. Otherwise, he condemns himself to an uncritical, closed and anthropomorphic religion of his own making.

We have noticed all along how theology and liturgy interact, how the *lex orandi* affects the *lex credendi* and vice versa. If theology is directed towards securing our union with God in the particular social and cultural circumstances in which we find ourselves, then it is fundamentally a language of prayer. We live spontaneously, sacramentally, orally. We should not be surprised to find that theology is, as John Coulson describes it, basically oral and doxological – expressed spontaneously in worship, created in the act of preaching or in the outpourings of contemporary Christian hymnography (Coulson 1981, p. 161). Theology is a language of reconciliation and communion, not of academic sophistication or of political conflict. We must bear these factors in mind when we try to discern the beginnings of new theological traditions in non-Western countries.

Modernism and extrinsicism

In every chapter of this book we have emphasized the privileged character of the symbol in the language of revelation. It was the characteristic error of the Catholic modernists at the turn of the nineteenth and twentieth centuries to believe that no valid inferences could be drawn from the traditional symbols of Christianity. They fell, as it were, between the two stools of traditional symbolism and rational explanation. Much the same dilemma afflicts many of the more recent secular theologians. John Hick's opposing of literal propositions to poetic or metaphorical language, which is merely the expression of subjective commitment, seems to echo this

dilemma very accurately. Modernists tended to reduce the Christian faith to
the expression of inner religious experiences which had no objectivity. They
downgraded the terms 'symbol', 'symbolism', 'symbolize', denying them
any element of real participation in, or unity-in-difference with, the objects
signified. For them, symbolism was 'mere symbolism', and it was in this
sense that the word was used, for example, in this demythologized creed of
Marcel Hébert:

> I believe in the objective value of the idea of God, of an absolute and perfect ideal,
> distinct, though not separated, from the world which He draws and directs towards
> the greater good, One and Three, because He can be called infinite activity, infinite
> mind, infinite love. And I believe in Him in whom there was realized in an
> exceptional or unique degree the union of the divine with the human nature, Jesus
> Christ, whose luminous superiority, impressing simple hearts, is for them
> symbolized by the idea of a Virgin Birth, whose powerful action after His death
> caused in the mind of the apostles and disciples the visions and appearances narrated
> in the Gospels, and is symbolized by the myth of a descent to Hell and an ascension
> to the upper regions of the sky. I believe in the Spirit of love (one of the aspects of the
> threefold Ideal) who (or which) quickens our souls, gives them an attraction, an
> impulse to everything that is true beautiful and good . . . I believe in the holy church
> universal, as the visible expression of the ideal communion of all beings . . . . I believe
> in the survival of that which constitutes our moral personality, in the eternal life
> which is already present in every soul leading a higher life, and which popular
> imagination has symbolized in the ideas of the Resurrection of the body and of
> eternal felicity (quoted in Bevan 1962, p. 226).

For this modernist priest, God and the Church had become 'ideals'; Jesus'
divinity, a 'luminous superiority'; his resurrection, 'a powerful action' on
the apostles' minds; life after death, a survival of the 'moral personality'.
And all this intangible and subjective experience is 'symbolized' by 'myths'
created by the 'popular imagination'. For Hébert, these are mere illus-
trations, mere comparisons or allegories, and the Bible is no more than a
book of fairy-tales.

The tragedy is that the Church of the time had no understanding of
symbol, myth and imagination available to it other than that put forward by
Hébert; it was therefore rightly suspicious of his ideas. In response to the
unsettling philosophical climate of the nineteenth century, the Church of
Pope Leo XIII adopted a policy of strict fidelity to the philosophy and
theology of St Thomas Aquinas, using it in a way which would have
horrified the Angelic Doctor himself, as a restraint upon all theological
exploration. The neo-Thomist system was grounded in an understanding of
revelation that was thoroughly transcendentalist and supernaturalist, but its
methods were rationalist – even positivist (Daly 1980, p. 19). It first
demonstrated the supernatural origin of revealed truth, as expressed in the
assertions of Scripture and tradition, by appealing to divine facts, mainly
miracles, and it then brought deductive reasoning to bear on these revealed

assertions. Its method was therefore rationalist. Its positivism consisted in presenting its sources as external facts, empirically observable by the senses and entirely extrinsic to human nature. There was no need, according to this system, to posit any intrinsic relationship between what is revealed and the nature of the one who believes. Neo-Scholasticism, or to be precise, neo-Thomism was therefore deeply suspicious of terms such as 'symbolism' or 'imagination' for they seemed to imply a faith that was vague, imprecise, subject to the vagaries and waywardness of human emotions and completely lacking in objective validity.

Theologians who were identified with the error of Modernism, condemned in 1907 by Pope St Pius X, raised a number of questions which neo-Thomism was unable to answer in the light of its own argument and conceptual scheme. Maurice Blondel dubbed neo-Thomism 'extrinsicism', and suggested that human experience was the point of departure for the awareness of God's self-revelation. For Blondel, the state of man was not either natural or supernatural, but 'transnatural', and there was a *de facto* connection between the natural and the supernatural orders. One passed from one's own inner religious life to a knowledge of the transcendent. He rejected a purely immanent religion, but advocated the 'method of immanence' for arriving at the transcendent. Lucien Laberthonnière's theory of 'Critical Mysticism' also attacked the speculative type of theology which was divorced from real life. He stigmatized the intellectualist neo-Thomist system as a form of supernatural rationalism. However, with Laberthonnière, the issue was not one of the relationship between nature and supernature, but of the mode of contact between the transcendent being (God) and human action. Laberthonnière condemned the Scholastic verbal expedient of analogy which leaves us in uncertainty. The consciousness of God, the certainty of his authority, had to be a part of the human self-consciousness.

Alfred Loisy attempted to rebut German Protestant arguments by appealing to the historical character of the Gospels. This historical approach prevented him from accepting the complete range of conclusions taught by the reigning 'non-historical' orthodoxy. Although he ended sadly as 'a weary and disillusioned sceptic' (Daly 1980, p. 61), he offered a formidable challenge to neo-Thomism. The latter system, he argued, led logically either to the denial of history as an intelligible reality, or to an exemption of revelation from the laws of history. If revelation takes place in history, then it is an interpretation of experience.

Finally, George Tyrrell appealed to the fundamental human need to worship and stressed the importance of the ministry of the Word. While this led him to attack the abstractions of a philosophical theology, it also led him to the belief that the transcendent makes contact with man in the symbolic, and the ability of man to form symbols, to live in them and to accept their limitations, prevents him from becoming an agnostic.

No doubt, the so-called modernists were far from orthodox on many issues, judged by criteria other than those of a Catholicism expressed solely in neo-Thomist categories, but the anti-modernist movement in the Church and the official equation of neo-Thomism with orthodoxy failed to silence them completely. Some of the questions they had raised refused to go away, and surfaced again in the New Theology of the 1940s and 1950s, associated with the names of Chenu, de Lubac, Le Roy, Sertillanges, Charlier, Congar, Draguet and others, while Karl Rahner and Bernard Lonergan attempted a synthesis of these insights within the thirteenth-century Thomist framework of faith and reason.

Thus it came to be accepted that revelation was ultimately personal, rather than propositional, and that, even if human beings can know God by the light of reason alone, this is not *de facto* the case. 'Pure nature' does not exist, but is already graced. Man is in fact orientated by God towards the supernatural life. It is significant that the documents of Vatican II prefer the word 'integral' to 'supernatural'. As Newman had declared more than a century before in his University Sermon of 1830, the human reason was not unaided by grace and 'no people has been denied a revelation from God'. In the next chapter we shall deal with this aspect of the theology of revelation more fully, and in the final section of this chapter we shall briefly examine the relationship of theology and history. We may conclude by noting that there has been a considerable progress from Pope Leo XIII's encyclical *Aeterni Patris* which virtually identified Thomistic philosophy with human reason itself, to the documents of Vatican II, which, while they subscribe to a theoretical pre-eminence of Thomism, have broken its practical hegemony and stimulated the growth of alternative theologies (cf. *Optatam Totius*, 16; *Gravissimum Educationis*, 10; *Ad Gentes*, 22).

History, theology and the development of dogma

Professor Ninian Smart has written: 'There is no way in which religion can claim to be other than revisionary in principle about its judgements, in line with any other form of intellectual exploration' (Smart 1978, p. 30). The whole context of doctrine and religious practice points to a focus, but can one discover what that focus is? Every epoch in the history of a religion attempts to provide a picture of the focus, but which picture does justice to the focus, and do we not – in any case – impose our own contemporary picture upon the pictures of the past? There is thus, concludes Smart, no answer to the question: 'What is Christianity?' (Smart 1978, pp. 18–30).

History has been called by Gabriel Daly the 'hair-shirt' of Scholastic theology (Daly 1980, p. 224). The latter could not accept that its massively objective system was vulnerable to the insecurities of historical criticism. We have already touched on this question when speaking of our ability to create meaning as well as to discover it in the historic faith-statements of the Church's *magisterium*. This is a comparatively recent admission by theologians. St Thomas Aquinas had no awareness of doctrinal change or renewal. When Popes or Councils made doctrinal *determinationes* (Aquinas' term), they did not enlarge the object of belief, but simply preserved and protected the real meaning of what had been previously believed. Both Reformation and Counter-Reformation theologians justified their conflicting positions by referring to primitive Christianity and were hostile to any idea of doctrinal development. For Catholics, 'reformation' was quite simply 'innovation'. Seventeenth-century theologians and preachers like Bishop Bossuet thought that all the dogmas believed by Catholics of the day were individually believed by the apostles, and that any variation in the teaching of the Faith must be a sign of error. Any development was in the form of a return to the pure and integral teaching of the apostolic Church (cf. Chadwick 1957, pp. 1–5).

The theology of doctrinal development appeared in the nineteenth century, as part of the general emergence of evolutionary theory and is associated with the names of Johann Adam Möhler and John Henry Newman. Newman's *Essay on the Development of Christian Doctrine* first appeared in 1845, the year of his conversion to Roman Catholicism; he proposed an organic idea of dogmatic development whereby the Christian idea flowers in the consciousness of the believing community under the influence of the Holy Spirit. Newman was interested in the theology of the community, the self-conscious faith of Christians, the language of which is imaginative. Newman derived his organic imagery from his faith in the living presence of the risen Christ in the community, and, just as the believer became sacramentally aware of the presence of Christ in his ordinary daily actions, so the truths of revelation had to relate to his present awareness. Doctrinal development was a growth in imaginative responsiveness on the part of Christians to the once-for-all self-communication of God in Christ.

This climate of thought, together with the prospect of revitalizing the papacy through papal dogmatic definitions, encouraged Pope Pius IX to define the Dogma of the Immaculate Conception of the Blessed Virgin Mary in 1854 and directly paved the way for the definition of papal infallibility by the First Vatican Council in 1870, and of the Blessed Virgin's Bodily Assumption by Pope Pius XII in 1950. The nineteenth century, therefore, saw the beginning of a new attitude on the part of the Church's *magisterium* towards dogmatic development, but since it did not undertake to demonstrate historically the way in which the dogmas it defined were part of the primitive deposit of revealed truth, it was left to the theologians to solve this particular problem.[2]

Some theologians, like Reginald Schultes and Francisco Marin-Sola, opted for a logical theory of dogmatic development. This approach regards the newly defined truths as being the result of syllogistic reasoning from premises in propositional truths known in apostolic times. While this method was convincing in some cases, it was not successful in showing that new dogmas such as the Immaculate Conception were already contained in the apostolic preaching. More fatal to the logical approach was the Church's abandonment of the idea that revelation consists in propositions. This led opponents of the logical theory, such as Karl Rahner and Edward Schillebeeckx, to go back to the ideas of Möhler and Newman and to develop a theory of homogeneous, organic development. This theory held that the self-communication of the divine surpasses what the human mind can comprehend or express in discursive thought or in propositional truths, but is grasped intuitively in its totality. Dogmatic development is therefore a vital process which takes place under the guidance of the Holy Spirit and by which the faithful instinctively know, through their meditation, their prayer and worship and their interpretation and application of Scripture, what is a valid expression (in dogmatic terms) of revealed truth. On this understanding, Marian dogmas do not have to be logically derived from statements about Mary in the Bible, but can be inferred from the relationships between Jesus and his Mother which the Biblical texts suggest.

Homogeneous theories of dogmatic development, whether syllogistic or organic, suggest a cumulative growth or expansion of knowledge in the Church, and do not really allow for the neglect, suppression or reformulation of faith-statements. Cardinal Newman, at one point, quotes St Vincent of Lérins:

> Let the soul's religion imitate the law of the body, which as the years go on develops indeed and opens out its due proportions, and yet remains identically what it was. Small are a baby's limbs, a youth's are larger, yet they are all the same (Newman 1887, p. 172; Lash 1975, pp. 64–75).

Such an image takes care of the problem of continuous identity, but it seems to suggest that the process of doctrinal development is one of irreversible expansion. Since the middle of the twentieth century, the growing pluralism and mobility of human society have made the homogeneous theories less plausible. Avery Dulles remarks that we do not need more dogmatic definitions, our problem is 'to grasp the meaning, relevance, and credibility of the statements already made' (Dulles 1978, p. 50). He prefers (ibid., p. 51) to describe the progress of dogma in terms of George Lindbeck's 'historical situationism' (Schillebeeckx 1967, pp. 138–139). According to this view, faith-statements are the outcome of a dialogue in history between God and his people. They are historically conditioned responses to, or interpretations of, the Word of God. New formulations and new doctrines are needed to maintain old truths and to give them relevance and credibility. Dogmatic development is not, therefore, merely a question of progress in historical time; it is also a question of interculturation or the mutual influencing of living cultures. Such a theory does not preclude faith in the charism of infallibility, which demands, not that a given formulation be always and everywhere imposed, but that its meaning be not directly contradicted. The Declaration of the Sacred Congregation for the Doctrine of the Faith, *Mysterium Ecclesiae* (1973), the provisions of which we shall consider more fully in the final chapter of this book, seems to correspond exactly with the requirements of historical situationism. Moreover, the theory parallels other theories of the development of human knowledge in the secular sphere, such as Thomas Kuhn's *The Structure of Scientific Revolutions* (Kuhn 1970). In the light of all that has been said so far in this book about the Judeo-Christian experience of God's self-revelation, it is now high time that we examine the experience of revelation in non-Christian religious traditions, and the relationship of the Christian religion to revealed religion in these other forms.

NOTES

1 A remark made in my hearing by Fr Pierre Benoît O.P.
2 In this account I am following Dulles 1978, pp. 45–62.

QUESTIONS FOR DISCUSSION

(1) How do we reconcile the unrepeatability of Christianity's 'originating experience' with the experience of God's continuing self-revelation?

(2) How is the 'sacred deposit of the Word of God' handed down in the Church?

(3) Why was the modernist controversy so crucial for the self-understanding of the Church in its role as teacher and guarantor of faith-statements?

(4) For further enquiry: What forms do you envisage theology taking in the contemporary world-church?

SELECT ANNOTATED READING LIST

Vatican Council II, 1965: *Dei Verbum, Dogmatic Constitution on Divine Revelation* in *Vatican Council II*, ed. A. Flannery (Dublin, 1975), pp. 750–765. Any study of the theology of revelation in the contemporary Roman Catholic Church must take this document of the *magisterium* as its point of departure. It is a relatively short statement about revelation in general and about the place of Scripture, in particular, in the process of that revelation.

G. O'Collins, 1981: *Fundamental Theology* (London). This readable introduction to the theology of revelation deals expertly with all the questions treated in our chapter. Its main emphasis is on the nature of divine revelation and its relationship to Scriptural interpretation, authoritative Church teaching and theology.

G. Daly, 1980: *Transcendence and Immanence – A Study in Catholic Modernism and Integralism* (Oxford). The merit of this book is that it demonstrates the wide diversity of opinion among modernists at the turn of the nineteenth century. It sets out the issues between modernism and anti-modernism clearly, and shows how the controversy has affected contemporary theology.

A. Dulles, 1978: *The Resilient Church – The Necessity and Limits of Adaptation* (Dublin). This book's basic theme is the problem of how the Church can undergo renewal while remaining faithful to its own traditions. Chapter III, on Doctrinal Renewal, is a very clear exposition of the history of the theory of dogmatic development and the positions being taken by theologians today.

R. P. McBrien, 1980: *Catholicism* (London), 2 vols. Volume I of this theological compendium sets out on pp. 220–238 most of the contemporary theological views on revelation. Earlier in the volume, on pp. 45ff., the author deals with the relationship of theology to faith and with the question of dogmatic development.

6

Hearing the Word

SALVATION AND REVELATION AS UNIVERSAL

The ultimacy of Jesus Christ as Saviour

In the light of the Word of God handed down in the community, Christians conceive it their duty to recognize the signs of the times, that is to say, those places, moments, words and actions, those lives and cultural traditions, in which God reveals his lordship and saving activity. The ancient Israelites came to understand that their God was 'Lord of the Universe' and that his salvation was offered to the whole of humankind. The apostles and their followers believed that God's final offer of salvation, God's 'last word', was embodied in the person of Jesus Christ and in the events of his life, death and resurrection. As St Peter told the Sanhedrin:

> There is salvation in no one else, for there is no other name under heaven given among men by which we must be saved (Acts 4:12).

Among the signs of the times which Christians are to recognize, a privileged place must be given to the living faiths of non-Christians, believers who do not accept Jesus Christ as the climactic embodiment of God's self-revelation. Equally important in a world of growing secularism is the attitude of those who reject or suspend all religious belief itself. The Christian has to ask himself: How is God's offer of universal salvation in Jesus Christ made available to people, believers or non-believers, who do not accept Christ's claims?

This question was posed very poignantly by an African scholar of religions, Dr Samuel Kibicho of Kenya:

> Was the God of African Traditional Religion . . . the One True God whom we Christians worship in Christianity, the Father of Our Lord Jesus Christ? If so, as most Africans believe, did our forefathers really know him adequately for their religious needs (salvation), or was their knowledge of him only partial and preparatory for the coming of the full revelation in the Christ of Christianity? (Kibicho 1978, pp. 370–371).

The Catholic theologian, in answering Dr Kibicho's question, would not accept its implication that the alternatives are exclusive. Yes, the exponents of African traditional religion *did* know God adequately for their religious needs and *were* capable of salvation. Yes, their knowledge of God *was* necessarily partial until the coming of the full revelation of God in Christ. The theologian is then faced with the further question of how salvation and partial knowledge can go together, and whether the supposition that they can do so does not downgrade the value of African traditional religion, or any non-Christian religion. In what sense, or to what extent, does the One True God reveal himself and offer his salvation to the adepts of non-Christian religions? And more to the point, how does this revelation and offer of salvation relate to the historic event of Jesus Christ?

The New Testament offers us no doubt at all that God wills the salvation of all human beings and that there is but one mediator between God and men, Jesus Christ:

> First of all then, I urge that supplications, prayers, intercessions and thanksgivings be made for all men, for kings and all who are in high positions, that we may lead a quiet and peaceable life, godly and respectful in every way. This is good and it is acceptable in the sight of God our Saviour, who desires all men to be saved and to come to the knowledge of the truth. For there is one God, and there is one mediator between God and men, the man Christ Jesus, who gave himself as a ransom for all, the testimony to which was borne at the proper time (1 Timothy 2:1-6).

There is also no doubt about the current teaching of the Catholic Church that God's universal salvific will is effective and that every human being is given a chance of salvation. Grace is offered to all. The Second Vatican Council taught explicitly that sincere non-Christians, believers and non-believers alike, are moved by grace when they follow their conscience, and so are capable of being saved.

> Those who through no fault of their own, do not know the Gospel of Christ or his Church, but who nevertheless seek God with a sincere heart, and moved by grace, try in their actions to do his will as they know it through the dictates of their conscience – those too may achieve eternal salvation. Nor shall divine providence deny the assistance necessary for salvation to those who, without any fault of theirs, have not yet arrived at an explicit knowledge of God, and who, not without grace, strive to lead a good life (*Lumen Gentium*, 16).

Speaking of the Christian's duty to struggle with evil in all its forms, as one who has been made a partner in Christ's paschal mystery and who goes forward to the resurrection, the Second Vatican Council adds the following:

> All this holds true not for Christians only but also for all men of good will in whose hearts grace is active invisibly. For since Christ died for all, and since all men are in fact called to one and the same destiny, which is divine, we must hold that the Holy Spirit offers to all the possibility of being made partners, in a way known to God, in the paschal mystery (*Gaudium et Spes*, 22).

The notion of 'baptism of desire' or the *votum sacramenti* or *propositum sacramenti* has long been a commonplace among Catholic theologians, as a way of explaining how the unbaptized can be saved. Following the teaching of St Thomas Aquinas, Piet Fransen has popularized the concept of the fundamental option for God, as a further explanation of the so-called 'baptism of desire' (Fransen 1967, pp. 67–122). This fundamental option can be concretely expressed in any form of authentic conversion of heart which is an implicit act of love for God. Every human being is confronted by two mutually exclusive forms of love, distinguished by St Augustine as *amor sui usque ad contemptum Dei*, 'the love of self that leads to the contempt of God', and *amor Dei usque ad contemptum sui*, 'the love of God that leads to the contempt of self'. There is no other option that a human being can make. Salvation is therefore available to all who do not freely make self-love the ultimate goal of their whole existence.

As a matter of fact, human beings exist in a supernatural order of grace and all human experience is open to the knowledge and self-communication of God. This openness to God and his self-communication is a reality of human existence, gratuitously bestowed. It is, in fact, the very condition of all experience and of all reflection on experience. The human being in his own subjectivity, in his own self-knowledge as the subject of experiences, knows God and has, through grace, a radical capacity to respond to God's self-communication. Karl Rahner calls this basic or general self-communication of God in human experience 'transcendental revelation'. The radical capacity to respond to God's self-gift, he calls the 'supernatural existential', and he sees it as a permanent modification of the human spirit which orientates it towards God (Rahner 1978, pp. 138 ff.; McBrien 1980, I, p. 160).

All of this remains at a highly abstract level. In fact, man's own self-understanding, self-interpretation and self-orientation in a fundamental life-option take place (as we pointed out in the first chapter) within a collective cultural tradition – a history. As Rahner stresses, transcendental revelation becomes explicit – but not necessarily or exhaustively so – in categories or themes which are developed in human culture and history. This process Rahner refers to as categorical or historical revelation. Piet Fransen also speaks of the individual giving expression to his fundamental life-option through a personal creed, which is simply the appropriation by him of a corporate or collective creed that provides him with the categories and symbols in which to express his own orientation and commitment (Fransen 1967, pp. 92–93).

We noted in Chapter 3 how the ancient Israelites recognized God's saving activity in the actions and traditions of other nations. The Christian Church, also, accepts that God is active in other religions, and that human beings are saved through their participation in these religions, not simply as individuals and in spite of them. The Second Vatican Council's Decree on the Church's Missionary Activity acknowledged that men and women are basically social beings and that evangelization must be directed to human groups and collectivities as much as to individuals:

> They [those who have never heard the Gospel message] constitute large and distinct groups united by enduring cultural ties, ancient religious traditions, and strong social relationships (*Ad Gentes*, 10).

The Declaration on the Relation of the Church to Non-Christian Religions states:

> The Catholic Church rejects nothing of what is true and holy in these religions. She has a high regard for the manner of life and conduct, the precepts and doctrines which, although differing in many ways from her own teaching, nevertheless often reflect a ray of that truth which enlightens all men . . . Let Christians, while witnessing to their own faith and way of life, acknowledge, preserve and encourage the spiritual and moral truths found among non-Christians, also their social life and culture (*Nostra Aetate*, 2).

This injunction was followed by the setting up of Vatican Secretariats for Non-Christian Religions and for Non-Believers, and by an even more explicit expression of respect for non-Christians in the Apostolic Exhortation on Evangelization in the Modern World which concluded the 1974 Synod of Bishops.

> The Church respects and esteems these non-Christian religions because they are the living expression of the soul of vast groups of people. They carry within them the echo of thousands of years of searching for God, a quest which is incomplete but often made with great sincerity and righteousness of heart. They possess an impressive patrimony of deeply religious texts. They have taught generations of people how to pray. They are all impregnated with innumerable 'seeds of the word' and can constitute a true 'preparation of the Gospel' (*Evangelii Nuntiandi*, 53).

In due course we shall examine the two phrases quoted from Justin Martyr and Eusebius with which this passage ends, because they raise the question of Christ as the ultimate Revealer in human history. We must first of all ask how the effectiveness of God's universal salvific will relates to Christ and to his paschal mystery.

In Chapter 4 we saw that the prologue to John's Gospel proclaimed the man Jesus as God and yet as a distinct, pre-existing divine person. This Gospel celebrates the profound unity in word and work between Jesus Christ and the Father. Thus the prologue, in words taken up later by the Nicene Creed, says:

> He was in the beginning with God; all things were made through him, and without him was not anything made that was made (John 1:2–3).

> . . . through him all things were made (Nicene Creed).

Jesus, therefore, in the mind of the apostolic Church took over the role attributed by the ancient Jews to the divine word and wisdom. He is the universal agent of creation, its model and its goal. Furthermore, in the incarnation, Jesus Christ united himself with each and every human being, so that, in experiencing God through our neighbour and bringing God's love to him, we are doing this through Jesus Christ. 'Truly, I say to you, as you did it to one of the least of these my brethren, you did it to me' (Matthew 25:40). The resurrection, freeing Christ's humanity from the limitations of a single lifetime, in a historical place and epoch, transformed it into a vehicle of universal salvation and released the Spirit to the whole world. Christ's universal lordship embodies therefore the ultimate reign of God over human hearts. The Christian believes, then, that Christ is the agent, the reality, the goal of salvation wherever and whenever it is offered by God.

The ultimacy of Jesus Christ as Revealer

It is one thing for the Christian to proclaim his faith in Christ as the principle of God's salvific activity in non-Christian religions; it is quite another to demand a conscious recognition of this fact by the adepts of these religions. Yet God 'desires all men to be saved and to come to the knowledge of the truth' (1 Timothy 2:4). The religious faith of believers is given expression by the community, as we have seen, in a 'creed' of religious beliefs. Bernard Lonergan has enumerated four types of expression: the imperative or moral, the narrative or historical, the ascetic or mystical, and the theoretical (Lonergan 1972, p. 118). Religious beliefs are made up of a compound of any or all of these forms of expression. They may emphasize one or another form. There may be an imbalance in the compound, and – from a Christian point of view – error or silence in any of the components. The relationship of faith to belief raises certain questions in Christian minds on the subject of non-Christian religions. Is God's universal revelatory will as effective as his universal salvific will? Can salvation take place in a human being without affecting his knowledge and understanding of what is taking place? Finally, can one separate the activities of salvation and revelation? Salvation demands at least implicit faith, and this is the teaching of the Second Vatican Council:

> ... in ways known to himself God can lead those who, through no fault of their own, are ignorant of the Gospel to that faith without which it is impossible to please him ... (Ad Gentes, 7).

A faith, therefore, is necessary, and theologians in the Catholic tradition such as Bernard Lonergan and Charles Davis are agreed about the implicit character of this necessary faith, and have explored its connotations

(Lonergan 1972; Davis 1970). A faith, however, which is born of love and which is implicit from a Christian point of view, has nevertheless cognitive aspects, and some of these may parallel the affirmations of Christianity. It would be surprising if this were not the case. Indeed, in so far as Christ is the goal of revelation and salvation, one would expect that God-given faith in non-Christian traditions would be capable of conscious development in the direction of Christianity.

It can, of course, be argued that God's will that the truth be universally known may only become effective in the future – perhaps not in this life or in history at all. Christ is, however, the agent and present object of revelation/salvation, and he is already at work outside, as well as inside, the Church. It is therefore legitimate for us to try and discern recognizably 'Christian' elements in the cognitive aspects of non-Christian faith. It is tentatively suggested here that perhaps implicit faith may denote in some cases a conscious acceptance of doctrines which go in the same direction as Christianity. If this is the case, the theologian requires the assistance of the student of religions in recognizing these doctrines.

In this area, the Second Vatican Council took up several images and ideas of the early Fathers of the Church. One of these is that of St Eusebius of Caesarea, the *praeparatio evangelica*, or 'preparation for the Gospel'. According to this idea, a non-Christian religion prepares its adepts for the explicit proclamation of the Gospel of Christ by a certain partial understanding of the truth. In so far as this idea implies what Samuel Kibicho calls 'a radical discontinuity' between the non-Christian religion and the Gospel which eventually supplants it, or else implies that the non-Christian religion has no contribution to make to an on-going Christian response to the Word of God, then it appears insufficient and hardly likely to commend itself to interested non-Christians. However, when it is complemented by other patristic concepts, the idea of a *praeparatio evangelica* may appear more fruitful.

Such other patristic concepts include the *vestigia Christi*, 'the footprints of Christ', and the phrase of Justin Martyr which was frequently adopted by the Second Vatican Council, the *semina verbi* or 'seeds of the word'. These ideas take the Logos-agent of creation as their basis, the so-called *logos spermatikos* or 'seminal logos'. Christ as agent of creation has implanted seeds or germs in the human mind and in the whole of reality as experienced by man. Moreover, the risen Christ acts 'spermatically', stirring up, and germinating in, human thought and human traditions, so that they participate in the truth. The Second Vatican Council speaks of uncovering 'with gladness and respect those seeds of the word' which lie hidden in the national and religious traditions of non-Christians (*Ad Gentes*, 11). Developing the image, the Council goes on to say:

> The seed which is the word of God grows out of good soil watered by the divine
> dew, it absorbs moisture, transforms it, and makes it part of itself, so that eventually
> it bears much fruit (*Ad Gentes*, 22).

This is a description of the way in which providentially supplied elements ('dew' and 'moisture') are transformed by the Word of God and enable it to grow and bear fruit. There are frequent allusions by the Council to the 'riches' of non-Christian traditions which must be brought to Christ, and the missionary decree speaks not only of 'borrowing' such elements, of 'reconciling' them with divine revelation, but also of their being 'taken up into a Catholic unity' (*Ad Gentes*, 22). In his speech to the bishops of Africa and Madagascar in Kampala in 1969, Pope Paul VI made it quite clear that non-Christian traditions had a part to play in the development of Christianity. He spoke of human values and characteristic forms of culture in Africa which would 'find *in* Christianity and *for* Christianity, a true superior fullness' (italics mine). It is evident that the principles of what we have called participant revelation are here at work and that the encounter of Christianity with non-Christian religions results in the affirmations of Christianity acquiring further meanings.

Nevertheless, one still has to decide the criteria according to which the authentic seeds of the word or footprints of Christ are to be recognized in other religions. Here there can be no doubt that an *a posteriori* evaluation of non-Christian religions is being made in the light of the Word of God to which the Church, in its tradition, is consciously faithful. Nothing can be called a 'seed of the word' which contradicts or diminishes what the Church already holds as revealed and affirmed. Such a 'seed' must be an element of tradition that is authentically religious, that is to say, it must exhibit a feeling for a further dimension to life, a communion with ultimate transcendent reality. It must offer hope in its approach to suffering and in its interrogation of human existence. And it has to be reconciling. To that extent it will be both Christological and Trinitarian, for Christ came to reconcile human beings with one another and with God, and he revealed a God who is not a dualistic complement of opposites, but who is essentially synthesis and concord. Three, as R. C. Zaehner has remarked, is the number of reconciliation (Zaehner 1970, p. 413). Not only does creation bear the impress of the Trinity, but so also, of necessity, does the authentic notion of God wherever he reveals himself.

At this point we must ask ourselves: 'Have we really resolved the problem we started with?' The Christian believes that Jesus Christ is the climactic embodiment of God's self-revelation, that this revelation happened in history, to be precise, in the specific culture-history of the Jewish people. We are still predicating a divine revelation in non-Christian religions which has no conscious link with the narrative memory of Jesus Christ as preserved and celebrated by the Church. The seeds of the word may be sufficient in God's eyes for the salvation of the non-Christians who subscribe to them, but they do not know them as seeds of the word. They do not recognize, indeed they might even repudiate, a reference to the historic Christ. Their 'Christian' character is the result of a *post factum* recognition by professed Christians, whose intervention could be interpreted as, at best, condescending or, at worst, gratuitously insulting. It is clear that any hypothesis about how divine revelation among non-Christians is related to the decisive revelation which took place historically in Christ must refer to an encounter, or the prospect of an encounter, with the narrative memory of Jesus Christ celebrated and proclaimed by the Church. The problem then consists in explaining how the various historical forms which divine self-revelation has assumed in the non-Christian religions relate to the one special history of revelation which culminated in Christ and which continues to live in the Christian Church.

Broadly, there are three types of answer to the problem. The first two deny one or other of the apparently conflicting premises. They produce an oversimplified solution either by denying salvation and revelation among non-Christians, or by denying the ultimacy of Christ and the existence of a special history of revelation. These are the exclusivist and relativist types of theory. The third type of theory may be called inclusivist, and it characterizes the Catholic approach to non-Christian religions, as will be readily appreciated from our discussion of ideas such as *logos spermatikos, vestigia Christi* and *semina verbi*. Inclusivist theories do, however, run the unacceptable risk of relativizing the Church and its God-given mission to proclaim the Good News of Jesus Christ, and they often do not take sufficient account of the historical nature of divine revelation in non-Christian religions. We shall now turn to a consideration of these three types of theory.

GOD'S SELF-REVELATION IN OTHER RELIGIONS

Exclusivist theories

The great German Protestant theologian Karl Barth asserted that the discovery of God is made known in Jesus Christ exclusively (Hick and Hebblethwaite 1980, pp. 32–51). He sharply disavowed any idea that the Gospel of Christ might relate to existing concepts in non-Christian religions. The whole of humanity is waiting for Christ, and its waiting is guaranteed by God's faithfulness. That faithfulness is established when we meet Christ, whose message is the proclamation of divine forgiveness. Barth had a strong sense of the sin of religions, of their propensity for idolatry and hypocrisy – for a repetition of the primordial apostasy. All human activity, he declared, is 'a cry for forgiveness', and God in Jesus comes not only to challenge all the temples of the world, but also to proclaim their cleansing or their rebuilding. What is more, he placed Christianity itself under the same judgement of the Word of God, making a radical distinction between Christ and Christianity. There is an obvious truth that Christians of all ages stand judged by the Gospel they proclaim, but it is not at all easy to see how the Word of God comes to us except within the Church community which holds it in trust, or why Christianity, however unfaithful in practice, should be placed on the same footing as non-Christian religions. Kenneth Cragg concludes that Karl Barth's theology had European issues firmly in mind and did not really come to grips with the reality of religions in other parts of the world (Cragg 1977, pp. 69–70).

Hendrik Kraemer, in his great missiological analysis *The Christian Message in a Non-Christian World* (Kraemer 1961), modifies Barth's position, but remains close to it. He does not reject all religious life outside Christian revelation, though, like Barth, he places empirical Christianity on the same level as non-Christian religions. For him, human religious aspirations are an impotent desire to realize the divine nature. This is revealed and conceded by Christ alone. Only the Bible has a 'radical religious realism', because it reveals God as condemning man radically and radically forgiving him. Christ, therefore, is the ultimate standard of reference and the 'crisis of all religions'.

Another instance of exclusivism is provided by the Lausanne Covenant, the declaration of the International Congress on World Evangelization held at Lausanne, Switzerland, in 1974, and by Evangelical commentators on this declaration. Article Three of the Lausanne Covenant contains the following:

> We recognize that all men have some knowledge of God through his general revelation in nature. But we deny that this can save, for men suppress the truth by their unrighteousness. We also reject as derogatory to Christ and the Gospel every kind of syncretism and dialogue which implies that Christ speaks equally through all religions and ideologies . . . . To proclaim Jesus as 'the Saviour of the World' is not to affirm that all men are either automatically or ultimately saved, still less to affirm that all religions offer salvation in Christ. Rather it is to proclaim God's love for a world of sinners and to invite all men to respond to him as Saviour and Lord in the wholehearted personal commitment of repentance and faith (Stott 1975, p. 14).

John Stott, in his exposition and commentary on the Lausanne Covenant, has this to say:

> What, then, about those ignorant of the Gospel? Are we to say that they are ignorant of God altogether, including those who adhere to non-Christian religions? No. 'We recognize that all men have some knowledge of God.' This universal (though partial) knowledge is due to his self-revelation, what theologians call 'his general revelation' because it is made to all men, or his 'natural' revelation because it is made 'in nature', both externally in the universe and internally in the human

conscience. Such knowledge of God is not saving knowledge, however. 'We deny that this can save', partly because it is a revelation of God's power, deity and holiness but not of his love for sinners or of his plan of salvation, and partly because men do not live up to the knowledge they have. On the contrary, they 'suppress the truth by their unrighteousness', and their rejection of the truth which they know then leads to idolatry, to immorality and to the judgement of God. So, far from saving them, their knowledge actually condemns them. And they are without excuse. Therefore, it is false to suppose that sinners can be saved through other systems, or that Christ 'speaks equally through all religions and ideologies'. We firmly repudiate 'every kind of syncretism and dialogue' which suggests this as derogatory to Christ and the Gospel. For these are unique, and non-Christian religions know nothing of them (Stott 1975, p. 15).

Later, commenting in the same passage about Christ's title of 'Saviour of the World', Stott writes:

Negatively, we mean neither 'that all men are . . . automatically . . . saved' for, alas, some will reject Christ and perish. Still less do we mean 'that all religions offer salvation in Christ', because plainly they do not. All non-Christian religions, if they teach salvation at all, offer it only as a reward for merit which has been accumulated by good works, whereas the Christian message is 'the Gospel of the grace of God', that is, Good News of his mercy to sinners who deserve nothing at his hand except judgement (Stott 1975, p. 17).

These passages draw heavily upon the first two chapters of the epistle to the Romans and upon an intellectualist interpretation of them. We have already discussed the hypothesis of a 'natural' revelation, that, of human beings deducing the existence and nature of God by the light of their reason from the works of nature. As an abstraction it is undoubtedly possible, and was, indeed, declared to be so by the First Vatican Council. However, we are not confronted with a situation of 'pure nature', but one of a world in which God's grace is active. Moreover, the ancient Jews and St Paul himself did not conceive of a world of nature that was exempt from the history of salvation, but rather one which was subordinated to it. Stott's approach denies all relevance to non-Christian religious systems as such, and treats their adherents as individuals scrutinizing natural events, following their consciences, and accumulating personal merit without reference to the testimonies of a tradition. In his view, non-Christian religions leave men to their own devices. Finally, Stott's assertion that God reveals only his power and not his love to non-Christians is itself derogatory to the true idea of God. If God truly reveals himself, he cannot reveal himself as other than he is – Love.

In fairness to Evangelical Christians it must be said that the positions taken at Lausanne have been modified on other occasions. For example, in conversations with Roman Catholic theologians at Venice in 1977, it was conceded that the activity of the Holy Spirit could not be limited apodictically by the visible frontiers of the Church or by the literal proclamation of Christ's Gospel alone, and that salvation outside the Church was at least possible, even if it was precarious and unlikely.[1] It must also be said that, contrary to the optimism about the salvation of non-Christians which usually reigns among Catholics and Anglicans, there are some writers of these confessions, such as Henri Maurier or Stephen Neill, who stress rather the insufficiency of non-Christian religious systems and their need for fulfilment in explicit Christianity (Maurier 1968; Neill 1970).

One must also point out that in a rigorously exclusive theory of revelation and salvation, such as those we have been considering, no apology is given for the undeniable ineffectiveness of Christianity or of the Christian Gospel in a world where millions of men, women and children live and die in ignorance of Christ. The question of how God's universal call to salvation in Christ can be linked to such a historically inadequate instrument is not confronted.

Relativist theories

The most extreme form of relativism quite simply denies the uniqueness and universal relevance of the Christ-event. This is especially the case when it is also denied that the historical man, Jesus Christ, was or is in any real sense God. For John Hick, as we have seen, to speak of the divinity of Christ is merely to use a poetic simile in order to describe a personal feeling or commitment. In Hick's view, Christians must simply abandon the doctrine of the divinity of Christ if they are to live at peace with neighbouring religions in the modern world (Hick and Hebblethwaite 1980, pp. 183–186; Hick 1976 and 1973). There must be a Copernican revolution according to which we envisage the various religions revolving around the One Real, as planets revolve around the sun. Religions need not be rivals any more than planets, each in their own orbit. Religions are not 'true' or 'false' any more than civilizations are. They are simply geographically isolated ways of expressing ultimate reality which have grown into mutually exclusive traditions. For Hick, a global theology is a possibility, based upon the limited affirmations about the nature of reality which are contained in religious teachings; but where the religions differ is in their poetic language, and this refers only to the attitudes of the believers themselves.

John Macquarrie has criticized Hick's theory for its élitism – its desire to find a lowest common denominator, or highest common factor, which is not part of the 'poetic' language of popular religion. Such a syncretistic, cosmic faith can have no reality (Macquarrie 1979, pp. 351–352). Kenneth Cragg finds Hick's religious planetary analogy suspect, since there is plenty of evidence for the historical interaction of religions in the past and for the intensification of their present interaction (Cragg 1977, pp. 75–76).

Moreover (as we have already pointed out in Chapter 4), Christian belief in the divinity of Christ is not purely subjective, but is founded in a historical actuality.

A less radical revision of Christian doctrine, but possibly a more radical form of relativism is exhibited by the writings of Ernst Troeltsch in the first quarter of the twentieth century (Hick and Hebblethwaite 1980, pp. 11–31). Like Hick after him, he asserted that peoples have experienced divine reality in different ways and have therefore expressed this experience differently. Each religion was supremely true for its own adherents and derived its life and power from its unique character and independence. Troeltsch is self-confessedly 'super-denominational'. He preserves the uniqueness of Christianity (as he does of each religion), but he sacrifices its claim to universality. In the present situation of the world it is, in any case, more and more difficult to uphold the independence of religious systems.

The contemporary scholar of religions Wilfred Cantwell Smith is able to preserve the universal reference of Christianity in a subtle, but ultimately negative, way (Cantwell Smith 1978). He believes that the identification of religions is in itself an arbitrary and selective process, carried out in terms of alien beliefs and presuppositions. This point of view evokes well-merited sympathy from scholars. Certainly, each religion should be studied in its own context and the question should be asked: 'What does a religion do for its own adherents?' before a further one is posed: 'What does a religion mean for the adherents of an alien religion?' Wilfrid Cantwell Smith is content to confine himself to the first question only. The duty of the Christian is to probe his own convictions. If he does this, Smith is persuaded that he will discover the truth and relevance of non-Christian religions. The kind of God revealed in Jesus Christ, his anguish and his love, must convince the Christian that the adherents of other religions also live in God's presence. This is an opinion apparently shared by C. F. D. Moule, the Biblical scholar. He ends his book *The Origin of Christology* with a consideration of the ultimacy of Christ, and decides that the distinctiveness of Christianity is found in the person of Jesus, whose achievement in life and death both includes and transcends human expectations (Moule 1977, p. 158). It is precisely because God became incarnate in Jesus Christ, in this historical person and in a particular historical place and time, that God can save men in other ways and through other circumstances. God limited himself in this instance; it is reasonable to expect him to do so in others. God continues to reveal himself therefore in man's constantly widening experiences. Thus, this revelation can still be meaningfully described as being 'in Christ'. We are on the brink of an inclusivist theory here, but no positive connection between the historical actuality of the incarnate Word and God's continuing revelation in other religions is claimed by Moule. This is, therefore, the reverse of Hick's position. The divinity of Christ is affirmed, but his universal reference is converted into a particular model or instance – a defining instance, maybe, but one, perhaps, among many. It is not unfair, then, to describe Moule's position in Wilfred Cantwell Smith's phrase as one of 'dynamic particularism'.

Paul Tillich was one of the leading Protestant theologians of the twentieth century and he professed, along with his fellow Germans Barth and Bonhoeffer and with Hendrik Kraemer, the sharp distinction, which we have already discussed, between religion and Gospel, or between religion and Religion with a capital 'R' (Hick and Hebblethwaite 1980, pp. 108–121). The Gospel or the one true Religion can only be attained, according to Tillich, if we can destroy religion, that is to say the religiosity which is expressed by myth (unhistorical, or unreal, imagery) and cult (false and hypocritical ritualism). It is clear that Tillich, in common with his contemporaries, used words like 'religion', 'myth' and 'cult' in a pejorative sense. It is the duty of every religion to commit suicide, as it were – to destroy its own religiosity and to attain the freedom of ultimate truth. Those religions which can do this will be the religions that will last. Tillich offers no prophecies about the capacity of non-Christian religions to do this, he only knows that Judeo-Christianity possesses this capacity and is engaged in this struggle. Christianity and every other religion has to break through its own particularity. It is then that unity will be achieved, not through syncretism, not through the end of real Religion, not through the victory of one particular religion over others, but through either the victory of each religion over itself or its self-defeat and annihilation at its own hands. Tillich's theory is once again a theory which precludes universal evangelization and which concentrates on a change of heart primarily among Christians themselves.

Inclusivist theories

John Henry Newman was frankly optimistic in his view of non-Christian religions. He spoke of 'natural religion', but he was at pains to point out that this was not some kind of abstract essence of religion deduced from created nature by the use of unaided human reason (Newman 1909). Newman distrusted mere reasoning in matters of religion and did not think that it could produce any religious certainty. The human moral conscience was not always a reliable guide either, but, in Newman's view, it offered a measure of certainty which anticipated the conclusions of reason. The conscience had to be obeyed because it pointed to the moral locality of the unseen God. A man who followed his conscience made an implicit act of faith and improved his moral nature so that more and more prospects opened up for him and he experienced presentiments of a future life and of divine judgement. The conscience, Newman believed, implied a relationship between the soul and a power that was both exterior and superior. Thus, to follow one's conscience implied habitual obedience to God.

However, the conscience could in fact be 'wavering', 'unformed' and 'incomplete', in spite of the certainty it conveyed. The fact was, so Newman claimed, that God did not leave people to the uncertainties of their reason, nor to the vagaries of a certain, but often unreliable conscience.

> Scripture informs us that revelations were granted to the first fathers of our race, concerning the nature of God and man's duty to him; and scarcely a people can be named, among whom there are not traditions, not only of the existence of powers exterior to this visible world, but also of their actual interference with the course of nature followed up by religious communications to mankind from them. The Creator has never left himself without such witness as might anticipate the conclusions of reason and support a wavering conscience and a perplexed faith (Newman 1909, p. 18).

The peoples of the world enjoyed a revelation from God which they expressed in one form or another, but this was not an authenticated revelation. It did not clearly reveal the personality of God nor his 'tangible history' as an object upon which human affections could be placed and human energies concentrated. Authentic revelation required 'personation', someone who, in the words of the first Epistle of John, could be 'seen and heard and handled'.

Yet Newman could describe the 'dispensation of paganism' as a 'large and practical religious creed', adding:

> It may even be questioned whether there be any essential character of Scripture doctrine which is without its place in this moral revelation (Newman 1909, p. 21).

He sketches an outline of this creed. It includes a principle which is exterior to the mind and which is attractive, infinitely exalted, perfect and incomprehensible; a surmise of a coming judgement; the knowledge of unbounded benevolence, wisdom and power as traced in visible creation; moral laws unlimited in their operation; something of hope respecting the availability of repentance; and an insight into the rule of duty. Although the history and study of religions was still in its infancy when Newman expressed these views, his reasoning from the nature of the moral conscience and from what was known of non-Christian religious traditions at the time led him to take this optimistic view.

However, Newman's optimism was tempered by a measure of realism. If such religious knowledge was attainable within non-Christian religions it was not actually attained. The incompleteness of the revelation vouchsafed to them, their ignorance of the incarnation, led to errors: 'the unworthy, multiplied and inconsistent images' of polytheism; fatalism; pantheism. Such errors occurred because men tried, by their own efforts, to attribute a personal and historical character to the Deity, or because they did not understand the personal character of the principle of good in themselves and in the universe. This was ultimately revealed in Christ. Newman, therefore, emphasized the continuities between non-Christian religions and Christianity, without condemning their adherents to perdition, and without embarrassment over the unique and universal character of the Christian revelation. What Christianity had to offer was a tangible, historical personalism. This was the revelation authenticated by God himself in human flesh.

Raimundo Panikkar, the Indian Catholic theologian, has offered us several approaches to the problem of other religions, particularly to the problem posed for Christians by Hinduism. These approaches are not contradictory, but they belong to different phases or contexts of his thought, as it were. With regard to Hinduism especially, Panikkar believes that no purely doctrinal or cultural encounter can take place. Hinduism believes in the relative equality of all religions and such a belief is fundamentally destructive of Catholic Christianity (Panikkar 1968 [and 1981]; Hick and Hebblethwaite 1980, pp. 122–150). Yet Christians cannot expect to win over Hindus to their own way of thinking by preaching a destruction or assimilation of Hinduism. Neither religion can escape a historical, existential encounter, and it is possible for them to meet at the level of mutual endeavour towards accomplishing the final goal of existence, the divine ultimate, however it is defined. For the Hindu, the two religions must either meet as two 'castes', striving towards the same end in their differences, or else forget their differences and accept each other in the divine basis of their origin as well as their goal.

For the Christian, the first alternative undermines his own faith. He is pledged to a meeting with other religions. But his own definition of the final goal of existence is Christ, who is the goal of revelation and salvation, indivisible from the God whom the Hindus would also probably accept as goal. Christ is both agent and object of revelation and salvation, and is already at work in Hinduism. This work, from the Christian point of view, is not yet complete; in Hinduism Christ has not yet suffered, died and risen. But the Christian must ultimately accept the Hindu challenge of sacrificing particular differences for the absolute goal. In existential dialogue a mutual *kenosis* or self-emptying has to take place, as both religions, each with the help of the other, visualize the absolute goal more clearly and draw closer to one another. This cannot happen through a conflict of formulas, but through 'naked faith, pure hope and supernatural love'. It is not enough for the Hindu to say 'We are the same'; the effort must be made by both Hindu and Christian to *be* the same.

Panikkar's vision is one of dialogue, although it plays down the cognitive aspects of this dialogue and the role of Christ as agent, as opposed to goal, of revelation. Its merits are that it places the encounter between the religions firmly in the historical sphere and stresses the dynamic character of Christianity itself. This is in the line of thinking which we laid down in Chapter 1, when considering the challenge of sociologists of religion, such as Peter Berger, who speak of the growing 'interpenetration' of religions. More and more theologians have come to describe the relationship in terms of 'dialogue', and it is clear that in any true dialogue there is both openness and commitment – openness to receive from others and commitment to one's own identity. Both these are necessary aspects of a common search for truth.

Stanley Samartha, another Asian theologian who is associated with the work of the World Council of Churches, sees the aspect of openness in dialogue as an authentic part of the process of revelation itself (Hick and Hebblethwaite 1980, pp. 151–170). The incarnation was itself the start of a finally effective dialogue between God and man. Moreover, argues Samartha, the purpose of the incarnation and paschal mystery is reconciliation of God with man, and of man with man in God. Furthermore, the Spirit has been given to us to lead us into the fullness of truth, and this search for truth cannot be conducted in isolation. It is a collective enterprise. For all these reasons, it is an essential part of the Church's task to listen – to hear what the Word is saying in the non-Christian traditions of the world, as well as what he is saying in the Church. We must listen to the Word whenever and wherever he speaks, and that (incidentally) is the reason for the choice of title to this chapter: 'Hearing the Word'. This fundamental attitude of openness has recently been very finely expressed by the German Protestant theologian of religions Horst Bürkle. His call is not for the 'multiplication of our own mode of ecclesiality' but for

> an openness to receive and participate in everything which the Church still has need of in the present in order to express [its] universality . . . (Bürkle 1977, p. 138).

Openness, in Bürkle's view, becomes a commitment of Christians towards the true nature of their own Church. A similar point of view is expressed by Bishop John V. Taylor, who sees the positive value of dialogue as one of exposing our own religious experience to one another's questionings while letting each other know what the unchanging absolutes are in our own experience (Hick and Hebblethwaite 1980, pp. 212–233).

John Macquarrie, the Scottish Episcopalian theologian, reminds us that a commitment to the truth of our own absolutes is not sufficient. Nor is it even enough to grope towards a fuller understanding of these absolutes, knowing that the fullness of truth resides in Christ, and that he can help us refine and reconceive our picture of the truth in the light of the questions put to us by other religions. Absolutizing demands the service of a universal truth, and therefore an altruistic sense of mission (Macquarrie 1979, p. 352). Does not the notion of dialogue, therefore, bring us back to the absolutist-inclusivist claim, in some form resembling the gentle and eirenic universalism of Newman?

The German Protestant theologian Jürgen Moltmann offers the image of 'catalyst' to describe the unique and universal role of Christianity in revelation (Hick and Hebblethwaite 1980, pp. 191–211). Christianity must renounce its claim to direct evangelization, but act as a 'critical catalyst'. Just as a catalyst causes elements to combine simply through its presence, so Christians, by their presence all over the world, will indirectly 'infect' other religions with Christian ideas, values and principles. Without, in fact, Christianizing these religions completely, it is the Church's task to prepare other religions for the messianic era to which Christianity herself testifies. Another interesting image is provided by the American Catholic theologian Richard McBrien; the 'key' and the 'master key' (McBrien 1980, I, p. 237). While non-Christians may have 'keys' to the knowledge of God and may perhaps know him more fully than many Christians, Christ is himself the 'master-key' which opens all the doors to divine knowledge without exception. Christian faith exists outside the Church and non-Christians can exceed Christians in their knowledge and love of God. The explicit knowledge of Christ, however, makes possible the fullest knowledge and love of God, if those who possess this 'master-key' care to use it.

These ideas and images are perhaps more satisfactorily expressed in the work of the German Catholic theologian Heinz Robert Schlette (Schlette 1966). Schlette affirms the real nature of non-Christian religions as religions, that is to say, as vehicles of revelation and salvation. He also maintains that the dialogue between Christianity and these religions will help Christians to acquire a more profound and a more explicit understanding of the truth revealed in Jesus Christ. However, the basis of that revealed truth is that God's Kingdom is proclaimed and that the end of sacred history has begun. In Christianity is proclaimed the abrogation of all religions. The position of non-Christian religions in the economy of redemption is, therefore, one of pre-Christian expectancy, of divine pedagogy or educative action. This means that the divine educative action is only apparent *a posteriori* from the standpoint of fulfilment or actual Christianization.

It will be plain that, at the end of this discussion, we are back where we started from. Apart from the idea of dynamic, on-going dialogue, we have not really postulated any actual connection between divine revelation in non-Christian religions and the explicit memory and proclamation of Christ in the Church. We shall now turn to the debate which has surrounded the theory of the Catholic theologian Karl Rahner to see what further light this sheds on the problem.

The theory of 'anonymous Christianity' and its critique

Karl Rahner's thesis can be summarized as follows (Rahner 1976 and 1981). Christianity is the one, absolute and universal religion to which all men are called and for which they are destined. However, until the Christian Gospel actually enters the historical situation and the consciousness of the individual, this individual can adhere to a non-Christian religion as a lawful religion, thus fulfilling his obligation to worship God in a social form. This religion can only be lawful if it offers positive means for helping the 'pre-Christian' to gain a right relationship with God, whatever errors and deficiencies the system may contain. This means that non-Christian religions possess supernatural or grace-filled elements, and that those who profess them, even though they are not in contact with the historical life and tradition of Jesus, still receive the Spirit and the effect of the transcendent and immanent mystery of Christ within their life and consciousness. According to Rahner, it is proper to call such 'pre-Christians' 'Christians', but in an anonymous sense, since they have no explicit consciousness of being Christians. They are recipients of revelation and salvation and these are Christic. There is no other revelation or salvation besides Christ's. The Christian missionary, nevertheless, still has a role to bring the 'anonymous Christian' to explicit consciousness of the 'latent Christ' who is the agent, object and goal of all salvation. Rahner's hypothesis of 'anonymous Christianity' has been the object of a number of criticisms, some of which we have already touched on. Evangelical Christians who deny the possibility, or at very least the normal possibility, of salvation outside the visible Church have attacked this kind of theory vehemently. This is a logical consequence of the kind of exclusivist position taken by the Lausanne Congress in 1974, for example. Humanity cannot, it is argued, find salvation in Christ without direct news of the Gospel. Men cannot encounter him anonymously.

But it is not only Evangelicals who criticize the theory. Bishop Kenneth Cragg offers two basic criticisms. One is that Rahner's 'chivalrous' position could well be reversed, and one could as well speak of 'anonymous Buddhists' or 'anonymous Hindus', an idea that Christians might find even harder to accept (Cragg 1977, pp. 77–78). This is echoed by John Macquarrie, who calls Rahner's theory 'a concealed kind of imperialism' (Macquarrie 1979, p. 350). Imperialism is at best only superficially chivalrous, and the problem is, after all, a peculiarly Christian one. Christianity has the problem of interpreting other religions to itself. The other religions are generally content to coexist in an unsystematized pluralism. It would not, in fact, occur to a Hindu to call a Christian an 'anonymous Hindu' or to a Buddhist to call him an 'anonymous Buddhist'. The second criticism by Bishop Cragg is that anonymity and faith, ignorance and grace are 'unconvincing alliances' (Cragg 1977, pp. 77-78). Yet from a Christian standpoint Rahner's theory is not based on complete anonymity or on total ignorance. The theory offers the possibility of recognizing authentic Christian elements in non-Christian religions. Moreover, even an implicit Christian faith is a conscious faith, holding out the possibility of a growth in perception even if there is no recognizably explicit link with the Gospel (Rahner 1981, p. 48).

Bishop Cragg, however, goes on to ask: 'Are we not sent to preach the kingdom rather than to assume it?' (Cragg 1977, p. 78). He feels that Rahner would be more logical in making mysticism the essence of all religions, in which doctrinal anonymity would not then be an issue. This suggestion, as Cragg himself realizes, implies abandoning all search for criteria of truth, as well as any reference to Christian historical actuality. We would be left with a position similar to that proposed by John Hick.

Certainly, we are sent to preach the Kingdom. The controversial Catholic writer Hans Küng has called 'anonymous Christianity' a 'pseudo-solution' and seems to opt for the position of Jürgen Moltmann in which Christianity is a critical catalyst (Küng 1978, p. 99). For Küng, a person can only be described as a Christian if the life and death of Jesus Christ are ultimately decisive for him. He must commit himself wholly and entirely to the Christian message. In other words, the phrase 'anonymous Christian' is a contradiction in terms.

This also resembles the basis of Johann Baptist Metz's sweeping criticism of Rahner's theory. Metz calls the theory of his former teacher 'a theological hedgehog trick' (Metz 1980, pp. 158 ff.). This uncomplementary epithet refers to an old north German folk-tale which tells how a hare undertook to race against a hedgehog in parallel furrows of a ploughed field. The hare sprinted again and again to either end of his furrow, only to find each time that the hedgehog was already there at the end of his. The hare had been tricked by the hedgehog who had placed his identically similar wife at the other end of the furrow, and simply did no running at all.

In Metz's theological appplication of the folk-tale, the hare stands for the Christian, running through history; while the two hedgehogs stand for the non-Christian who is, from the point of view of salvation, 'already there'. The historical tradition which goes back to Christ is rendered pointless and the hare is harassed to death by the hedgehogs with their alternate cry of 'I am already here!' The theory of anonymous Christianity, therefore, guarantees the victory of Christianity without the experience of Christian history and praxis. The narrative memory of Christ is relativized and rendered unnecessary.

Rahner's reply to this kind of criticism is ingenious (Rahner 1981, pp. 47-49). He sees effective memory, *memoria*, as looking forwards, as well as backwards. It is, of course, true that *memoria* is eschatological – a future expectation, but with roots in the past, as Schillebeeckx has described it. *Memoria*, according to Rahner, is already active among non-Christians as an *a priori* possibility of historical experience. It seeks and watches for the absolute bringer of salvation who communicates it finally through a specific historical proclamation. Rahner leaves it to historians of religion to identify such anticipations and the historical forms which they take.

Rahner and Metz are on different 'wavelengths', as it were, but the anticipation of a disclosure of meaning does not exclude the fact of meaning already discovered in an unfolding historical praxis. The non-Christian is 'already there' through such experience. Moreover, eschatological expectation requires 'roots in the past'; and the historical traditions of non-Christians have to be accepted in their full historicity as vehicles of revelation and salvation.

Rahner's theory would seem to provide a starting-point for deeper reflection about the relationship of non-Christians to the Church, and it certainly goes beyond the Barthian notion of 'guaranteed waiting'. Rahner's anticipation is more than a passive waiting, and, as such, it demands further enquiry into the possibilities of a thoroughgoing historical approach to the question. What follows in this chapter is not claimed, by any means, to be a fully-fledged answer to the problem, but merely to glimpse the avenue along which the most fruitful line of enquiry may be pursued.

THE PLACE OF CHRIST IN A UNIVERSAL HISTORY OF REVELATION

Practical imitation of Christ

Echoing the optimism of John Henry Newman, the World Council of Churches expressed its commitment to the solution of this intractable problem:

> We believe that in addition to listening to one another, we need to know what people of other faiths and no faiths are saying about Jesus Christ and his followers. While we cannot agree on whether or how Christ is present in other religions, we do believe that God has not left himself without witness in any generation or any society. Nor can we exclude the possibility that God speaks to Christians from outside the Church. While we oppose any form of syncretism, we affirm the necessity for dialogue with men and women of other faiths and ideologies as a means of mutual understanding and practical co-operation (World Council of Churches, 1976, Section I, no. 25).

Statements like this about a dynamic dialogue with people of other faiths tend to lay stress on the cognitive aspect, and this, too, is characteristic of the theory of anonymous Christianity which we have just been discussing. Certainly, we should not abandon the cognitive aspect; otherwise, we fall into the trap of the vague mysticism condemned by Kenneth Cragg. Nevertheless, we must recognize, with R. C. Zaehner, that the religions of the world represent an interpenetration which produces a 'concordant discord' which no amount of philosophical or theological discussion can render homogenous or uniform. Zaehner has rather colourfully criticized the speculative tendencies of Christians:

> Christianity has, from the beginning, been plagued with theology; it has been plagued with the rational spirit of the Greeks, prying into what theology itself calls 'the mysteries of faith', busily defining the indefinable (Zaehner 1970, p. 16).

Zaehner called for a more pragmatic approach to the religions of the world and one which could go beyond tolerance, to experience other religions historically. All religions are in a process of creative evolution and the other religions share in this process in one way or another. As we saw, when speaking of dogmatic development at the end of the last chapter, the Church's understanding of itself is neither static, nor a question of simple, homogeneous or linear evolution. It is the outcome of interculturation, or the mutual influencing of living cultures, and lived situations.

As we have also seen, Raimundo Panikkar places the dynamic encounter of religions in the historical sphere, and calls upon Christianity to undergo a purifying transformation. Panikkar also believes that the development of all religions towards unity can be assisted by the actualization of the Church's catholicity (Panikkar 1973). In becoming more truly universal, in seeing itself through an alien religious experience, Christianity is not being imperialistic. Nor is it acting consciously as a critical catalyst. It is not precluding any other attempted synthesis which is the product of true dialogue (one that takes account of differences as well as of similarities), and which adopts as starting-point a non-Christian religion. It is simply issuing an invitation to understand the fundamental insight and tendency of all religious consciousness, which links together the 'infinitude' of man tending towards God, and the 'finitude' of God who is the *finis* or end of man. This vision of reality Panikkar calls 'theandric'. There are not two realities, God *and* man; but neither is there only one reality, God *or* man. Reality is theandric, and God and man are in close 'constitutive collaboration for the building-up of reality, for the unfolding of history and the continuation of creation' (Panikkar 1973, p. 75).

For Johann Baptist Metz, the 'inviting *logos* of Christianity' encourages imitation:

> It has a narrative structure with a practical and liberating intention. If this is expressed in Christological terms, it means that the salvation that is founded 'for all men' in Christ does not become universal via an idea, but via the intelligible power of a praxis, the praxis of following Christ. This intelligibility of Christianity cannot be transmitted theologically in a purely speculative way. It can only be transmitted in narrative – as a narrative and practical Christianity (Metz 1980, p. 165).

For Christian theology, the universal meaning of history has already been established in Christ. There can be no other point of departure. Humanity has already been saved long ago by the definitive action of God in Jesus Christ. In Christ, there is, in fact, only one history of salvation and the 'special' history of salvation has become paradigmatic of the whole of salvation history. Salvation does not occur only in virtue of, and with reference to, an anticipation of future historical events, a future proclamation of the Gospel of Christ. It happens here and now, in every history, and the yardstick with which to measure its occurrence is simply practical conformity to, consistent imitation of, Christ.

Every religion, therefore, is an unfolding history of the intelligible power of Christ, transmitted through historical lives and the historical interaction of people, events and cultures. Christianity is itself the product of such a history and interaction, and becomes more truly itself as its universality and interculturality is further actualized. In Christianity this is truly of the essence. Its identity and uniqueness, going back to the historic actuality of Christ himself, consists in the fact that its vocation is to be at the centre of man's search for meaning. The tradition or narrative memory of Christ, preserved and celebrated in the Church, is an effective sign of the ground of all religion and of all being. It points to this 'ground' or this 'meaning' and it helps to put people in touch with it.

Christianity does not deny to other religions elements of its own insight. On the contrary, Christians are bound to look for evidence that their insights are shared. That is the meaning of the patristic phrases *vestigia Christi* and *semina verbi,* and of the World Council of Churches' and the Second Vatican Council's call to hear the Word speaking to Christians from outside the visible bounds of the Church. However, they must not see these elements as static, propositional truths, as a purely, or mainly, notional Gospel. The Gospel is a way of life, and Christ reveals his lordship and his saving activity through events and relationships of love, compassion and hope; freedom from sin and guilt and suffering; in a word, through reconciliation. Other religions are incomplete, but so is Christianity. The Christian pilgrimage is still continuing, and its future form will depend to a very great extent on the repercussions which it experiences from interpenetration with other religions. Equally, Christianity does not deny to other religions the right to make their own reading of universal salvation history.

The originality of this viewpoint, which we derive from theologians such as Metz and Panikkar, with the aid of the objective studies of religions by such scholars as Zaehner, Bowker and Smart, is to abolish the separate historical 'furrow' of 'special' salvation history. This is not done in any sense that could possibly diminish in Christian eyes the uniqueness and finality of God's self-revelation in Jesus Christ. Instead of the parallel furrows borrowed from the north German folk-tale, another image is needed. Perhaps a suitable one could be found in the incandescent lamp (familiar to missionaries!), which, as it is gradually turned up, reflects more and more light from the mirrors, glasses and other shiny objects in the room. In the same way, the Word made Flesh, the 'inviting *logos* of Christianity' is already present and active in the whole of human history, successively and – for the most part – cumulatively imparting and borrowing more and more light from the religious traditions of the world. God-in-Christ reveals himself – witnesses to himself – in every truly religious history. Praxis is accompanied by knowledge and intelligibility, and this is a growing phenomenon which attains fuller consciousness when baptized people who are consistently faithful to Christ witness explicitly in word and work to the decisive revelation contained in the Gospel and to the activity of Christ's Spirit in the non-Christian tradition to which they come, or of which they have been a part.

Panikkar rightly argues that the meeting of dynamic religious traditions cannot take place on neutral ground, or in a no-man's-land (Panikkar 1973, pp. 5-6). If Christians can hear God speaking to them in other religions, that voice will come from the very heart of these traditions. It will also bear the Christological-Trinitarian traces of true 'seeds of the word', bearing in mind that each non-Christian religion will have its own emphasis and that its insights will carry the Christian further in the understanding of his own tradition. Generally speaking, however, trinitarian parallels in other religions are not couched in personal terms. Yet the Trinity (according to Panikkar) is the 'junction where the authentic spiritual dimensions of all religions meet' (Panikkar 1973, p. 42).

The apophatic Word of Buddhism

The Second Vatican Council had this to say about the Buddhist religion:

> Buddhism, in its various forms, testifies to the essential inadequacy of this changing world. It proposes a way of life by which men can, with confidence and trust, attain a state of perfect liberation and reach supreme illumination either through their own efforts or by the aid of divine help (*Nostra Aetate,* 2).

Convinced of the illusoriness of the world, the Buddha not only found prevailing ideas of God implausible, he found language totally inadequate to do justice to the goal of human life, that final illumination he called *nirvana*. The Buddha's language was apophatic. That is to say, he affirmed by denying and conveyed meaning through silence. The state of enlightenment transcended anything that could be conceived or experienced in this world, but the Buddha did not want to identify himself as an eternalist or as an annihilationist. That was why, in reply to the venerable Malunkyaputta's questioning, he said:

That the world is eternal has not been explained by me, Malunkyaputta; that the world is not eternal . . . that the world is finite . . . that the world is not finite . . . that the life-principle and the body are the same . . . that the life-principle is one thing and the body another thing . . . that after dying the Tathagata [the 'Thus Gone One'] is . . . is not . . . both is and is not . . . neither is nor is not has not been explained by me, Malunkyaputta. And why, Malunkyaputta, has this not been explained by me? It is because it is not connected with the goal [. . .] does not conduce to turning away from, nor to dispassion, stopping, calming, superknowledge, awakening nor to *nibbana* [*nirvana*] (Foy 1978, p. 218).

R. C. Zaehner argued that the silence of the Buddha implies, at the very least, that the state of enlightenment itself exists, and that this is really a way of speaking about an eternal state of being or an entirely new mode of existence, guaranteeing immortality like the Christian idea of the resurrection (Zaehner 1970, p. 102). However, the Buddha's silence was also a silence about God and God-relatedness, and he refused to describe *nirvana* in theistic or personalist terms.

The Buddha's teaching concerns the absolute transcendental, the final mystery, which cannot be affirmed or denied because he refused to speculate about the continuity of the knowing subject or whether, indeed, there was a self. Only in death itself can the Buddhist be proved right or wrong (Bowker 1978, p. 306). And yet, the Buddha's teaching and example bear witness to an attitude of humility and responsiveness towards the ultimate mystery of life, and they also testify to a power of attraction for others. The theistic paradox, which is most evident in the cult of images of the Buddha, endowed with the Buddha's living presence, is not so much a 'back-door' corruption, nor even a yearning to fill the 'God-shaped blank' left by the Buddha's silence, as a paradox at the heart of Buddhist teaching. *Nirvana* is rationally inconceivable, and the discipline of self-restraint in its service does not logically demand that one show love, and compassion, for others (Bowker 1978, p. 256; Gombrich 1971, p. 322). This, according to Zaehner, is an 'ingrained' contradiction in Buddhism (Zaehner 1970, p. 175). Richard Gombrich, however, in his study of Buddhist precept and practice in Sri Lanka, sees the Buddhist religion operating at an affective level which appears sometimes to contradict the cognitive level of explicit teaching (Gombrich 1971, p. 140).

Buddhism offers the Christian an extreme example of religious apophatism. Not only does it see into the nothingness of life, it also looks into what Panikkar calls the 'no-face' of God. The source of being cannot be just being. God is a 'total silence', the silence of being, beyond negation, beyond affirmation, impervious to atheistic speculation. Yet, historically, the apophatism of the Buddha creates confidence and trust. He is the revealer, a human, and not a divine, guarantee, but one through whom – as Buddhist history shows – the divine has been experienced affectively. The cult of the Boddhisattvas even displays its own trinitarian form, with the *Trikaya* or three bodies, of ultimate foundation, of bliss and of transformation for earthly presence.

Buddhism throws light upon the God described by the New Testament as the Father of Jesus Christ. For this is a God who is fundamentally silent and unknowable, except as he is seen and known in the Son. 'No one has ever seen God; the only Son, who is in the bosom of the Father, he has made him known' (John 1:18); '. . . no one knows the Father except the Son and any one to whom the Son chooses to reveal him' (Matthew 11:27); 'He [Christ] is the image of the invisible God' (Colossians 1:15). More, perhaps, than the Old Testament, the writers of the New Testament lay stress on the unknowability and inapproachability of God, who is only known and approached through Christ: 'He who has seen me has seen the Father' (John 14:9). As Panikkar has written in this context: 'there is nothing else to see of the Father, except the result of his paternity, namely, the Son' (Panikkar 1973, p. 49). The insight of the Buddha may serve to highlight this aspect of Christian Trinitarian doctrine and the unique mediating role of Jesus Christ.

Cosmic consciousness in Vedic and in traditional ethnic religion

It has already been mentioned in Chapter 1 that in traditional ethnic religions there is a symbolic interaction between human society and the world of nature. Religion always offers mankind a unifying dimension through which to interpret experience, and the problem of the unity and multiplicity of reality seems uppermost in the ethnic religions. The two words which most often spring to the lips of a scholar of religions who is trying to understand the ethnic religions are 'polytheism' and 'pantheism', and yet both these terms do these religions an injustice. The religious practitioner is not scandalized by a philosophical absurdity or by a confusion of categories. He is simply expressing his experience in terms of images that are in dialectical tension or an evolutionary profusion.

The ancient Vedic religion of India, to judge by the collection of hymns it has bequeathed to us, expressed this cosmic consciousness through the interplay of men and gods and of matter and spirit. The divine was over all, through all and in all, and no clear distinction could be drawn. However, it could not be said that divinity *was* all. The following quotations from a hymn about the creation suggest that spirit evolved from matter:

> There was not non-existent nor existent;
> there was no realm of air, no sky beyond it . . .
> Death was not then, nor was there aught immortal;
> no sign was there, the days' and nights' divider . . .
> Thereafter rose desire in the beginning,
> desire the primal seed and germ of spirit . . .
> The gods are later than this world's production;
> who knows whence it first came into being? (Ballou 1940, p. 3).

Later, in the unusual hymn to the primal man, the world appears to be one part of a sacrificially divided spiritual being:

So mighty is his greatness;
yea, greater than this is Purusha,
all creatures are one fourth of him,
three fourths are the immortal in heaven (Ballou 1940, p. 20).

In the religion of the Vedas, the divine is projected in personal images of gods. These are the protagonists of Vedic mythology, which eludes critical historical analysis.

This is not the case necessarily with the personifications of, for example, African ethnic religions. The same continuities between God, divinities and the world, and between divinities and human beings, are there, but frequently there is a discernible historical basis. A historical personality is a bearer of revelation. In Uganda, for example, Kintu is one of the divinities credited with a human existence (Nsimbi 1974). He was the first king of the Ganda people, and was alleged to be of semi-divine parentage. He taught people how to worship and how to live moral lives. At his death, his tomb became a shrine, a focus for liturgical celebration and for the recitation of his moral teachings. There are numerous other religious 'founders' of this kind in Africa: Nyikang of the Sudanese Shilluk, Kyala of the Tanzanian Nyak-yusa or M'Bona of the peoples of the Zambezi valley, to name but a few.

Ideas of reincarnation were not perhaps so widespread or so literal in Africa as in India, but they have been present at many times and in many places. At their most explicit, they are to be found among the Ashanti of Ghana, who believe that a person is reincarnated again and again until his life-work is complete and he is qualified to enter the world of the ancestors. In African religion, as among all ethnic religions, the typically supreme value is the transmission of human life, which links human beings with divine reality, usually through the ancestors who play the role of divine plenipotentiaries, but sometimes also through the persons of divine rulers whose psychological and biological life are bound to the rhythms of the world of nature, rulers like the Yoruba kings of Nigeria, the Ashanti king of Ghana or the paramount chief of the Bemba of Zambia.

An example of the interaction betweeen human ancestors and God is provided by the following short prayer used by the Mende of Sierra Leone. In asking God to let the prayer reach the ancestors, the Mende resemble the Kimbu of Tanzania (on the other side of the African continent), who call upon God to witness that prayer to the ancestors has been offered.

O God, let it reach to Kenei Momo,
Let it reach to Nduawo,
Let it reach to all our forefathers
Who are in your arms (Harris 1950, p. 201).

In a few lines it is impossible to do justice to the depth and variety of religious belief and feeling among the ethnic religions. Their cosmic consciousness testifies to the interrelatedness of all reality, but it is, perhaps, as Zaehner calls it, largely 'a mysticism of the body' (Zaehner 1970, p. 52). More important, perhaps, as 'seeds of the word', are the ways in which the adherents of these religions look for icons or images of divine reality in personal form, and particularly in human, incarnational form.

Personalism and mutual love in the *Bhagavad Gita*

The *Bhagavad Gita,* 'the Song of the Lord', is the chief written expression of the classical Hinduism which was a devotional development of Vedic religion. Devotion (*bhakti*) and love are the normal ways in which a personalist spirituality develops. What is involved is interpersonality, mutual giving, mutual acceptance. God does what a person does: he loves, forgives, judges, punishes, rewards. He is a mystery of love, far, far superior to human love. Classical Hinduism personalized the philosophical concepts of the heterogeneity of God and self, and their complementarity, by using developed forms of the Vedic gods. Shiva represents the first and Vishnu the second – the highest Brahman and the highest self, true transcendence and true immanence. Vishnu takes on human and animal forms in order to restore harmony in the world. Krishna, the human incarnation of Vishnu, steps out of mythology to become the mentor of the song's hero, Arjuna.

The Upanishads had already used the notion of the 'Lord' as representing the unity underlying the diversity of the world:

> By the Lord enveloped must this all be –
> whatever moving thing there is in the moving world.
> With this renounced, thou mayest enjoy.
> Covet not the wealth of anyone at all (Iśā Upanishad, 1; Foy 1978, p. 83).

Now Krishna's guidance is to be accepted in self-discipline and 'stabilized mentality'. Yoga is the keyword of the *Bhagavad Gita.* It is the self-restraint of the spiritual athlete who renounces the fruits of action, instead of action itself, and whose detachment leads to attachment. In this he acknowledges God's lordship and does his duty for the sake of the Lord. The song celebrates the right attitude of devotion which must be shown to the Lord, and the bonds of reciprocal love which unite him to the sinner who calls upon him. R. C. Zaehner sees the *Gita's* ideal of 'attachment' as on a higher plane than the Buddhist ideal of *nirvana.* It is union with God. In Zaehner's words, the *Bhagavad Gita* is 'the most significant sacred text in the whole history of religion' (Zaehner 1970, pp. 128, 177).

> The Blessed One said:
> With mind attached to Me, son of Prthā,
> Practising discipline with reliance on me,

Without doubt, Me entirely
How thou shalt know, that hear! (Foy 1978, p. 110).

But those whose sin is ended,
Men of virtuous deeds
Freed from the delusion of the pairs,
Revere Me with firm resolve.

Unto freedom from old age and death
Those who strive, relying on Me,
They know that Brahman entire,
And the over-soul, and action altogether.

Me together with the over-being and the over-divinity,
And with the over-worship, whoso know,
And [who know] Me even at the hour of death,
They truly know [Me], with disciplined hearts (Foy 1978, pp. 113–114).

Arjuna, the devotee in the song, experiences the ecstasy of being loved, possessed and ravished by God. He is vouchsafed what Ninian Smart calls a 'shattering experience', the vision of God, clothed in the mythological emblems of the cult of Vishnu.

But thou canst not see Me
With this same eye of thine own;
I give thee a supernatural eye:
Behold my mystic power as God!

Samjaya said:
Thus speaking then, O King,
Hari [Vishnu] the great Lord of Mystic Power,
Showed unto the son of Prthā [Arjuna],
His supernal form as God:

Of many mouths and eyes,
Of many wondrous aspects,
Of many marvelous ornaments,
Of marvelous and many uplifted weapons;

Wearing marvelous garlands and garments,
With marvelous perfumes and ointments,
Made up of all wonders, the god,
Infinite, with faces in all directions (Foy 1978, p. 115).

Arjuna said:
I see the gods in Thy body, O God,
All of them, and the hosts of various kinds of beings too,
Lord Brahma sitting on the lotus-seat,
And the seers all, and the divine serpents (Foy 1978, p. 116).

Thou art the Primal God, the Ancient Spirit,
Thou art the supreme resting-place of this universe,
Thou art the knower, the object of knowledge, and the highest station,
By Thee the universe is pervaded, Thou of infinite form (Foy 1978, p. 119).

The Song of the Lord represents a supreme moment in the Hindu revelation, of God imaged in human form, and of interpersonal union between God and man. Yet, as Zaehner remarks, this God of Hinduism is never entirely divorced from his creation, and his epic, the *Bhagavad Gita*, is not rooted in historical events perceived and experienced as such. This unfolding of Hindu mystical experience, no less than that of the Upanishads and the Vedanta which we shall consider shortly, can be for the Christian an approach to the life of God in the Trinity, and, as the Second Vatican Council says in speaking of Hinduism generally, of 'recourse to God in confidence and love' (*Nostra Aetate*, 2).

Iconomorphism in Judaism and Islam

It may seem strange to speak of icons or images of God in Judaism and Islam, religions which proverbially ban all iconography or representation of God, but, as Panikkar points out, the iconomorphic spirituality does not require idols or pictures, and may even repudiate them with vehemence. It needs to speak of God, not in silence and apophatism, but in terms of symbols culled from experience. Creaturely forms, mental or material, have to be attributed to God if he is to be known as Other. Basic anthropomorphism is necessary, for the icon stands for the homogeneity which subsists between God and his creature. It is this homogeneity which comes to the fore in the Vedic and ethnic religions and which is developed with greater affectivity in the personalism of the *Bhagavad Gita*. In Judaism and Islam the holiness or otherness of God is represented in an exclusive pattern which stresses the provisional nature of the symbols used, and points to the underlying reality. If God were totally Other, he could not be known as Other, and so Yahweh and Allah are described in anthropomorphic terms.

About Judaism much has already been said in this book. The religious experience of the Jews has been one of closeness-in-separation where Yahweh was concerned. Their theistic language in speaking of him was never questioned, and it was able to take its final form (from the Christian point of view) in Jesus Christ, for whom the relationship with the transcendent God of Israel was a dialogue between persons. Judaism has survived without the acceptance of the incarnation, and many Jews look upon Christ as the 'true Jew', the classic Jewish healer and holy man.

An important reason for the survival of Judaism is that the Jewish experience of God is bound up with the fortunes of a people. They have been convinced of the exclusive character of their revelation, of which the corner-stone is the Torah. This is not to say that their religion is literally a religion of the Book. Rather, it is a form of spiritual Zionism – 'a resettlement in the Lord' through the Torah, as one Jewish writer has expressed it (Z. H. Kallischer in Foy 1978, p. 415). Israel's particularism has never been wholly exclusive. Jews are not spiritual supermen with a special genius for religion. They have been chosen to fulfil God's purposes, in the service of, and as a sign to, others.

Already in the New Testament Christians asked themselves what message lay in the survival of Judaism. St Paul hinted at a stupendous revelation accompanying the final inclusion of Israel in the salvation brought by Christ; 'For the gifts and the call of God are irrevocable' (Romans 11:12, 29), while the Gospel of Luke suggests that there is a specific period of Gentile supremacy and that Jerusalem will be trodden down 'until the times of the Gentiles are fulfilled' (Luke 21:24). Perhaps the Jewish religion is destined to survive as a sign of the conquest of suffering and of the, as yet, unfulfilled mission of Christianity. For the Jews, however, it cannot be said that the 'dividing wall' between Israel and the uncircumcised has been broken down in Christ (Ephesians 2:14).

Hendrik Kraemer has said that the greatness of Islam lies in its 'question-less and answer-less' character. Certainly, much of its attraction lies in the stark and consistent simplicity of its affirmation that Allah is, its assertion of God's 'findability'. However, not only is the rejection of Christianity apparently inherent in Islamic faith, so also is its ultimate rejection of mysticism. There is little personalism in Islam, for the personality of Allah is engulfed in the 'burning heat' of his attributes and of his sublime names (Kraemer 1961, pp. 217, 220–221).

Man is lost without a code of conduct and this is provided in an externalized revelation in the form of immutable, divine words. In Islam the Word is not made flesh, the Word is made Book:

> The unbelievers of the people of the Book
> and the idolaters would never leave off,
> till the Clear Sign came to them,
> a Messenger from God, reciting pages purified,
> therein true Books.
> And they scattered not, those that were given the Book,
> excepting after the Clear Sign came to them.
> They were commanded only to serve God,
> making the religion His sincerely,
> men of pure faith, and to perform
> the prayer, and pay the alms – that is
> the religion of the True (Qur'an, 98; quoted in Foy 1978, p. 473).

The Clear Sign from Allah, given through Muhammad, in the celestial and pre-existent Qur'an, provokes fierce loyalty and absolute surrender. There is (in Kraemer's words) a 'hyperbolic theocentricity' which almost abolishes the place of man in the God–man relationship (Kraemer 1961, p. 221). So for Islam, the intimate union of the soul with God in the experience of Muslim mystics borders on blasphemy. It also implies a personalist relationship of love which raises the question of the organic unity of God. Abu Yazid was one Muslim mystic who saw that where there is love there is trinity: 'Lover, Love and Beloved are all one, for in the world of union all must be one'. Muslim mysticism is, perhaps, both a derivative from Christianity (as R. C. Zaehner suggests), and a yearning for the liberation of man in the divine freedom which the approach to God in a personal relationship guarantees (Zaehner 1959, p. 106). There have been many revelatory moments in the history of Islam, and John Bowker is prepared to place the experience of Muhammad on Mount Hira beside that of the mystic al-Ghazali (Bowker 1978, pp. 191–240). Meanwhile, the modern Islamic revolution recalls a confused world to the 'Clear Sign' of conformity with the divine order.

Upanishads and Vedanta: The non-duality of the Real

That we return once more to the Indian religious experience is testimony to the immense richness that is to be found there. The speculations of the Upanishads take the experience of cosmic consciousness much further than the majority of the Vedas. Their most important contribution is their meditation on the unity of the soul, the world and God. As the Catholic theologian Piet Schoonenberg has suggested, to describe our experience of God as two persons reaching out to one another from their own mutual limitation and ultimate loneliness is ultimately inadequate (Schoonenberg 1977, p. 90). God is already with us. He is all. He is the 'ground of our being', 'nearer to me', as St Augustine wrote, 'than I am to myself'. And yet a pantheistic, or a purely immanent God, is not more knowable, let alone more plausible, than a purely transcendent God. It was with this problem that the Upanishads wrestled, while preserving other personalist and theistic modes of God-talk.

The Upanishads treat of the mystery in the depths of the human soul and of the liberation of man from his human condition into an absolute form of existence, while seeking to avoid regression into the elemental consciousness that pre-existed his consciousness of incommunicable selfhood. In this attempt, they are forced to pass beyond the limitations of the human reason and beyond logic or the law of contradiction. Like the salt dissolved in water, as described in the Chandogya Upanishad, the divine being pervades the whole world and its distinction from the world is unperceived by the senses. Yet the Upanishads are not proclaiming a crude monism. The key to their message is contained in the word *advaita*, 'non-duality'. God and the world are one, and they are also not one, at the same time. They are not one thing and they are not two things. The Mandukya Upanishad puts it in more abstract form than the Chandogya Upanishad:

Not that which cognises the internal, not that which cognises the external, not that which cognises both of them, not a mass of cognition, not cognitive, not non-cognitive. Unseen, incapable of being spoken of, ungraspable, without any distinctive marks, unthinkable, unnameable, the essence of the knowledge of the one self, that into which the world is resolved, the peaceful, the benign, the non-dual . . . . (Mandukya Upanishad, 7; Radhakrishnan 1953, p. 698).

This perspective of divine reality defies logic. It can only ultimately be known in mystical abandonment, in revelation, in the grace of faith. It is a vision of total union with God in dialogue. It does not affirm through denying, or through silence. It is not apophatic. It both affirms and denies. It both says and unsays, holding on, as it were, to two ends of a chain without being able to say how they are joined.

The search for a fuller expression of this liberating experience continued among the teachers of the schools known as the Vedanta in the medieval period of Hinduism. These can be described as an attempt to reconcile the conclusions of the Upanishads with the theistic traditions of the Vedas. One of the great exponents of these schools was Shankara, whose monistic tendencies are mitigated by his theory of the two levels of thought, or two phases of divine reality. These are a lower and more personal conception and a higher, less determinate conception like that we have been considering in the Upanishads. Shankara could not ultimately admit that God is a pure monad. Once again – as in the thought of Abu Yazid – the God revealed in loving dialogue turns out to be trinitarian in some sense. Shankara admitted a pluralism in the absolute ground of all reality. It is *saccidananda*: 'being' (*sac*), 'awareness' (*cit*), 'bliss' (*ananda*). The Ground of being turns out to be, not a sort of fundamental energy in matter but a living God, almost identical, as Zaehner notes, with the Christian Trinity: Substance, Logos and Love, but ultimately lacking the Christian insistence on a personal dimension (Zaehner 1957, p. 140).

The Trinity, revealed in reflection by the first Christians on the climactic experience of Jesus Christ, is thus not only the meeting-place of the religious insights we have been considering, but is somehow enhanced by them. Thus Panikkar is able to recognize the 'unseen' Father of the New Testament in Buddhist apophatism, the Son 'in the bosom of the Father' in the iconomorphism and personalism of the theistic religions of Asia and Africa, Judaism and Islam, and the Spirit 'who fills the whole world' in the non-dual God of Vedantic Brahmanism. And we note, also, how each of these religious emphases aspires to the others, finding in some cases a synthesis which parallels the Christian Trinity.

Atheism, humanism and the search for meaning

The Second Vatican Council dealt with a phenomenon of increasing importance in the Western world, if not in the world at large. A growing number of men and women of intellectual and moral worth deny, or suspend judgement about, the traditional affirmations of religion, particularly those of Christianity. Distinctions must be drawn between different attitudes, and it must be recognized that religion in general and Christianity in particular can derive positive gains from such attitudes. In some cases these people are simply rejecting a false understanding of God which may have been given them by a misguided emphasis on the part of believers themselves, or they may be prompted by a violent protest against evils which they deem to be incompatible with belief in God. Both these causes can be helpful to believers in their own self-questioning and self-identification, as various other sections of this book have shown. Other causes of non-belief are a rational-positivist outlook or the general apathy and lack of intellectual curiosity induced by the bourgeois consumer-society. In some Third World countries aggressive colonialism has sapped the credibility of traditional non-Christian religions, while Christianity has been presented in an uncongenial, metaphysical form. This has led – particularly among intellectuals – to forms of non-belief.

Kenneth Kaunda, President of Zambia, has said that atheism demands a peculiar form of heroism (Kaunda 1973, pp. 22–23). Can one achieve the same kind of certainty about the non-existence of God, as one can about faith in him? True atheism is basically a thirst for the absolute, which drives the non-believer beyond everything that has existence – beyond meaning itself – unless, as often happens with the Marxist intellectual, he invests the material universe with a kind of spiritual vitality which causes spirit to emerge from matter. This kind of atheism, is as Raimundo Panikkar points out, 'an eloquent spokesman' for the divine transcendence which defies all human initiatives in seeking and describing it (Panikkar 1973, p. 78). It is, if you like, the illogical belief in a transcendental principle that is unknowable because it has no roots in immanence. In the Marxist form it is not unlike (as R. C. Zaehner shows) certain types of cosmic consciousness (Zaehner 1970, p. 74).

The agnostic is more cautious, and more logical, in suspending belief about the existence of God. In this, he certainly approaches the apophatism of certain kinds of Buddhism. The humanist exalts man by denying, or casting doubt upon, God. All these positions are compromises or half-truths. In many ways they even resemble some of the religious beliefs we have just been considering, but without the opening on to theological development, further discovery of meaning, or radical renewal. The militant atheist or convinced humanist cannot be content to live in a world devoid of meaning. His theoretical position demands, as we have said, a commitment to continuing research, just as religion itself is similarly committed. Above all, living in this world demands a commitment to humankind, and this implies, as David Jenkins argues, a commitment to the triumph of personalism over the threatening determinism of the impersonal (Jenkins 1967). Reality is theandric, and this theandric reality is guaranteed for all time by the incarnation of the Word, Jesus Christ, who reveals the 'unseen God' and introduces the spirit of harmony and interrelatedness among all beings – Jesus Christ who reveals the pattern of fulfilment of every human being as person.

NOTE

1   Unpublished memorandum, Evangelical/Roman Catholic Dialogue on Mission, Venice, 19–23 April 1977.

QUESTIONS FOR DISCUSSION

(1)   What are the problems in reconciling the notion of implicit faith with historically experienced revelation-salvation?

(2)   How can a definitive Christian revelation relate credibly to non-Christian religious traditions without denying their right to exist?

(3)   In what sense was J. H. Newman correct to say that 'no people has been denied a revelation from God'?

(4)   For further enquiry: How far do the different forms of atheism in the modern world present a special problem for inclusivist theologies of salvation?

SELECT ANNOTATED READING LIST

P. Fransen, 1967: 'How Can Non-Christians Find Salvation in their Own Religions?' in J. Neuner (ed.) *Christian Revelation and World Religions* (London), pp. 67–122. In a few pages Fransen sums up the thought of contemporary Catholic theologians on implicit faith and salvation outside the Church.

C. Davis, 1970: *Christ and the World Religions* (London). A fuller statement of the problem of salvation in non-Christian religions and of the Christian theology of world religions.

K. Rahner, 1981: *Theological Investigations*, Vol. 17 (London). In pp. 40ff. Rahner reconsiders his theory of anonymous Christianity and answers his critics. The section is entitled: 'Jesus Christ in the Non-Christian Religions'.

J. Hick and B. Hebblethwaite (eds.), 1980: *Christianity and Other Religions* (Fontana, Glasgow). This is a helpful book of readings which gives the whole spectrum of opinions, Catholic and Protestant, about the relationship of Christianity to other religions.

W. Foy (ed.), 1978: *Man's Religious Quest* (London). This is a large paperback (more than 700 pages) but very worthwhile as a comprehensive review of religions. It is a compendium of readings from sacred texts of all the world religions and of comments by scholars and religious thinkers. The book was designed as a textbook for the Open University.

7

The Ingrafted Word

THE ACT OF FAITH

Revelation, the cause of faith

St James exhorted his Judeo-Christian community, and indeed all Christians, to receive with meekness the 'implanted' or 'ingrafted' word of truth (James 1:21). This word of truth, otherwise called by him 'the law of freedom' is all that God has revealed to the human race definitively and ultimately in Jesus Christ. For James it is a pure gift from the 'Father of Lights' which begets us to a new life and which moves us from simple hearing to zealous action.

The ultimacy of God's self-revelation in Christ is, as we have just seen, an inclusive, dynamically orientated ultimacy. The Second Vatican Council teaches that God does not deny the assistance necessary for salvation to any man or woman of goodwill and that his self-gift is not remote from them, even if they have no explicit knowledge of the Gospel of Christ or seek the unknown God in 'shadows and images' (*Lumen Gentium,* 16). Furthermore, we have claimed that, if Christianity is to actualize its own catholicity, it must undertake an historical encounter with the living faiths in which God's grace is also active and in which Christ's power is also being revealed and unfolded.

For Christians, God's supreme act of self-revelation was the revelation of Christ as risen and alive. St Paul, referring to his experience on the Damascus road, said simply ' . . . he who had set me apart before I was born, and had called me through his grace, was pleased to reveal his Son to [or in] me' (Galatians 1:15–16). The apparition stories are passing moments in this process of revelation. They describe an initiative that comes from God in the shape of a mysterious 'catechist', a young man, a pair of angels in white, 'the angel of the Lord' or even Christ himself at first mistaken for a fellow pilgrim, a gardener, a ghost or a fisherman on the lake shore. In the case of Paul, it is a blinding light accompanied by a voice. The inconsistencies of the apparition accounts reflect the confusion of the witnesses. There is a mixture of recognition and unfamiliarity, of faith and doubt, of fear and joy, of closeness and separation.

As a result, they are convinced that Jesus is alive, but known to them now in a new way, and they proclaim him as such, as 'Christ' and 'Lord'. From the apparition stories and from the Easter kerygma itself, it is clear that the New Testament writers are not simply using non-factual imagery to describe the survival of their faith in Jesus beyond his passion and death. It is equally clear that they are not merely speaking of the resuscitation of a person who was in some sense dead (as the 'clinically dead' are sometimes resuscitated). Nor is the Risen Christ a disembodied personality, for his personality reveals itself in the apparitions in bodily form. However different or 'spiritual' Christ's body became after the resurrection, it shared in his personal reality, as the body does in the personal reality of every human being who is alive.

The Risen Christ revealed himself as recognizably the same, and yet as radically different, a new reality. Through the resurrection Jesus was transformed to the very roots of his humanity. His personality received its fullest and most overwhelming expression. His followers experienced him as totally and fully alive, unlimited in his presence to them and closer to them than he could possibly have been in an ordinary, physical body. Yet their experience of him went even deeper than this. He communicated himself to them, pictorially experienced and expressed in the apparition accounts through his sharing of food with them and his table-fellowship, redolent of the messianic feast. The Risen Christ revealed himself in them as 'Lord', as a life-giving spirit endowing them with new power and life through personal communion with him.

The Risen Christ was known to be alive and with God. He did not just 'die into God' but lives now to God and to humanity. He was now felt palpably by the apostles in their own lives, in their own new-found capacity for a self-sacrificing love capable of overcoming all the destructive forces inside and outside themselves. Jesus was now experienced as the source of the Spirit, the agent of a spiritual revolution or renewal which drove people forward to carry on his mission of a reconciling and healing love. The resurrection was the continuation of Christ's own mystery in the lives of his followers. They were to be baptized into his death and into his rising. They were to continue and to complete his sufferings. They were to say with Paul: 'For me to live is Christ and to die is gain' (Philippians 1:21). They were to witness to the resurrection, not so much through words, as through a changed life.

The resurrection is the supreme revelation of God's gift of love to humanity, and faith is 'falling in love' with the Risen Lord who is given. As Bernard Lonergan reminds us, you cannot reason yourself into being in love (Lonergan 1972, p. 123). The apostles are our witnesses. They had the originating or foundational revelation of the Risen Christ, and they have proclaimed it to the ends of the earth and across the centuries. But the faith of us who 'have not seen', of us who come after the apostolic age, does not depend on mere hearsay. We do not merely believe in Christ on the authority of the apostles, great as it is. Our faith is a response to God's own self-gift to ourselves. We recognize that gift in the light of the authentic tradition which goes back to the apostles and to the first Easter, but the experience is our own. Nobody can have it for us. God's love comes to us, and that alone is the beginning of our faith, a share in the revelation which was granted to the apostles – our participant revelation. God reveals his Son in us and he becomes the 'place' in which we dwell by faith.

Faith, the response to revelation

In the preceding section we have noted what James Mackey has called 'the faith-creating role of the Resurrection' (Mackey 1979, p. 87). Faith is part of God's own self-gift as Love. It is a personal relationship in which the believer places himself in total submission to God's self-gift. Not only is the revelation God's gift, so also is the faith-response of the believer. Only God gives the gift, for 'every perfect gift is from above' (James 1:17). No amount of reasoning or logical inference can produce the virtue and 'habit' of faith, because it is born of love. Nevertheless, the gift is not overwhelming or irresistible. God's infinitely free act of self-disclosure activates our own liberation, and our own self-realization in him, but it remains possible for us to resist and reject him. Faith, therefore, is a way of referring to our encounter with God as a person, our experiential knowledge of him. Like the other so-called 'theological virtues', faith has God as its direct object, and it is inseparable from love and from hope, which are other aspects of this same encounter. We believe in a person – God.

However, as Karl Rahner reminds us, it is not the case that we have nothing to do with God until we become aware of him, or make him real to ourselves, or form concepts of him (Rahner 1978, p. 151). Man is himself an instance of the free self-communication of God. God is at the centre of everything that exists, and is therefore already present in man as an 'existential', that is to say, as a capacity to accept God's self-gift, a capacity which transforms and orientates him and which has a history. The whole of human history, of individuals, of nations of the human race itself, would be 'blind' and purposeless if it were not orientated towards God's glory, and this transcendent quality which gives history its meaning is necessarily mediated by that history. All history thus becomes a history of salvation, of a call to realise its transcendent purpose. As we have seen, salvation history reached its climax in God's self-revelation in Jesus Christ.

We dispose ourselves for the gift of faith by confronting our own being in freedom and responsibility, in discovering the root of our own personality, in the self-interpretation of man which takes place in human cultures and traditions. We affirm God's existence and his loving nature by living our lives and using our talents and faculties. In one way or another God makes his presence felt to every human being. He is experienced as 'the ground of our being', as somehow not apart from our own selves, but he is also experienced as a 'Thou', as another person in whose being and life we share, in whose world we participate and to whom we disclose ourselves as he does to us.

In the light of the apostolic testimony, we recognize God's offer of himself to us at its most clear and explicit in Jesus Christ as our risen Lord. All religious faith occurs within a tradition and a community of faith, and this is especially true of Christianity. The testimony of the apostles to the originating experience of the resurrection comes to us through a community of faith which is the Church, and each individual achieves faith within that community. Within that community, moreover, his or her faith is continually activated and deepened. The preaching of the Good News about Jesus Christ is indispensable to our Christian faith, but it is not sufficient to bring faith about. An interior illumination, which is the direct action of God's Spirit, is also necessary. As St Paul puts it:

> Now we have received not the spirit of the world, but the Spirit which is from God,
> that we might understand the gifts bestowed on us by God (1 Corinthians 2:12).

The content of faith, or orthodoxy, has no meaning for us if it is not grasped by a confession of faith and a giving of faith to the God in whom we believe. It is by his power that this commitment takes place, both the orthodox confession of faith's content and the orthopraxy which answers the question posed by faith: 'What shall I do, Lord?' (Acts 22:10).

Theologians used to stress the rational presuppositions of faith and faith's cognitive aspects. Today, they are unanimous in emphasizing the difference between faith and beliefs, and in asserting that where faith is concerned love precedes knowledge and knowledge is born of love. To say that religious faith is reasonable is not to say that its certainty reposes on conclusive evidence or on an ability to explain or understand its content. To say that faith is reasonable is to say that reliable evidence exists for God's self-revelation, but that we must go beyond the evidence. In Chapter 4 we devoted a good deal of space to discussing the historicity of Jesus of Nazareth, but it is not the kind of evidence that offers a once-for all, exhaustive proof of the Christian Good News – of the meaning of Jesus' death and resurrection. One cannot put the evidence through a computer and come up with an irrefutable equation. If one could, then faith would, of course, disappear. The whole point about faith is that it leaves the mind swinging, that it creates in the believer what the Jesuit poet Gerard Manley Hopkins called 'the ecstasy of interest' (quoted in Pick 1966, p. 409). Wonderment and awe are the stuff of faith, not mathematical proof. Hopkins was trying to describe the notion of 'mystery of faith' to his friend Robert Bridges. Such a mystery, he said, was not mysterious because it was uncertain. A mystery of faith was not 'an interesting uncertainty' but 'an incomprehensible certainty' (quoted in Pick, *ibid.*). The question then to be asked is: How does one become certain (in faith) of things that one cannot satisfactorily comprehend or explain? As John Coulson has recently shown, this was the question which absorbed Cardinal Newman's attention (Coulson 1981, p. 45).

Newman's answer to the problem rests on the supposition commonly held today by Catholic theologians that religious faith is to be compared to the judgements of value and the commitments of a person in love. Love and knowledge are not opposed in the act of faith, but faith is, as Bernard Lonergan describes it, 'the eye of love' (Lonergan 1972, p. 117). It is the gift of God's love which reveals who God is and what he asks of us, and which elicits from us an apprehension of transcendent values, drawing us further and further out of ourselves and into the deifying light which gives a goal and a purpose to our lives. It is the mutual indwelling of the Johannine Last Supper discourses:

> In that day you will know that I am in my Father, and you in me, and I in you . . . .
> If a man loves me, he will keep my word, and my Father will love him, and we will
> come to him and make our home with him . . . . Abide in me and I in you (John
> 14:20, 23; 15:4).

Faith is not simply a believing of things to be true, but a dwelling in the Truth. The commitment of love makes possible the confession of faith.

Newman did not equate the intellect with the reason. There was also the power of the imagination, which Newman believed to be primary where the act of faith was concerned. For him, the imagination was not simply a process of imaging, or of receiving reflected impressions. It was the means by which experiences were apprehended in creative fashion and made real to the intellect, striking the mind, stirring up the affections and stimulating conduct. For Newman the pure reason was concerned with purely mental objects, with inferences from experience, which were logically and chrono-logically posterior to the imaginative apprehension of experience. Such inferences do not affect our conduct and require no apprehension of what is inferred. This analysis was the basis for Newman's distinction between real assent and notional assent (Newman 1903, pp. 89–90). Real assent is imaginative assent. Notional assent is rational assent. This distinction, moreover, corresponds to that between faith and beliefs.

John Coulson is at pains to point out that Newman was very far from ad-vocating the ascendancy of feeling over rational demonstration (Coulson 1981, pp. 51–55). He did not think that the imagination should usurp the function of the reason, but he did hold that nothing could be conceived which had not first been imagined, and that imagination provided the conviction and the intensifying power for rational research. Science does not, in fact, proceed on the basis of radical doubt or of habitual scepticism. Its hypotheses are founded on imaginative vision and a hope grounded in conviction that an answer will be found. As Thomas Kuhn describes them, this is precisely how scientific revolutions take place and how the crises of normal science are resolved through the intuitive processes of great minds (Kuhn 1970).

The certitude of faith, then, is not just a simple act of the will. It is a state of mind dominated by the imagination which affects the whole person and enables him to grasp and interpret his experience of God through the symbolic forms provided by his community of faith. These are, as it were, the social framework of his creative imagination. This we have already discussed at greater length in the first chapter of this book. Gerald O'Collins has quite rightly linked the hope aspect of the believer's disposition with the power of imagination. He speaks of the 'imagination of hope' which sets the believer free to go forward confidently in anticipation of a future with God (O'Collins 1981, p. 149). He also explains that this imagination is linked to 'those permanent structures of the human person which render faith possible'; it was Newman's interest to describe those structures in his analysis of the psychology of faith. To sum up then, the image of God is brought before the mental vision of the individual who is thus convinced that he is thereby placed in communion with the person whom the image represents. To this vision the moral sense and the moral judgement adhere, so that the individual's whole temperament, character and volition are unified within the disposition we call faith. The object of faith is embraced, not because its truth can be ultimately demonstrated, but because of its divine character which convinces the believer that he possesses and is possessed by the truth.

Imagination and reason are not, however, at loggerheads, but are organically united. The presence of God to the believer remains a question, an incomprehensible mystery, and all the problems of God's nature and existence and of his dealings with humankind are, as Bernard Lonergan describes them, 'the questions of a lover' seeking more complete knowledge (Lonergan 1972, p. 116). This he does (in Bergson's phrase) through the activity of the 'intelligence immobilizing the real', grasping and generalizing the fleeting moments of a process which the creative imagination knows intuitively to be a process of becoming. Alternatively, the problems of God's existence and nature may also be the questions of an unbeliever resisting the impressions of God's self-revelation, and seeking to escape him. In the man who submits, however, the light of faith becomes the ground of reasoned affirmations of belief.

Revelation and the life of faith

The life of faith here refers to the mutual indwelling of God and the believer. It goes by many names: supernatural life, spiritual life, life of prayer. It is also called 'the life of grace'. *Charis* or 'grace', as it is used in the New Testament, means the favour or free gift of God. It is God's sovereign and benevolent love for humanity, his act of love towards the human race. The greatest grace of God was the appearance of God on earth in human form, the incarnation of the Word.

> For the grace of God has appeared for the salvation of all men, training us to renounce irreligion and worldly passions, and to live sober, upright, and godly lives in this world, awaiting our blessed hope, the appearing of the glory of our great God and Saviour Jesus Christ, who gave himself for us to redeem us from all iniquity and to purify for himself a people of his own who are zealous for good deeds (Titus 2:11–14).

Grace is a new way of life, a new mode of existence in which we experience salvation. The life of faith means accepting to be guided by the Spirit of God in grace and thus to live in a loving communion with God. Many images are used in the New Testament to express this salvation: being adopted as a child of God, being freed, rescued, ransomed etc. from the enemy, being reconciled after a dispute, making recompense or atonement and so forth. In the Gospel of John the favourite image is 'indwelling'. 'Dwell in me' occurs no fewer than thirty-eight times. The Gospel of John is essentially the Gospel of Faith. Its authors and editors present the 'beloved disciple' as the follower who went furthest in seeing and in loving. Jesus is the icon of God, the sign of the Beyond, and every event in his life and ours has a further meaning or message. Every moment is privileged. In John, the mystery of Jesus is a mystery of revelation.

In the Johannine way of thinking, faith is the means by which we draw out the full implications of what it is to be human. The human is the most expressive language about God, and in Jesus God takes a human face. God turns out to be more 'normal', more 'human' and more 'natural' than we are; for, as Pierre Simson has put it: 'We are not just failed supernaturals; we are sub-natural!'[1] The Gospel of John was written to provoke the response and the life of faith:

> Now Jesus did many other signs in the presence of the disciples, which are not written in this book; but these are written that you may believe that Jesus is the Christ, the Son of God, and that believing you may have life in his name (John 20:30–31).

To believe in Jesus as the Word of God is to believe that God is Love and that he enters into loving converse and communion with us. Love is the absolute priority. In practical terms this means going beyond the present moment and 'seeing' God's love purifying and transforming every human situation. It means entering into the love of God and accepting the Cross of Christ as the sign of that love. It means allowing God to accomplish and complete his love in us.

The life of faith is a growth or a becoming; it is an ever more profound revelation of God to us. It is a call to obey the great commandment of love, which underlies all the commandments. It is a call to fraternal love, to recognize the sign of the stranger – the Risen Christ who reveals himself in the anonymous pilgrim to Emmaus (Luke 24:13–35), and in the mysterious fisherman on the shore of Lake Tiberias (John 21), and in all the strangers of other classes, creeds and cultures. It is a call to universality and interculturality. There is no end to this seeking, to this going beyond.

The Epistle to the Ephesians is, perhaps, one of the most eloquent New Testament texts where the life of faith, conceived as a deepening and broadening of love, is concerned:

> For this reason I bow my knees before the Father, from whom every family in heaven and on earth is named, that according to the riches of his glory he may grant you to be strengthened with might through his Spirit in the inner man, and that Christ may dwell in your hearts through faith; that you, being rooted and grounded in love, may have power to comprehend with all the saints what is the breadth and length and height and depth, and to know the love of Christ which surpasses knowledge, that you may be filled with all the fullness of God (Ephesians 3:14–19).

The life of faith, then, is a continuing revelation to the believer of the love of God, and it takes place through the power of the Spirit. The Spirit is the 'Go-Between God', the means of this 'beyondness', who enlarges our consciousness and our world of relationships (Taylor 1972). It is the Spirit who develops our personality, and who guides our discernment. Finally, it is the Spirit who gives us the necessary strength for the self-sacrifice demanded by unselfish love. In the strength of the Spirit, we are growing towards an ever fuller revelation of God in Jesus, towards a fuller participation of his experience, and particularly of his 'Abba experience', so that, with the Spirit of God's Son in our hearts we can cry 'Abba! Father!' (Galatians 4:6) like Jesus himself.

FAITH IN A SECULAR AGE

Honest to what?

In Chapter 1 of this book we dealt very briefly with so-called Secular Theology and with the ambiguities involved in the attempt to speak of God in secular terms. We also suggested that modern secularism itself was, up to a point, an outgrowth or an 'occupational hazard' of Christianity. In this section – by means of a few examples – we shall try to show how the secularist dilemma derives from certain erroneous presuppositions about the nature of faith.

The 1960s were the heyday of Secular Theology, typified in the English-speaking world perhaps by two books: Harvey Cox's *The Secular City* (Cox 1965) and John A. T. Robinson's *Honest to God* (Robinson 1963). Both authors were influenced to a greater or lesser degree by the ideas of Rudolf Bultmann, Dietrich Bonhoeffer and Paul Tillich. The basic premise common to these writers was that there is what John Coulson calls 'a great divide' between the modern secular city and the pre-industrial village, that mythology in general, and the mythology of the Bible in particular, no longer speak to modern man, and that when the Biblical myths are de-mythologized into metaphysical truths, they do not constitute part of his experience (Coulson 1981, pp. 6, 15).

Harvey Cox did not proclaim, like Nietzsche before him or Thomas Altizer and William Hamilton (Altizer 1966; Hamilton 1966) after him, that God is dead, but he did declare that God was a hidden God. His doctrine was not atheism but non-theism. For Harvey Cox, there was no theophany or appearance of God in Jesus of Nazareth, but merely a final affirmation of the divine hiddenness and of God's turning the world over to man as his responsibility. Even after the mythological and metaphysical layers of the Bible have (to use Harvey Cox's phrase) been 'scraped away', God is not discovered to be modern man himself, nor is he a particular quality in man or another name for human reciprocity and love. There is still a transcendent, but this is experienced in non-theistic terms, in the events of social change, in history and in politics, wherever an aspect of experience cannot be transmitted into an extension of ourselves. The images men have of God are therefore only names which refer to particular social and political experiences. When social and political structures change, then the names, too, must change with them. They do not have any permanent cognitive value. It is, perhaps, significant that towards the end of his book, Harvey Cox confesses that he is unable to confer a new name on God. A new name will come when God is ready. The most he can do is to propose a moratorium on the use of the name 'God' so as to see whether a new name will emerge, or whether the three-letter word 'God' will reassert itself. Not a God that is dead therefore, but a God without a name.

The basic flaw in Harvey Cox's proposal is that, if modern man has no experience of a God with a name, he is unlikely to experience – let alone celebrate and worship – a nameless God. Modern man will not recover his experience of God without making the kind of imaginative assents that are necessary to mediate religious faith. What is needed is the recovery of symbol and myth, that is to say the symbolic statements which interpret the meaning of events for us and of the Christ-event above all, not the 'scraping away' of mythology and its metaphysical paraphrases. But Harvey Cox is right, up to a point. Modern man does not experience God, at least in the secularized industrial societies of the Western world.

What is the reason? John Coulson asks if it is not so much because man has come of age, or has shouldered his responsibility for the world, as because his sensibility is impoverished (Coulson 1981, p. 6). It is impossible (as we noted earlier) to recast our theology in non-Biblical and non-symbolic terms. The mythical 'code' is necessary for us to become aware of the transcendent. After all, symbolic thinking is very far from being a thing of the past, and the arts, music, poetry and literature are necessary today as in previous ages, perhaps more necessary. The problem is not one of a divorce between science and religion, but between culture and religion, and this is as much the fault of the theologians as it is of the artists and writers. 'The split between the Gospel and culture is without a doubt the drama of our time . . . ' wrote Paul VI (*Evangelii Nuntiandi*, 20).

'The great divide' stands between our own pluralistic age and previous ages when the contemporary culture incarnated the reigning religious faith. Can this 'great divide' be overcome? John Coulson thinks it can, because the divide is not basically one between a homogeneous 'age of faith' and an 'age of religious pluralism', but one between an age which accepted imaginative language as the primary form of religious faith, and one which has equated faith with the conceptual language of belief. Now that theologians accept the distinction between faith and beliefs, the stage is set for the recognition of the primacy of faith. Among modern writers there are a few outstanding examples – T. S. Eliot would be one – of creative minds who have shown us how a new religious symbolism can remain open to the God revealed in the literary forms of Scripture. The answer to Harvey Cox's problem lies therefore in the recovery of an imaginative and experiential theology, not in its abandonment.

For the then Bishop of Woolwich, John A. T. Robinson, the starting-point of *Honest to God* was similar to that of *The Secular City*. Biblical symbolism is a scandal for modern man, because God is neither physically nor metaphysically 'up there' or 'out there'. Robinson went on to ask whether Christianity – and indeed transcendence – need necessarily be identified with a personalist and theistic understanding of the deity. The idea of transcendence must be stated in other terms than those of a nonsensical mythology. Robinson adopted the phrase (first coined by Gerard Manley Hopkins) which describes God as 'ground of our being'. This ground is not, according to Robinson, a divine person, existing in himself, but is the love which concerns us ultimately and which is the depth of personal relationships among human beings. 'God, the final truth and reality "deep down things" [Hopkins, again] *is* love' (Robinson 1963, p. 49). Robinson was not, as was widely thought, attacking the existence of God, but rather a particular personalistic image of God which he believed discredited the theistic conviction of the ultimacy of the personal.

However, there was an ambiguity as to whether this personalness held any divine guarantee, since it was inseparable from human reciprocity. Even Jesus of Nazareth, who typified the love called 'God', was simply the most successful example of a man completely united with the ground of his being. Robinson's brand of non-theism turns out to be an anonymous form of pan-entheism, according to which human beings achieve their fulfilment within an all-embracing, but unidentified, 'God'.

The personalist image of God in fact guarantees *his* freedom and love more than it helps to explain the ultimacy of love in human relationships. We cannot abandon the idea of God as personal, even if, as we noted in Chapter 1, his personalization represents in Newman's words, 'the confession of an insoluble question' (quoted in Coulson 1981, p. 66). But the image of God as person is not important in itself, it is God's freedom and love which must be safeguarded. The extremely personal way in which Jesus experienced his Father and spoke about his and our relationship with him does just this. The knowledge that God is somehow personal purifies our experience of human persons (Schoonenberg 1977, p. 90).

The other strong impression which Robinson's book conveyed was that he did not understand analogy or symbol, for he certainly offered no third way of knowing God, besides that of taking the Biblical images as either literally physical or as abstractly metaphysical. Sixteen years later, Bishop Robinson published *Truth is Two-Eyed* (Robinson 1979) and vindicated all the criticisms made here of his earlier book. In fact, the positions he now adopts are very close to those put forward throughout this present study of revelation and its interpretation. It becomes clear that Robinson's main pre-occupation is to correct an imbalance in popular Christianity: that of 'super-naturalism' or 'interventionalism'. Christianity has stressed communion at the expense of union, the personal at the expense of the impersonal, the uniqueness and historicity of Christ at the expense of God's universal and eternal action. But in other religions – and Robinson takes the example of Hinduism – there is a reverse emphasis. The balance must be held between the two poles. Religions can therefore correct one another when they come into contact. In *Truth is Two-Eyed* a corrected theory of pan-entheism is put forward which safeguards God's distinctness and 'thou-ness'. The full implications of Gerard Manley Hopkins' poetic theology are also drawn out, the 'thou-ness' of God guaranteeing the 'thou-ness' of everything and leading the poet to coin the words 'inscape' and 'instress' in order to express the unique particularity of all created things, which reflects the distinctness and uniqueness of the Creator (Robinson 1979, p. 28).

There is also in Bishop Robinson's later book a deep appreciation of the Johannine Gospel and of its affirmation (which we noted earlier in the chapter) of both the divinity and the 'normality' of Jesus Christ. Robinson shows here a full understanding of the nature and working of religious symbolism. In his statement 'where the greatest tension is there also is the possibility of the greatest creativity' he anticipates John Coulson's present-ation of imaginative language as both 'saying and unsaying' and revelation as both 'light and darkness'; and he has also accepted in advance Coulson's understanding of the incarnation as the basic model for all symbolism, for all imaginative language and for all theology of icons or images which nurture the act of faith (Robinson 1979, p. 67; Coulson 1981, p. 126).

From non-theism to anti-theism . . . and atheism?

If *The Secular City* and *Honest to God* typified the Secular Theology debate in the 1960s, then *The Myth of God Incarnate* edited by John Hick (Hick 1977) certainly typified the Christological debate in the Protestant English-speaking world of the 1970s. This is not the place to discuss all the essays contained in that book, the main argument of which is that Jesus Christ was deified from having simply been 'a man approved by God' (Acts 2:22). A full discussion of the issues would have to take place in a study of Christo-logy, and we have in any case (in Chapter 4) agreed with C. F. D. Moule, for example, that Christology was a drawing out of what was implicit from the beginning, rather than a switch from Adoptionism to Incarnationalism. Moreover, we have agreed with James Dunn that Jesus' divinity was recognized in practice before the doctrine of the incarnation was fully spelt out. Incarnation theology began when the exalted Christ was spoken of, by the Epistle to the Hebrews and by the later Pauline Epistles, in terms drawn from the Wisdom imagery of pre-Christian Judaism. It became explicit in the Johannine writings and these influenced Christological investigation in subsequent centuries.

Here we shall single out one essay from the controversial symposium and trace the later development of its author's thinking.

Don Cupitt, in 'The Christ of Christendom' (Hick 1977, pp. 133–147), is perfectly aware of the nature of imagery and symbolism. He is also well aware of the relationship of the Byzantine theology of icons to that of the incarnation. As Theodore the Studite argued, it was because of the reality of the incarnation that the painted icon could be venerated as a real image or manifestation of God, whose Son it represented (cf. Meyendorff 1975, pp. 45–48). The appearance of icons in the fourth-century Church was a novelty that gained acceptance with considerable difficulty in a Judeo-Christian tradition which strictly prohibited representations of God, as compromising his spirituality and total transcendence. Don Cupitt quotes John of Damascus's justification of their introduction as comparable to the introduction of new Christological dogmas.

Cupitt is undoubtedly right to trace the influence of Byzantine court models on the portrayal of the Christ of Christendom in the icons, and to scoff at the crudely anthropomorphic and even tritheistic representations of the Godhead which later developed, following the imperial and papal models of the Middle Ages. Where it is no longer possible to follow him is in his claim that the orthodox dogma of the incarnation emerged at the same time as the icons, and was part of the bid to Christianize the ideas and structures of the pagan Roman Empire. In other words, incarnational theology emerged only with the great Christological dogmas. As we have already seen, although dogmatic development continued in the first centuries of the Church's existence, the appearance of the fully fledged incarnational theology goes back to the Johannine circles and is anchored in the historical reality of Jesus himself.

Moreover, Cupitt's objection to incarnation and the icons is somewhat different from that of the Iconoclastic emperors and their supporters in the eighth century. Whereas for Cupitt, icons were the logical outcome of the early Christological dogmas, for Constantine Copronymos it was the reverse. Iconoclasm was the logical outcome of the Christological debates and of a particular interpretation of the Councils which saw the deification of Christ's humanity as suppressing its properly human individual character, in spite of a formal rejection of Monophysitism. The Iconoclasts failed to take account of the Chalcedonian definition that each nature in Christ preserves its own manner of being.

Cupitt believed that Chalcedonian Christology was 'a remote ancestor of modern unbelief', for it first encouraged a notion of the deity as a super-human person – no different ultimately from the deified emperors or Helle-nistic kings – and secondly, it contradicted Jesus' emphasis on divine trans-cendence and the need for a choice between the human and the divine. The cult of a divine Christ entailed the relegation of the deity to the background. Quite apart from Cupitt's controversial view of Christ's own teaching, it is highly arguable whether, in the Roman Catholic tradition, popular devotion has emphasized Christ's humanity sufficiently. While this has happened in liberal Protestantism, and Cupitt may be correct to say that the doctrine of the incarnation has collapsed in the minds of leading Anglican churchmen today, in popular Roman Catholicism, Christ's humanity is very often swallowed up in his divinity, so that Christ becomes a kind of heavenly 'half-breed' or 'God-in-disguise', very much in the Docetist or Monophysite fashion. This unconscious flaw in popular Catholic devotion was pointed out by Frank Sheed in *Theology and Sanity* many years ago.

In his latest book *Taking Leave of God* (Cupitt 1980) Don Cupitt has come a long way from the positions evaluated above. It is no longer a question of rejecting the incarnation and divinity of Christ, but of rejecting all objective theism in the shape of an 'immense cosmic or supracosmic mind', and of a life with God after death. Cupitt considers the mythological or affirmative way of speaking about God, as well as the apophatic or negative way. One can argue with his somewhat over-subjective approach to symbolism. For him, meanings do not interpret or 'half-create' the experience that is – up to a point – given. Interpretation generates the experience *tout court*. However, Cupitt is sufficiently at home with symbols to understand their value. Although he thinks that the modern development of science has 'annihilated' the mythological understanding of a created world or an objective God, since mythology yields no conclusive evidence that can satisfy the scientist, he nevertheless finds mythology serviceable in order to speak about the claims of spirituality, of self-transcendence and of radical freedom. He therefore retains the word 'God' and God-talk generally in order to symbolize a Kantian type of moral imperative (Cupitt 1980, p. 94), 'the religious requirement', as the following quotations show:

> What then is God? God is a unifying symbol that eloquently personifies and represents to us everything that spirituality requires of us. The requirement is the will of God, the divine attributes represent to us various aspects of the spiritual life, and God's nature as spirit represents the goal we are to attain. Thus the whole of the spiritual life revolves around God and is summed up in God. God is the religious concern, reified (Cupitt 1980, p. 9).

> And what is God? The Christian doctrine of God just is Christian spirituality in coded form, for God is a symbol that represents to us everything that spirituality requires of us and promises to us (p. 14).

> So the resurrection is a religious reality . . . . It consists in the maximal degree of liberation from the power of evil and of spiritual individuation, creativity and responsiveness. The enjoyment of this through Jesus is, by definition, faith in his resurrection. Compared with this tremendous religious reality, 'historical' claims about walking corpses and empty tombs are foolish and irrelevant (p. 45).

> In religion there is no independent being whose existence validates the practice of worship . . . . There does not need to be such an independent being, for the aim of worship is to declare one's complete and disinterested commitment to religious values (p. 69).

And so we come at last to Cupitt's concept of faith, which is the final key to his whole theory:

> Faith is not theoretically cognitive and on the account I have given we do not have any reliable information about a world-transcending God at all. Faith is practical, a way of binding oneself. I impose the religious requirement upon myself to the pursuit of religious values. I choose my religion, all of it (p. 126).

In Cupitt's view, faith is a gift by oneself to oneself. Just as Napoleon snatched the crown from the Pope's hands and crowned himself, so the modern 'believer' snatches faith from an impotent and non-objective God to bestow the gift upon himself, and salvation becomes auto-salvation, with the man Jesus as model (if one cares to choose Jesus as such).

Cupitt's objections to theism are not merely because theism is too personalistic (cf. Robinson), but because theism is unreal. Theism cannot be proved or even be symbolically experienced in any objective form. His non-theism is much more of an anti-theism, and despite his God-talk, is discovered in the end to be an atheism. He sometimes refers to his position as 'Christian Buddhism', but it is his own atheistic interpretation of Buddhism that attracts him. He is perhaps more candid when he compares his position to that of the self-confessed Western atheist. This he does particularly in the area of worship. Both Christian and atheist turn out to be worshipping, not God, but a projected ideal, the self they have not yet become (Cupitt 1980, p. 64). The reader of *Taking Leave of God* cannot but be convinced that its writer has really taken leave of God, and that he uses 'God' as a symbol of his ideal self. In which case the idea of God has been emptied of meaning and it is waste of time to talk about religious faith. Don Cupitt's faith is the faith of a well-intentioned atheist.

Dionysos in the Third World

If a split has occurred between the Gospel and culture in the countries of Western Christendom, there is an even more dramatic split in the countries of the so-called Third World. On the one hand, the ancient cultures of the non-Western world were religious cultures and accepted an imaginative language as the language of their faith, whereas, now under the impact of Western education, science and technology, this language of symbol and ritual is either being discarded or trivialized as a tourist spectacle. On the other hand, secularist and anti-theistic ideas are being purveyed from the post-Christian West, and are influencing leading thinkers and writers. The Church has played its part in discrediting the ancient non-Christian faiths. It was, of course, necessary for her to challenge these faiths constructively, but very often the first generations of missionaries displayed a self-confident and indiscriminate hostility to whole religious systems together with their cultural expressions, and tragically introduced a Christianity couched in the metaphysical language of beliefs rather than in the imaginative language of a living faith.

In this situation even the most humane and articulate thinkers, although they are strongly attracted by Christian imagery and the values which it represents, can nevertheless be finally impervious to religious faith in general and Christian faith in particular. It is instructive to consider one example here before concluding this section on faith in a secular age. It is the example of a poet and playwright who is probably the most accomplished writer and dramatist in Africa today, the Nigerian Wole Soyinka. Soyinka was born in 1934 into a Protestant family in Abeokuta, but he was profoundly influenced both by the religious and humanistic culture of his own people, the Yoruba, and also by the classical theatre of ancient Greece to which he was introduced by his university studies in Britain and his association with the European theatrical tradition. His career – apart from writing and producing – has been that of a university lecturer in his own country.

His plays exhibit a fascinating vacillation between Christ as Saviour and the Yoruba god Ogun. The latter's contradictory attributes of creator and destroyer prompt Soyinka to identify him with the Greek Dionysos and to make him the ultimate symbol of man himself. It may be that the humanism, pessimism and anti-theism of Nietzsche have influenced Soyinka in this identification, but Soyinka retains his liking for Christian symbolism and his confidence that 'inner reality' can be found in man-as-victim, rather than in a race of supermen.[2]

Soyinka's early plays were those of a moralist-critic of traditional society and its failure to come to terms with modern development. In *The Swamp Dwellers* the forces of reaction are led by the traditional village priest, but there is a further enslavement to the elusive and ultimately fatal ideal of urban prosperity (Soyinka 1977 [1973]). The role of prophet is played by a blind beggar whose moral superiority and whose association with obvious symbolic clues from the New Testament (such as the washing and anointing of his feet by a woman) reveal him as a saving Christ-figure. In *The Strong Breed* the teacher and healer Eman offers himself as scapegoat in a village purification rite in place of his protégé, an idiot boy (Soyinka 1977 [1973]). Eman's sacrifice is consciously modelled on that of Christ. In *Kongi's Harvest* Soyinka transfers his moral critique from the traditional social scene to that of politics in independent Africa, and mercilessly satirizes an autocratic African dictator who usurps both traditional and Christian symbolism in his aspirations towards godhead (Soyinka 1974). In this play the saviour-challenger who espouses pain to end pain and who speaks out against terror fails in his mission, and the story ends on a note of uncertainty as to whether the social visionary can ever hope to re-educate the tyrant.

Behind this play lies perhaps an implied critique of Christianity. Soyinka had already written *The Road*, two years before, in which a mad professor, in search of immortality and the conquest of death, arranges 'accidents' and runs a shop to sell the loot from crashed vehicles (Soyinka 1977 [1973]). The characters are both predators and victims, living on the confines of a church and cemetery beside the road. The Professor, formerly a reader in the church, has now been barred from it, and has turned his attention to the road. There is more than a hint that the road symbolizes Ogun-Dionysos and that the locked church stands for Soyinka's rejection of 'rigid Christian orthodoxy' as relevant to Africa's human problems. The road, which offers both livelihood and inescapable death to the play's characters, wins in the end. Soyinka's pessimism gathered strength during the Nigerian civil war and his own experience of imprisonment. *Madmen and Specialists* is a gruesome commentary on the violence of contemporary African society

(Soyinka 1974). It is violence in the cause of a power which serves nobody, and which is therefore without meaning. A group of mendicants in the play, crippled by the violence to which they have been subject, contrive nonetheless to maintain and prolong the violent system. They are disgusted with everything but themselves and purgation can only be achieved by self-disgust.

Finally, Soyinka comes out into the open with a free translation from the Greek of the *Bacchae* of Euripides (Soyinka 1977 [1973]). In this play the Greek Dionysos is a thinly disguised Ogun who wreaks a horrific revenge upon the ruler who would seek to penetrate the secrets of his mysteries. Here Soyinka is the explicit activist and revolutionary, proclaiming that leaders who reap the benefits of power must also bear the burden of sacrifice. Moral conversion on the Christian model is ineffective. Rather, thinks Soyinka, the experience of creativity and destruction in man's world demands that conversion be complemented by subversion.

For Soyinka, African traditional religion is dead and Christianity (on its own metaphysical terms) is irrelevant. Since no one can re-create a religion, the mythological patterns of the past must be reconstructed in order to yield a secular meaning, while remaining open to universal values and to the symbol-systems of non-African cultures and religious traditions. Presumably Soyinka would agree with a sentence written by the late Camara Laye, the Guinean novelist, a few year before his death:

> ... The Black Continent is groping in the dark. It is a continent in quest of a vanishing spirituality, a continent pursued by a too-immediate reality, a continent in search of itself (Laye 1980, p. 32).

From a Christian point of view, the tragedy about Wole Soyinka is that Christianity was brought to him in unpalatable form, a form incapable of producing the imaginative assent of faith. Soyinka's principal character in *The Road*, the Professor, is tempted to play God in order to discover the secrets of life and death and he complains: '...why may I not understand...?' (Soyinka 1977 [1973], p. 224). A young East African critic has answered that question: 'In my view, the Professor cannot understand because God can only be found when he reveals himself' (Chagenda 1981, p. 17). Soyinka has not yet been able to recognize God revealing himself in the situations of contemporary Africa with which he deals, but his secularism and humanism are sympathetic, for he remains open to a 'conditioning by strangers' and his search for light among the wretched of the earth is leading him to the right place. It is certainly among them that God reveals himself.

CELEBRATING THE WORD

Religious faith, ritual and life

Faith, as we have described it, is fundamentally an imaginative assent, and as such, it is both discovered and expressed with a system or order of symbols. That is to say, it is discovered and expressed within a community which possesses a common symbolic language and tradition, a community of faith which is also a worshipping community. The imagination is not autonomous as Don Cupitt suggests. Nor is the act of faith merely the self-imposition of a religious requirement. Still less is the act of worship merely a declaration to oneself (whether or not in the presence of others) of one's commitment to religious values. Again, society does not rediscover the inner meaning of human life in the world and reconstruct its values (especially in Africa) by means of an élitist tragic theatre, as Wole Soyinka imagines. On the contrary, the rediscovery of, and commitment to, ultimate values takes place within a worshipping community.

In Chapter 1 we described religion as 'a living communion with divine reality', and we said that symbolic actions and words expressed this communion through what is called 'worship'. Worship is at the heart of all religion. It is the way in which a community is formed and renewed in faith, the way in which believers respond to the revealed Word of God, and therefore a 'place' of continuing revelation. Worship is not the action of a madman talking to himself; it is the the action of the wise man, in his right mind, listening to God. In valid worship there is an awareness of the presence of God, a submission to him and a willingness to be led by him in love. In the words of the Benedictine mystic Augustine Baker, 'Praying is Loving'.

What is the shape and direction of worship? Worship informs us of God's presence and establishes our communion with him through the oblique language of symbolic words and actions – in a word, through ritual. Ritual has been given a bad name by the psychologists. Eric Berne, for example, uses the word to refer to stereotyped complementary transactions, programmed by external social forces, which relieve guilt-feelings, offer rewards and generally reassure people who are basically insecure in life. In such a definition rituals are dead things, performed in order to keep people imprisoned in an unreal world. One thinks of Mervyn Peake's Gothic fantasies and the figure of the Earl, performing his daily meaningless rituals in a labyrinthine castle. Certainly symbols can be a snare, a vehicle for self-deception. Out of context they assume other meanings. Or they may be prized for themselves. This has certainly been a hazard of Catholic liturgy and sacramental theology. The Western, empirical mind began to shift its attention in the Middle Ages from the meaning of ritual action to the nature of sacred objects. It was more interested, for example, in what happened to the bread and wine than in questions about the meaning of the Eucharist, and priests whispered the words of consecration to the altar-bread in their hands, instead of speaking them – as was intended – to the faithful assembled around the altar: 'This is my Body which will be given up for you' (Guzie 1974, pp. 61, 70).

Ritualism is a decided danger and it has triggered off a revolt against ritual itself. Modern Western man has been loath to recognize the symbolic and ritual element in his life, and has felt it to be 'primitive' and disreputable, when it was not confined to the psychiatrist's couch or the poet's irrelevant muse. 'That's just poetry', he says when he expresses his disbelief. There is no doubt that symbols must be pruned from time to time in a liturgical renewal, but there has been much rationalistic iconoclasm in recent liturgical development – a trend that has been earthily dubbed 'the kitchen-sink' liturgical mentality. The mysteries disappear in a liturgical 'laying of tables' and a liturgical 'washing-up'. The shape and direction of worship have often been misunderstood.

Ritual is at the heart of worship. It is the bridge between individual and community, between ideas and lived experience, between faith and action. Ritual 'speaks' to us, through the reading of texts, through the exposition of preachers and commentators, through verbal prayer formulas and hymnody, through movement and gesture, through images, music, art and architecture, through natural elements such as fire, water, oil, food and drink. Ritual manufactures its symbols in a complex drama or rehearsal of life, into which process the individual is drawn. Deeply shared meanings are thereby expressed and the awareness of God's presence is heightened. More than this, God's love is revealed to us and guides us into greater certitude.

> Deep within us, shared among us,
>   may we ever keep
> The mind and heart of Jesus Christ.

So runs a contemporary Christian folk hymn which accurately sums up the general purpose of Christian liturgy. Ritual speaks to the whole man, to his emotions as well as to his imagination and reason. That is why different celebrations are characterized by different emphases, from a stately cathedral liturgy to the enthusiasm of a charismatic prayer group. 'For where two or three are gathered in my name, there am I in the midst of them' (Matthew 18:20). The two indispensable conditions of that presence are the gathering, that is to say the depth of the spoken and unspoken sharing, and the fact that it takes place 'in my name'. The second condition refers to a shape or style in religious ritual which produces an emergent authenticity or truth, that makes it succeed and pass the test of the believer's own internal criteria as well as those of external guarantees, such as are contained in liturgical directives, books and rubrics. If these conditions are contravened, either there is no divine presence or it is robbed of its power – for example, where there is hatred or division in the community, or where questions of meaning are swallowed up in a shallow empiricism and in the mundane concerns which indicate a preference for one's own will, and a reliance on one's own powers, rather than God's. That is the state of mind of the person who rejects the holy-water sprinkler at Rogation time (which represents our confidence in God's providence) in favour of fertilizers and pesticides. The true believer accepts all these things because he sees no contradiction between the levels at which they operate.

The believer lives doxologically, or worshipfully, and the liturgy exercises an influence on every aspect of his life. Ideally his whole life becomes a prayer. Not only does he perform all his duties of state with a pure intention, but he discovers personal prayer and interior silence as an outgrowth of the community's public worship. This may achieve a greater or lesser level of mystical intensity, dispensing ultimately even with words and images. It is obvious that communities of contemplatives create a special environment in which the liturgy can be celebrated at considerable psychological and spiritual depth, and in which the deeper levels of mental prayer can flourish. However, one should not underestimate the capacity of ordinary men and women to allow their faith, and its liturgical expression, to influence their lives in the world, and to become what Ignatius of Loyola called 'contemplatives in action'. The dividing line between contemplation and action is not always easy to draw.

The social anthropological concept of 'flow' is relevant here, and helps to elucidate the power of liturgy to influence action. This concept, elaborated by Victor Turner and Mihali Csikszentmihalyi, is that of a state in which action follows action with no need of conscious intervention on our part (Turner 1976). There is a unified flowing from one moment to the next, with little distinction between self and environment, between stimulus and response, or between past, present and future. The state provides coherent demands for action and clear feedback, but it has no rewards outside itself. 'Flow', then, describes what happens in a successful ritual action. Ritual structure does not simply reflect the social structure, nor can it be crudely imposed from above by a kind of liturgical conditioning, assumptions which have been too readily made by those responsible for the contemporary liturgical renewal.

The anthropologist Arnold Van Gennep introduced a classic concept into the study of ritual with his idea of 'rites of passage' (Van Gennep 1960). His thesis was that almost every kind of ritual one can think of is structured as a transition or passing over from one state to another. This remarkable insight applies quite conspicuously to religious ritual in general and to the Christian liturgy in particular. All liturgy is essentially a rite of passage. It is a passage from death to life and from darkness to light. All liturgy, therefore, has a paschal and a revelatory character. Of course, there are different kinds of death and darkness, as there are of life and light. There is the death of self, as well as what T. S. Eliot called 'the darkness of God'.

> I said to my soul, be still, and let the dark come upon you
> Which shall be the darkness of God . . .
> I said to my soul, be still, and wait without hope
> For hope would be hope for the wrong thing; wait without love
> For love would be love of the wrong thing; there is yet faith
> But the faith and the love and the hope are all in the waiting (*Four Quartets: East Coker,* III, 12–13, 23–26).

As we remarked in Chapter 1, there is a passive and a pathic quality in worship. The waiting can sometimes be a lengthy process, but it is constituted by faith, love and hope. God is present in the darkness, and the light is his gift when it comes. The life of faith and worship both hides and discloses the love of God. Though there be moments of profound consolation in prayer, it is often only when one looks back over one's life that one discovers an overall pattern of transition and illumination.

Revelation in the New Temple

The Temple in the history of ancient Israel became a privileged place of revelation and covenant-renewal. In the New Testament it is Luke who emphasizes, perhaps more than the other evangelists, the focal role of the Temple in the life and ministry of Jesus. It is in the Gospel of John that Jesus is most clearly presented as the new Temple, the place where God is worshipped in spirit and in truth:

> In the temple he found those who were selling oxen and sheep and pigeons, and the money-changers at their business. And making a whip of cords, he drove them all, with the sheep and oxen, out of the temple; and he poured out the coins of the money-changers. And he told those who sold the pigeons, 'Take these things away; you shall not make my Father's house a house of trade.' His disciples remembered that it was written, 'Zeal for thy house will consume me.' The Jews then said to him, 'What sign have you to show us for doing this?' Jesus answered them, 'Destroy this temple and in three days I will raise it up.' The Jews then said, 'It has taken forty-six years to build this temple, and will you raise it up in three days?' But he spoke of the temple of his body. When therefore he was raised from the dead, his disciples remembered that he had said this; and they believed the Scripture and the word which Jesus had spoken (John 2:13–22).

> Jesus said to her [the Samaritan woman], 'Woman, believe me, the hour is coming when neither on this mountain nor in Jerusalem will you worship the Father . . . . But the hour is coming and now is, when true worshippers will worship the Father in spirit and in truth, for such the Father seeks to worship him. God is spirit and those who worship him must worship in spirit and truth' (John 4;21–24).

All the Synoptists record Jesus' prophecy of the destruction of the Temple, and the symbolic tearing of the curtain which divided the Holy of Holies from the Holy Place at the moment of Jesus' death on the cross. That was the 'hour' when the new messianic sanctuary was inaugurated, the Body of Christ.

There is a polyvalence or multivocality about this symbol, 'the Body of Christ', for it signifies Christ's own glorified humanity, the Church in whose assembly he is present and his sacramental presence in the Eucharist. The Eucharist realizes the mystery of the Church because it brings about our communion in the glorified Body of the risen Christ (in whom, of course, the Crucified is perennially present). This is achieved sacramentally. Among the Church's sacraments, the Eucharist recapitulates in a very special way the whole mystery of Christ, using as it does a rite especially instituted by Christ himself on the eve of his passion. The centrality of the Eucharist is receiving new emphasis these days in the Roman Catholic Church, through the introduction of 'ritual Masses': other sacraments, including baptism, are being celebrated more and more within the context of the Eucharistic liturgy.

Again, it is the authors and editors of the Johannine writings who under-score Eucharistic symbolism and its vital link with Jesus, the new place of encounter between God and man. Chapter 6 of John's Gospel contains the symbolic answer to the question: 'Who do you say that I am?' Jesus Christ is food for others. He is the Bread from Heaven. He is the bread broken and shared among us, so that we might live the life of the Trinity, the life of endless love and total unity. ' . . . and the bread which I shall give for the life of the world is my flesh' (John 6:51). In Luke and in John, it is clear that the celebration of the Eucharist in the early Christian communities has influenced the structure and phrasing of the accounts of meals which Jesus shared with others, expecially the multiplication of the loaves and fishes and the messianic meals in which he revealed himself to his disciples after the resurrection. This is especially true of the Emmaus story.

> When he was at table with them, he took the bread and blessed, and broke it, and gave it to them. And their eyes were opened and they recognized him; and he vanished out of their sight. They said to each other: 'Did not our hearts burn within us while he talked to us on the road, while he opened to us the scriptures?' And they rose that same hour and returned to Jerusalem; and they found the eleven gathered together and those who were with them, who said, 'The Lord has risen indeed, and has appeared to Simon!' Then they told what had happened on the road, and how he was known to them in the breaking of the bread (Luke 24:30–35).

Jesus was known to Cleopas and his companion in the breaking of the bread. The Church affirms that in the Eucharist the real and saving presence of Christ's glorified humanity is 'known', which is to say 'experienced' (in Biblical vocabulary). The Eucharist is food and drink to be received, and in them Jesus gives us himself as he really is, not physically of course, but sacramentally.

The sacrament is a symbol of a special and unique kind. All true symbols, as we have never tired of repeating, participate in the reality they signify. The sacrament participates directly in the reality of God himself. The deified humanity of Jesus is truly an icon or image of God. He is, according to the Greek theologians, *the* icon *par excellence* of God, the *imago patris* or 'image of the invisible God' (Colossians 1:15) (Meyendorff 1975, pp. 201–207). If Christ is truly human, then his humanity and his history can be described and represented, and such secondary icons or images are really images of what Jesus Christ truly is – God! Ritual and liturgical arts are inseparable from faith and theology, and they affirm the historicity of the incarnation, not some kind of abstract, universal humanity assumed by the Word of God. The Church understands the Eucharist as more than a mere representation or evocation of our salvation history, as possessing an even deeper level of participation in the reality of Christ himself than the Byzantine understanding of icons as participative symbols. Through the Eucharist Christ not merely carries out his saving action, but gives himself whole and entire as the bread which is broken and shared among us. The Eucharist is a *memoria*, an effective 'narrative memory' (to use the phrase favoured by Johann Baptist Metz).

It follows, therefore, that the Eucharist, which is at the heart of the sacramental system, is a mystery of real participation in the glorified Body of Christ and the high point of God's continuing revelation of himself to us. It is in the Eucharist that Christ's Body is most clearly and frequently experienced as the place of encounter between God and man, in Spirit and in truth. The Eucharist is effected by the power of the Holy Spirit, and through it, our faith tells us, we are taken up into Christ and brought by him to the Father. In a real way, therefore, the Eucharist celebrates and expresses what we believe in, and is a mystery of revelation and salvation for us.

> When He has sheaved us in his sheaf,
> When He has made us bear his leaf. –
> We scarcely call that banquet food,
> But even our Saviour's and our blood,
> We are so grafted on His wood (G. M. Hopkins: *Barnfloor and Winepress*).

Theology as contemplation

We noticed in Chapter 5 that the popular understanding of theology in the Church is of a discipline which operates strictly within a rational and conceptual framework and which deliberately excludes any appeal to the imagination or to symbolism. We also quoted the opinion of Charles-André

Bernard that systematic theology had consequently been cut off from contact with the Church's ascetical and spiritual tradition, although so great a master of metaphysical theology as St Thomas Aquinas was also a poet and a mystic. It was necessary for a theologian to lead 'a double life' as it were, keeping the disciplines of systematic theology and spirituality in separate compartments. The Church, however, as Bernard points out, never lost sight of the importance of conveying the message of the Good News through symbolism and imaginative language (Bernard 1980, p. 57). Not only were great theologians such as St Gregory the Great, St Augustine of Hippo, St Albert the Great, St Thomas Aquinas and St Bonaventure proclaimed 'Doctors' of the Church, but so also were great mystics and spiritual writers whose style of language was frankly symbolical. Such were the 'Doctors' St Bernard, St Catherine of Siena, St Teresa of Avila, St John of the Cross and St Francis de Sales. St Bernard and St John of the Cross were poets in their own right, and the writings of all these Spiritual Doctors of the Church were nourished by Biblical symbolism, by art, by the sacraments and by their own mystical experience. 'Fire', 'blood', 'being wounded', 'mystical marriage', the trappings of feudal sovereignty, were all part of recognized spiritual vocabulary.

In so far as we are returning today to an experimental basis for theology, to praxis, to history and to a hope that predicts future liberation, we are opening the door to a more imaginative, and a less conceptual, type of theological language. It is a language more directly in tune with the act of faith and the primary symbols which spark that faith. But modern theology is not, as Johann Baptist Metz and Nicholas Lash point out, merely to be identified with the concrete historical or political process or with utopian predictions (Metz 1980; Lash 1979). Faith must find a means of self-expression in every human situation, and that self-expression, we have suggested, is basically doxological or worshipping. If it is to follow, and to serve faith, then theology can only be a form of prayer.

It is an old axiom of the Church that *lex orandi est lex credendi*, 'the law of worship is the law of belief', and theologians must turn again to the liturgical sources of their discipline. We use the word 'theoretical' as being synonymous with 'conceptual' and 'abstract'. It should not be forgotten that it derives from the Greek word *theoria* which means a 'seeing', 'a gazing' or a 'contemplation'. Theology should be a contemplation of the mysteries. This, at any rate, has always been the Eastern view of theology (Meyendorff 1975, pp. 8–9). In the liturgy great use is made of Biblical texts and imagery. Great use has also traditionally been made of the Book of Psalms, corrected as it must be, and made to undergo 'the test of the Cross', with the aid of antiphons, responsories and readings. But in our liturgy there is also a vast treasury of hymns, which constitute a poetic encyclo-paedia of theology and spirituality. The liturgy, too, is the place in which theology can clarify the act of faith, where creeds which are acts of allegiance, professions of orthodoxy, and therefore true 'symbols of faith' are recited by the faithful. What John Meyendorff has written of Greek theology in particular should be true of all theology, that it is 'a vision of the saints' and that it is a presentation of revelation as a living truth, directly accessible to human experience (Meyendorff 1975, pp. 8–9). The Christian believer enjoys a sacramental – and thus direct – experience of God's presence in the Church assembled for worship. This worship must be more clearly seen today as the source and expression of a theology which is loyal to the community of faith.

NOTES

1 Pierre Simson in a lecture at St Anne's, Jerusalem on the Johannine writings, July 1981.
2 Soyinka 1976 expounds his literary and philosophical theory. I am also indebted to an unpublished dissertation by Wandera Chagenda (Chagenda 1981) on Soyinka as a social visionary.

QUESTIONS FOR DISCUSSION

(1) How does the supreme revelation of Christ's resurrection possess a unique faith-creating role in the Christian community?

(2) In what ways do contemporary secular theologies often undermine the notion of religious faith itself?

(3) Why is liturgical worship central to an understanding of God's continuing revelation?

(4) For further enquiry: Explore the possibilities contained in the Eastern understanding of theology as contemplation.

SELECT ANNOTATED READING LIST

B. Lonergan, 1972: *Method in Theology* (London). In a clear and succinct exposition, chapter 4, on 'Religion', studies the nature and working of faith, as well as the antecedents of faith.

G. O'Collins, 1981: *Fundamental Theology* (London). Chapter 5, on 'Experiencing the Divine Self-communication in Faith', concentrates on the act of faith itself, analysing it from the various points of view: reasoning, knowing, loving, imagining.

J. Coulson, 1981: *Religion and Imagination* (Oxford). This stimulating book about the inter-action of religious faith and the literary imagination contains, in chapter 2, a valuable discussion of J. H. Newman's approach to the act of faith: 'Newman's Grammar of Imagination and Belief'.

J. Meyendorff, 1975: *Byzantine Theology* (London). Byzantine theology is especially relevant to our discussion of revelation in the Christian liturgy and the link between liturgy and theology. This book provides a useful summary.

T. Guzie, 1974: *Jesus and the Eucharist* (New York). This is a very helpful account of the place of the Eucharist and its significance in the life of the Church and in the narrative commemoration of Christ's mystery.

D. Cupitt, 1980: *Taking Leave of God* (London). This highly controversial, but deeply sincere, book by the Dean of Emmanuel College, Cambridge, offers the student a perfect example of the logical result of a secularist approach. The author writes with clarity and frankness.

8
The Word Fully Known

REVELATION AND MISSION

The task of evangelization

It is in the context of suffering for others that the New Testament presents Paul as minister of the Word. Paul became a servant of the Church to 'fulfil the Word of God' or 'to make the Word of God fully known'.

> Now I rejoice in my sufferings for your sake, and in my flesh I complete what is lacking in Christ's afflictions for the sake of his body, that is, the church of which I became a minister according to the divine office which was given to me for you, to make the word of God fully known, the mystery hidden for ages and generations but now made manifest to his saints (Colossians 1:24–26).

It is very clear in the New Testament accounts that mission is a direct fruit of God's self-revelation in the Resurrection of Jesus Christ. At every appearance of the Risen Christ there is a sending: 'Do not be afraid; go and tell my brethren to go to Galilee and there they will see me' (Matthew 28:10); 'Go, tell his disciples and Peter that he is going before you to Galilee' (Mark 16:7); 'Peace be with you. As the Father has sent me, even so I send you' (John 20:22). The sending is a universal mission: 'Go therefore and make disciples of all nations, baptizing them in the name of the Father and of the Son and of the Holy Spirit, teaching them to observe all that I have commanded you; and lo, I am with you always, to the close of the age' (Matthew 28:19–20); 'You shall be my witnesses in Jerusalem and in all Judaea and Samaria and to the end of the earth' (Acts 1:8).

The idea of witnessing is present in all the resurrection accounts, and the apostles confess that they are impelled by an interior force (which is none other than the Spirit) to proclaim what they have seen and heard. As Peter and John told the chief priests and the other rulers: 'We cannot but speak of what we have seen and heard' (Acts 4:20). 'The love of God controls us . . .' was how Paul described it (2 Corinthians 5:14). The word which was preached was 'Word of God', 'Word of life', 'Word of truth', but also 'Word of the Cross', for to preach a risen Christ is also to preach a 'Christ crucified, a stumbling block to Jews and folly to Gentiles...' (1 Corinthians 1:23). The word 'martyr' means 'witness', and witnessing entails sharing in Christ's sufferings, instancing his self-sacrificing love, even giving up one's life if need be.

> For while we live we are always being given up to death for Jesus' sake, so that the life of Jesus may be manifested in our mortal flesh. So death is at work in us, but life in you (2 Corinthians 4:11–12).

Jesus is the Gospel we preach, the 'Good News'. We do not preach Christianity, but Christ. It is very important that this should be understood at a time when the Church's right to carry out mission work is sometimes called into question. We are not foisting an alien ideology on to unwilling people. 'We speak of what we know' and 'the love of God controls us'. We have been baptized into the life and death of Christ, the universal and ever-lasting man, given to the world in every age and place by the resurrection. There is something wrong with our faith, if we are not mission-minded. We are servants of the Word and that Word is 'Go!' That is the final spoken word of the Word made flesh. We do not go out upon our mission with mere speech. Preaching is an indispensable part of it, of course, but the totality of the Gospel is a way of life, a transforming encounter with the person of Jesus Christ. We preach Jesus and his style of life, and Jesus imparts his own personal, 'participant' revelation to those who receive the Good News – his own personal invitation to give the assent of faith.

We preach Christ and the lordship or the kingdom of Christ. These are absolutes. They are a reversal of worldly values, exalting what the world rejects, proclaiming God's mercy to all generations, as Mary exclaimed in her canticle: 'His mercy is on those who fear him from generation to generation' (Luke 1:50). That means, as we have already seen, salvation, reconciliation among all groups of people who are divided from, or opposed to, one another. It means breaking down barriers and liberating people from every kind of oppression. That is the full meaning of *shalom*, 'Peace!', the greeting of the Risen Christ. It means a change of heart for every individual, a *metanoia*, or radical conversion.

To preach the Good News is to preach the kingdom and the lordship of a crucified God. The sign that this kingdom is coming is Christ's own self-sacrificing love, his taking upon himself the sins and the sufferings of humanity, his concern for the humble and the poor. These are the means by which the Good News is preached and the proof that it is he, himself, who is at work in his missionaries and evangelizers. This was how Jesus carried out his evangelizing activity, and it is the chief means at the disposal of the Church whose mission is born of that activity.

Accepting the Good News means establishing a community of faith, a community of salvation, and this community becomes, in its turn, an evangelizing community. That is the clear consequence of the revelation of Christ's resurrection and a sign of his permanent presence in the world until 'the close of the age'. It means that this community (the Church) is not the owner or the master of the message, and it means that it is constantly being evangelized itself. Pope Paul VI put this very forcibly:

> The Church is an evangelizer, but she begins by being evangelized herself. She is the community of believers, the community of hope lived and communicated, the community of brotherly love; and she needs to listen unceasingly to what she must believe, to her reasons for hoping, to the new commandment of love. She is the People of God immersed in the world, and often tempted by idols, and she always needs to hear the proclamation of the 'mighty works of God' which converted her to the Lord; she always needs to be called together afresh by him and reunited. In brief, this means that she has a constant need of being evangelized, if she wishes to retain freshness, vigour and strength in order to proclaim the Gospel (*Evangelii Nuntiandi*, 15).

Pope John Paul II described the same need of the Church as one of being in a constant state of conversion:

> Authentic knowledge of the God of mercy, the God of tender love, is a constant and inexhaustible source of conversion, not only as a momentary interior act but also as a permanent attitude, as a state of mind. Those who come to know God in this way, who 'see' him in this way, can live only in a state of being continually converted to him. They live, therefore, *in statu conversionis*; and it is this state of conversion which marks out the most profound element of the pilgrimage of every man and woman on earth *in statu viatoris* (*Dives in Misericordia*, p. 67).

Christian evangelization, therefore, which flows from God's climactic self-revelation in Jesus Christ, demands a renewal of humanity, an interior change in both the personal and the collective conscience. This means that there is a commitment to preach the Good News in wider geographical areas and in increasing numbers, in ever-changing human groups and cultures, at differing levels within society and culture. The Church has to maintain a world-wide presence if its catholicity is to be at all credible, although this does not imply a numerical or cumulative universality. It does, however, mean taking advantage of every new opening, every new possibility that is afforded by the Holy Spirit, who is forever opening doors.

Evangelization is not merely a spatial phenomenon; it is a phenomenon of greater or lesser depth and intensiveness. The Good News constitutes a challenge which is designed to upset ordinary human criteria of judgement. Human cultures and ways of life are to be profoundly evangelized, and in a vital way. Although collective and impersonal methods may be employed, nothing can rival the effectiveness of the witness of life and of person-to-person contact. The Gospel is transmitted only by a living preaching, by a life which is certainly not wordless or lacking explicitness, but primarily by a *life*, and one lived in a community which is a sign of the transformation being effected. This transformation affects all aspects of human life, both personal and social. It proclaims a liberation which is not merely a declaration of rights under a just social order, but a call to a full human life which does not accept the primacy of things over persons.

Pope John Paul II in 1980 gave a timely warning that justice is not enough, especially when it is conceived of as victory over an enemy, entailing his annihilation or total dependence:

> The experience of the past and of our own time demonstrates that justice alone is not enough, that it can even lead to the negation and destruction of itself, if *that deeper power, which is love,* is not allowed to shape human life in its various dimensions (*Dives in Misericordia*, p. 60).

It is only the power of love, as revealed in Jesus Christ and contained in his Gospel, that can give human beings true interior freedom and complete human fulfilment.

Promoting the unity of the faith

Evangelization and the movement for Christian unity are closely linked both in concept and in practice. Unity is an indispensable dimension of Christ's own special commandment of love, and Christ himself intended it to be a sign to the world which would inspire faith in his own mission.

> I do not pray for these only, but also for those who believe in me through their word, that they may all be one; even as thou, Father, art in me, and I in thee, that they may also be in us, so that the world may believe that thou hast sent me (John 17:20–21).

The embarrassment of Christian denominations competing in the same mission fields, and the consequent confusion that this caused, led directly to the modern ecumenical movement. This is a commonplace of recent church history. The opening words of the Second Vatican Council's Decree on Ecumenism stated the problem very clearly from the point of view of evangelization:

> Christ the Lord founded one Church and one Church only. However, many Christian communions present themselves to men as the true inheritors of Jesus Christ; all indeed profess to be followers of the Lord but they differ in mind and go their different ways, as if Christ himself were divided.' Certainly, such division openly contradicts the will of Christ, scandalizes the world, and damages that most holy cause, the preaching of the Gospel to every creature (*Unitatis Redintegratio*, 1).

Pope John Paul II has posed the problem again and again in his regular addresses and during his pastoral visits to various countries when he has gone out of his way to meet leaders of other Christian communions. This is what he had to say in Nairobi in 1980:

Whether they live in Africa or in Europe, in Asia or in America, Christians are the
heirs of sad divisions that have to be first faced in a dialogue of mutual understanding
and esteem, 'speaking the truth in love' (Ephesians 4:15), and then dealt with in
accordance with the promptings of the Holy Spirit. This task is, I repeat, an urgent
one. Jesus calls us to bear witness to him and to his saving work. We can do this adequately only when we are completely united in faith and when we speak his word
with one voice, a voice that rings with warm vitality which characterizes the whole
Christian community when it lives together in full communion. [1]

But it is not only the scandal of a divided witness which prompts Christians
of different communions to rediscover their unity. Christians are, as Peter
Berger observes, discovering a relative proximity in a new world situation
(Berger 1980, p. 158). At the time of the great Christological controversies
which divided the early Church, and even at the time of the Reformation
controversies of the sixteenth century, the world was a smaller place. Today
the *oikumene* is much more comprehensive, and ecumenicity looks towards
far more distant horizons. Other polarities than those which caused the
Christian divisions are becoming important today, and the new-found
dialogue and familiarity that has sprung up among churches may be teaching
Christians to live with a certain degree of tension. Tension may be a
necessary element in a united Christianity.

The concept of dialogue, now accepted by most Christian churches,
implies a spirit of openness to God's Word coming to us in each other's traditions. It also implies a readiness to change and to meet the just demands of
others. This openness and this risk of self-examination and change are truly
characteristic of the response to divine revelation. These are the very attitudes that revelation demands of us. Dialogue demands first of all a clarification of one's own position and a loyal commitment to it that avoids all
false conciliatory approaches. It also involves an honest definition and confrontation of differences, and a whittling down of such differences where
they concern non-essentials and particularly non-theological obstacles.
Finally it includes the ability to learn from others, to accept others' differences where one's own principles are not compromised by so doing.
Dialogue, certainly in so far as it concerns theological self-clarification and
the definition of differences, must be an informed dialogue, avoiding the
false eirenicism of which we have spoken, but this does not mean that it has
to be 'a dialogue of the deaf'. A great deal can be achieved by discussion between the accredited representatives of the churches, as the mounting number
of officially agreed statements testify. However, learning to accept each other
is a long-term objective which includes ordinary Christians at every level in
the churches. Dialogue is not a purely conceptual, or even verbal, process, and
the foundations of a rediscovered communion cannot ultimately be laid at
theological meetings, but only in the shared experience of ordinary believers,
chipping away at the cliff of prejudice and non-theological factors.

Our common baptism is the effective sign of faith in God's self-revelation in Jesus Christ. We have a duty to profess that faith, to defend it unambiguously and never to deny it, even merely externally or even in order to save our lives. We have moreover the duty, as we have just seen in the preceding section, to spread the faith, to evangelize by a form of 'lived preaching' in the same way as Jesus, our Master, evangelized. We also have the duty, in virtue of our baptism, of promoting the unity of the faith. Ecumenism, even though it has come into prominence relatively recently, is not optional for a baptized Christian. It is not a religious luxury which he is free to take up or put down. It is a clear duty which derives from baptism.

> Baptism, therefore, constitutes the sacramental bond of unity existing among all who through it are reborn. But baptism, of itself, is only a beginning, a point of departure, for it is wholly directed toward the acquiring of fullness of life in Christ. Baptism is thus ordained toward a complete profession of faith, a complete incorporation into the system of salvation such as Christ himself willed it to be, and finally, toward a complete integration into Eucharistic communion (*Unitatis Redintegratio*, 22).

If such is the purpose of baptism, then the obligations of the baptized are clear. Christians must constantly examine their consciences to see if they are really promoting a complete profession of faith and a complete incorporation. Every Christian is obliged first of all to know, and be faithful to, the real and authentic tradition of the Church and to avoid an intransigent insistence upon non-essentials. If he or she is equipped for theological dialogue, then opportunities for it should be sought. All have the serious duty of public and private prayer for Christian unity and of joining in shared prayer services to this end where these take place. There are countless opportunities for joint action between the churches in development and relief work and other areas of social life, thus avoiding the wastage of resources and the useless duplication of projects, buildings and so on. The sharing of spiritual resources is recommended by most churches within certain limits which vary from church to church. Certainly the sharing of church buildings is a welcome new phenomenon, as are the various aspects of joint pastoral care and collaboration in the field of catechesis. The Roman Catholic Church's discipline for the unilateral, and in some cases the reciprocal, sharing of the sacraments, particularly the Eucharist, are fairly clear, though the theological basis for the practice laid down is a subject of discussion among theologians. But whether Catholics can, or cannot, as Church, share reciprocally in the Eucharist with Christians of other churches, there is no doubt, as the quotation from Vatican II cited above stresses, that Eucharistic communion is an aspect of full ecclesial communion, towards which our common baptism orientates us, and towards which we are pledged to work by every legitimate means.

Ecumenical activity, then, flows from God's self-revelation accepted by us in faith, just as surely as does the task of evangelization and the making of disciples. The shape of the great, united Church of the future is perhaps still hidden from us now, as is the moment of its realization in or out of historical time. Nonetheless, our faith lays upon us the urgent task of shaping it as a concrete reality here and now.

Wider ecumenism among world religions

In the first chapter of this book we described religions in Clifford Geertz's phrase as 'cultural systems'. Religious experience of the transcendent receives objective expression in a historical tradition, and this tradition focuses on a matrix of dynamic images. We tried to give a thumbnail sketch of five great areas of religious tradition. Later on, in Chapter 6, we returned to the question of the implications for other religions of the Christian belief in the ultimacy and uniqueness of Jesus Christ. Every great religious tradition has what Charles Davis has called a 'centre of symbolic structure' (Davis 1970, p. 103). In Islam it is the Book, the Qur'an. In Judaism it is spiritual 're-settlement' through the Torah. In Hinduism there is a multiplicity of structures and centres, united nevertheless by the socio-religious caste system. In Buddhism there are several structural levels and the central symbol of the Buddha receives different forms and interpretations. In traditional ethnic religion the variations are almost without number, but the basic characteristic of the symbolic centres is a continuity between human society and the world of nature.

The central symbol of Christianity is Jesus Christ, the crucified and risen Lord. As Davis points out, faith in Christ rests on the Judeo-Christian conviction that God reveals himself, not merely in a subjective experience which becomes institutionalized in an external historical form, but also in the order of objective historical knowledge or experience (Davis 1970, p. 124). Bernard Lonergan shows how God's inner word of Love in the hearts of believing non-Christians becomes an 'outer word' of Love, that is, becomes historical as well (Lonergan 1972, pp. 118–119). Charles Davis does not think that the recognition of prophetical religion (that is, revelation in the order of objective knowledge) in non-Christian religions is incompatible with faith in Christ, and God is free, after all, to make use of what instruments he pleases to reveal himself (Davis 1970, pp. 122–124). However, God cannot contradict himself, and the recognition of prophetical religion existing outside the Church inevitably raises questions of truth or falsity with greater insistence, since we are speaking of an objective order of knowledge. The problem is particularly acute where relations between Christians and Jews and Christians and Muslims are concerned.

The uniqueness of Christ as prophet consists basically in the fact that his message is merged with his own person and that he *is*, in an objective sense, God's Word. He is also a living presence for people everywhere and at all times. In his person are merged both the objective content of God's revelation and the subjective union of man with God. If this faith is denied, then Christianity loses its distinctive character and ceases to be recognizable.

Christ's ultimacy is, however, open-ended. Not only must Christians recognize an implicit and saving faith in other religions which denotes a divine self-revelation and an expression of faith that has become historical, but Christians could perhaps dare to go a little further. They must, in any case, accept that they can learn from other religious traditions, that other religions have a function in God's providential plan, even a positive place in the whole economy of salvation won by Jesus Christ. In Chapter 6 we went so far as to suggest that the implicit faith by which non-Christians are able to be saved could perhaps indicate a conscious acceptance of themes which go in the same direction as Christianity, and we tried very tentatively to show how the world religions might find a meeting-place in Christianity (following, in particular, Raimundo Panikkar's Trinitarian scheme).

Such an attempt to identify the 'seeds of the Gospel' or of the 'world-seeding Logos' was not intended in any way to predict a possible religious synthesis. We cannot assume that such a synthesis, which necessarily entails a conscious and explicit knowledge of Christ, will be historical rather than eschatological. What we were concerned with was a Christian field of encounter for the religions, a shape for dialogue, or a direction for channelling the religious interpenetration taking place in the contemporary world.

The question we have to ask in the context of evangelization and mission is: What are the conditions and the priorities for inter-faith dialogue at the present moment? A first and fundamental condition is laid down by Raimundo Panikkar. The encounter between religions is not merely rational. A doctrine which can be brushed aside as cumbersome and divisive has not been seen as a doctrine that derives from a lived faith. For doctrines to be understood, they must be experienced as a lived reality, and religious dialogue must try to spell out the consequences of such a reality (Panikkar 1968, pp. 1–13. 20, 24). Davis makes the same point that it is dangerous to envisage each religion as a set of doctrinal propositions which are to be subjected to comparative analysis (Davis 1970, p. 103). Dialogue is historical, a concrete meeting of men in society. It is also a religious act in itself. It is demanded for Christians, because our own understanding of other religions is part of our own growing knowledge of Christ. Revelation continues in the process of interculturation – through the questions which our interaction with the world religions forces us to put to the Christ whom we have experienced and whom we believe to be the same Christ originally experienced by the apostles.

The Vatican Council's document *Nostra Aetate*, and the guidelines on relations between Christians and Jews subsequently issued by the Vatican, have been attempts to outlaw in theory and in practice all forms of anti-Semitism, as being totally at variance with the spirit of Christianity itself and the demands of humanity. The resistance of the Jewish people to Christian evangelization, and their presence as alien communities dispersed throughout Christianized Europe, drew down upon them persecution, massacre and exile in generation after generation. To the lasting shame of Christians this persecution was often justified on theological grounds which were a travesty of Christ's own attitude before his accusers and judges. The liquidation of six million Jews in the Nazi death camps was the unspeakable nadir of anti-Semitism and of racial discrimination in any form. Today, in Jerusalem, one approaches the Yad Vashem, or memorial exhibition and archive of the Holocaust, along the avenue of the Righteous Gentiles, where every tree commemorates a non-Jew who helped protect or rescue Jewish people from the Nazi terror.

Nevertheless, it is understandably difficult for Jews to overcome their deep-rooted antipathy to the Cross which has been for them a symbol, in every age, of Christian cruelty and anti-Semitism. Yet, in spite of this, dialogue with Christians can only be centred on that Cross. Jews and Christians can discuss their common heritage in the Old Testament and also their common liturgical heritage which derives from the same source, but ultimately the role of Jesus Christ as 'exegete' of the Jewish Bible cannot be circumvented. Christianity constitutes an interpretation of the Torah which Jews must seriously consider, and Christians have a duty to invite Jews to examine and respond to the writings of the New Testament in the light of their own tradition and experience since the time of Christ. It is fortunate that a small, but growing, number of Jewish scholars is doing just this. It is also fortunate that a small, but vigorous, Judeo-Christian community is also asking what it means to be both a Christian and a Jew.

It has been noted that Judaism's central symbol is that of a people, regenerated through fidelity to the Torah. It has also been noted that the identification of Jewish religion with this people has never been wholly exclusive. Modern Jews sometimes say that their people has been chosen by God for a purpose, but that this fact does not exclude the possibility of God's choice of other peoples for other purposes. An important aspect of Jewish-Christian dialogue must be precisely this question of the significance of ethnicity, and whether ethnic barriers can be superseded, as Christ's Good News proclaims.

The centrality of the Qur'an for Muslims makes them especially vulnerable to the threat of historical criticism, flowing with the tide of modern consciousness from the West. This threat has provoked a fierce fundamentalism in several corners of the Muslim world, a fundamentalism which rejects the Western experience in its totality, as irredeemably decadent and irreligious. This attitude is shared to some extent by Eastern Christian communions embedded in the Muslim world of the Near East. As we argued in Chapter 1, following Peter Berger, the fundamentalist option is doomed to failure in the long run. The Muslim crisis can only be resolved by dialogue and discernment.

The vital question for Muslim theologians to answer is whether the Qur'an, particularly in what it has to say about Jesus, Son of Mary, is a truth forever fixed by divine decree. The Qur'an minimizes Jesus' titles and privileges, and it attempts to demythologize his divinity. Christians are said to have forgotten part of the divine 'reminder' they received, and Jesus is not thought to be the Word of God himself, but merely an outward manifestation of that Word. His quality of 'servant' of God is interpreted as being opposed to the claim that he is God's Son. The Qur'an contains what Michael Fitzgerald (Fitzgerald 1981, pp. 11–12) has called 'a cry of horror' at the very idea that God should have a Son:

> They say the All-Merciful has taken to himself a son . . . the heavens would almost be rent, the earth split, the mountains come crashing down . . . .It is not fitting for the All-Merciful to take a son (Qur'an 19, 88–92).

There is an inscription in the Dome of the Rock at Jerusalem, which was built on the Temple site by Abd-al-Malik in the seventh century, as a rival to Constantine's Basilica of the Holy Sepulchre:

> O you people of the book, overstep not bounds in your religion and of God speak only the truth. The Messiah Jesus, son of Mary, is only an apostle of God, and his word which he conveyed into Mary, and a spirit proceeding from him. Believe therefore in God and his apostles and say not Three. It will be better for you. God is only one God. Far be it from his glory that he should have a Son.

If Muslims are convinced that they hold the ultimate truth about Christ, then they dispense themselves from dialogue with Christians. The Algerian scholar Ali Merad (quoted in Fitzgerald 1981, p. 9) is disposed to believe that the Qur'an aims to provoke questions regarding the mysterious character of Jesus and his place in God's plan, and not give definitive answers. In any case, if dialogue is to take place, Fitzgerald lays down the same condition as Panikkar and Davis. Christians must witness to the divinity of Christ and the reality of the Trinity by showing that these are not incomprehensible doctrines, but an experience and a praxis, operative in their own lives (Fitzgerald 1981, p.12). It is especially through the Eucharist, and the effectiveness of the Eucharist in ordinary life, that Christians can witness to Muslims about the truth of Jesus. Even the Qur'an in the *sura* of *The Table* apparently refers to the Eucharist as a sign given to Jesus by God, and a confirmation of the truth of his message (cf. Qur'an 5, 112–113, and probable influence of 1 Corinthians 11:27ff.).

Christians have to persuade Hindus also of the value of dialogue. Panikkar believes that Hindus are tempted to fall in love with their past and with the immense and varied riches of their religious traditions, to the extent that they are reluctant to continue the search in dialogue with other world religions (Panikkar 1968, pp. 20–24). Dialogue implies a denial of complacency and an acceptance of the need to go forward. Hinduism has a history of profound theological reflections and of equally intense mysticism and asceticism. The unfolding of this rich religious experience and its historical expression in successive forms is not a process that is over. The same can surely be said for Buddhism. In these great Oriental traditions there are tensions and polarities which ensure a continuing 'intra-faith' dialogue quite apart from an 'inter-faith' dialogue with Christianity or other world religions. External dialogue, however, is also relevant to the internal process; in fact, in the present world situation it is not unconnected. The boundaries between the great religions are shifting ones, and Christianity is certainly accepting questions, if not influences, from the East.

The modern Hindu thesis of the mystical unity of all religions is an invitation to Christianity to co-exist with Hinduism in a religious caste system of its own making. Such a thesis depends on a mystical interpretation of religion in general and means, as Charles Davis points out, the elimination of Christianity on its own terms as a historical and prophetical religion (Davis 1970, p. 122). Thus Christianity is welcomed as a religion similar to the various forms of Hinduism, and is even offered a place within the manifold Hindu structure. Panikkar adds:

> That is the reason why Hinduism thinks itself to be tolerant, though Christianity is afraid that this seeming tolerance is the highest form of intolerance: only to allow to others the place it has allotted to them (Panikkar 1968, p. 14).

It is also the reason why Hinduism does not fear the modern Western consciousness as Islam does, and why it is able to offer secularized Westerners attractive mystical and ascetical disciplines which can operate at a level remote from objective historical knowledge. In Christianity the historical is closely bound up with an emphasis on the personal, and it is this factor in Hinduism which requires attention from Christians while they, in their turn, reflect upon the Hindu contribution to the understanding of God's universal and eternal action. In Buddhism, the dialogue with Christians must help to make explicit the tensions which illustrate Buddhist history, as between what Gombrich calls cognitive and affective religion, and between negative and positive religious ideals.

The spread of the modern consciousness has not by any means extinguished the traditional ethnic religions of the world, but it probably means that their survival can only be ensured in circumstances that are somewhat marginal and abnormal. This is because they belong to societies in which relationships are essentially small-scale. The normal choice is not, as the

Nigerian playwright Wole Soyinka seems to believe, between a tourist spectacle and a traditional mythology revamped by secular philosophy. The secularist alternative is certainly realistic, though perhaps less as a sophisticated literary humanism than as a rank, unthinking materialism. The other option, however, is an appropriation of the traditional religious heritage within a missionary world religion, which in most cases will be either Christianity or Islam. For such an appropriation to be valid, a genuine 'intra-faith' dialogue has to take place in which Christians and Muslims frankly recognize the presence of unabsorbed ethnic-traditional elements within their religious borders. The modalities of this process will be discussed – for Christianity – later in this chapter.

THE THIRD CHURCH

A new ecclesiology

The phrase 'Third Church' was coined a few years ago by Walbert Buhlmann in a book called *The Coming of the Third Church* (Buhlmann 1976). He was referring, not to a Church of the Third World existing alongside the Church of the Old and New Worlds, but to a new mode of existence for the Church Universal. Historically, the Church began as a Jewish-Christian community or communities. From the Jewish world it was transplanted into the Hellenistic world to which Rome and Western Europe succeeded as the cultural heirs. Christianity flourished on the pagan soil of the Roman Empire, and the second great epoch of its history, the Gentile Church whose language was Latin, has lasted down to our days. The Third Church has been called by Bishop Christopher Butler 'the Church of the Nations' and by Karl Rahner 'the World Church'. In this World Church it is certainly true that the Church of the Third World is making its impact and that the centre of Christian gravity is unmistakably shifting towards the Third World (cf. Shorter 1979). This was Buhlmann's thesis and it is borne out by statistics. Already, in the Roman Catholic communion alone, more than half of the membership is to be found in Third World countries, and by the year 2000 it will probably approach three-quarters.

Karl Rahner has confidently identified the 'leap to World Church' as taking place at the Second Vatican Council (Rahner 1979). It may be that the indigenous episcopates of the Third World were not represented in a correct proportion to those of Western countries, but at least indigenous bishops came in their own name and were not only represented by missionary surrogates. 'For the first time', writes Rahner, 'a world-wide Council with a world-wide episcopate came into existence and functioned independently . . . . At the Council a Church appeared and became active that was no longer the Church of the West with its American spheres of influence and its

export to Asia and Africa' (Rahner 1979). The great symbol of this qualitative 'leap forward' was the abandonment of Latin as the universally
necessary language of worship. The introduction of vernacular worship had
linguistic implications that were not simply semantic, as Pope Paul VI
pointed out in 1975, but were 'anthropological and cultural' (*Evangelii
Nuntiandi*, 63).

With regard to the doctrinal decrees of the Second Vatican Council,
although they take a European understanding of the various questions as
their starting-point, they are not nearly so closely conditioned by the style of
Neo-Scholastic theology as the pre-conciliar schemata which they replaced.
Moreover, as Rahner makes clear, the Council makes (or clarifies) certain
doctrinal presuppositions fundamental to the self-understanding of the
World Church.

> Doctrinally the Church [at the Council] did two things which are of fundamental
> significance for a world-wide missionary effort. In the Declaration on the Relation
> of the Church to Non-Christian Religions, a truly positive evaluation of the great
> world religions is initiated for the first time in the doctrinal history of the Church.
> Furthermore . . . the documents on the Church, on the missions, and on the Church
> in the modern world proclaim a universal and salvific will of God which is limited
> only by the evil decision of human conscience and nothing else. This implies the
> possibility of a proper salvific revelation-faith even beyond the Christian revelatory
> word. As a result, in comparison with earlier theology roughly to our own time,
> basic presuppositions for the world mission of the World Church are fashioned
> which were not previously available (Rahner 1979).

The Declaration on Religious Liberty and the Decree on Ecumenism can
also be interpreted in a similar perspective.

Karl Rahner is convinced that the break between the new, World Church
and the old, Latin Church of the West is as significant as that between
Judeo-Christianity and the Pauline Christianity of the Gentiles, with its
abolition of circumcision and the framework of the Mosaic law (including
the Sabbath), and the removal of the Church's centre from Jerusalem to
Rome. The difference between the situation of Jewish Christianity and the
situation into which Paul transplanted Christianity is not greater than the
difference between Western culture and the contemporary cultures of Africa
and Asia. Rahner accurately remarks that today's difference may be hidden
to some extent by the layer of rationalism and technology which the West
has imposed on the whole world. Up to this moment Western Christianity
has sought to impose itself – without risking a really new start – on those
religious cultures which welcomed Western cultural exports, and not on the
resistant world of Islam and the religions of the East. Rahner sees the alternatives before the Church with great clarity:

> This, then, is the issue: either the Church sees and recognizes these essential differ-
> ences of other cultures for which she should become a World Church and with a
> Pauline boldness draws the necessary consequences from this recognition, or she

remains a Western Church and so in the final analysis betrays the meaning of Vatican II (Rahner 1979).

Rahner asks a number of further pertinent questions which are implied in the dilemma he has defined.

> How can a unity of faith be maintained and verified when you have plural proclamations, and how can the highest ecclesial body in Rome work for this, since the task is apparently entirely different from what the Roman authorities on faith have previously assumed within a common Western horizon of understanding? It is also self-evident that a significant pluralism with respect to canon law (and other ecclesial praxis as well) must be developed in the great local churches – even apart from the fact that genuine progress towards ecumenical unity cannot otherwise be expected (ibid.).

The beginnings of an answer at a theoretical level are certainly to be found within the documents of Vatican II themselves and especially, perhaps, in Paul VI's Apostolic Exhortation *Evangelii Nuntiandi* which followed upon the fourth Rome Synod. This is not the place to give a fully fledged ecclesiology of the World Church, even if it were yet possible to do so. What follows is simply an outline appropriate to the present context of a discussion on revelation and mission at this moment when the World Church is taking its first faltering steps. Moreover, we shall reserve the question of inculturation or interculturation until the next section of this chapter, and the question of pluralism, theological, liturgical and catechetical, to the final three sections.

Lumen Gentium, Vatican II's Dogmatic Constitution on the Church, introduced the concept of 'particular churches' and stated that 'it is in these and formed out of them that the one and unique Catholic Church exists' (*Lumen Gentium*, 23). Particular churches, however, are not independent churches. They are only *the* Catholic Church in a particular place to the extent that they are in communion with other particular churches and especially with the privileged particular church of Rome, whose bishop, the Pope, is a visible personal sign and instrument of this communion. The particular church *is* the Catholic Church in a particular place because it is bound to other particular churches in love, faith and loyalty, in receptiveness to the Church's teaching authority and in the *lex orandi* which is also the *lex credendi*. Paul VI adds:

> Legitimate attention to individual [particular] churches cannot fail to enrich the Church [universal]. Such attention is indispensable and urgent. It responds to the very deep aspirations of peoples and human communities to find their own identity ever more clearly (*Evangelii Nuntiandi*, 63).

The Pope sees the bond of communion as being strengthened by a mutual enrichment among the particular churches, which communicate their own insights and experience – their own vision of Christ – to the Universal Church.

How does this take place? It is not merely a verbal or semantic phenomenon, not merely a question of translation. It is a mutual experiencing and a mutual self-revelation, an ecclesio-cultural bilingualism. Particular churches influence one another through the contagion of example, through personal links and through innumerable other structured links, many of which have come into existence in the wake of the Second Vatican Council. Pride of place should perhaps be given to the post-Vatican pastoral journeys of Popes. Then there is the somewhat limited exchange which takes place at the triennial episcopal synods in Rome, but which throws into relief the Church's practical pluralism. There are also continental and regional episcopal associations. There are international meetings of theologians. There is the growing internationalization of religious orders and even of missionary congregations, with their increasing Third World membership.

In these processes, the Church in the Third World is certainly influencing Western Christianity. Western Christians are being brought into contact with the freshness and optimism of the Church in the Third World, with its poverty, with its insistence on the primacy of practice and on the need to change concrete circumstances of life, rather than to alter theological formulations. Third World Christians are participating to a greater degree in missionary work, extending beyond their own local situation. They are attempting to describe the objectives of evangelization in their own terms, through 'conscientization', through 'life-centred catechesis', through the formation of basic Christian communities, through the inspiring figure of a religious foundress like Mother Teresa of Calcutta, with her formula: 'by the Third World for the Third World'.

Nonetheless, practice in the Church still lags behind theory and there are even questions of theory which cry out for urgent clarification. Karl Rahner puts his finger on one crucial question which still remains unclear, 'the lasting and timely significance' of collegiality. It is not yet theoretically clear how the highest plenary authority in the Church actually exists and acts in two subjects which are at least partially different, that is to say, in the Pope acting alone and also in the General or Ecumenical Council of the whole Catholic episcopate, acting with and under the Pope. The bishops form a college with the Pope, and the doctrine of collegiality stresses the word *with* rather than *under*, without opposing or denying the second word. Until constitutional changes of one kind or another take place, it will not be clear how the collegial principle, so necessary to the idea of the World Church, is to operate. In Rahner's own words:

> In a true World Church some such change is necessary, since a World Church simply cannot be ruled with the sort of Roman centralism that was customary in the period of the Piuses (Rahner 1979).

Adaptation, inculturation, interculturation

There is no human community in the world, however isolated it may be, which is not, at least to a small extent, influenced by strangers. Every cultural tradition absorbs elements that come to it from other cultural traditions, and often makes innovations under the stimulus such elements provide. This process is largely unreflective and is difficult to plan or to programme. A World Church is a Church which takes human cultures seriously. This was the message of a speech at the 1977 Synod by Cardinal Otunga of Nairobi: Take us seriously and help us to take ourselves seriously. Faith necessarily uses the resources of human culture, even if it is distinct from it. The Second Vatican Council spoke of faith 'entering into communion with different forms of culture' (*Gaudium et Spes*, 58), and it emphasized that the proclamation of the Good News was not tied to any one form of culture or way of life. This is entirely in line with the explicit universalism which characterized the originating experience of Christianity, Jesus Christ's own attitude towards strangers and the limitless character of the Easter proclamation. It is a necessary consequence of our participation in the life of the Risen Christ. As the Epistle to the Colossians puts it:

> Do not lie to one another, seeing that you have put off the old nature with its practices and have put on the new nature, which is being renewed in knowledge after the image of its Creator. Here there cannot be Greek and Jew, circumcised and uncircumcised, barbarian, Scythian, slave, free man, but Christ is all, and in all (Colossians 3:9–11).

Brian Hearne has noticed how Pope John Paul II re-phrased a saying of Paul VI's in his own characteristic personalist terms. Whereas Pope Paul had told the Bishops of Africa and Madagascar in 1969: 'You may and you must have an African Christianity', Pope John Paul declared during his pastoral visit to Africa in 1980: 'Not only is Christianity relevant to Africa, but Christ, in his members, is himself African!' (Hearne 1979).

It is clear that the Roman Catholic Church, confronted by the growing reality of a World Church and its theoretical and practical implications of pluralism, is in a very different situation from that which obtained before the Second Vatican Council. It is no longer a question of one already evangelized part of the world evangelizing the rest of the world, along the lines of its own cultural presuppositions, but of a much more complex reality of cultural interaction and exchange. It is a situation in which the whole Church is being transformed. But the vision of World Church dawned slowly, even at the Council itself. The documents produced in the earlier sessions of the Council, like the Constitution on the Sacred Liturgy, employed the notion of 'adaptation'. They took for granted that a single universal Latin rite would be maintained, but that provision would be made in this rite for the admission of 'adaptations', 'variations' or 'elements from the traditions and cultures of individual peoples'. It was also conceded that in 'some places and circumstances' and 'in mission countries' 'a more radical adaptation of the liturgy is needed' (*Sacrosanctum Councilium*, 38, 39, 40 and 65). These principles guided the revision of the liturgical books after the Council and determined the shape of the post-conciliar liturgical directives.

The Constitution on the Sacred Liturgy decreed that 'a wider use of the vernacular' (no. 36) was to be permitted, and this has meant not only the effective replacement of Latin by the vernacular in almost all celebrations involving the participation of the people, but also that demands are being made for a pluralism of liturgies. The Council already noted the intimate connection between rite and words (*Sacrosanctum Concilium*, 35). It was left to Paul VI, after the Council was ended, to draw attention to the intimate connection between language and culture. In Kampala, Uganda, in 1969 he spoke of the 'language and mode of manifesting this one Faith' as including 'the tongue, the style, the character, the genius and the culture of the one who professes this one Faith'. He admitted 'a certain pluralism' in the fields of pastoral, ritual, didactic and spiritual activities. This was a very cautious and diffident approach to pluralism, and it was soon to be replaced by a more confident one (cf. Shorter 1979).

At the Roman Synod of 1974, Third World Bishops were outspoken in their condemnation of 'the theology of adaptation' and they demanded an 'incarnational theology', thereby echoing a concept which had appeared in the Decree on the Missionary Activity of the Church (*Ad Gentes*), produced in the Second Vatican Council's final session. Pope Paul VI's Apostolic Exhortation *Evangelii Nuntiandi* of 1975 was the response to this appeal. This document contained the following striking passages:

> What matters is to evangelize man's culture and cultures (not in a purely decorative way as it were by applying a thin veneer, but in a vital way, in depth and right to their very roots) . . . (*Evangelii Nuntiandi*, 20).

> The individual Churches, intimately built up not only of people, but also of aspirations, of riches and limitations, of ways of praying, of loving, of looking at life and the world which distinguish this or that human gathering, have the task of assimilating the essence of the Gospel message and of transposing it, without the slightest betrayal of its essential truth, into the language that these particular people understand, then of proclaiming it in this language.
>
> The transposition has to be done with the discernment, seriousness, respect and competence which the matter calls for in the field of liturgical expression, and in the areas of catechesis, theological formulation, secondary ecclesial structures and ministries. And the word 'language' should be understood here less in the semantic or literary sense than in the sense which one may call anthropological and cultural (*Evangelii Nuntiandi*, 63).

These texts reveal a notable progress of thought. The cultural implications of the process here called 'transposition' are clearly stated, and the process is deemed to apply to theological formulation and to structures and ministries, as well as to liturgy and catechesis. The document also makes liberal use of the terms 'incarnation' and 'incarnational'.

The Decree *Ad Gentes* had likened the missionary process to the Incarnation of the Word:

> ...just as happened in the Incarnation, the young Churches, which are rooted in Christ and built on the foundations of the apostles, take over all the riches of the nations which have been given to Christ as an inheritance. They borrow from the customs, traditions, wisdom, teaching, arts and sciences of their people everything which could be used to praise the glory of the Creator, manifest the grace of the Saviour, or contribute to the right ordering of the Christian life (*Ad Gentes*, 22).

According to this theological image, therefore, the Word becomes flesh in successive cultures and traditions. This analogy with the Incarnation enjoyed a vogue in missiological circles after Vatican II, until it was pointed out that the basic analogy ought not to be the Incarnation alone, but the whole mystery of Jesus Christ. When the self-revelation of God becomes explicit in a given human tradition or culture through the proclamation of the Good News of Jesus Christ, there is a necessary process of dying and rising. The Gospel both challenges and transforms cultures. The Second Vatican Council clearly recognized this when it called for theological investigation in 'each of the great socio-cultural regions', and for a re-examination of the truths of revelation in the light of the philosophy and wisdom of the peoples being evangelized to see 'how their customs, concept of life and social structures can be reconciled with the standard proposed by divine revelation' (*Ad Gentes*, 22).

The term 'incarnation', as applied to the active process of missionary evangelization, has now been largely replaced by the term 'inculturation'. This word is, of course, theologically neutral, but it nevertheless possesses certain drawbacks. It still envisages the problem in terms of each single culture to be evangelized, even if the process is more than a 'clothing' of an abstract message with cultural 'flesh'. Theologians and the *magisterium* sometimes convey the impression that inculturation merely consists in detaching 'the essence of the Gospel' (*Evangelii Nuntiandi*, 63) from one cultural form and of 'transposing' or 'inserting' it into another cultural form. Even Bernard Lonergan, who distinguishes between the cognitive meaning, the constitutive or lived meaning, and the effective or practised meaning of the Gospel, seems to assume that a preacher can simply learn another cultural language as a system of communications and express the Gospel's essential truth through this other system or language (Lonergan 1972, pp. 328–329).

The actual facts are otherwise. For one thing, we are dealing with meanings expressed in symbols and images even at the cognitive level. For another, it is not easy to detach essential meaning from a first cultural form, let alone re-express it in another. Rahner is right to strike a note of caution:

> None of us can say exactly how, with what conceptuality, under what new aspects the old message of Christianity must in the future be proclaimed in Asia, in Africa, in the regions of Islam, perhaps also in South America, if this message is really to be present everywhere in the world. The people in these other cultural situations must themselves gradually discover this – and here, of course, it cannot remain a question of formally declaring the necessity of such other proclamations, nor simply of deriving them from an inherently problematic analysis of the special character of these peoples (Rahner 1979).

It never happens that meanings alone are communicated from one culture to another. On the contrary, the reciprocal borrowing of cultural elements also takes place. But this raises the further problem of pluralism of meaning. Symbols acquire their meaning from the position they occupy in a given symbolic matrix, as well as from the way they operate. Symbols which are detached from one symbol-system and inserted in another run the risk of acquiring a new and perhaps altogether different meaning. However, the possibility of an interaction between symbol-systems, so that a transfer of meaning takes place, is not to be excluded. What has to be avoided is syncretism, or the absorption of one symbol on the terms of another symbol-system, if meaning is to be preserved. The transfer of religious meaning from one symbol-system to another cannot occur without dramatic modifications of symbolic patterns on one side or the other.

Old patterns cannot acquire new meanings without a dialectic taking place. The conflict has to be worked out largely at the unconscious level in highly personal situations, such as the crises which occur at moments of conversion or of vocation. A recent study by Bishop Bengt Sundkler of the Lutheran Church in Bukoba, Tanzania has demonstrated the all-important role of dreams in the appropriation of symbols and in the fashioning of an authentic African symbol-system in which to express the new experience of the Christian faith (Sundkler 1980). Sundkler analysed no fewer than 865 dreams of Lutheran Christians and pastors. Evangelization, therefore, results in a largely unconscious process of interculturation (to use the word coined by Bishop Joseph Blomjous), rather than in a conscious programme of one-way inculturation (Blomjous 1979). What ensures a valid transfer of Christian meaning is the personal and historical character of evangelization, its character as testimony or – to use the word favoured by Lonergan – its intersubjectivity. In Christianity, the ultimate religious meaning is personal, and it is experienced and transmitted through personal communion. The interpersonal nature of Christian evangelization and witness is intimately linked to the meaning of the Gospel itself. Consequently, it is to be distinguished from the teaching of an ideology, or of any set of abstract propositions. Evangelization sparks off a historical process, and is itself part of a historical process, of interculturation, in which human beings reveal themselves and their religious faith to one another.

Evangelization, integral development and social justice

In the Third or World Church, as we have called it, there is a grossly unequal distribution of the world's goods. The World Church is divided into rich and poor. Proclaiming the Good News of God's self-revelation in Christ necessarily entails facing up to all the realities of the present world situation. God reveals himself to us now through the signs of the times. Through poverty, suffering and injustice, God reveals to us his concern for the poor and for those who suffer. He goes even further. He reveals his concern through *our* concern, his involvement through *our* involvement. Evangelization, therefore, entails an involvement in the whole movement for human renewal. The preacher whose inaction and passivity belie his preaching is guilty of counter-witness. Orthodoxy and orthopraxy go hand in hand. From the very beginning there were inequalities in the Christian community which undermined its credibility. James was particularly scathing about them:

> My brethren, show no partiality as you hold the faith of Our Lord Jesus Christ, the Lord of glory. For if a man with gold rings and in fine clothing comes into your assembly, and a poor man in shabby clothing also comes in, and you pay attention to the one who wears fine clothing and say, 'Have a seat here, please,' while you say to the poor man, 'Stand there,' or 'Sit at my feet,' have you not made distinctions among yourselves and become judges with evil thoughts? Listen, my beloved brethren. Has not God chosen those who are poor in the world to be rich in faith and heirs of the kingdom which he has promised to those who love him? (James 2:1–5).

> If a brother or sister is ill-clad and in lack of daily food, and one of you says to them, 'Go in peace, be warmed and filled,' without giving them the things needed for the body, what does it profit? (James 2:15–16).

As Pope John Paul II has written, 'Catechesis is closely linked with the responsible activity of the Church and of Christians in the world' (*Catechesi Tradendae*, 24).

Development can be looked at in two ways. On the one hand it can be viewed as a progressive liberation from evils, such as poverty, suffering and injustice. On the other hand, and more positively, it can be viewed as a progressive humanization of man and his environment, man fulfilling the creator's command to subdue the earth and to be a faithful steward of its riches. But human development cannot be merely material or social. There must also be an openness to God, revealing himself, otherwise man degrades himself and becomes dehumanized. Integral development and the establishment of full social justice depends on personal faith and conversion, and on a commitment to work for justice that springs from the knowledge and the confidence that one is forgiven by God. Certainly we should 'hunger and thirst' for justice. We should work for it as something which is continually being brought into being. Whatever else it is, justice is not static. The search for true justice demands a social critique. Every human being has a right to those things which are necessary in order to live humanly, and private possessions must never be used in a way that conflicts with the common good.

There is an element of injustice in every situation, and our faith must certainly move us to work for practical changes. This involves the replacement of unjust structures and the removal of those who abuse authority. However, there is a tendency to believe that unjust people are products of unjust structures, rather than *vice versa*. There is often also a naïve belief in the possibility of a utopia, of a revolution which will create better, or even perfect, structures. Unfortunately, there is a constant tendency for just structures to become unjust, and the remedy does not consist in greater foresight and increased efficiency, but in conversion. Structures are unjust because they reflect the corruption that lies in the heart of man. The key factor in injustice is man's corruption. Therefore, the building of a just world depends on the confession of personal sinfulness and on the acceptance of God's forgiveness, incarnate in Jesus Christ.

The World Church must truly be a New People of God, that is to say, it must help men and women to discover their true identity in Jesus Christ. God not only reveals who *he* is in Jesus Christ, he also reveals to us who *we* are. He reveals that we are persons, having our own life history which we write ourselves, and having an openness to a future which we can ourselves begin to create, in the light of a transcendent purpose. This revelation comes to us with God's free gift of faith; and our real identity – the real truth of our existence – is the fruit of this religious experience. Johann Baptist Metz is right to see the greatest contemporary injustice as the denial of dignity and identity to individuals and to whole peoples, and the silencing of their voices of protest (Metz 1980, pp. 151–152). This is one of the effects of an imbalance of riches and technology in the world, as well as the 'unfeeling rationality' that rules it. It is also a product of the fear of an uncontrolled development of technology which may finally destroy man himself. The Church has to give people and peoples a voice and an identity. This it can only do by proclaiming the Good News of Jesus, that 'God has chosen those who are poor in the world to be rich in faith' (James 2:5)

REVELATION AND PLURALISM

Theological pluralism and the unity of faith

Two years before Pope Paul VI, in *Evangelii Nuntiandi*, called for a transposition of the Gospel message into the varied cultural languages, in the fields of theological formulation, liturgical expression and catechesis (*Evangelii Nuntiandi*, 63), the Roman Congregation for the Doctrine of the Faith issued an important Declaration (*Mysterium Ecclesiae* of 1973) which showed how doctrinal formulation could be conditioned in four ways. These ways were: the context of faith and human knowledge; the differing contemporary concerns; changing categories and conceptions; and, finally, the expressive power of living human language (*Mysterium Ecclesiae*, 5). If, as we have seen, 'theology follows', it is obvious that theologians will have differing opinions on the interpretation of events and on what is, and what is not, relevant to theological research. There will be not only different (cultural) languages, but different areas and levels of consciousness, and different areas of questioning and concern.

Pluralism is one of the characteristics of the world in which we live and attempts to 'paper over the cracks' with political ideologies and truculent totalitarian systems cannot succeed; we shall have to live with these ideologies and with these systems. They are all a part of the context in which theology is done. Theology used to be the exclusive preserve of the leisured intellectual. It was also the preserve of the clergy, and therefore made assumptions which suited the dominant male Westerner. Today the emphasis is on context – the practical situations in which human beings live their faith in Jesus Christ. We are now confronted by the prospect of indigenous theologies, such as Indian theology or African theology, also by the influential Latin American liberation theology which is, in practice, a response to the challenge of Marxist ideology. There is also Black theology, which seeks to respond to the growth of self-consciousness among blacks in a world of white oppressors, and there is a growing theology of Woman that parallels the movement for women's liberation. At a similarly general level, one finds a Third World theology, which aims to mobilize theologians of various Christian churches in the Third World and to distinguish areas of theological concern from those of Western or 'North Atlantic theology', although it is difficult enough in all conscience to recognize a unified 'White' or 'Western' theology. The Western world, while submitting more and more to influences that originate outside its frontiers, remains very much a clearing-house for theological opinion, standing, as it does still, at the centre of a world-wide network of communications media.

What happens to the unity of faith when Christian theology begins to reflect the pluralism inherent in the modern world? Certainly, the unity of faith can be endangered by this process, but it can also be endangered by a conservative or classicist refusal to give credence to contextual theologies. Pluralism can only be prevented from becoming schism when the claims of legitimate diversity are upheld. The problem is not one of verbal adaptation or translation. It is more than a mere communications problem. In accepting the gift of God in Jesus, one is accepting 'the sign of the stranger'. One is accepting not only the possibility, but the actual beginning of a universal reconciliation that spans centuries and continents. This reconciliation begins and ends with the imaginative assent of faith and the conversion of the moral conscience. It implies a constant openness to God revealing himself in other people and other situations. It entails a commitment to Jesus, the stranger from another century and another culture, but a stranger who really lived and who teaches us to live – for others. It calls for solidarity with all the men and women who found faith in Jesus, in this age and in past ages. It relies on the conviction that in Jesus we are brought closer to one another. It cherishes communion, and, when communion is lacking, dialogue that builds communion.

The dangers to unity of faith and the communion by which it is expressed are mainly threefold. One is contestation. This is often a danger when theology takes its starting-point from the special situation of a race, a class or any category that refuses to recognize the separate identity of others, even when those others can rightly be termed oppressors. It is a theology which needs an enemy for its own self-definition, and to this extent it ceases to be Christian. A Christian theological solution cannot exclude any category from salvation. Moreover, it has the self-confidence to borrow from other sources and to name them without fear of ridicule or alienation.

The second danger is to reduce theology to the terms of its own context, and to equate it with social or political action alone, to say that salvation is only another name for a historical process. If this happens, theology dwindles to mere ideology – perhaps to something akin to Marxism. The final danger is to create a theology which operates at a high level of abstraction and which tends to be divorced both from the primary symbols of faith (provided by the originating experience of the New Testament) and from the symbols of contemporary religious experience. Theological language must be a language of communion and a language of prayer.

Authentic worship and liturgical pluralism

Pope Paul VI spoke of pluralism in the field of liturgical expression, although, at the time and subsequently, his remarks were clearly seen to exclude the possibility of a pluralism of rites, and to offer only minor variations in a universal rite in all the areas of the world evangelized by missionaries of the Western Church. In a world which has experienced the diaspora of large numbers of Christian refugees belonging to Eastern rites, as well as the missionary activity of some of these churches, the Greek Orthodox for example, the prospect of a pluralism of rites in a World Church looks perhaps less daunting. It is certainly a question which cannot be evaded indefinitely. A plurality of rites exists, of course, already in the Catholic

Church, although it affects a relatively small number of Christians compared with the masses of those who belong to the 'Latin' or Western patriarchate of Rome. Since the Second Vatican Council, Eastern Catholics of Maronite, Melkite, Chaldean, Jacobite, Armenian, Coptic and Ethiopic rites have striven to uphold their various liturgies as a form of pluralism which should be taken for granted in the Church Universal and not be treated as something exceptional. They have also posed, increasingly convincingly, as spokesmen for the separated Christians who share their individual liturgical traditions, but not their communion with Rome.

The Second Vatican Council's Decree on the Catholic Eastern Churches was at pains to stress that the Eastern churches or rites were of equal rank with the Western church or rite (*Orientalium Ecclesiarum*, 3). It also referred to them on occasion as 'particular churches', the phrase employed by the Dogmatic Constitution on the Church (*Lumen Gentium*) for the communities in which, and out of which, the one, universal Church is formed. *Lumen Gentium* itself even went so far as to compare episcopal conferences of Latin rite to the Eastern, patriarchal churches which unite a multiplicity of local churches in their own liturgical and other usages (*Lumen Gentium*, 23). The unity and authenticity of the mystery of faith celebrated by Catholics in communion with one another is clearly unaffected by differences of liturgical rite.

Whether or not Western Catholicism legislates in the future for a plurality of rites, the introduction of vernacular worship and the stimulus already given to liturgical creativity by post-conciliar reforms is encouraging the growth of local liturgical traditions. This is basically because a vernacular liturgy calls a whole new range of hymns into existence. Professional theologians rarely compose hymns. They are the work of clergy and laity, reflecting on their own faith-experience and responding to the Word of God in their own way. Hymns establish themselves through actual usage, and become in effect an expression of the consensus of believers and eventually a rule of faith. The same can also be said for variant prayer formulas introduced into the renewed liturgy according to local taste and usage.

It is instructive to compare the genius of different cultures at work in writing hymns and composing prayer texts. Let us take first of all the penitential rites of two Eucharistic liturgies which have not yet received official approbation from Church authority. The first comes from a Eucharistic Rite for India:

Celebrant: You are the great refuge of all.
   People: Lord, in you we take our refuge.
Celebrant: You are the most merciful.
   People: Lord, extend to us your mercy.
Celebrant: You are the eternal purity.
   People: Lord, purify us.

Celebrant: You are the spotless one.
People: Lord, remove our stains.
Celebrant: You are the destroyer of sin.
People: Lord, pardon our failures.
Celebrant: You are the protector of the just.
People: Lord, give us your justice.
Celebrant: You are the remover of ignorance.
People: Lord, lead us to the truth (Amalorpavadass 1976).

The Indian preoccupation with divine attributes, with truth, virtue and purification, is altogether different from the African emphasis on strength, power and possession by the Spirit. This penitential formula is taken from the Eucharistic Rite for Zaïre:

Celebrant: Lord our God, like the insect that sticks onto our skin and sucks our blood, evil has come upon us. Our living power is weakened. Who can save us? Is it not you, O Father? Lord have mercy!
People: Lord have mercy!
Celebrant: Before you, O Father, before the Virgin Mary, before all the Saints, we confess that we have done wrong. Give us the strength we need to lead better lives. Christ have mercy!
People: Christ have mercy!
Celebrant: Before our brothers, before our sisters, we confess that we have done wrong, save us from falling back into the shadows, Lord have mercy!
People: Lord have mercy!
Celebrant: Most Holy Father, weaken in us whatever drives us to evil; forgive our faults because of the sacrifice of your Son, Jesus Christ. May your Spirit take possession of our hearts and may our sins be drowned in the deep and silent waters of your mercy. Through Christ Our Lord.
People: Amen.

A second comparison can be made between Indian and African approaches to the Eucharist. The Indian text exalts the Eucharist as an 'elixir' of eternal life:

This is the Bread that came down from Heaven. Whoever eats this Bread will never die. This is the cup of immortal nectar. Whoever drinks of this cup will live for ever. For the Lord said, 'he will have eternal life, and I will raise him up on the last day . . . ' (Amalorpavadass 1976).

An African Eucharistic hymn from Tanzania, however, appears to stress the continuity between earthly and heavenly life. This hymn consists of a series of verses with a recurring refrain:

Refrain: This is the Body of Life
This is the Bread of Life
This is the invitation to Life

Verses: Jesus is Bread of life
Jesus is Blood of life
Jesus is True Life

Jesus is King of life
Jesus is Lord of life
Jesus is Friend of life

Jesus is our Heritage of life
Jesus is our Gift of life
Jesus is our Love of life

Jesus is the Bringer of life
Jesus is the Giver of life
Jesus is True God of life

Jesus is the Happiness of life
Jesus is the Light of life
Jesus is the Path of life

Jesus is the Beginning of life
Jesus is the Continuation of life
Jesus is for ever Life.[2]

Such examples illustrate the variety of spiritual interpretation and emphasis in the liturgical language of newly evangelized peoples, contemplating the same mystery of faith. Texts such as these present God's self-revelation as a living truth which people can experience through worship in the community of faith.

From faith to vision – making the many one

Catechesis – perhaps better termed Religious Education – is inseparably linked to both theology and liturgy. Catechesis is an indispensable part of the continuing process of revelation. Its aim is to create the conditions in which a human being can enter into communion with the God who reveals himself in Jesus Christ. It seeks to activate what Karl Rahner has called 'the supernatural existential' in man, to awaken his capacity to respond to God's prior self-gift, and having achieved this, to continue to deepen this communion by rendering the knowledge that is born of love ever more conscious and decisive in his life. Thus in his own decisions, in his freedom and in his interchange with his community of faith and with the tradition he has accepted to inherit, he experiences God's revelation ever more fully.

When we speak of Religious Education, we inevitably think of human growth. Catechesis has to be tailored to fit different ages – pre-school, infant school, primary and secondary school, institutions of higher learning, preparation for marriage and the on-going religious formation of adults. The whole educational process has to be designed to serve a Christian community of adults and to bring the power of the Word into the heart of any and every human grouping throughout the world. It has to cater for all stages of growth and all crises in the life of a human being from the cradle to the grave. Education never ends. Neither does the communication and comprehension of God's revelation.

Like theology and liturgy, catechesis demands a plurality of cultural expression, and this has been the constant message of the post-conciliar catechetical congresses of Manila in 1966, Medellín in 1969 and Rome in 1971. It was also the message of Pope John Paul II in his Apostolic Exhortation *Catechesi Tradendae*, which presented the findings of the 1977 Rome Synod on Catechetics for Our Time. The Pope has this to say:

> We can say of catechesis, as well as of evangelization in general, that it is called to bring the power of the Gospel into the very heart of culture and cultures. For this purpose, catechesis will seek to know these cultures and their essential components; it will learn their most significant expressions; it will respect their particular values and riches. In this manner it will be able to offer these cultures the knowledge of the hidden mystery and help them to bring forth from their own living tradition original expressions of Christian life, celebration and thought. Two things must however be kept in mind.
>
> On the one hand the Gospel message cannot be purely and simply isolated from the culture in which it was first inserted (the Biblical world or, more concretely, the cultural milieu in which Jesus of Nazareth lived), nor, without serious loss, from the cultures in which it has already been expressed down the centuries; it does not spring spontaneously from any cultural soil; it has always been transmitted by means of an apostolic dialogue which inevitably becomes part of a certain dialogue of cultures.
>
> On the other hand, the power of the Gospel everywhere transforms and regenerates. When that power enters into a culture, it is no surprise that it rectifies many of its elements. There would be no catechesis if it were the Gospel that had to change when it came into contact with the cultures.
>
> To forget this would simply amount to what Saint Paul very forcefully calls 'emptying the cross of Christ of its power' (1 Corinthians 1:17) (*Catechesi Tradendae*, 53).

In this passage the Pope accurately describes the process of interculturation. Individually and collectively the human race receives an ever fuller knowledge of the God revealed in Jesus Christ. It is a process of on-going reconciliation and reintegration in the spatio-temporal sphere of human history. Will this process ever be completed? On earth, maybe. But what of heaven?

St Paul seems to say that faith and hope will pass away when we enjoy the final, face-to-face vision of God:

> Love never ends; as for prophecies, they will pass away; as for tongues, they will cease; as for knowledge, it will pass away. For our knowledge is imperfect and our prophecy is imperfect; but when the perfect comes, the imperfect will pass away. When I was a child, I spoke like a child, I thought like a child, I reasoned like a child; when I became a man, I gave up childish ways. For now we see in a mirror dimly, but then face to face. Now I know in part; then I shall understand fully, even as I

have been fully understood. So faith, hope, love abide, these three; but the greatest of these is love (1 Corinthians 13:8–13).

St Paul's image of childhood is a helpful one. Faith, like the knowledge of the child, does not cease to be. It is perfected and grows to maturity. Theologians have always taught that the face to face knowledge of God is an unimaginable person to person union which dispenses with any of the other objective elements which are present in our earthly knowledge. However, this direct 'vision' of God does not imply that all distinction between Creator and creature is at an end in heaven! What it means is that we can at last know and love God, as God in the glorified human nature of Christ knows and loves us. Of this knowledge Christ remains the eternal mediator, and in his glorified humanity we experience God directly. Christ remains forever the Revelation of God. He is our revelatory communion with God, the fullness of that revelation (cf. Moran 1973, pp. 179–188). When we say that revelation never ends, we are obviously applying our own experience of history and the space-time dimension symbolically. In heaven there is no history in the strict sense and no space or time. Yet, if every person is a mystery of unending self-revelation, how much more true must this be of the infinite and eternal God? Heaven provides the fullest possible knowledge of God that we can achieve, and this knowledge is still the result of God's self-revelation, and of the everlasting movement of the human creature into the incomprehensible truth and love of God. Perhaps the most that can be said about this everlasting revelation must be said apophatically with St Paul:

> 'What no eye has seen, nor ear heard,
>   nor the heart of man conceived,
>   what God 'has prepared for those who love him'
> God has revealed to us through the Spirit (1 Corinthians 2:9–10).

Faith on earth is not merely a preparation for eternal life, but a beginning of that very life, as our receptiveness to God's self-gift increases and our participation in the revelatory communion which is the Word of God made flesh grows deeper. Heaven marks the disappearance of the very last trace of self-love. Thenceforth, the progress of revelation is unstoppable and is lifted to a level that surpasses all earthly imagination and symbolic perception.

NOTES

1 Pope John Paul II at Nairobi, 7 May 1980: *Information Service* of The Secretariat for Promoting Christian Unity, no. 44 (1980), p. 83.
2 Hymn composed at Kipalapala, Tanzania, by A. Ntapambata; my tr. from the Swahili.

QUESTIONS FOR DISCUSSION

(1)   How is the finality of God's self-revelation in Christ linked in practice with the tasks of evangelization and ecumenism in the contemporary world?

(2)   Why are the concepts of revelation and interculturality so closely linked?

(3)   What are the implications of saying that theological language is a language of communion and prayer?

(4)   For further enquiry: It would be useful to carry further the discussion of the implications for the theology of revelation of the unending, direct vision of God in heaven.

SELECT ANNOTATED READING LIST

Pope Paul VI, 1975: *Evangelii Nuntiandi - Evangelization in the Modern World* (C.T.S., London). One of the most important documents of the pontificate of Paul VI. It is the final presentation of the work of the 1974 Rome Synod on Evangelization, and offers the most developed official statement on inculturation and World Church.

Pope John Paul II, 1979: *Catechesi Tradendae - Catechesis in our Time* (C.T.S., London). This document sums up the work of the 1977 Rome Synod on Religious Education or Catechesis. It shows how participant revelation continues in the action of preaching and teaching.

W. Buhlmann, 1976: *The Coming of the Third Church* (Slough). This missiological analysis by a former missionary in Tanzania draws far-reaching conclusions for the whole Church. The book is a remarkable synthesis and interpretation of Christian trends in every continent.

B. Lonergan, 1972: *Method in Theology* (London). Bernard Lonergan deals specifically with theological pluralism on pp. 267–294 and 326–329.

G. Moran, 1973: *Theology of Revelation* (London). An excellent summary of the whole theology of revelation, with special reference to the catechetical aspects. The final chapter on 'Revelation in Heaven' is particularly interesting.

Bibliography

Bible

All Scripture quotations are taken from the Revised Standard Version of the Bible, copyright 1946, 1952, 1957 and 1971 by the Division of Christian Education of the National Council of the Churches of Christ in the United States of America.

Documents of the Church's Magisterium

Vatican Council I

Dei Filius: Dogmatic Constitution on the Catholic Faith in H. Denzinger, *Enchiridion Symbolorum* (Freiburg, 1963), nos. 3000–3045.

Vatican Council II

N.B. References are in all cases to:
A. Flannery, 1975: *Vatican Council II – The Conciliar and Post Conciliar Documents* (Dublin)

Ad Gentes: Decree on the Church's Missionary Activity: pp. 863–902.
Dei Verbum: Dogmatic Constitution on Divine Revelation: pp. 750–765.
Dignitatis Humanae: Declaration on Religious Liberty: pp. 799–812.
Gaudium et Spes: Pastoral Constitution on the Church in the Modern World: pp. 903–1001.
Gravissimum Educationis: Declaration on Christian Education: pp. 725–737.
Lumen Gentium: Dogmatic Constitution on the Church: pp. 350–426.
Nostra Aetate: Declaration on the Relationship of the Church to Non-Christian Religions: pp. 738–742.
Optatam Totius: Decree on the Training of Priests: pp. 707–724.
Orientalium Ecclesiarum: Decree on the Catholic Eastern Churches: pp. 441–451.
Unitatis Redintegratio: Decree on Ecumenism: pp. 452–470.

Encyclical Letters, Synodal and Other Documents

Pius XII, 1943: *Divino Afflante Spiritu* in *Selected Letters and Addresses of Pius XII* (Catholic Truth Society, London, 1949), pp. 111–146.
Paul VI, 1975: *Evangelii Nuntiandi – Evangelization in the Modern World* (Catholic Truth Society, London).
John Paul II, 1979: *Redemptor Hominis* (Catholic Truth Society, London).
John Paul II, 1979: *Catechesi Tradendae – Catechesis in our Time* (Catholic Truth Society, London).

John Paul II, 1980: *Dives in Misericordia* (Abbots Langley, Herts).

Sacred Congregation for the Doctrine of the Faith, 1973: *Mysterium Ecclesiae – Declaration in Defence of the Catholic Doctrine on the Church* in *Catholic Mind*, no. 71 (October) pp. 58–60.

Books and Articles

T. J. Altizer, 1966: *The Gospel of Christian Atheism* (Philadelphia).

D. S. Amalorpavadass, 1976: 'Indigenization and the Liturgy of the Church', *International Review of Missions* 65, no. 258 (April), pp. 164–181.

K. Appiah-Kubi and S. Torres (eds), 1977: *African Theology en route* (New York).

R. O. Ballou, 1940: *The Bible of the World* (London). Includes Hymns of the Rig Veda.

H. W. Bartsch (ed.), 1972: *Kerygma and Myth – A Theological Debate* (London).

R. Bastide, 1978: *The African Religions of Brazil* (London).

P. Berger, 1980: *The Heretical Imperative* (London).

C. A. Bernard, 1980: 'Le défi symbolique', *Kerygma* (Ottawa) 34, pp. 51–67.

E. Bevan, 1962: *Symbolism and Belief* (Fontana, Glasgow) (first pub. London, 1938).

J. Blomjous, 1980: 'Inculturation and Interculturation', *African Ecclesial Review* 22, no. 6 (December), pp. 393–398.

T. Boman, 1960: *Hebrew Thought Compared with Greek* (London).

M. F. C. Bourdillon and M. Fortes (eds), 1980: *Sacrifice* (London).

J. Bowker, 1978: *The Religious Imagination and the Sense of God* (Oxford).

R. Brown, 1973: *The Virginal Conception and the Bodily Resurrection of Jesus* (London).

W. Buhlmann, 1976: *The Coming of the Third Church* (Slough).

H. Bürkle, 1977: *Einfuhrung in die Theologie der Religionen* (Darmstadt).

H. Butterfield, 1949: *Christianity and History* (London).

W. Cantwell Smith, 1978: *The Meaning and the End of Religion* (London) (3rd ed.).

O. Chadwick, 1957: *From Bossuet to Newman* (Cambridge).

W. Chagenda, 1981: 'Wole Soyinka: The Social Visionary', unpublished dissertation presented to the University of Bristol, Department of Theology and Religious Studies.

R. G. Collingwood, 1963: *The Idea of History* (Oxford).

J. H. Cone, 1970: *A Black Theology of Liberation* (New York).

F. Coplestone, 1942: *Friedrich Nietzsche* (London).

J. Coulson, 1981: *Religion and Imagination* (Oxford).

H. Cox, 1965: *The Secular City* (New York).

      1970: *The Feast of Fools* (New York).

A. K. Cragg, 1977: *The Christian and Other Religion* (London).

D. Cupitt, 1977: 'The Christ of Christendom' in J. Hick (ed.), *The Myth of God Incarnate* (London), pp. 133–147.

      1980: *Taking Leave of God* (London).

G. Daly, 1980: *Transcendence and Immanence – A Study in Catholic Modernism and Integralism* (Oxford).

C. Davis, 1970: *Christ and the World Religions* (London).

P. Donovan, 1979: *Interpreting Religious Experience* (London).

M. Douglas, 1970: *Natural Symbols* (London).

A. Dulles, 1969: *Revelation Theology* (London).

      1978: *The Resilient Church* (Dublin).

J. D. G. Dunn, 1980: *Christology in the Making* (London).

W. Eichrodt, 1961: *A Theology of the Old Testament* (London).

E. E. Y. Evans-Pritchard, 1962: *Nuer Religion* (Oxford).

M. Fitzgerald, 1981: 'Jesus, a Sign for Christians and Muslims', *Vidyajyoti – Journal of Theological Reflection* (May), pp. 1–14.

W. Foy (ed.), 1978: *Man's Religious Quest* (London).

P. Fransen, 1967: 'How can Non-Christians find Salvation in their own Religions?' in J. Neuner (ed.), *Christian Revelation and World Religions* (London).

C. Geertz, 1966: 'Religion as a Cultural System' in M. Banton (ed.), *Anthropological Approaches to the Study of Religion* (London), pp. 1–46.

B. Gerhardsson, 1979: *The Origins of the Gospel Traditions* (ET: London).

R. Gombrich, 1971: *Precept and Practice: Traditional Buddhism in the Rural Highlands of Ceylon* (Oxford).

B. Griffiths, 1976: *Return to the Centre* (London).

G. Gutiérrez, 1973: *A Theology of Liberation* (New York).

T. Guzie, 1974: *Jesus and the Eucharist* (New York).

W. Hamilton, 1966: *The New Essence of Christianity* (New York).

A. Hanson and R. Hanson, 1980: *Reasonable Belief* (Oxford).

R. Harjula, 1969: *God and the Sun in Meru Thought* (Helsinki).

W. T. Harris, 1950: 'The Idea of God among the Mende' in E. W. Smith (ed.), *African Ideas of God* (London), pp. 183ff.

B. Hearne, 1979: 'Christology and Inculturation' *African Ecclesial Review* 22, no. 6 (December), pp. 335–341.

B. Hebblethwaite, 1976: *Evil, Suffering and Religion* (London).

F. Heiler, 1932: *Prayer: A Study in the History and Psychology of Religion* (London).

J. Hick, 1968: *The Centre of Christianity* (London).
    1973: *God and the Universe of Faiths* (London).
    1976: *Death and Eternal Life* (New York).

J. Hick (ed.), 1977: *The Myth of God Incarnate* (London).

J. Hick and B. Hebblethwaite, 1980: *Christianity and Other Religions – Selected Readings* (Fontana, Glasgow).

E. Hill, 1964: 'Remythologizing, the Key to the Bible', *Scripture* 16, no. 35 (July), pp. 65–75.

R. Horton, 1971: 'African Conversion', *Africa* 41, no. 2, pp. 85–108.

D. E. Jenkins, 1967: *The Glory of Man* (London).

W. Kasper, 1977: *Jesus the Christ* (London).

K. Kaunda, 1973: *Letter to My Children* (London).

M. Kayoya, 1968: *Sur les Traces de mon Père* (Bujumbura, Burundi).

S. G. Kibicho, 1978: 'The Continuity of the African Conception of God into and through Christianity: A Kikuyu Case Study' in E. Fasholé-Luke *et al.* (ed.), *Christianity in Independent Africa* (London), pp. 370–388.

H. Kraemer, 1961: *The Christian Message in a Non-Christian World* (London) (5th ed.).

T. Kuhn, 1970: *The Structure of Scientific Revolutions* (Chicago) (2nd ed.).

H. Küng, 1978: *On Being a Christian* (Fontana, Glasgow).

N. Lash, 1975: *Newman on Development* (London).
    1979: 'Liberation from the Citadel', *The Month*, no. 1345, vol. 240 (October), pp. 341–344.

R. Latourelle, 1966: *The Theology of Revelation* (New York).
    1978: *L'Accés à Jésus par les Evangiles* (Paris).

C. Laye, 1980: *The Guardian of the Word* (Fontana, Glasgow).

E. Leach, 1970: *Lévi-Strauss* (Fontana Modern Masters, Glasgow).

C. Lévi-Strauss, 1966: *The Savage Mind* (London).

B. Lonergan, 1972: *Method in Theology* (London).

M. Machoveč, 1977: *A Marxist Looks at Jesus* (first pub. London, 1976).

J. P. Mackey, 1979: *Jesus the Man and the Myth – A Contemporary Christology* (London).

J. Macquarrie, 1967: *God-Talk* (London).

               1979: 'Commitment and Openness: Christianity's Relation to Other Faiths', *Theology Digest*, 27, no. 4 (Winter), pp. 347–355.

H. Maurier, 1968: *The Other Covenant: A Theology of Paganism* (New York).

J. S. Mbiti, 1971: *New Testament Eschatology in an African Background* (Oxford).

R. P. McBrien, 1970: *Catholicism* (London), 2 vols.

J. L. McKenzie, 1974: *A Theology of the Old Testament* (London).

               1976: *Dictionary of the Bible* (London).

J. B. Metz, 1980: *Faith in History and Society* (London).

J. Meyendorff, 1975: *Byzantine Theology – Historical Trends and Doctrinal Themes* (London).

J. O. Mills and W. S. F. Pickering (eds), 1980: *Sociology and Theology: Alliance and Conflict* (Brighton).

G. Moran, 1973: *Theology of Revelation* (London).

C. F. D. Moule, 1977: *The Origin of Christology* (Cambridge).

M. W. Murphree, 1969: *Christianity and the Shona* (London).

J. Murphy-O'Connor, 1976: 'Christological Anthropology in Philippians 2:6–11', *Revue Biblique* 83, pp. 25–50.

R. Murray, 1975–6: 'The Theory of Symbolism in St Ephrem's Theology', *Parole de l'Orient* 6 and 7 (Paris).

S. Neill, 1970: *Christian Faith and Other Faiths* (Oxford).

J. H. Newman, 1887: *An Essay on the Development of Christian Doctrine* (London) (5th ed.).

               1903: *An Essay in Aid of a Grammar of Assent* (London) (2nd ed.).

               1909: *Fifteen Sermons Preached Before the University of Oxford* (London).

               1961: *On Consulting the Faithful in Matters of Doctrine*, ed. J. Coulson (London).

F. W. Nietzsche, 1901: *Nietzsche as Critic, Philosopher, Poet and Prophet*, selections from his works ed. T. Common (London).

M. Nsimbi, 1974: 'Kiganda Traditional Religion', paper read to meeting of Vatican Secretariat for Non-Christians, Gaba, Uganda.

G. O'Collins, 1981: *Fundamental Theology* (London).

R. Panikkar, 1968: *The Unknown Christ of Hinduism* (London) (and 2nd ed. 1981).

               1973: *The Trinity and the Religious Experience of Man* (London).

W. Pannenberg, 1969: *Revelation as History* (London).

J. Pick (ed.), 1966: *A Hopkins Reader* (New York) (first pub. Oxford, 1953).

S. Radhakrishnan (ed.), 1953: *The Principal Upanisads* (London).

K. Rahner (ed.), 1975: *Encyclopedia of Theology: A Concise Sacramentum Mundi* (London).

K. Rahner, 1976: *Theological Investigations* 14 (London).

               1978: *Foundations of Christian Faith* (London).

               1979: 'Towards a Fundamental Theological Interpretation of Vatican II', *Theological Studies* 40, no. 4.

               1981: *Theological Investigations* 17.

B. M. G. Reardon (ed.), 1978: *Religious Thought in the 19th Century*, Cambridge (1966).

H. Reisenfeld, 1957: *The Gospel Tradition and Its Beginnings* (London).

A. Roberts and J. Donaldson (eds.), 1868: *The Writings of Cyprian* (Ante-Nicene Christian Library, VIII; Edinburgh).

J. A. T. Robinson, 1963: *Honest to God* (London).

           1972: *The Human Face of God* (London).

           1979: *Truth is Two-Eyed* (London).

J. A. T. Robinson and D. L. Edwards (eds.), 1963: *The Honest to God Debate* (London).

H. H. Rowley, 1944: *The Missionary Message of the Old Testament* (London).

C. Rycroft, 1979: *The Innocence of Dreams* (London).

E. Schillebeeckx (ed.), 1967: *Man as Man and Believer* (New York) (G. A. Lindbeck: 'The Problem of Doctrinal Development and Contemporary Protestant Theology', pp. 138–139).

E. Schillebeeckx, 1979: *Jesus, An Experiment in Christology* (London).

           1980: *Christ: The Christian Experience in the Modern World* (London).

           1980*: *Interim Report on the Books Jesus and Christ* (London).

H. R. Schlette, 1966: *Towards a Theology of Religions* (London).

M. Schmauss, 1968: *God in Revelation, Dogma*, vol. 1 (London).

P. Schoonenberg, 1977: 'God as Person(al)' in *A Personal God?*, ed. E. Schillebeeckx and B. Van Iersel (New York), pp. 80–93.

R. Schutz and M. Thurian, 1968: *Revelation Theology: A Protestant View* (New York).

A. Shorter, 1979: 'The Third Church', *The Way* (April), pp. 116–125.

N. Smart, 1977: *The Religious Experience of Mankind* (Fontana, Glasgow).

           1978: *The Phenomenon of Religion* (London) (2nd ed.).

W. Soyinka, 1974: *Collected Plays*, vol. 2 (Oxford).

           1976: *Myth, Literature and the African World* (Cambridge).

           1977: *Collected Plays*, vol. 1 (2nd ed.) (1st ed. 1973).

J. Stott, 1975: *The Lausanne Covenant: Exposition and Commentary* (Minneapolis).

B. Sundkler, 1980: *Bara Bukoba* (London).

M. L. Swantz, 1970: *Ritual and Symbol in Transitional Zaramo Society* (Uppsala).

M. J. Swiatecka, 1980: *The Idea of the Symbol* (Cambridge).

J. V. Taylor, 1972: *The Go-Between God* (London).

C. Tresmontant, 1956: *Essai sur la Pensée Hébraïque* (Paris).

           1962: *Origins of Christian Philosophy* (London).

I. Trethowan, 1971: *The Absolute and the Atonement* (London).

T. Tshibangu, 1980: *Théologie comme Science au XXième Siècle* (Kinshasa, Zaïre).

V. W. Turner, 1976: 'Ritual, Tribal and Catholic', *Worship* 50/56 (November).

E. B. Tylor, 1903: *Primitive Culture*, 2 vols (London).

A. Van Gennep, 1960: *The Rites of Passage* (London).

A. Vergote, 1980: 'The Chiasm of the Subjective and Objective Functions in the Symbol', *Kerygma* (Ottawa) 34, pp. 27–50.

G. Vermes, 1973: *Jesus the Jew* (London).

G. von Rad, 1965: *Old Testament Theology* (London), 2 vols.

           1972: *Wisdom in Israel* (London).

R. A. White, 1980: 'The Church and Media Ethics', *Communication Research Trends* 1, no. 1 (Centre for the Study of Communication and Culture, London).

C. Williams, 1966: *Faith in a Secular Age* (Fontana, Glasgow).

World Council of Churches, 1976: *Confessing Christ Today* (Geneva).

T. C. Young, 1940: *Contemporary Ancestors* (London).

R. C. Zaehner, 1957: *Mysticism: Sacred and Profane* (Oxford).

           1970: *Concordant Discord: The Interdependence of Faiths* (Oxford).

Zaïre Rite for Mass, 1975: 'The Zaïre Rite for the Mass', *African Ecclesial Review* 17, no. 4, pp. 244–248.

Index